ALSO BY STEVEN UJIFUSA

*A Man and His Ship: America's Greatest Naval Architect
and His Quest to Build the S.S.* United States

BARONS OF THE SEA

And Their Race to Build the World's Fastest Clipper Ship

STEVEN UJIFUSA

Simon & Schuster

New York   London   Toronto   Sydney   New Delhi

Simon & Schuster
1230 Avenue of the Americas
New York, NY 10020

First Simon & Schuster hardcover edition July 2018

SIMON & SCHUSTER and colophon are registered trademarks of Simon & Schuster, Inc.

For information about special discounts for bulk purchases,
please contact Simon & Schuster Special Sales at 1-866-506-1949
or business@simonandschuster.com.

The Simon & Schuster Speakers Bureau can bring authors to your live event.
For more information or to book an event, contact the Simon & Schuster Speakers
Bureau at 1-866-248-3049 or visit our website at www.simonspeakers.com.

Interior design by Carly Loman

Manufactured in the United States of America

10   9   8   7   6   5   4   3   2   1

Library of Congress Cataloging-in-Publication Data
Names: Ujifusa, Steven, author.
Title: Barons of the sea : and their race to build the world's fastest
   clipper ship / Steven Ujifusa.
Description: New York : Simon & Schuster, 2018. | Includes bibliographical
   references and index.
Identifiers: LCCN 2017037340 (print) | LCCN 2017037569 (ebook) | ISBN
   9781476745992 (Ebook) | ISBN 9781476745978 (hardcover : alk. paper)
Subjects: LCSH: Clipper ships--United States--History--19th century. |
   Merchant marine--United States--History--19th century. | Shipping--United
   States--History--19th century.
Classification: LCC VM23 (ebook) | LCC VM23 .U37 2018 (print) | DDC
   387.5/4092273--dc23
LC record available at https://lccn.loc.gov/2017037340

ISBN 978-1-4767-4597-8
ISBN 978-1-4767-4599-2 (ebook)

To my wife Alexandra

There be three things which are too wonderful for me, yea, four
   which I know not:
The way of an eagle in the air; the way of a serpent upon a rock;
   the way of a ship in the midst of the sea; and the way of a man
   with a maid.

—PROVERBS 30:18–19

See what ambition will do. A man worth 250,000 dollars
relinquishing the joy of society, of wife and children to scramble
among the herd for a few more dollars. Every man for his taste.

—WARREN DELANO II,
letter to Abiel Abbot Low, December 23, 1840

CONTENTS

FOREWORD

With their unprecedented speed and lithe, angelic beauty, American clipper ships harnessed the power of the ocean winds to transform the young United States from a fragile agrarian republic to a muscular international maritime power. Between 1840 and 1860, the clippers revolutionized global trade by getting Chinese tea, porcelain, and other exotic goods to market twice as fast as rival British ships. The clippers also helped transform California from a remote outpost on the Pacific Ocean, where residents subsisted on fishing and farming, into the Golden State it is today, connected by trade and culture to the commercial centers of the East Coast and beyond.

Yet the clippers also kept company with conflict and violence. The China trade was built on lethal, highly addictive opium, a drug that led to two wars between China and Great Britain and the start of China's so-called Century of Humiliation. The captains who plied the seas could be harsh, sometimes driving their ships and crews to the brink of destruction for the sake of profit and glory.

Their masters, the Americans who owned the clipper ships and their cargoes—men with names such as Delano, Forbes, and Low—amassed wealth so great that they became the pillars of the American Establishment. These were the dynastic fortunes that built lavish estates, funded prep schools and universities, and financed much of the new enterprise on which the country would be built: the mines that fueled national growth, the railroads that carried people and goods through the vast interior, and the transatlantic cable that connected the continents. In power and philanthropy, the owners of the clipper ships saw themselves as modern-day merchant princes, much like the grandees of Europe's most famous maritime city-state: the "Most Serene Republic" of Venice. Their cultural and political influence lasted well into the twentieth century. It is no surprise that the grandson of one of the most successful of them would become president of the United States.

BARONS OF THE SEA

THE PATRIARCH

He cared little for outsiders, but would do anything for his own family.

—Sara "Sallie" Delano[1]

Warren Delano II loved sitting at his big desk at Algonac, his Hudson River estate. Around him were treasures of Chinese art: temple bells, porcelains, silk wall hangings. This day, through the wavy glass panes of the library windows, he could see a fall breeze rustle the red and gold leaves on the trees, and the sun glitter on the river. The air was crisp, and a coal fire glowed in the hearth. Penning letters to family and friends, with advice on business and stern judgments about character, he was at home, in charge, and seemingly at ease, managing a business empire that spanned the globe.

Fifty years old in the fall of 1859, Delano was a tough man to the core: well over six feet tall, with chiseled features, a hooked nose, a leonine beard, and bristling sideburns. Suspicious of strangers, he loved his family without reservation. All coldness melted away when his six children tumbled around the library, as they often did while he worked. If two of them got into a fight over a toy, he would look up from his desk, smile, utter firmly, "What's that? Tut, tut!" and the squabble would stop. It was not fear of the patriarch but fear of disappointing him that kept his children well behaved. He never spanked them. Nor did he share his worries on days when letters brought ill news. In the words of one daughter, he had a remarkable knack for hiding "all traces of sadness or trouble or news of anything alarming."[2] To be a true Delano, one had to keep a pleasant disposition, no matter what life threw at you.

The Delano clan had been risking their lives on the high seas ever since the Flemish Protestant adventurer Philippe Delannoy first made the Atlantic crossing to the Plymouth Bay Colony in 1621. Building the family's maritime fortunes required spending much of life apart from those they loved, and demanded a delicate balance of poise on land and toughness at sea. It was a fact of life in seagoing New England: the longer the absence and the larger the risks, the greater the financial rewards. The old whale-hunting cry "A dead whale or a stove boat!" could well have been the family's motto.*

For two centuries, the clan had sacrificed much to attain modest prosperity. But Warren Delano's opulent fortune had sprung from his mastery of another kind of maritime gamble: trading in tea and opium. He had made two visits to China as a young man, first as a bachelor, and then with his wife, Catherine, whom he had married only a few weeks before they set sail. They had lost their first-born child in that country, a tragedy that had driven his young bride to near-suicidal despair. Another child would come home chronically ill.

Yet Warren was expert at keeping his private emotional life divorced from the grand vision by which he and his contemporaries had transformed the world. Their hard work had made a young republic into one of the world's great commercial sea powers, with a fleet of fast ships that challenged Great Britain's maritime supremacy. The success of Yankee clippers, which Delano helped mastermind, shook Old Britannia's complacency, cracking ancient, restrictive trade laws that had kept foreign-built vessels out of British ports. "We must run

---

* *Stove* as in broken, holed, or smashed by an angry whale.

a race with our gigantic and unshackled rival," snarled the *London Times* upon the first visit to London of a Yankee clipper, in 1850. "We must set our long-practiced skill, our steady industry, and our dogged determination against his youth, industry, and ardor."[3] The American clipper in question, *Oriental*, had cut the trip from China to London nearly in half, from six months to a mere 97 days, and her cargo of tea sold for a whopping $48,000. This was at a time when an average American worker made between $10 and $12 a month.[4]

Delano's great wealth from trade had allowed him to remove his family to Algonac, a sixty-acre estate north of New York City. The mammoth scale of the house was in no small part inspired by a great rambling palace Delano had seen on the banks of China's Pearl River many years before, while it also reflected the latest in nineteenth-century American architectural fashion. The architect, Andrew Jackson Downing, was a proponent of the "picturesque": a whimsical Gothic window here, a wood-and-glass cupola there. Downing seems to have understood his seagoing but home-loving client. As a self-taught tastemaker, Downing skillfully used his pen to appeal to the longings of his prosperous but increasingly harried bourgeois clientele. "The mere sentiment of home," Downing mused in *The Architecture of Country Houses*, "has, like a strong anchor, saved many a man from shipwreck in the storms of life."[5]

For Delano, Algonac did exactly that. The tan stucco house, designed in the Tuscan villa style and adorned with towers, gables, and wide porches, was his fortress—a refuge from all of the uncertainties that had dogged his early life. Screened in by stone walls and tall trees, Warren was the realm's benevolent yet exacting ruler. Here, all of the world's problems were kept at bay, and all of life's questions answered. He played games with his children and tended his fruit trees. He and Catherine wrote what they called their "Algonac Diaries," lovingly describing their children's "explosions of firecrackers," and one particularly "splendid bonfire in the henyard."[6] The crash of a gong summoned the family to their evening meal, in an east-facing dining room with a spectacular view of the Hudson River.

Yet Warren didn't tell stories to his children about his time in China as a young man—the violence he had lived through, or his loneliness there before Catherine, or facing down the hard edges of life on the other side of the world. He was determined that his children not go through what he'd experienced. For all his present comfort, he knew what it had taken to make his money, in a foreign country, skirting the fringes of the law.

At Algonac, there was a silent witness to the source of his wealth, in spirit if not in life: a Chinese patriarch was enshrined in an oil painting that hung in the paneled library. He had a thin, pinched face and melancholy eyes, and he was dressed splendidly in flowing silk robes, necklaces of bright jade. A close-fitting cap, topped with the red coral button that denoted his high "mandarin" social status in the Chinese governmental hierarchy, sat next to him on the table.

This was Houqua, the great Chinese merchant whose favor had helped make Warren Delano one of America's richest men. By 1859, the man in the painting had been dead for more than ten years. But through the first half of the nineteenth century, he had been one of the wealthiest men in the world, and a financial father to Delano and other young American merchants of that time. The painting at Algonac was a gift from Houqua himself. Every partner at Delano's firm, Russell & Company—the largest and most profitable American enterprise in China—brought home a portrait of Houqua. His visage adorned counting rooms in New York, Boston, and Philadelphia. So revered was the great merchant that one of Delano's partners named his tea-carrying ship, arguably the first of the sleek Yankee clippers, in Houqua's honor.

In the years since his time under Houqua's patronage, Warren Delano had invested the fortune he had made from his Chinese business into more clipper ships, and then into copper and coal mines, Manhattan real estate, and railroads. Delano himself had achieved

tremendous stature, not only for his wealth but also for his character. One contemporary wrote, "He was a man of quick perceptions,
accurate judgment, indomitable will, and possessed in a remarkable
degree the rich endowment of common sense . . . the result of clear
thinking and strict adherence to the facts."[7]

Yet by that fall day in 1859, the business letters Delano was writing from the library at Algonac were getting increasingly frantic.
A financial panic two years earlier, triggered by speculation in railroads, had caused his investments to suffer. His clipper ships were
particularly hard hit. Within several months of the crash, he had
gone from being a millionaire to being close to penniless. Despite
Delano's obsession with privacy at Algonac, there was no way to
keep this financial cataclysm away from his family hearth. Meanwhile, America was hurtling toward the reckoning between North
and South, a conflict from which even the gates of Algonac could not
shelter the Delanos.

Warren Delano had a big family, an expensive house, and above
all, a reputation to maintain. He had taken big risks throughout his
life, and now, staring at bankruptcy, he was not about to sit still. He
saw only one way to avoid certain ruin: he would return to China
and the opium and tea trade.

His wife and six children would remain at Algonac. Warren
promised Catherine, several months pregnant with their seventh
child, that he would be gone only two years. She did her best to keep
calm as he packed his bags and prepared to leave. She knew firsthand the danger of ocean travel and the volatile political situation in
China, a country where Westerners were not welcomed as guests but
rather derided in the streets as *fanqui*. Foreign devils.

When Warren Delano boarded ship in the Port of New York, the
sounds and smells around him would not have differed greatly from
the scenes of his first voyage more than a quarter century before:

the tang of salt water, the shouts of the sailors, the thunder of the canvas as it dropped from the yards and captured the wind, and the gentle motion of the deck as the vessel glided through the Upper Bay and then out into the gray expanse of the North Atlantic. In his ears would be the sonorous calls of the chanteymen, singing work songs to keep time as they hauled in the lines and spun the capstans—old sailing songs, tuned to the new clipper era:

> Down by the river hauled a Yankee clipper,
> And it's blow, my bully boys, blow!
> She's a Yankee mate and a Yankee skipper,
> And it's blow, my bully boys, blow!

The name of the ship that took him on this voyage is lost to history, but it was almost certainly one of those rakish, swift vessels that he helped pioneer: majestic clippers, flying before the wind like great birds of prey, their vast spreads of canvas stretched taut, their deep, sharp bows piercing wave after wave. On such a vessel, the trip would take fewer than three months. When Warren had first gone to China in 1833, six months was considered an acceptable run. In this respect alone, time spent aboard ship had changed.

Still, life on a long sea voyage would have quickly worn thin: dinners with the captain; letter writing; endlessly rereading the same books and outdated periodicals such as *Harper's Weekly*; listening to other passengers tell stories, play the piano, or sing. Delano had played the guitar as a young man. Perhaps now he sang a few songs with his fellow passengers to pass the time.[8] But this private man likely despised being forced into the shipboard company of people he didn't know. At night, his huge frame jammed into a narrow berth built for a much smaller man, he may have stared out his port light and yearned for Algonac and his family.

An ocean away, his five-year-old daughter, Sara, found the separation from her beloved Papa hard to bear. She later remembered her father vanishing without explanation. As many Yankee children lamented, "Dear papa done Tanton [gone Canton]."[9] When Warren's letters began to arrive, young Sara steamed off the stamps and pasted them in her collection.[10]

The letters meant that Warren Delano had arrived safely. Renting a large house called Rose Hill and settling into his Russell & Company duties, Delano was going back to the work he knew. He missed his family, but he was making money—as he had done thirty years ago.

Chapter i

THE CANTON SILVER CUP

In these days of steam and telegraph, it is difficult to conceive of the state of isolation in which we lived. When a ship arrived, she often brought news five or six months old from home, but as the success of her voyage depended upon keeping private all intimations about the market which she had left behind, not a letter or newspaper was ever delivered until she had bought her cargo, very often not until she lifted her anchor to go off.

—John Murray Forbes,
partner at Russell & Company[1]

Imperial Chinese edicts forbade sexual relations between Western-ers and Chinese. They also forbade boat racing and the opium trade. The Westerners had and did them anyway.

It was 1837, and on the banks of the Pearl River, twenty-seven-year-old Warren Delano lowered himself into a six-man rowing boat christened the *Not So Green*. Delano and his fellow Americans were in pursuit of the Canton Silver Cup, to be awarded by the newly formed Canton Regatta Club. Here he was, junior partner of the small Boston-based firm of Bryant & Sturgis, halfway around the world from his close-knit New England family, racing amidst the grandeur and squalor of one of the world's great trading ports. The statues of five goats—which represented five elements of the Chinese zodiac and the nucleus of an ancient, sprawling Taoist temple—gave Canton the nickname the "City of Rams."

The two competing boats—one British, one American—headed up to the starting line, their oars pulling through yellow waters choked with trash and sewage. Occasionally a dead dog or cat would float past, grotesquely bloated, paws turned toward the heavens. Glancing over at the vast Whampoa harbor, the anchorage just downriver from Canton, Delano could see the big East Indiamen riding at their moorings, preparing to sail home loaded with hundreds of crates of fragrant tea. His *Not So Green* was tiny in comparison: low to the water, the artful sheer of her planked hull curving gracefully upward toward her bow and stern. The elegant craft was most likely the handiwork of the old Chinese shipwright Mo-Pin ("No Pigtail"), whose exacting workmanship was popular with the rich men of Canton's "Golden Ghetto," the foreign merchant community.[2]

Other small craft bobbed past. Schooners that shuttled Westerners downriver to the Portuguese island colony of Macao. Coastal junks, their bows adorned with painted eyes, trundling from Canton to the Chinese ports forbidden to Westerners, Shanghai and Xiamen. Then there were the "flower boats," gaudy floating brothels that drifted past seductively, with Chinese women doing their best to tempt the "foreign devils" from their months of enforced celibacy. Warren's cousin Amasa Delano, who had traveled to China as a ship's officer twenty years earlier, was horrified at what appeared to be the corpses of mixed-blood babies bobbing in the Pearl River, mingled with the dead animals and trash.[3]

At least one trader couldn't repress his desire for illicit companionship. American William Hunter kept a Chinese mistress at Macao, out of sight of the authorities, and had two children with her. When he sailed home alone after twenty years away, he grew so sad that he got on another ship bound for Canton to be with her again. "The man must be insane," wrote a colleague. "A man who has been from home since 1825 . . . and amassing more than $200,000, return[ing] to

China and his miserable Tanka mistress."[4]* Unlike his fellow Americans, Hunter also learned Chinese in secret and came to understand the culture deeply. This was also an act of defiance: the government forbade foreigners from learning the Chinese language, and any exchange beyond what was proscribed by law was furtive at best.

Hunter was a rare exception. The Western traders pulling the six-man gigs that day were not thinking about Chinese culture. Rather, they were focused on competition between England and her former colonial possession, the United States of America. The gun went off, and the *Not So Green* sprung forward, her sharp bow cleaving through the Pearl River. Delano and his five crewmates strained hard, groaning with every stroke as the oars clanked in their locks and the wooden blades gripped the water in unison. Sweat streaming, muscles burning, and the palms of their hands chafing raw, the Americans tore past the other boat, and an intense ten-minute effort swept across the finish line. They had won the Canton Regatta's highest prize, the Silver Cup. The racing committee, attired smartly in pressed white linens aboard a flower boat hired for the occasion, applauded. But the American merchants watching from the balcony of their nearby warehouse broke into wild cheers. "What with our national flags and much other bunting," wrote William Hunter of the celebration, "displayed on tall bamboos from the flat roof of the flower boat, the gathering of so many Fankwaes [or *fanqui*, the foreign devils], their numerous boats manned by English and American jacks well got up, with the Lascars† in tidy white and fresh turbans, it was indeed a gay scene . . . on the Pearl River by the City of Rams."[5]

---

* Known today as Daahngā, this Southern Chinese ethnic subgroup lived on junks and made their living from the sea. The Han Chinese looked down on them as outcasts. For their part, the Daahngā had comparatively few reservations about having sexual relationships with Westerners.
† South Asian and Arab militiamen working for the British Crown.

Back at work in the days that followed, Delano must have basked with pride at his part in the triumph over their British rivals. A descendant of *Mayflower* Pilgrims, he would one day consider changing his Anglicized family name back to the original French Protestant Delannoy. His dislike of the English had been learned from his father, who had been captured by the British navy in the War of 1812 and nearly died aboard a prison ship. "I would sooner grow a tail and become a Chinese in customs, manners, and religion than be an Englishman," Delano wrote later. "Still, I have no prejudice."[6]

There would be other races in the months ahead, but Delano's part in winning the Silver Cup would not divert him for long from his true contest in Canton. "Between you and I," Warren wrote his younger brother Franklin back in America, "I have the prospect of joining an old established house here, and if I can succeed in so doing, it will be far more advantageous to my pecuniary interests than anything I could expect to do by going home. I should repeat, in case of my joining this house, that it would involve the necessity of my remaining in Canton 3 or 4 years longer, but am sure should be disappointed were I to go home seeking business or employment, I must . . . submit to this privation. Of one thing you may be assured— that if I soon do get money enough to enable me to live at home in a very moderate degree of comfort, I shall soon turn my back upon Canton."[7]

All foreigners who lived in Canton (modern day Guangzhou) were confined within the whitewashed colonnades of the so-called Factories. The classical architecture and low-slung roofs stood out against the ochre and browns of the rest of the city. Flags of many nations fluttered from the poles on the wharves just beyond: England, France, Sweden, Holland, and, newest of all, the Stars and Stripes of the young United States of America.

The Factories didn't really make anything; their title was derived from the word *factor*: a merchant or broker. In this case, the residents of the Factories were brokers of Chinese export goods. The first floors of the Factory were for storing those riches: Bohea tea from the Wuyi Mountains and young hyson tea from Anhui; luxury goods such as nankeen,* silks, jades, lacquer, and porcelain; medicinal herbs such as camphor (used to treat colds and fungal infections); and exotic foodstuffs such as rhubarb. Of everything there, young hyson (Cantonese for "flourishing spring") reigned supreme. Picked before the first spring rains, the leaves were first fired in a wok, and then twisted into brow-shaped knots and fired again. It was crates of hyson tea that the members of the Boston Tea Party heaved into Boston Harbor in 1773.

The second and third floors of the Factories contained offices and single sleeping rooms for merchants, clerks, and the occasional Christian missionary. Chinese servants waited on the Westerners from dawn to dusk, making their beds, drawing their water, cooking their meals, and emptying their chamber pots. In the American Factory—which housed the firms of Russell & Company, Wetmore & Company, and others—great counting rooms were lined with wooden desks where clerks and literary men (known as "writers") kept track of business transactions and meetings. Each seat was equipped with a quill, ink, a big ledger, and a dome-shaped bell, which the office worker could ring if he needed a drink or a snack.

Canton's Factories gathered together a few hundred young men from all over the world. Most were from Great Britain: younger sons of the nobility; Scottish merchants; a few missionaries hoping to convert the Chinese. There were traders from Holland and France, as well as a handful of Indians and Sephardic Jews from the Middle East. The Americans were the newest arrivals, not having

---

* A firm, yellowish Chinese cotton cloth.

established a beachhead in Canton until after independence from England.

The Portuguese were the luckiest. Because they had arrived in China first, they had their own colony—architecturally a little bit of Lisbon—on the island of Macao, sixty miles downriver, near where the Pearl River drained into the South China Sea. Since no Western women were permitted on the Chinese mainland, Macao became home for the wives of Canton's other foreign merchants. There the few women who braved the long journey to the East could raise their children, see their husbands as often as they could, and try their best to re-create the social life they knew back in New York, Boston, or London. During the winter off-season, a young trader could waltz until the wee hours of the morning. "I had never seen so brilliant a party anywhere, not even at the garrison fancy ball at Gibraltar," wrote the young American merchant John Murray Forbes. There, lit by crystal chandeliers and surrounded by swirling skirts, a young man would climb on a chair, raise his glass, and toast: "To the bright eyes of Macao!"[8]

Back in Canton, the atmosphere was hypermasculine, a work-hard-play-hard routine of long hours punctuated by cricket games, gambling, and eating and drinking to excess. "You can form no idea of the enormous extravagance of this house," wrote one trader, noting, "the consumption of the article of Beer alone would suffice to maintain one family comfortable in Salem. Our young men finish an entire bottle at each dinner, a dozen bottles are drunk at table at ordinary occasions & frequently 1-1/2 dozen bottles."[9, 10] Despite servants and many creature comforts, the Factories were still claustrophobic. "If you could see the packed-up way we have to live here, crammed as close to each other as jars of sweetmeats in a box of bran," complained one American missionary—"no yard, no out-houses, no trees, no back door, even—you would feel as keenly as I do the plea-sure of sometimes seeing growing green things."[11]

During the busy trading months in spring, summer, and fall, the

American merchants worked as many as twenty hours a day, rising early for a breakfast of rice, tea, toast, curry, eggs, and fish. A light lunch was served at noon, and a big dinner at six thirty, washed down with wine, beer, and India ale, and topped off by brandy and strong draws from Manila cheroot—a thin cigar made of tobacco, roots, and bark, cut at both ends.[12] Supposedly, smoking a cheroot warded off fatal tropical diseases such as malaria. Work then continued into the night, no matter how much they'd had to drink.

Foreign merchants were restricted to trading with a government-approved Chinese guild, the Cohong. Based on the Americans' best guess of what the demand would be back home in six months' time, they would make an offer to one of the guild's dozen or so Chinese merchants, who made up the formal Cohong association.[13] The foreign merchants were called *yanghang*, or "ocean traders." If the tea market back home was oversupplied and weak, a bad buy could ruin the Yankee merchant. If the tea market was strong, he would make a nice profit.

To buy the tea, the American merchants would use a combination of cash, usually in the form of silver, and promissory notes. The Chinese merchant was paid in full (plus interest) only after the tea had gone to auction back in America. An example from 1805 illustrates one such transaction: a Rhode Island trader purchased from his Chinese counterpart fifty chests of souchong tea for $1,533.12. Rather than paying the full amount at once, he put up $383.12 and promised to pay the balance of $1,150 (plus interest) the following season. To avoid confusion, the notes and proceedings were recorded in both Chinese and English.[14]

Back in the Factory, the clerks would make a note of the amounts paid for the tea crates, dutifully recording all transactions in ledger books and carefully preparing hundreds of invoices to send to their bosses back home. The accounting side of the business was tedious and exacting, perfect for bean counters but aggravating for poets. As Russell & Company partner Abiel Abbot Low wrote home to his younger, *bon vivant* brother, William Henry, who was considering a trip to Canton to make his fortune: "Let me repeat that a thorough knowledge of bookkeeping is absolutely necessary to one who designs to act a responsible part; at least the principle of double entry should be so familiar that you could readily carry it into practice." He also urged his younger brother to improve his handwriting.[15]

While the clerks worked, others prepared the tea crates for shipment home. The quicker the tea got to New York—especially the coveted first picking of young hyson—the higher the price it fetched at auction, and the better the reputation of the firm. In Canton, each sealed crate was marked with the name of the merchant or consignee. Some were opened randomly to ensure that the contents did not include sticks, stones, or dried weeds. Like sommeliers in the wine trade, tea traders had to develop very acute senses of taste and smell. "A dirty business," one trainee described the constant sniffing, tasting, and weighing, "the tea getting into the nostrils, soiling the hands, etc."[16] A fragrant luxury coveted by consumers back home quickly became a noxious nuisance to the merchants selling it.

The foreign tea ships rode at anchor at Whampoa. From June to September—months when ships from America and Europe could take advantage of the seasonal monsoon winds, blowing them eastward to Canton across the South China Sea—the harbor became a forest of masts, with colorful flags fluttering. On hot summer nights, the air was damp and thick, and the calls of tropical birds mingled with the cries of passing boatmen. The Western captains would clear their ships' imported cargoes with officials, go ashore to meet with their assigned hong merchant, exchange presents (*cumshas*), and receive the so-called Grand Chop: the official clearance document, stamped with the seal ("chop") of the *Hoppo*, or head Chinese customs official.[17]

Trips were timed with the seasons. Homeward bound vessels generally rode at anchor at Whampoa between July and October. If they didn't, they would have to beat against the strong winds of the southwest monsoon. In the fall, the monsoon shifted, bringing winds that blew toward the southwest, which helped the foreign ships sail home faster. While they waited for the winds to change, the captains would go ashore to the Factories to lodge, dine, and network with the partners of the shipping firms. The sailors stayed aboard the ships, maintaining them and preparing for the hundreds of tightly packed tea chests expected on the voyage.

Before these could be loaded, the crew would seal up all hatches and portholes, and light a fire down below to smoke out the rats and cockroaches. The cockroaches, one sailor wrote, "are really more troublesome than the rats, for they eat the labels off tea chests. They will gnaw your toe nails and eat your books and your oil clothing, and will fly in your faces; on one occasion, they drove all the watch below deck." Once the fire was put out, a team of Chinese laborers would then cart away up to thirty bushels of dead bugs before the holds could be loaded with tea chests.[18]

Finally, when the winds were right and the cargo fully loaded, the ships weighed anchor and set sail for home. Their route took them west through the steamy South China Sea, through the Sunda Strait to the Indian Ocean, and onward around Africa's Cape of Good Hope. The ships would then ride the southeast trades northward to the equator. There the paths of the British and American ships would diverge: the former tacking northward to London's West India Docks; the latter westward across the Atlantic to New York's South Street or Boston's India Wharf.

The ships that made these voyages had not changed much in design during the past two centuries. A typical American or British "Indiaman" was about 175 feet long and 30 feet wide, with a full hull and deep draft (hull depth before the waterline) and characteristic rounded topsides (hull above the waterline)—a feature known to sailors and builders as tumblehome. The British vessels, usually converted fourth-rate warships, boasted ornate sterns with latticed glass windows that glowed at night, when captains hosted other masters and friendly Chinese mandarins over claret and port.

Since Elizabethan times, popular shipbuilding consensus was that below the waterline, a ship's hull should resemble the body of a fish: a bluff bow and a narrow, tapered stern. "Cod's head and mackerel tail," was how wags described a typical merchant ship's hull of that period.[19] And while these burdensome, full-bodied ships carried plenty of cargo, their average day's run was slow. They were built of oak, teak, and other heavy materials, their bottoms coppered to repel boring mollusks—built for strength, not dispatch. "Safety and comfort were the watchwords, with no desire or effort for speed," wrote Captain Arthur Hamilton Clark, one of America's most astute chroniclers of the clipper ship era. "No one ever knew how fast these vessels could really sail, as they never had anyone on board who could get the best speed out of them."[20] A six-month voyage from Canton to London was seen as a perfectly respectable passage. It didn't really matter which ship got to England first, as prices were fixed in London. In fact, until the 1830s, the British traders had worked for a Crown-sanctioned monopoly, the East India Company. But even after its exclusive China trading rights ended, there were no significant changes in ship design on either side of the Atlantic.

The American ships were of similarly full-bodied build, although they generally carried less ornamentation. (They did, however, persist in painting faux gun ports on their topsides.) But the impetus for new ship design was great. Without the kind of government support that protected British profits, the US owners were under economic pressure to get their cargos to market faster. There was little room for fripperies such as gilded heraldry and luxurious cabins on American ships—for tightfisted shipowners, such things wasted time, money, and speed. Thanks to the Revolution and the War of 1812, Britain had little interest in shipping tea and China goods to its pesky former colonies. American merchants were more than happy to fill this void. Unlike the mercantilist British Crown, the federal government took a laissez-faire attitude toward the China trade. All Congress cared about was collecting duties, the main source of federal revenue at the time. As a result, skilled ship-wrights and opportunistic merchants had been collaborating for a couple of decades to revolutionize ship design, with a focus on increasing speed in smaller vessels.

The fruits of this Yankee ingenuity would be sailing full tilt into a greatly changed China within a few years.

To most Chinese, the few hundred fair-skinned people huddled in Macao and Canton were at best inconvenient guests—at worst, little better than rats. The Americans were the "flowery flag devils," after the stars and stripes that flew from their ships. The Danish were the "yellow flag devils," and the English, "red-haired devils."[21]

There were no Chinese-flagged vessels bound for Europe. For almost four hundred years, the country had insulated itself from direct contact with the Western world. In 1492, when Christopher Columbus sailed from Spain on his first voyage across the Atlantic to find the Celestial Kingdom described by Marco Polo, China's own overseas commerce had essentially already been stopped. In 1371, more than a century before Columbus's overseas gamble, the emperor and his mandarins declared a series of sea bans (*haijin*) that made the unauthorized construction of an oceangoing junk a capital offense. Gone were the massive trading junks of the Ming dynasty "treasure fleet," which had ventured as far as the east coast of Africa. Although Chinese maintained a thriving international trade with the Philippines, the East Indies, and Vietnam, China tried to ignore the barbarians of the West.

China was, after all, the Middle Kingdom, whose emperor ruled by the Mandate of Heaven. It was big enough and rich enough to ignore and snub the outside world. The Chinese grew all the food they needed and produced all the luxuries (porcelain, silk, jade) that its most privileged citizens required to adorn their palaces with an opulence of which the monarchs of Europe could only dream. China also saw itself as too big and strong to subjugate and colonize.

19

But Europeans wanted China's products too. When Portuguese captain Jorge Alvares sailed into Canton Harbor in 1513, his ship packed with tempting goods, the Chinese grudgingly agreed to trade. One new delicacy the Portuguese introduced to China—Mexican chilies—would forever put a fiery kick into the native cuisine.

As for the *fanqui* merchants of later years, there were many beautiful and exotic Chinese items to ship back home to sell, but the most coveted (and profitable) were the dried leaves of a plant that could not be grown in Europe's temperate climate. Tea (*Camellia sinensis*), which the Chinese used as medicine, came from a mysterious evergreen shrub that, when dried and boiled in water, produced a beguiling beverage. Its kicks of caffeine, theobromine, and theophylline soothed the nerves, while its rich taste delighted the palate. A subtropical plant, it thrived on the banks of the Pearl River in southeast China, alongside mulberry bushes, host plants for silkworms. When the Portuguese traders introduced tea to the West, Europeans could not get enough of it. By the mid-1700s, England was hooked. Because of its expense and exotic origins, drinking tea became an elaborate social ritual. For the rich, this also meant purchasing new precious objects—filigreed silver and porcelain tea sets—that were manufactured in their home countries.

The passion for tea found its way across the Atlantic to England's American colonies. Tea helped spark the American Revolution, when a new parliamentary tax on imports to the colonies provoked a group of revolutionaries dressed as Native Americans to dump 342 chests of the prized shrub into Boston Harbor. One ditty urged American patriots to drink tea brewed from clover, called labrador tea:

Throw aside your Bohea and your green hyson tea,
And all things with a new fashioned duty;
Procure a good store of the choice labrador,
For there'll soon be enough here to suit ye;

There do without fear, and to all you'll appear

Fair, charming, true, lovely, and clever;

Though the times remain darkish, young men may be
    sparkish,

And love you much stronger than ever.[22]

The Boston Tea Party was as much a revolt against a cartel as it was against taxation without representation. As elsewhere in the British colonies, the Honorable East India Company had a lock on the tea trade; only it could sell the in-demand drink.

After independence, Americans retained their thirst for tea, especially green tea. (The British tended to favor black.) With the Honorable Company monopoly out of the way—only countries in the British Empire could remain part of her tea supply chain—US merchants had to start dispatching their own ships to China. On February 22, 1784, the Baltimore-built *Empress of China* sailed from New York with a cargo of ginseng, becoming the first American ship to arrive in Canton.[23] The Chinese market had long coveted the American variety of ginseng over the native strain for its superior taste and strength.[24] The trip's backers were a constellation of the young nation's richest men, including Robert Morris, known as the "financier of the Revolution" for using his business connections to equip and pay General George Washington's troops. Fourteen months later, when *Empress of China* arrived triumphantly back in New York Harbor, the cargo brought auctioneers stampeding to the wharf. The American people, tea-starved during the lean years of the American Revolution, were finally getting their fix.*

For its part, the *Empress of China* syndicate enjoyed a 25 percent return on its investment. The successful venture attracted mer-

---

* Tea would not be cultivated in Britain's colony of Kenya until the early nineteen hundreds.

chants from other American commercial cities—Boston, Salem, New York, Philadelphia, and Baltimore—to dispatch ships in the *Empress*'s wake.

The men who sailed these ships—and mostly single men braved the long and treacherous journey—were the soldiers of fortune of the new era of global trade. Most came from comfortable backgrounds, well connected but not independently wealthy. To go to China as a young bachelor and risk everything took a lot of guts, and to get an apprenticeship with a merchant firm usually meant procuring a letter of introduction from richer relatives.

Young Warren Delano II of Fairhaven, Massachusetts, fit the bill exactly. His family was established and esteemed but hardly wealthy. The Delanos still had to work for a living, and in their native Fairhaven, that meant either plowing rocky New England soil or braving the cruel sea. Fairhaven was just across the Acushnet River from New Bedford, Massachusetts, America's whaling capital and arguably the richest city per capita in the United States. Many of Warren's forebears, including his father Warren Sr., had commanded whaling ships, harpooning the colossal beasts from slim whaleboats rowed by crews of six men. One of Warren's cousins, Captain Amasa Delano, made a trip to China in 1794 aboard the *Massachusetts,* writing in his memoir that China "is the first for greatness, riches, and grandeur of any country ever known."[25]

Tough men such as Warren's father, one historian would rhapsodize later, were "great types of our American manhood" who practiced a "handicraft in which courage, resourcefulness, agility, clear eye, and steady nerve were the very common places of the calling."[26] At the city's peak in the 1830s, the merchant princes of New Bedford owned almost seventy whaling ships, which sailed to as far away as Antarctica and the Sea of Japan to bring back barrels of the precious oil used for candles and industrial lubricants. Charles Francis Adams, son of President John Quincy Adams and grandson of John Adams, the second president of the United States, wrote admiringly of New Bedford, saying that, "it had risen like magic, and . . . presents more noble-looking mansions than any other in the country."[27] The whaling wealth of New Bedford spilled over into Fairhaven, which had a whaling fleet of its own.

Warren's father, a gruff old salt if there ever was one, lived in a Greek Revival wood-frame structure, paid for with the modest fortune he had earned from the sea. Early in the Anglo-American War of 1812, he had been captured by the British while running a blockade and nearly starved to death in captivity. On his release, he returned home to his family sick but safe. Then, in 1814, the British bombarded the New England coast, burning Essex, Connecticut, to the ground and threatening Fairhaven and New Bedford. A still-frail Warren Sr. and his wife, Deborah, spirited their young sons Warren, Frederic, Franklin, and Edward, inland to avoid the exploding British shells. When the war ended in 1815, the elder Delano retired from the sea, and went to work as a ship agent and whale oil broker.

The Delanos were smart, resourceful, and tough minded. As one descendant wrote later, although a "courageous and self-respecting lot . . . they must have had a very hard and up-hill struggle for existence."[28] The elder Warren and his wife wanted better for their children, grooming Warren II and his brothers for a commercial career from a very young age. He attended Fairhaven Academy, the local private school, which cost $2 per quarter in tuition and educated boys and girls (albeit in separate classrooms). The curriculum included English, French, Greek, Latin, music, and drawing. "Particular attention will be given to the culture of the moral character," boasted a Fairhaven Academy advertisement.[29]

None of the Delano boys was bound for college. The Delanos, like many prosperous families of Puritan stock, valued intelligence, but of the mercantile rather than bookish kind; that is, unless the young man in question were destined for the clergy or law, in which case, the family would pack him off to Harvard or Yale. Although no intellectual slouch—Delano became a prolific letter writer as an adult—Warren fit the description of his near contemporary Moses Grinnell, another scion of a leading whaling family: "not burdened with special predilections for scholastic pursuits, and determined to become a shipping merchant."[30]

At the age of sixteen, Warren Delano II headed north to Boston to work as an apprentice clerk at a firm with strong New Bedford roots: the Boston-based firm of Hathaway & Company. One Hathaway, Francis, had been among the first New Bedford merchants to break into the China trade, which had previously been the domain of men from Boston, Salem, and New York. The Hathaways and the Delanos almost certainly knew each other socially, although, unlike the Unitarian Delanos, the Hathaways were Quakers, known formally as the Society of Friends. Even in the New World, the "Friends" kept a low profile, dressing in plain clothes and keeping businesses within families.

Perhaps Warren found the sweet fragrance wafting from the Chinese tea chests on the Hathaway ships more appealing than stinky barrels of whale oil. He kept his sights on the China trade. Moving to New York, he took a position at another merchant firm, Goodhue & Company, where work was gentlemanly and lucrative: "they sell a cargo of teas and China goods (worth perhaps $400,000 at auction) at auction or by brokers with less noise than an eighth avenue dealer in tea and soap displays in an hour."[31]

New Bedford connections continued to favor the Delanos. Warren's younger brother Franklin was hired by Moses Grinnell to work in his firm's New York office. The bread-and-butter of Grinnell, Minturn & Company was the transatlantic packet trade, run under the flag of the Swallowtail Line, which carried passengers (mostly immigrants) and British-manufactured goods (mostly crockery and textiles) across the North Atlantic. Yet the most valuable items on the manifest were the so-called bills of exchange: the European promissory notes that were greasing the financial wheels of the growing

American economy. These notes were issued in England by banks such as Baring Brothers & Co. to a select group of American business partners. Once the ink had dried, the precious bills of exchange would be placed aboard a sailing packet departing from Liverpool or London.[32] In an era before America had a national currency, bills of exchange backed by gold were safer to transport than gold itself."[33]

The Grinnell firm was also in the whaling business. (One wag joked that the Grinnell firm "sold two kinds of oil, good and bad.")[34] It was a business that both Delano brothers hoped to leave behind. Tea was an imported luxury product that tempted the palate. Whale oil, while a necessity that lit the lamps of the nation, was rendered from slaughtered animals on filthy ships. Harvard student-turned-sailor Richard Henry Dana, author of the hugely popular memoir *Two Years Before the Mast*, wrote disdainfully of one such "slovenly" whaler: "She had a false deck, which was rough and oily, and cut up in every direction by the chines of oil casks; her rigging was slack, and turning white, paint worn off the spars and blocks." He found her "slab-sided Quaker" captain just as unappealing. These descriptions insulted the residents of Nantucket and New Bedford, who mailed complaints to the author, but Dana replied cheekily that his description was "not exaggerated" and that the whaling ship was indeed "ugly to behold."[35]

Warren Delano wanted to avoid the whaling business for another reason: money. On a good voyage, a New Bedford whaling ship could expect to earn $16,000—after years on the high seas. A few Yankee whalers got really lucky: one ship came in with a haul of 4,100 barrels of whale oil worth $109,000. But such profits still had to be divided up among the owners, the captain, and more than thirty crew members, as well as local charities.[36] A typical captain would receive about 1/8 of the profit, perhaps no more than $900, while a sailor who had shipped out for the first time would receive only about 1/350 of the profit (or "lay," as seamen called it in *Moby-Dick*)—sometimes as little as $25 for several years' work.[37]

This is the life Warren's father had known, and he had been one of the lucky ones. In China, Warren knew he had the potential to earn much, much more. His goal was a lifetime "competence": a bankable sum large enough to make a man independently wealthy. In the mid-nineteenth century, a competence was the equivalent of $100,000, earned over five to ten years away from home. Earning this from trading tea and opium wouldn't be easy. Most men didn't have the connections to get into the trade and, once there, couldn't do the intense work. Warren Delano II had and could.

The Americans who went to China included a smattering of New Yorkers, Philadelphians, and southerners, but Delano's Yankees prevailed. Originally a derogatory term used by the Dutch settlers of New Amsterdam (later New York) to describe their British neighbors to the north, *Yankee* meant New Englanders, usually descendants of Pilgrims, Puritans, and other Protestant dissidents who fell afoul of the Church of England and fled to North America. Buttressed by uncompromising faith and toughened by the severe climate, Yankees excelled at commerce, the cutting-edge technology of the time, and the art of seamanship. Self-reliance was the ultimate virtue. Sentimentality had no place in their lives. At least in public.

Warren Delano II most likely made his first China connection at Goodhue or Hathaway. By 1833, he'd left New York for Canton. Being a merchant in China was a big step up; his family expected great things of him. He was only twenty-four.

Delano traveled aboard the brig *Commerce* as a "supercargo"—the onboard representative—of his new employer Bryant & Sturgis, a firm with branches in New York, Canton, and Manila. It was a Bryant-owned ship that Harvard's Dana crewed with on his famous voyage, a vessel carrying "spirits of all kinds (sold by the cask), teas, coffee, sugars, raisins, molasses, hardware, crockery-ware, tinware, cutlery, clothing of all kinds, boots and shoes from Lynn, calicoes, and cotton from Lowell, crapes [*sic*], silks; also shawls, scarves, necklaces, jewelry, and combs for the women; furniture; and, in fact, everything that can be imaged, from Chinese fireworks to English cart-wheels,—of which we had a dozen pairs with their iron tires on."[38]

As the *Commerce* set her sails and headed out to sea on her six-month voyage, Delano knew that he had hard tasks ahead. He had to get to Canton alive, he had to stay healthy in the strange land, and he had to ingratiate himself with his trading associates—not only as a hard worker but also as good company.

His employer had invested considerable resources in sending him to China. The passage alone cost about $600, a good tradesman's income in the 1830s.[39] The longer he stayed, and the harder he worked, the more money he could make for the firm. If he did not die of tropical disease, an accident in the harbor, or alcohol poisoning, he had a shot at his goals: a partnership at a big firm that could lead to the competence he needed to return home a success.

In Canton, Delano's immediate supervisor was the unflappable, intelligent Russell Sturgis. Only four years older than Delano, Sturgis was everything that a China merchant should be. He had a killer instinct for making money and had the right connections: he was a great-nephew of Colonel Thomas Handasyd Perkins, one of the first Americans in the China trade. Sturgis considered himself lucky to have his second wife, Mary, and his four children with him. (Mary Sturgis would never come home, dying in Manila in 1837.)

Delano worked hard for Sturgis, and it paid off. In 1835, two years after his arrival in China, he made partner at the firm.[40] It was an unusually fast rise. Yet Delano remained unsatisfied. He saw Bryant & Sturgis as a second-tier concern, and he hadn't come to China to accept second place. He wanted to break into the most prestigious and profitable operation of them all, one boasting deep relationships with the Chinese merchant community that gave its partners unparalleled access to the tea and opium trade. That firm was Russell & Company, which had the fastest vessels in the American merchant marine: trim, loftily rigged schooners with huge spreads of white canvas when flying before the wind. Russell & Company far out-classed its American rivals in profits, earning $240,000 in one particularly good year.[41] Much of this was due to Houqua's relationship with two of Russell & Company's partners: brothers John Murray Forbes and Robert Bennet Forbes. One rival firm despaired: "They now have a fearful advantage over us, backed as they are by Houqua on one side and Barings on the other."[42]

With luck, young Delano could use his partnership to engineer a merger between Bryant & Sturgis and the greater firm. But there was one problem: he was a nobody.

CHAPTER 2

BREAKING INTO THE FAMILY

I shall not go into any argument to prove that I considered it right
to follow the example of England, the East India Company, the
countries that cleared it for China, and the merchants whom I had
always accustomed to look up to as exponents of all that was hon-
orable in trade,—the Perkins's, the Peabody's, the Russells, and
the Lows.[1]

—ROBERT BENNET FORBES

"It" was opium, smuggled into China from India by the British and
from Turkey by the Americans. Of all the American firms trading
tea in Canton, only the Quaker-run Olyphant & Company refrained
from the opium trade. (The partners of the rival firms called them
"Zion's Corner.") One calming buzz fed the other, although the Chinese craving for opium was far more potent, addictive, and deadly
than the Western craving for tea. And no American company excelled at the business better than Russell & Company.

Russell & Company was a family affair, staffed almost entirely by
a network of cousins connected through the craggy-faced founder of
America's trade in China, Colonel Thomas Perkins. It was Perkins
who had introduced Turkish opium to the Chinese market, breaking the British monopoly on the drug from India. According to his
biographer, Thomas Cary, Perkins "became well acquainted with

the habits of the Chinese, and collected a fund of information concerning trade there in all its branches."[2] So much so that Perkins became one of America's first millionaires, worth $3 million at his death in 1854.

In Canton, Colonel Perkins's operation was called the Boston Concern. After Perkins, a Yankee from Connecticut would take over. The affable yet shrewd Samuel Russell built upon his predecessors' pattern of trade: selling the Chinese ginseng, beaver and other animal pelts, cotton, and sandalwood (and, covertly, opium); and buying Chinese tea, silk, porcelain, and other luxury goods to sell back in the United States. Few mastered the game of risk better than Russell. "There was about him a suavity and charm of manner under which no circumstances ever deserted him," wrote Russell's business partner William C. Hunter, the same man who kept a Chinese mistress during his many years in Canton.[3] "Of his considerable forbearance under great provocation I can vouch from personal experience."[4] The Perkins men felt that they could do business with their fellow Yankee, even if Russell wasn't a relative. In 1827 Perkins and Russell merged into a new partnership under the Russell moniker: Russell & Company.

Perkins and Russell knew American success would rest on favorable ties with the Chinese Cohong, the guild that held the monopoly on foreign trade. And no member of that guild was more important than its leader, the mighty Wu Ping-Chien, known to foreigners as Houqua. In portraits, a slight man with a wispy white beard and rather sad eyes, Houqua was in life a mandarin powerhouse, paying no mind to the dictates of the ancient Confucian social hierarchy, in which a merchant had no standing. Bedecked in shimmering silk robes and clattering jade necklaces, he met and entertained the *fangai* merchants so hated in China, building his fortune by selling, buying, and making loans against the foreigners' future profits. He always made it a point to forgive debts to preserve a relationship. According to one story, when an American merchant owed him $100,000 (a full competence), Houqua told the desperate man in pidgin: "You and I are No 1. olo flen; you belong honest man, only no got chance." He then opened his safe, ripped up the promissory notes, and threw them in the trash. "Just now have settee counter, alle finishee; you go, you please."[5]

Eventually worth some $26 million, Houqua became by far the richest merchant—perhaps the richest nonsovereign—in the world. However, his position was not without risk. As head of the Cohong, he was held personally responsible by the authorities for the foreigners' good credit and law-abiding conduct. (Their illicit opium trading would become a source not only of profit but of danger to him.) What's more, high-born Chinese resented his getting around the ancient, presumptive meritocracy. But in Canton, both Chinese and foreigners admired his mettle, brains, and money.

To the Americans in Canton, Houqua held the keys to the Celestial Kingdom, the keys to the money. They revered him almost as if he were a deity. Perkins established a strong relationship with the great merchant early on. When Russell arrived, he too became a protégé. In fact, Houqua liked Russell so much that, to the chagrin of the British, he decided to do business exclusively with Americans— and in time with Russell's firm almost exclusively. Eventually the numerous relations and partners of Russell & Company were to become Houqua's surrogate sons. "You know it is an ambition common to my countrymen to have many sons," he wrote one of them.[6] As a businessman who dealt with foreigners, Houqua couldn't wholly trust his fellow Chinese, especially the government in Peking, but he could create his own fraternity of impressionable young men.

The fraternity soon included Perkins's nephews Robert and John Murray Forbes, who arrived in Canton in the 1820s to carry on in their uncle's footsteps, spending their bachelor days in China to develop connections and earn the competences they craved. The brothers were the poor relations of the Perkins clan, their father having failed as a merchant and died destitute. Robert and John had felt duty bound to provide for their mother, the colonel's sister, and both eventually left school to go into Uncle Thomas's business.

Robert, age thirteen, went to sea on his uncle's ships. "He has become so useful that I really regret to let him go away," a cousin at home complained, "but as he has set out to make a sailor, it is best to let him persevere; and I will answer for his being at the top of his profession within a few years."[7] Dashing, adventurous, a lover of sea stories, Robert rose through the ranks to become a ship's captain before joining the company in Canton.

Younger brother John Murray preferred to keep his nose in the ledger books. Introverted and solemn, he had received a liberal education at a boarding school in Northampton, Massachusetts. Its lessons were not merely scholarly. Remembering his schooldays later, John wrote, "The history of my life at Round Hill School would not be complete if I forgot fisticuffs. My notion then as now was, after Polonius' advice—Avoid getting into a fight by all honorable means, but, once in, so conduct the war that your adversary would not soon hanker after another."[8]

His father's death had a profound effect on John's outlook on life and business. While Robert sought adventure, John sought stability. His letters journal the intense family burden many of these young Americans felt when they left home to seek their fortunes in China. He remembered his mother's "patient patching, my sister Emma's vigilant eye to our wants, corporeal and spiritual, and especially the latter on Sunday afternoon, when she always read to us our Bible and hymns."[9] When he left Round Hill for Canton at the behest of Uncle Thomas, John must have been overwhelmed by the pressure to succeed. But at the same time, he knew that his reputation and future financial stability depended on his success.

"You may be sure that I shall receive your advice and wishes as to my conduct as anything rather than those of a taskmaster, and I trust that I shall observe them more strictly than if they were so," John wrote his brother Robert in 1828, as he prepared to set sail to join Robert in Canton. "I can hardly say that I was surprised at your determination as to my going to Canton. It is true that it must be painful to me to leave all our friends here, but I feel that it is better to make any sacrifice than to be a useless member of our family."[10]

Of the two brothers, it was John who forged the closest relationship with Houqua. He even looked a bit like a Yankee version of the great merchant, with a long, pinched face, prominent nose, high forehead, and prematurely receding hair. His tact and attention to detail led Houqua to transfer all of his tea business to Russell & Company, stipulating that John Forbes handle it personally.[11]

When the younger brother, John, eventually returned to Boston, having "made his competence" in Canton, the connection with Houqua remained. As John began investing his wealth into American enterprises—including the era's new transportation technology, railroads—Houqua entrusted him with a few hundred thousand dollars to invest and manage on the great merchant's behalf.[12]

To be awarded stewardship of such a huge chunk of foreign capital was unprecedented for an American businessman. And if the Russell men were masters of risk in tea speculation, they were extremely careful when it came to overseeing Houqua's fortune. "Remember, security is my first object!" Houqua wrote regarding a shipment of teas and silks via Turkey. "I desire to run no unnecessary risks, and want, if possible to have the accounts closed early."[13] From Houqua, John learned the ultimate negotiating trick, as he explained to a relative: "The great art of making bargains is to find out other people's ultimatum without letting out yours, and this can be done with most people by letting them talk."[14]

Robert Forbes, too, had made his competence and returned to Boston, but his financial outcome was not as happy as his brother's. In a series of setbacks following the Panic of 1837, triggered by rampant over speculation in Western states, he lost the fortune he had made in the China trade, as well as his townhouse on Temple Place in Boston's tony Beacon Hill. At thirty-five, he was terrified of dying a melancholy, burned-out, and humiliated old man. He had to make a new competence. Leaving his wife, Rose, and infant son, Robert Jr., in Boston, Robert Forbes returned to China, resolved to take back his place as the head of Russell & Company in Canton.

To get the position, Robert needed to replace the firm's managing partner there, which he did by pressuring the man to return to his original employers in New York.[15] Forbes then began canvassing the other Americans in the Factory to find a new partner and so grow the company. In a letter to his wife, he mused that "Russell Sturgis & Delano make an efficient house," and would make ideal business partners.[16]

Warren Delano, especially, must have been good company, for he and Forbes started dining together. The two combined work with social activity. They stuck close by other Yankees such as Sturgis (Robert's second cousin and Delano's boss) and Francis Hathaway of New Bedford (whose firm was the first tea trader Delano had worked for, at age sixteen). Forbes joined the Union Club of Canton, an elite group of "much sociability and festivity" founded by his younger brother John a few years earlier. "We are by rule all hosts & all guests wherever we go, have a supreme right to find fault with the wine or anything else & to call for whatever we want," Robert Forbes wrote. "[T]his abuse of constraint makes it pleasant, they meet weekly, go or not just as you please."

This was the inner circle of Americans and British who bonded over games of leapfrog on the dikes, cricket, and boat racing. While they played late-night games of whist, poorly paid junior clerks were abed in their stuffy little rooms in the Factories, worrying whether or not they would get tapped one day for membership.[17] The blending of competition with bonhomie was always a difficult balance. Some of the younger men spilled out their hopes and fears in long letters back home. Others kept their thoughts to themselves, staring at the ceilings of their dark bedrooms as the smells of Cantonese cuisine, the rap of sandals against cobblestone, and the cries of beggars wafted into their rooms. In front of the Factories was an open public square, usually filled with hordes of unfortunates. "Cash, foreign devils, cash!" they shouted at passing Westerners, banging their tin cups on the pavement.[18] Nearby, the only streets open to Westerners, Hog Lane and Old China Street, were narrow, dank alleys barely wide enough for two men to walk abreast. Hawkers hollered in pidgin at passing sailors, pushing everything from knickknacks to prostitutes.

For his part, Delano learned that the best approach was to maintain a hardboiled exterior, not burdening his family back home with the sad or seamy side of Canton life. The camaraderie made life a bit easier. It helped that Forbes shared Delano's love of boats and racing. Indeed, Robert, a bona fide sea captain, loved nothing more than a boat race, whether with oars or sail. There was a legendary story that once, while stocking up a cargo of sandalwood in Honolulu, he had challenged Captain Catesby Jones of the American sloop-of-war USS *Peacock* to a rowing race. Forbes later recalled proudly how Jones told him that it was a race "between gentlemen . . . for the trial of the speed of the boats and the endurance of the men."[19] It ended in a dispute over a buoy marker, so in this trial, the better man was not decided.

As their friendship grew, Delano and Forbes spent evenings rowing together in the *Not So Green*, making their way between the junks, barges, and flower boats. His goal, Robert wrote, was to "exercise every day so as to win a *silver cup*."[20] After their workout, the men retired to the Factories to play whist until the wee hours, as Chinese servants brought them drinks and other refreshments. With the sun setting on the Pearl River, the men could forget about invoices and ship loading and concentrate on more personal matters: homesickness, fears of what awaited them in this strange place, their dislike of the English, Houqua's generosity—and whether or not the mandarins would stop taking bribes and finally crack down on the opium trade by force.

They also must have mused over Delano's marriage prospects back home. When Forbes's cousin John Perkins Cushing had returned to Boston from Canton several years earlier, bringing with him a huge fortune and a retinue of Chinese servants, beautiful young women had "beset him like bumblebees about a lump of sugar."[21] Cushing loved to visit the Boston mansion of his august uncle Thomas Perkins, with whom he frequently played backgammon and enjoyed the cambric teas, dipped toast, gingerbread toast, East Indian preserves, and other culinary memories of his time in China.[22]

Warren could dream.

Forbes was always thrilled to leave the confines of the counting-house to be on the open water. In letters, he makes no mention of rowing the *Not So Green* with Delano in any of the Canton regattas. But in the fall regatta of 1838, Robert took the helm of the sailing yacht *Ferret* and piloted her to victory against the British competitors *Rat* and *Mouse*. After he beat the nearest rival by four minutes, the spectators on the water erupted into a "deafening shout of applause." The sight of so many graceful sailing yachts, flying along silently like white-winged birds over the surface of the water, was thrilling. In his ships-captain viewpoint, Forbes thought that winning the sailing race "gave more satisfaction to the public than all the rowing matches."[23]

Boat racing was one of the few ways to break up the tedium of Canton life. In a letter to Rose—Forbes felt chummy enough with his wife that he freely told her about all of his shenanigans in the rowdy boys' club that was Canton—the merchant could barely contain his excitement at his winnings: "Entrance fee $5—cost of boat race $15—gain a cup worth $75—deduct $20 as above—$55 dollar gain by boats thus far—& I have bought a sail boat!!! costing something over $200 but worth $300—gain thereby $100 hey!!!" Forbes must have then realized that his wife would be infuriated that he was spending money on yachts and skylarking with his coworkers while she was living in reduced circumstances and caring for their infant son. "Here comes the cloven foot say you," his letter continued. "There's the sock he has already split open." Although, he added jauntily, "This is not so," insisting that his more cautious (and still rich) brother John Murray Forbes would agree. "As John will say, health is capital here & health can only be retained by relaxation from the desk for an hour or two every day after dinner—the boat is my capital."[24]

As for Houqua, looking on as his protégés amused themselves, the old man hated the idea of any type of boat race. He disliked the betting that took place and feared that the illegal racing would attract the attention of the Chinese authorities. "Mus take care! Mus take care!" he would splutter.[25] The advice fell on deaf ears. But his American sons never lost his friendship, and Houqua continued to offer a hand to new traders who impressed him. In the ultimate kiss of approval, Houqua invited Robert Forbes and Warren Delano to a dinner at his country villa on Honam, across the river from Canton.

There Delano and the others marveled at the retreat the great merchant had created for himself. Decorative ponds shimmered in the golden glow of the morning sun. Lush shrubs and languid trees shaded the strolling paths. The various buildings were a riot of bright colors: blood red, periwinkle blue, and chocolate brown. Silk lanterns swung lazily from the eaves. In the marble-floored banquet hall, soft-footed servants started to serve the first course at noon. The delicacies flowed from the kitchen to the table until the wee hours of the morning: plovers' eggs, sturgeon's nose, sea slug soup, and other pungent dishes.[26] The guests did their best to look grateful as they consumed food both gooey in texture and fiercely spicy. They dared not turn down a course, no matter how exotic. They rarely if ever ate Chinese food in the Factories, as their servants had been trained to serve them more familiar Yankee fare such as roast beef and boiled fish.

But Houqua's taste and hospitality made a lasting impression.

The frail little man—clad in flowing silk, head topped with his customary red-buttoned mandarin cap—was a true merchant prince, unpretentious in manner but generous to those who had made him rich. As the dinner came to an end and Houqua bade the Americans good night, Warren Delano must have realized that he was no longer the mere son of a Yankee whaling captain. He was now Warren Delano, China merchant, a member of one of the most exclusive, secretive, and profitable clubs in the world.

One wonders as he sailed down the swirling Pearl River, back to the confines of the Factories, if Delano's thoughts strayed to the great Hudson River estates he had seen from afar as a teenager. Those were days of high adventure, when his father brought him to New York to witness the 1825 opening of the Erie Canal. Along the riverbanks, he had seen columned mansions of brick and stone, regal and remote as fairy castles. These were the homes of the old New York patroon families, landed gentry who in some instances had owned their vast manors since the seventeenth century: Stuyvesants, Van Rensselaers, Livingstons. To the Delanos, like most citizens of the young republic, the residents of these homes were as unapproachable as the Olympian gods. Their estates were mysteriously beautiful and grimly forbidding.

Now, halfway around the world, Warren Delano had been welcomed through the gates of the promised land and hosted by a man far richer than any Livingston, in a house more beautiful than the finest mansion in the Hudson Valley. Perhaps he wondered if one day he might live in his own version of Houqua's villa, where he could shelter his family in pastoral comfort and peace, far away from the cruel, ruthless sea from where his forefathers had made their livelihoods.

As he occupied the world of the Pearl River, Delano would find that Houqua's hospitality was legendary but offered only to those chosen few merchants—mostly Americans such as the Forbes brothers and Samuel Russell—whom the great man liked. Back in the Factories, the social scene tended toward British-style bacchanalia. Many of the Yankees did their best to abstain. But few wanted to be seen as a bluenose.

One proud abstainer was Abiel Abbot Low, a key partner in Russell & Company. Low, called Abbot by his family, was a cautious, round-faced young man, measured in everything he did. His connection to the Russell firm came from his late uncle William Henry Low I, the first of the family to break into the China trade and a business partner of Samuel Russell. The Lows brought to Canton an austere Puritan ethos. These were men for whom opulence was utterly foreign, however enticing. Abbot knew sybaritic temptations could erode even the most diligent merchant. "If you have secured any permanent occupation at home, it would be well to stick with it," he wrote his sensitive, dandyish younger brother, William Henry Low II, back in New York. "I find it impossible to acquire studious habits [in Canton]. You take care to do better, while you are younger. I mean to improve."[27]

Harriet Low, sister to the two brothers, who had spent time in China in the 1820s as a companion to their bachelor uncle, also took a harsh view of the social goings-on. Harriet had found Macao, where foreign women had to reside, enchanting—it looked like a bit of sunny Portugal brought over to China—and had once dressed up as a man to get a look at Canton, too. (The Chinese authorities quickly found her out and ordered her back to Macao.) Still, in their trips to Macao to visit their wives and families, Harriet saw Canton's foreign merchant community at leisure. "The men are a good-for-nothing set of rascals," she wrote in her journal. "All they care about is eating, drinking, and frolicking."[28]

Abiel Abbot Low must have kept to his Yankee resolve to "improve," for he had done well for himself. As a Russell partner, he garnered one-sixteenth of the firm's profits, or about $25,000 a year.[29] Head partner Robert Bennet Forbes was most likely pocketing twice as much, with junior clerks earning perhaps only $500 to $1,500. Yet as Abbot Low prepared to return home with a handsome fortune, his brother William Henry was already sailing for China. The younger Low would face Canton's dangers to turn around his own fortunes: during his New York bachelorhood, whether from card playing, haberdashery, booze, or a combination of all three, he had racked up over $2,000 in debt (a middle-class income in 1830s America).

William Henry Low would join Russell & Company under a managing partner who embraced Canton's work-hard, play-hard ethos wholeheartedly. Robert Forbes may have gone broke back in Boston, but here he was a social lion, a man people looked up to. As someone who had risen through the sailor ranks as a young man, he retained his love for that salty lifestyle and couldn't resist a good betting opportunity or yarn, especially while he was away from his family. What Rose Forbes thought as she cradled their baby back in Boston is unknown. But she probably resigned herself to the fact that her husband was working to rebuild the fortune, and at that, he was doing the best he knew how.

The biggest bash at the Factories during these years in Canton took place on January 22, 1839, in honor of William Jardine, who was preparing to return home. Trained as a physician, the Scottish-born Jardine had become the most powerful British merchant in Canton. For six years, his firm, Jardine, Matheson & Company, had filled the breach left by the end of the British East India Company's government-backed monopoly of the China trade. Ruthless, flamboyant, with a nearly endless supply of Indian opium at his disposal, he had become immensely rich. He was also feared. One coworker described Jardine as "steady and ardent as a friend, equally steady and implacable as a foe."[30] The Chinese merchant community hated Jardine, nicknaming him "the Iron Headed Rat."[31]

Present at the farewell dinner were Warren Delano and Robert Forbes, among other representatives of the big American trading firms. The party took place in the main banqueting hall of the English factory. Eighty guests—British, American, and Indian—sat down at tables crowned with gleaming silver candelabras, the flicking candles illuminating oil portraits of traders and royalty. A cut-glass chandelier, fueled with whale oil, sparkled from the ceiling. The tables were set with snowy white linens. Above all hung a portrait of the late King George IV, the fat, dandyish son of the monarch who had lost the American colonies a half century earlier, and the uncle of the newly crowned Queen Victoria.[32]

Feasting, dancing, and toasting went on into the wee hours of the morning. Robert Forbes stood up on a chair, raised his glass, and declared that they, the Americans and British, should cast all divisions aside, as they were bound by common heritage and blood, as well as commercial interest. "*Union*—not merely political, not merely commercial, but the union of principle, the *union* of heart and soul!" he shouted.[33]

The dinner continued, with port, claret, and champagne served in rapid succession. The orchestra played waltzes, gavottes, and gallops. In the mayhem, Forbes noted gleefully, Delano was "let go of by his partner & tumbled headlong against a flower pot & cut a gash in his head an inch wide."[34] Was the dancing "partner" one of the other men? Or did the merchants bring in other company, from among the flower boat women who caught their eyes?

Everyone woke up with throbbing headaches the next morning. Warren Delano would later insist that, "Canton was, and is, a most stupid place."[35]

Yet the hijinks and loneliness of the "Canton bachelors" would bind this group of men together for the rest of their lives. "We pursued the even tenor of our way with supreme indifference," Russell & Company partner William Hunter wrote, "took care of our business, pulled boats, walked, dined well, and so the years rolled by as happily as possible."[36] Their unique social experience created a sense of loyalty that could not be replicated in any other setting in America, and in the years to come, these connections would carry over into their business lives. They would marry one another's cousins, invest in one another's ventures, and even rescue one another financially when times grew hard.

Soon after the festivities, Jardine set sail for England, where he was looking forward to a long and luxurious retirement.

Warren Delano was also looking forward. On January 1, 1839, a few weeks before the Jardine bash, the partners of Russell & Company drew up a new charter, in which the old partnership was dissolved. Delano's firm, Bryant & Sturgis, was absorbed into the new Russell & Company. Robert Bennet Forbes remained the head, while Warren became a full-fledged partner of the most profitable American firm in China—and one of the most secretive and lucrative businesses in the world.

Yet in the year to come, a zealous new Chinese official had decided that the high-living foreign devils had outstayed their welcome. There followed a trial by fire in which Jardine, Forbes, and Delano would all play a role. This misadventure would also bring about the genesis of the fastest merchant ships the world had yet seen.

CHAPTER 3

OPIUM HOSTAGES

I took it:—and in an hour, oh! Heavens! what a revulsion! what
an upheaving, from its lowest depths, of the inner spirit! what an
apocalypse of the world within me! I sometimes seemed to have
lived for 70 or 100 years in one night . . . a vast march—of infinite
cavalcades filing off—and the tread of innumerable armies . . . the
weight of twenty Atlantics was upon me.

—THOMAS DE QUINCEY,
Confessions of an English Opium-Eater, 1821[1]

The Americans and British called their spectral little schooners
"opium clippers," or simply "clippers." The speedboats of their time,
they carried small amounts of valuable cargo through treacherous
waters as quickly as possible. In the best conditions, a sharp-nosed
opium clipper could make fourteen knots, fast enough to outrun
anything else afloat. Captains hated the rough weather that might
force them to take in sail, which slowed them down. Captain Philip
Dumaresq, a native of Maine and one of the most celebrated opium
clipper masters, scrawled in his log angrily, "Fresh breezes, thick
weather, double-reefed topsails!!!!"[2]

Part of the opium clippers' mystery lay in the illicit nature of the
trade. They and their crews were the shadow actors of a publicly "respectable" industry. All the merchants of Russell & Company were

initiated into this underworld, starting with opium's arduous trip to China. It was they who built the ships to carry it; they who dutifully recorded costs and receipts. As a young man, company partner Robert Forbes supervised the construction of the storeship *Lintin* in 1830 at the Samuel Hall Shipyard in East Boston and personally kept the opium accounts for Russell & Company aboard her.[3] Handwritten account books during Forbes's time unashamedly noted "smuggler" in the source columns. A decade later, the lumbering, barque-rigged vessel still stood sentry at the gateway to Canton Harbor.

Robert Bennet Forbes explained in a letter to his wife, Rose, how the opium supply chain worked. In addition to carrying opium itself, Russell & Company made much of its money lending cash to speculators who bought opium on margin and then hoped to make a profit by selling it for more than they'd paid for it.

> A speculator in India has ten thousand dollars *more or less* he wishes to buy forty or fifty thousand dollars' worth of Opium to send to Mr. Smith in China for sale with this ten thousand Dollars, so he applies to Mr. Smith's friend or agent in India who allows him to draw a bill on Mr. S requesting him to pay forty thousand dollars to a third party [Russell & Company]—this bill sells for cash which is given with the ten thousand dollars to pay for the fifty thousand dollars' worth of Opium, the Opium is sent to Mr. Smith's consignment & the person who bought the bill also sends it to his friend here for collection, when it is due here say 30 or 60 days after the arrival of the Opium Mr. Smith must pay for it.[4]

If the opium sold for more than $50,000 plus the interest on the note, the speculator made a nice profit on his $10,000, as did Russell & Company on its loan of $40,000. If he didn't, he was ruined, and Russell & Company would lose money on the loan. The company's opium clippers and *Lintin* were key links in the chain connecting the speculators to the buyers. The faster the opium got to China, the shorter the duration of the loan, and the quicker Russell and the speculator collected their money.

William Hunter, the partner with the Chinese mistress, recalled later (without apparent shame) an opium-selling trip from Singapore to the Chinese coast. "We owned at the time a Boston clipper schooner called the *Rose*," Hunter wrote, "which, in 1837, was about leaving for that anchorage with a quantity of opium sold at Canton for delivery there, and an additional number of chests to try to market. The whole consisted of nearly 300 chests."

It was valued at some $300,000—the equivalent of tens of millions of dollars today.

Such opium imports had been forbidden by imperial edict in 1799, but that had no real effect on business. By the 1830s, the clipper drug runners were part of normal coastal traffic. Everyone knew they were illegal, but the Chinese government was nervous about using force to crack down on the trade. Craving for the drug had overwhelmed all means of enforcement. So had bribery.

When the *Rose*—almost certainly named after Robert Bennet Forbes's wife—arrived off the coastal city of Namao, the captain formally welcomed aboard a Chinese customs inspector, whom the crew scrupulously referred to as "His Excellency." The captain plied the official with cigars and wine, and gravely explained to him that the *Rose* had dropped anchor to "replenish her wood and water" after a rough voyage.

The Namao official pulled out a document and handed it to his secretary, who read it aloud. The Americans were reminded sternly that Canton, not Namao, was the only port open to Western trade. But, read the secretary, the Chinese emperor, whose compassion was "as boundless as the ocean, cannot deny to those who are in distress from want of food, through adverse seas and currents, the necessary means of continuing their voyage."

Once these formalities were over, "His Excellency" got down to business. How many chests of opium are on board? he asked. Are they all bound for Namao? Then, pocketing the expected bribe, the mandarin departed the *Rose*. As if on cue, a fleet of small Chinese merchant junks and "fast crabs" came up alongside the opium clipper. The balls of opium, Hunter noted, "had been already packed in bags, marked and numbered" for delivery to buyers.[5]

Time was money: the smugglers paid the Americans $5 per chest delivered on schedule; $2 a chest if it was late. These *cumsha* payments went right into the coffers of the foreign merchant.

The merchants came to believe that the trade was perfectly moral. "I insist that [the opium trade] has been fair, honorable, and legitimate," Warren Delano wrote in one letter home.[6] The Americans argued that they were merely following suit in a business the British regarded as aboveboard, and that the American share in the opium traffic was small by comparison. Moreover, they argued, it wasn't just the British and Americans who were in on it, but also Indian and Turkish growers and suppliers.

Indeed, both British and American merchants held that it was the *Chinese* trade system that was corrupt and cumbersome, and that confining foreign merchants to the single port of Canton was unfair and condescending on the part of the government in Peking. What they wanted, above all, was to be treated as equal trading partners. Opium smuggling was merely a way to circumvent an already rigged and rotten system. And easily-paid-off Chinese officials were in on the cartel.

Customs officials on the docks were not the only players. While the Canton Cohong trade guild profited from all cargo moving among China, Europe, and America, it was opium from India and Turkey that was the real moneymaker. By the early nineteenth century, thanks to the addictive power of opium, silver was starting to flow out of China rather than into it, severely depleting the imperial treasury. But some of the silver was, in fact, flowing back into the Chinese economy: from the drug addicts, to the dealers, to the foreign suppliers, and then into the trade guilds' pockets in exchange for tea and other Chinese goods. In the 1818–19 trading season, for instance, Americans coordinated the importation of an estimated $7.3 million worth of silver specie into China. By 1838, however, that sum had plummeted to $678,350. At the same time, tea exports from China to America rose from an estimated $1.3 million to $5.8 million.[7] In other words, opium filled the trade imbalance, allowing Western merchants to rob Peter (the Chinese addicts) so they could pay Paul (the Co-hong merchants).

As with the boat races on the Pearl River, Cohong leader Houqua claimed official ignorance of the opium trade. As one top American trader said, "I am aware that Houqua . . . never liked the flavor of opium"—the great Chinese merchant "always knew" where the money came from but was "willing to shuttee eye."[8] The arrangement, although complicated, was good for both sides. The Americans went home rich, and Houqua accumulated so much cash that he began to wonder what to do with it. That was where the proto-venture-capitalist Forbes brothers came in.

To protect himself, Houqua tried to leave no fingerprints on the opium side of his American friends' business. His greatest fear was that the Chinese government would seize his assets to punish him. As rich as he was, he knew that his position in Chinese society was tenuous. He, along with the other merchants of the Cohong, were personally liable for the conduct of the *fanqui* camped out in Canton. His father-son relationship with his favorite US merchants was his gentle way of keeping tabs on his charges, as well as keeping them loyal to him. But although Houqua did his best to avoid any direct connection with the sale of opium, the business was just too profitable to avoid.

The drug, of course, had terrible social consequences. Once the pastime of the wealthy, opium smoking had spread to all strata of society, affecting countless middle-class and poor Chinese. Unlike taverns, which were social (and often political) gathering places, opium dens were antisocial spaces. Pipe-smoking addicts would lie comatose, surrounded by pungent blue smoke, drifting into their own private dreams. Addicted breadwinners spent themselves into debt and left families destitute. If an addict didn't get his fix, the withdrawal could be excruciatingly painful.

But these ills could be ignored by those who profited from the trade, especially the Western merchants cocooned in the luxurious seclusion of the Canton Factories. Addicts got their fix out of sight, hiding from the authorities in back alleys and opium dens. "Opium was never for sale in Chinese shops in Guangzhou," Hunter observed, "nor were there any signs by which one could judge it was being prepared for smoking, it being used in no other form."[9]

The merchants had other excuses for their industry. The opium trade was not unlike the liquor business back home, they argued. Alcohol was seen to be ruining countless lives in America, where men drank away their wages on cheap whiskey and demon rum. And yet the sale of alcohol remained legal (although temperance would soon become a major political movement). Why, thought the merchants, should selling opium in China be condemned as worse?

Thus, while merchant Robert Forbes acknowledged that "there can be no doubt that [opium smoking] was demoralizing to a certain extent," he qualified this: "not more so, probably, than the use of ardent spirits." His memoir went on to divide "twenty or thirty thousand chests" of opium into the (then) population of 350 million Chinese and conclude that opium "had a much less deleterious effect on the whole country than the vile liquor made of rice, called 'samshue.'"[10] He definitely knew otherwise.

The other merchants also knew better. Opiate addition was rampant in Europe and America, as well. Laudanum, an alcohol-based herbal medicine containing about 10 percent opium, had been used as a painkiller and sedative since the sixteen hundreds; mothers and nurses soothed cranky infants with it. Now it had become popular among the creative figures of the Romantic Era; for example, the poet Lord Byron relished the euphoria it produced. Other opium-based quack "patent medicines" were being sold, advertised as good for every conceivable ailment: migraines, tuberculosis, insomnia, cancer, menstrual cramps, mental disorders such as depression and schizophrenia, and that mysterious, catchall female ailment of nineteenth-century medicine, "hysteria." The eighteen hundreds also brought a new, even more potent opiate when in 1805 a German chemist named Friedrich Sertürner turned poppy seeds into what he called morphine (from Morpheus, the Greek god of dreams).[11] Morphine addiction would balloon out of control as the nineteenth century progressed, especially in American cities.

Moreover, at a time when the United States was struggling to define itself as a virtuous republic, the suffering that came with the opium trade was, for some contemporary observers, a contradiction perhaps as great as the existence of slavery in the South. Yet American merchants had sailed through such moral battles in the past. Before the slave trade had ended in Northern states, Yankee merchants such as the Browns of Providence built fortunes transporting captured Africans to the sugar plantations of the Caribbean and the tobacco farms of the Southern states. If that was acceptable, how could trading in opium be so bad? Selling the deadly, addictive drug was only the regrettable means to a good end, part of an American merchant's rite of passage to the wealth he desired.

Yet things were changing in China. In 1838, as Western traders shipped ever more opium to Chinese shores—and Robert Forbes and Warren Delano trained to win the coveted Canton Silver Cup—Chinese emperor Min-ning appointed Commissioner Lin Zexu as the new governor general of Canton. Lin, a scholar who had risen through the ranks of the Confucian bureaucracy, decided it was time to show the *fanqui* who was boss. A first step was to confiscate the opium that was draining China of resources and lives.

Lin wasted little time. In March 1839, with the emperor's blessing, he sent the Western merchants in Canton an ultimatum: hand over twenty thousand chests of opium to the authorities (estimated value, $10 million; in the hundreds of millions of dollars today), or the Chinese would cut off food to the Factories and starve them into submission. Two months after William Jardine's farewell dinner, the old ways and good times seemed to be coming to an end.

The British, who controlled most of the opium in question, refused to submit to the Chinese demand. American firms also refused—although most of the drug crates that Russell & Company had on hand were not their own, being held on consignment from British traders. When the merchants' reply was made known to the Chinese, Lin put his plan into action. All Chinese servants were ordered to leave the Factories at once. Guards were posted to stop supplies from coming in. A row of lashed boats blocked all access to the Factories' docks. It was an unprecedented action. The merchants were shocked. Robert Forbes was particularly indignant that his return home to Rose and their child would be delayed, as he refused to leave Canton empty-handed. He began to fear he might not return at all. Years before, an older brother, Thomas, had never come home from a trip to China; he had drowned when a typhoon sank his ship as it sailed out of Canton. Robert's long-suffering mother, Margaret, should not have to lose another son.

Lin took other measures to squelch the opium trade, threatening execution by beheading to any Chinese citizen caught smoking an opium pipe.[12] Trapped inside the compound, Forbes, Warren Delano, Abiel Abbot Low, William Hunter, and several dozen other Westerners were forced to fend for themselves. No white man had ever entered the kitchen of the American Factory before, Forbes noted wryly. After he produced a breakfast of ham and eggs that looked and tasted like shoe leather, Delano took over as chief cook. "We laughed rather than groaned over the efforts to roast a capon, to boil an egg," wrote Hunter. But everyone helped. "We could all clean knives, sweep the floors, even manage the lamps."[13] They were amused by how well they were getting on despite Lin's best efforts. "The Chinese guards outside filled the square," Forbes snickered, "and they imagined we lived primarily on rats and beer." But Houqua had made sure that the Americans did not starve, by smuggling in supplies of food under cover of darkness. All that really bothered the captives was that they had to empty out their own chamber pots.

Yet the laughter inside stopped when an angry mob paraded a convicted Chinese opium smuggler in front of the American Factory. They marched him to the pole from which the American flag flew in the breeze and prepared to hang him beneath. The Americans watched in horror from the balcony. To hang someone beneath the Stars and Stripes was a disgrace, especially since this square, by long tradition, was considered "neutral ground." Several of the Americans rushed out to stop the hanging, but before violence broke out, the Chinese army arrived and dispersed the mob, and the smuggler, battered but alive, skittered into the alleys of Canton.

A month after the siege began, in April 1839, the Americans and British were summoned to meet with the imperial authorities in the hall where the Cohong merchants ran their affairs. There Forbes was horrified to see Houqua—the richest merchant in the world—with chains around his neck. His mandarin button, the indicator of his noble rank, was missing. The mandarins told the *fanqui* in no uncertain terms that if they did not hand over all their opium, Houqua would be executed.

To the Americans, the threat to their adoptive father was terrifying. Such acts seemed to confirm the common Western view of the Chinese as an uncivilized people (although Robert Forbes quickly wrote to reassure his wife that his hosts were "by no means so barbarous a nation as you would suppose from their late acts"[14]). Yet the Canton merchants decided to protect themselves for the time being. Russell & Company took the lead, announcing formally that it would withdraw from the opium trade. The risks to the safety of its partners, and to Houqua's welfare, were just too great.

"The unexpected proceedings of the imperial commissioner may be considered as having crushed the opium trade," agreed the *Friend of China*, an English-language publication printed by the merchant colony. "No merchant possessed of ordinary prudence can justify to himself or his constituents the outlay of any further capital in so forlorn an enterprise."[15] Yet the British companies refused to comply with the Chinese order or acknowledge the illegality of the trade. Opium was their lifeblood, and their trade in the drug was their royally granted prerogative.

The Chinese government dug in, refusing to be intimidated by the threat of British force. In the end, after a three-month siege, British trade superintendent Charles Elliott capitulated and handed over the twenty thousand chests of opium to Commissioner Lin, including about a thousand chests under Russell & Company's care. Lin promptly ordered the $10 million hoard dumped into a ditch on the banks of the Pearl River, where the estuary tide washed the foul mix of opium and mud into the South China Sea.

Houqua kept his head, his mandarin button, and his fortune. But the British traders, led by Elliott, left in a huff, vowing to return again with force.

Russell & Company had declared it would abandon the opium trade, but head partner Robert Forbes refused to leave Canton. When asked by a departing British merchant why he was sticking it out while most other Westerners were leaving, Forbes declared that he had no queen to bail him out. But with the British ships gone, Russell now had a golden opportunity to make money by playing clever games with its fleet. "Russell & Company shipped teas in American bottoms to the Dutch port of Rhio, and there transferred them to British ships," Forbes wrote. "This was thought to be a dangerous move, and our English friends predicted failure." But Forbes believed the British government would want the revenues from tea duties too badly to refuse the cargo, even if it was coming from China in this time of crisis. Besides, England knew, wrote Forbes, that "other markets would be found" by the Americans if it did not accept their crates of tea. "The result proved the wisdom of our course."

Forbes was proud of his team. "At this time, when all of the energies of R. & Co. were taxed to the upmost, Messrs. W. Delano, A. A. Low, Edward King, and William C. Hunter were most able and efficient co-operators," he recalled in his memoir, "and to them the concern was much indebted for its success during the unprecedented high pressure trade from May to December 1839."[16]

Delano was so busy that he called off the shipment of a guitar from Boston. "By the way, if the guitar is not already bought, don't give yourself any trouble about it," he wrote home. "I find that after all the stoppage of trade and the utter want of something to do, I have my hands full of work and but little time for music."[17] The hard work and camaraderie in the face of great risk would not be forgotten by the Russell & Company men in the years to come.

As the British departed, the American team was only getting stronger, as fresh young members—William Henry Low among them—arrived after the siege of the Factories. Abbot Low was more than ready to leave Canton, but before he did, he advanced his younger brother $3,000 as well as another $8,000 from the company's coffers, all of which William was to use to purchase tea to send home to New York at a hoped-for handsome profit.

Warren Delano's younger brother Edward, known as Ned, had also arrived.[18] Unlike Warren, who was whippet thin, twenty-year-old Ned Delano was pudgy and unathletic, and burdened by a nagging sense of insecurity that never quite left him. When his ship dropped anchor at Whampoa, Ned hadn't seen his brother in more than ten years. He was dismayed to find that the siege had taken a toll on Warren's health. "I should not have known him under circumstances different from which I was now placed," Ned wrote home of their first meeting. "[H]e appeared to me worn out—a yellow cadaverous visage [Warren was recovering from an attack of jaundice] added to a slow gait and body [a] little inclined forward."[19]

Having family near did Warren good. As the two brothers sailed up the Pearl River on the eighty-mile journey from Macao to Canton, Ned saw Warren let down the guard he had carefully raised during his six years in Canton. "A delightful frolic . . . biting and pulling ears, pinching flesh, etc.," Ned would write of their time together. "We amused ourselves with shooting birds, snipes, and magpies, the boatmen swimming on shore after them."

During the days, Ned Delano and William Henry Low were busy with shipping Chinese goods to New York, some on commission from the absent British firms. But the departure of the British had not changed the Factory's work-hard, play-hard ethos, no matter how the Americans had complained of the corrupting English influence. During their precious off-hours, the Russell men continued to enjoy games of whist, curry dinners washed down with claret, and relaxing rows on the river. Ned noticed the temptations of the young women who drifted by in the flower boats. "Played the gallant to a young lady in a boat," he wrote. "Modesty would not force a kiss from me, and I left her with only a squeeze of the hand. Chinese laws being against foreigners entering the boats *de plaisir*, I did not venture my person in the lady's chamber."[20]

Yet the lucrative idyll was brief. The British vowed to return to Canton, and return they would, with guns. The only question until then was whether or not the Americans would find themselves in the crossfire of an international conflict. The conflict about to ensue would be known as the First Opium War.

Back in England, William Jardine, infuriated by the loss of his company's opium, beat the drum in Parliament to punish the Chinese for their insolence. He sent a letter to Prime Minister Lord Palmerston urging military action against the Chinese government. The goal was reparations for the lost opium—and more. Jardine also pushed for seizing an island colony for British trade and opening additional Chinese ports to the west. The letter, known as the Jardine Paper, does not survive, but a letter from Jardine to his business partner, James Matheson, from around the same time hints that the "Iron Headed Rat" was eager to punish the Chinese for stealing his company property—especially since the American firms still in Canton were making money, while his firm was not. As he wrote quite succinctly: "You take my opium - I take your Islands in return - we are therefore Quits - & thenceforth if you please let us live in friendly Communion and good fellowship."[21]

A committed imperialist, Lord Palmerston listened eagerly to Jardine's demands, and Parliament acted. A British naval squadron arrived in June 1840 to blockade the mouth of the Pearl River, cutting off Canton from all trade.

Yet life in the Factories went on. As the noose tightened around the city, the Americans kept their eyes to the future. Having achieved his competence in the prosperous months without British competition, Robert Forbes set sail for home, leaving new partner Warren Delano in charge of Russell & Company's Chinese operations. "All will be well under Mr. Delano's control," Forbes wrote an associate, "and I shall be satisfied with whatever he may think right, should he require my cooperation."[22]

Ned could not help but marvel at Warren's newfound sophistication and worldliness. "Of course he feels his authority—yet he does not abuse it—a *young man* of 31 at the head of R & C[company]," Ned wrote admiringly. "He can carve a duck, eat curry, be interesting in conversation, be sarcastic in his remarks, tell a good story, and do many other things 'too numerous to mention.'"[23]

Warren Delano had achieved his supreme ambition of being anointed chief partner of the firm. It had not happened in the best of circumstances, but he now had his brother at his side, and if the two had fears, they left no record of them. Besides, the Americans gambled that the British would not dare open fire upon the residents of the Factories. Or if they did, the merchants would receive ample warning to evacuate.

Business continued the old New England way: smuggling, with assistance from Houqua. "I tell the Hong Merchants also that if the Mandarins are allowed us to send teas to Macao for transshipment to American ships, they must do so immediately and without making any noise about it," Warren wrote, "for if the English hear that such things are being done, the inner passage will be blockaded, inasmuch as they will not consent to us Americans doing trade while the English are cut off. Howqua [sic] will see the *Quangchowfoo* [mayor of Canton] this p.m."[24]

The elderly Houqua had reasons to be happy, despite his recent humiliation at the hands of Commissioner Lin. "The old gentleman is in good health," Delano wrote Abbot Low, "and still vigorous if we can judge by the *reported* fact of his having taken to himself a *nice, beautiful, and blooming* wife of sixteen years only three or four months since."[25] Indeed they all had reason to be happy. "A magnificent profite [sic]," Ned Delano wrote of the fortune he, his brother, and the Russell partners had made with the British gone, "the like of which I think cannot again accrue."[26]

It seemed only a matter of time before China capitulated and opened up to further Western trade. Delano wrote to Robert Forbes, now back safely in Boston (and in Delano's words, "in fine health and spirits"), that in preparation for this new economic landscape, Russell & Company would require a new type of ship.[27] She should be as "plain as possible, inside and out, but strongly fastened and of good, sound, and sufficiently heavy timber." Above all, in Delano's furtively underlined words, this new ship, which should be able to carry around 1,500 tons of tea and other Chinese goods in her hold, must be able to "*sail fast*." Deferring to Robert Forbes's knowledge of shipbuilding—and perhaps to stroke the former sea captain's ego— Delano added, "You understand these matters better than we do."[28]

Robert's brother John Murray Forbes was jubilant about not just his brother's return to Boston but also the huge boost the war had brought to their family's fortune. "My trade operations since I began business when a boy in Canton, or, if you take a fairer test, since I returned from China, in 1837, have not averaged over six percent interest on the amount invested if you *take out* the first lucky hit of the *Acbar* [*sic*]* by being out during the China war, and the very nice tea speculation to England that was made for me at the same time," Houqua's "American" son wrote years later. "Without these two operations, I am sure my profits have not been over six per cent, and I am inclined to think that *with them* they would not be much over six."[29]

Warren Delano was getting ahead of himself about the construction of a new type of ship. In the closing weeks of 1840, it was clear that the Royal Navy was prepared for an assault on the city of Canton. Although younger brother Ned professed public support for the impending British arrival, in private he hoped that the British would not use violence to get their way, not to mention to expand their overseas dominions. He and his brother had grown up knowing the stories of their father's harsh imprisonment by the British in the War of 1812. "I truly wish that John Bull [the British equivalent of Uncle Sam] would meet with one hearty repulse," Ned wrote in his diary, "for why should he enter their peaceful habitations and commit the horridest brutalities upon the women?"[30] His observations perhaps reflected more hatred of the English than respect for the Chinese.

Older brother Warren had a different view of the whole situation. Whatever harm the British had visited on their father during the War of 1812 had to be forgiven in light of the current conflict. "Great Britain owes it to herself and to the civilized world," Warren wrote home, "to knock a little reason into this besotted people and

---

* The *Akbar* was one of the largest and fastest of John Murray Forbes's vessels at the time.

teach them to treat strangers with a common decency."[31] By "civilized world," of course, he meant the West.

On January 7, 1841, six months after the blockade began, the British naval squadron made its move up the Pearl River, and the Chinese were aghast at the sight. The junks of the Chinese navy were no match for the steam-powered beasts headed for Canton, belching black smoke, paddle wheels thrashing, oak flanks bristling with cannon. As the HMS *Nemesis* led the British squadron upriver, they fired. Plumes of water erupted from the Pearl River as the shells fell around the junks of the forlorn Chinese navy. One by one, the ships blew up and plunged to the bottom. Finally, the *Chesapeake*, an old English merchant ship that the Chinese had seized and turned into a warship—complete with incongruous bright eyes on her bow— went up in a huge fireball as a shell hit her magazine. The shock reverberated across Canton, sending plaster tumbling from the ceilings of the Factories, shaking the crystal glasses in the sideboards, and causing the glittering cut-glass chandeliers to sway.

The Chinese shore forts returned the British ships' fire in vain: their guns were fixed and could fire only when an enemy ship passed directly in front of them. The forts were reduced to ruin. Hundreds of Chinese defenders were cut to ribbons by shells, shrapnel, and flying debris.

Warren Delano observed the defeat with awe and a strange sense of delight: "the rabble look up on us with a sort of stupid astonished gaze . . . The British ships of war are close at hand, and the Chinese know that they will strike again if they [the Chinese] do not move cautiously." In pidgin, he mocked them: "Poor Fokee, how you are humbled!"[32]

The residents of Canton panicked as the British ships approached. Some fled for their lives. Others formed an angry mob outside the gates of the Factory compound. Inside, the remnants of the once-bustling Golden Ghetto prepared for the worst. They felt assailed on two fronts: by the British on the water and the Chinese on land.

The British were striking other cities simultaneously. To the north, the queen's troops went ashore and marched inland, crushing the Chinese army at the port cities of Shanghai and Xiamen.

In May 1841 came the coup de grace: as the Royal Navy rode at anchor on the Pearl River, six Americans—the Delano brothers; William Henry Low; Russell & Company smuggling captain Philip Dumaresq (commander of Russell's trading ship *Akbar*); and two others—sailed out to the waiting British HMS *Calliope* to ask that the blockade let American ships to continue upriver. They were, after all, neutral vessels. The British commander replied curtly that he was about to intimidate the Chinese government with yet another show of firepower. Would the Americans like to watch? From the safety of their schooner, William Henry Low observed the British warships fire broadside after broadside into the Chinese fortifications at North Wangtong, fifty miles downriver from Canton. At the same time, infantry soldiers stormed ashore from the HMS *Nemesis*, butchering the defenders. When the smoke cleared, William could see the Union Jack fluttering over the battered fortifications.

Coming ashore at the invitation of the British, the Americans met an unforgettable sight. If they had shielded themselves from the horrors of the opium trade, they now saw firsthand the horrors of military might. "The dead, the dying, and wounded lay in one indiscriminate mass, many of them with their clothes on fire," William wrote his brother Josiah, "praying for water, or for an end to be put to their sufferings."[33] The sights and sounds of that day would haunt him for the rest of his life. Unlike the other American merchants, he felt some culpability for this conflict. He lacked a certain sangfroid that his Yankee colleagues had in spades.

Low and his comrades sailed back to the safety of the Factories, hoping that the British and the Chinese would work out a diplomatic solution. But the Chinese were not going down without a final fight, this time bringing their rage to the hated foreigners' front doors.

Later that month, a furious mob descended on the Factories, determined to rid Canton of the *fanqui* once and for all. This time the American merchants knew the jig was up. Low and Delano quickly loaded all of Russell & Company's goods into boats and fled the Factories to Macao, which was still under Portuguese protection. Of the Americans, only one remained in the Factory: Russell partner Joseph Coolidge, who stayed behind hoping to save what remained of his company's property from the angry mob.

The others left just in time. Tearing down the gates, the horde rampaged through the compound. They smashed furniture, slashed portraits (likely including the likeness of King George IV), destroyed crockery, and carried off the silver flatware and candelabras. In one last, desperate act of vengeance, the mob set the Factories on fire. Coolidge and several other Westerners were captured and tortured before being freed by the British troops who stormed ashore as Canton burned. His Portuguese secretary was not so lucky: beaten unconscious, he was thrown into the Pearl River and drowned.

"The English landed at Canton yesterday," Ned Delano wrote in his diary. "Hoisted the Br. Flag on the 'Company's hall' + recommenced negotiations—only 2 or 3 men killed in Canton—1 an Englishman by his office—the British killed some 40 or 50 men in silencing the little forts in the neighborhood—W. (Warren) G. and S. were on and in the factories while the shots were flying—so was Ryan—2 or 3 shot went very near them."[34]

Only Houqua could save the city of Canton from complete destruction. Under a flag of truce, the old man was rowed out to the British squadron. There he told the British commander that he and the other members of the Cohong would pay a ransom that would make the British whole for their lost opium, plus damages. Houqua paid the British $1.1 million; the other Cohong merchants put up another $900,000.[35] Shaken but alive and well, William Henry Low decided it was high time to join his brother Abiel Abbot Low at home. He had earned a decent sum during his short stay in Canton—not enough to be independently wealthy but enough, he felt, to propose to his beloved Ann Bedell back in Brooklyn, New York. Maybe one day he would return and become a partner, but only after the situation in China had calmed down. "There was no satisfaction in living in China in times such as these," he wrote home in frustration.[36] Yet William also proudly told his sister Harriet that he had made $15,000 from a series of shipments of silks, pearl buttons, and hyson tea—more than enough to pay off his debts from his bachelor days.

Warren Delano was not as bothered by what had transpired. When he set sail for New York in January 1843 after nine years abroad, he saw more opportunity than ever before.

Before his departure, Houqua threw his American "son" Warren Delano a final banquet in his honor. Canton was still in ruins, the Factories were burned, and the British Empire was victorious over the Celestial Kingdom, but the generous Houqua was in no mood for austerity when it came to the head of Russell & Company. One attendee noted that the dinner included "about 15 courses—bird's nest soup—shark fins—pigeons eggs—quail &c—sturgeon's lip, etc. We had 13 hours getting thro' with it. It is many years since Howqua [*sic*] has given a Chinese dinner at his own house, and perhaps never before did he give to a friend the like of this."[37]

As he sat in Houqua's glittering banquet hall, Delano was probably pinching himself. To be accorded an honor so rare, again especially after having survived such a harrowing siege! He had received Houqua's kiss of approval, reaffirming his membership in a select fraternity of American men. He then bade farewell to his Chinese godfather, as well as brother Ned, and set sail for the United States, leaving the wreckage of Canton behind him.

Even after nine years, Delano didn't carry home much understanding or respect for the Chinese. "With two or three exceptions," he snarled to the Russell & Company men back in America, "the Chinese with whom we are acquainted, talk and think like foolish little children, and of late, I keep as clear of them as I can."[38] But there was one important exception.

Packed in Delano's luggage were three portraits. Two were of Delano himself, painted by the Chinese artist Lam Qua. ("In my humble opinion," he wrote, "neither of them look any more like me than they do—like—like—like Martin Van Buren."[39]) The third portrait was of Houqua, by the same artist. Warren Delano treasured the Houqua portrait for the rest of his life.

The Chinese formally capitulated to the British in the Treaty of Nanking in 1842, which ceded the island of Hong Kong at the mouth of the Pearl River as a Crown colony. In addition, it granted Western traders access to four additional Chinese ports: Xiamen, Fuzhou, Ningbo, and Shanghai. As a final insult, the Chinese government was obligated to pay a staggering £21 million indemnity to the British Crown, due in full by December of the following year. Only upon receipt of a first portion of the payment, the treaty asserted, would Her Britannic Majesty's forces retire and "no longer molest or stop the trade of China." For the Chinese, the treaty ending the First Opium War was the start of the Century of Humiliation."[40]

When news of the Chinese defeat reached the United States, Congressman (and former president) John Quincy Adams declared that the Chinese had been at fault: "[T]he cause of the war is the Kotow!—the arrogant and insupportable pretentions of China, that she will hold commercial intercourse with the rest of mankind not upon terms of equal reciprocity, but upon the insulting and degrading forms of relation between lord and vassal."[41] (A Kotow was when Westerners were forced to act in a deeply subservient manner to Chinese officials.) Opium, Adams declared, had nothing to do with the conflict.[42]

The year the treaty was signed, Ned Delano, still in China, lonely and lost without his brother, sailed to Singapore for company business. There he made his first visit to an opium den. "Found smokers in all of them," he wrote in his diary. "One man was prostrate under its effects—pale, cadaverous, death-like . . . for when I took his pipe from his hand, he offered no resistance, though his eyes tried to follow me."

In the same journal, Ned decried the evils of slavery in the American South by jotting down the following bit of verse:

> A boasted flag of Stripes and Stars
> Once fluttered oe'r the waves
> Hangs dripping down in deep disgrace
> Wet with the tears of slaves.[43]

Then Ned Delano got back to work, earning the competence that would allow him to return home and get married. His brother Warren, in New York, was planning not only to do just that but also to invest his newfound riches in a new type of ship, one that would exploit the newly opened China.

CHAPTER 4

YANKEES IN GOTHAM

I am a Yankee of the Yankees—and practical; yes, and nearly barren of sentiment, I suppose . . . Well, a man like that is a man that is full of fight—that goes without saying.

—MARK TWAIN,
A Connecticut Yankee in King Arthur's Court, 1889

Franklin Hughes Delano had smoothed the path for his younger brother Warren's arrival back in New York. As Warren and his fellow Canton bachelors dined at Houqua's villa, Franklin climbed Manhattan's social ladder. The Yankee lad from Fairhaven distinguished himself in the shipping business as a partner at Grinnell, Minturn & Company, where he worked diligently at the firm's South Street office. Yet he also was very popular after hours. Like his brother, he was tall, but he was also an easy talker and blessed with extreme good looks. He excelled at the waltz and the gavotte.[1] One young lady, the granddaughter of one of New York's richest men, found the whaler's son irresistible.

Yet not all New Yorkers were so welcoming toward the Delanos and the New Englanders who were pouring into the growing metropolis.

Washington Irving, America's first professional author, was one of them. He had gained international fame as the creator of Rip Van

Winkle and the Headless Horseman. He moaned that New York, founded in 1625 as the dignified old Dutch settlement of Nieuw Amsterdam, was now being overrun by the crassly commercial, money-grubbing Yankees: "a long-sided, raw-boned, hardy race of whoreson whalers, woodcutters, fishermen, and pedlers [sic], and strapping corn-fed wenches; who by their united efforts tended marvelously toward populating those notable tracts of country called Nantucket, Piscataway [New Jersey], and Cape Cod."[2] To Irving, the Old Dutch families, whose wealth came from large feudal tracts of farmland in Manhattan and the Hudson Valley, meant gentry and good manners. Irving coined a name for this aloof and insular elite: Knickerbockers. He also came up with a lasting nickname for New York: Gotham.

Irving's nostalgic portrayal of old New York sold books but had little basis in the factual past; the city had never been particularly dignified. Nor did the musings of Irving's alter ego Diedrich Knickerbocker stop New York's continuing transformation into what De Witt Clinton, governor of New York State, called "the emporium of the world."

New York in the early 1840s was the nation's largest city, with almost three hundred thousand residents. It had displaced rival Philadelphia to the south as America's financial center and Boston to the north as its busiest port. The impetus that triggered and sustained the transformation was the completion of the Erie Canal in 1825, a 363-mile-long ditch dug by thousands of mostly Irish laborers. The waterway stretched between Albany on the banks of the Hudson and Buffalo on the shores of Lake Erie, and made moving grain out of the interior to the Port of New York and then to Europe easy and cheap—cheaper than sending it floating down the Ohio and Mississippi Rivers to New Orleans.

The Erie Canal boom launched some of the new nation's first great fortunes. Ironically, the richest man in this "new" New York was neither a Knickerbocker nor a Yankee. He was an uneducated German-born musical-instrument maker turned capitalist named John Jacob Astor, who had amassed a multimillion-dollar fortune in the fur trade and then multiplied that many times over by buying up New York real estate as the city crept northward up Manhattan Island.

Still, it was the new Yankee initiative that was driving growth. And few industries exemplified Yankee ascendancy more than the growth of New York shipping, which was firmly in the control of a group of families with New England roots. Ships and commodities, not rent payments and land, had produced their fortunes. They were the masters of New York's global trade—centered on its thriving seaport, which was bringing in greater riches with every year that passed.

New York in the early nineteenth century drew its lifeblood from its waterfront. In addition to the lucrative China trade, it was home to America's first fleet of regularly scheduled transatlantic packets, sailing under the house flag of the Black Ball Line. Starting service in January 1818, not long after the end of the trade-crippling War of 1812, the line had a fleet of four ships, enough to schedule monthly sailings between New York and Liverpool, England. "[T]he regularity of their times of sailing," the first advertisement proclaimed, "and the excellent condition in which they deliver their cargo, will make them very desirable opportunities for the conveyance of goods."[3]

The island of Manhattan, as poet Walt Whitman rhapsodized in his poetry anthology *Leaves of Grass*, was encircled by ships, and the sights and sounds of ocean commerce were never far away from its residents:

> Saw the white sails of schooners and sloops, saw the ships at
>   anchor,
> The sailors at work in the rigging or out astride the spars,
> The round masts, the swinging motion of the hulls, the slender
>   serpentine pennants,
> The large and small steamers in motion, the pilots in their
>   pilot-houses,

The white wake left by the passage, the quick tremulous whirl
    of the wheels,
The flags of all nations.[4]

When the thirty-four-year-old Warren Delano arrived in New York Harbor in the spring of 1843 and the great city unfolded before him, the newly wealthy merchant must have swelled with pride. True, China had made him rich, but New York was the real land of opportunity. He resolved to settle down in this city, the burgeoning center of America's unregulated, unchecked capitalist system. Here were opportunities to invest his $100,000-plus competence in a bewildering number of new enterprises, as coal, iron, cotton, railroads, real estate, and ships all sang the siren songs to the speculator.

Delano was returning to a city he had known well. He had clerked in New York at the merchant firm Goodhue & Company on his path to the larger fortunes of the China trade. But now, after having lived on the other side of the world for nearly a decade, he no doubt felt like a real-life Rip Van Winkle—few Americans of his time spent so long abroad, let alone strayed more than a few miles from their home. In his years away, the whole country had been changing. American capitalism had been loosed by President Andrew Jackson's successful destruction of the Second Bank of the United States—the "many-headed monster" that had attempted to bring some semblance of federal control to the nation's freewheeling financial system. Arkansas, as a slave state, and Michigan, as a free state, had been admitted to the union. Railroads were spreading fast throughout the United States: by the early 1840s, the country boasted almost five thousand miles of track, a tenfold increase since Delano set sail for China.[5]

Of course, the speed and the potential profits of the steam-powered iron horse had not gone unnoticed by the merchants of the China trade. Comfortably rich John Murray Forbes contemplated coming out of "retirement" to bet his competence (and Houqua's cash hoard) on the railroads. Yet the business was still a treacherous one, full of shady speculators and frauds as well as brilliant operators and real opportunities. Ultimately, Forbes decided to hold off, while others engaged in international shipping failed to share his enthusiasm for transportation over land. Convinced that America's future lay with the sea, John's brother Robert wanted to use his fortune and influence to build better and faster ships, giving Boston's shipbuilders a chance against New Yorkers in the same business.

For New York was a tough competitor, powerful and growing quickly. It was still largely a low-rise city of brick, wood, and brownstone—spreading northward rather than skyward for some years to come. Most New Yorkers lived in single-family rowhouses, except for those unfortunates crammed into the fetid tenements of Lower Manhattan's Five Points slum. Yet the largest buildings occupied by working people were still no more than six stories high. The tallest structures in Manhattan were churches: the spire of Trinity Church at the head of Wall Street would soon soar 281 feet in the air, making it the tallest building not only in New York but also in the entire United States. Only after the invention of the elevator and the steel-frame skeleton in the decades to come would the city start growing skyward. People would call these buildings by the name sailors gave to a triangular sail set from the truck and skysail yardarms: skyscraper.

Yet as Trinity's spire rose above, the city stank below. Sewage ran in the streets, especially in the slums. Pigs rooted through piles of trash dumped in alleys. The Collect Pond, for two hundred years the main source of water for New York, had long since been fouled with waste from tanneries. Cholera, typhoid, and other epidemics raged through the city on a regular basis. In 1830, after a cholera outbreak killed one in thirty-nine New Yorkers, the city fathers took action by planning a public works project comparable to the construction of the Erie Canal a few years earlier. In 1842 the Croton Aqueduct had opened, bringing thirty-five million gallons a day of clear, upstate water to the city's residents. Soon even this would not be enough to satisfy the growing demand.

When he landed in 1843, the trim, sunburned Delano almost certainly stepped ashore at South Street, New York's "Street of Ships." Around him were the raucous sounds and foul smells of a thriving port. The East River, like Canton's Pearl, was choked with commerce: packet ships, cargo sloops, and smoke-belching, clanking passenger steamers. Wharves were stacked with bales of southern cotton and barrels of flour destined for Liverpool, 3,100 miles across the Atlantic. Stevedores unloaded crates packed with English-woven calico and Staffordshire pottery, Jamaican sugar, Indian spices, and, of course, tea and silks from China—most in the care of Delano's august firm of Russell & Company. Just across South Street from the bustling wharves and the ships' jutting bowsprits and leering figureheads were the offices of all the great New York shipping houses, where men who sat at high-topped mahogany desks, wielding steel-nibbed pens, coordinated sailings and managed freight inventories with military precision. The buildings were faced with granite on the first floor, the upper stories with brick. Heavy oak joists supported the floors, while large windows admitted daylight into the counting rooms.

In an era before international investment banks and multibillion-dollar venture capital funds, no New Yorker was socially loftier than a wealthy merchant. He not only sold goods from abroad and owned fleets of ships but also served as a source of capital, funding all sorts of new enterprises. As one merchant scion declared proudly, "The word *merchant* did not mean a greengrocer or a haberdasher as it means today, but described a man with large capital who was an exporter of domestic and importer of foreign goods, who owned his own ships and usually their cargos, as well."[6] A merchant was a social leader and arbiter who determined who was in the club and who was out. During this era of growing American confidence, New Yorkers eagerly compared their city to the "Most Serene Republic of Venice," which derived its wealth from the sea and was ruled by a council of merchants. As one resident said at the time: "[A] New Yorker of no very extended acquaintance could tell the names of all the principal merchants and where they lived."[7]

As a new member of the club, Delano knew and respected the names above the doors on South Street. There was Howland & Aspinwall at 54-55, run by the intensely private and extremely shrewd William Henry Aspinwall, a New Yorker with whaling roots in Delano's native Fairhaven, Massachusetts. His ships flew a flag marked by a blue-and-white cross. Aspinwall had extensive interests in the Mediterranean and South America. An alluring manifest from an Aspinwall ship landing in New York from Valparaiso, Chile, included "satin, crepe, Florentine shawls, ribbons of all kinds, foulard silks, horse-skin gloves, openwork white silk hose, ladies' and men's white kid gloves, Irish linens, Russian sheetings" and much more, worth a very substantial $121,435.[8] Full faced, square jawed, and dark haired, Aspinwall, according to one descendant, apparently had a "rare faith in the honesty of his fellow man." When confronted with someone who could not pay a debt fully, he would supposedly say, "Very well, we will settle on those terms."[9]

South Street was also home to the shipping firm of N. L. and G. Griswold, whose ships flew a blue-and-white checkered flag. Stevedores joked that "N. L. & G. Griswold" really stood for "No Loss and Great Gain." The shrewd partners, Nathaniel Lynde Griswold and George Griswold, were two imperious six-foot-tall brothers from Old Lyme, Connecticut, who had become major players in the China trade. Their most famous commercial sleight of hand occurred when an especially fine crop of tea arrived from China on their ship *Panama*, in crates stamped with the ship's name. In an early example of branding, the Griswolds built two additional ships in succession named *Panama* so that more of their tea could be sold as "Panama Tea." Nathaniel was taciturn. The somewhat more outgoing George was known for having a "very speculating turn of mind."[10] The firm had strong social and business ties with the Russell partners: George's son John N. A. Griswold spent many years in Canton working as a Russell clerk, making him one of the few who had no family ties to the earliest partners—although that would change when his sister Sarah Helen married Russell partner John C. Green.[11]

Then there was the shipping firm recently founded by Abiel Abbot Low, Delano's old Russell colleague and Canton comrade-in-arms. At A. A. Low & Brother, Abbot, the eldest and richest of the Low siblings, was supported not by one "Brother" but four: William Henry II, Josiah, Edward, and Seth Haskell Low. Abbott had started his shipping company to provide expanded service to the several newly opened Chinese ports. Although it was technically separate from Russell & Company, he hoped to benefit hugely from shipping tea and other goods on consignment from his old firm. When Low was a Russell partner, his ships had flown the Russell & Company flag, with its distinctive blue-and-white diagonal quadrants. Now he proudly flew his own new banner: a red-and-gold flag with a white *L* in the center. In time, the *L* would be replaced by the first letter of the ship's name.[12]

Finally, there was Grinnell, Minturn & Company, the ships of which flew the company's red-and-white, swallowtail-shaped pennant. Its busy transatlantic trade between New York and Liverpool had become a worthy rival to the old Black Ball Line. Moses Grinnell of New Bedford had started the firm partnered with a curiously named old salt named Preserved Fish, who had since retired. Another, more-junior partner at the Grinnell firm was Warren Delano's own brother Franklin. Disgruntled with his position there—exactly why seems lost to history—Franklin was looking for an out, and his complaints seem to have given Warren a useful eye on the competition.

Grinnell, Minturn & Company and other shipping businesses plying the transatlantic routes carried more than cargo. They were bringing to New York—and through its portal, to all of America—thousands of European immigrants, mostly poor and desperate for opportunity. Men, women, and children stumbled onto the South Street wharves after spending weeks, even months, crammed into the packets' tween decks: a dark and fetid section of the ship known as steerage.

To New York mayor, diarist, and social arbiter Philip Hone, the new arrivals from England, Ireland, and Germany were an even greater scourge than the Yankees were to Washington Irving. "All of Europe is coming across the ocean," Hone complained. "All that part at least who cannot make a living at home. And what shall we do with them? They increase our taxes, eat our bread, and encumber our streets, and not one in twenty is competent to keep himself."[13] Within a few years, the steady tide of immigrants arriving in New York by packet ship would turn into a flood, thanks to the Potato Famine that sent millions of starving Irish across to the New World looking for food and work. British and American shipping companies would profit handsomely from the human tidal wave. Thousands died from disease and malnutrition on the "coffin ships." Those who did make it to New York alive found themselves shoved into the crowded, noxious Five Point slum, where robbery, prostitution, and murder flourished in the open. Other dangers included attacks by nativist gangs who feared these Roman Catholic newcomers would depress workers' already low wages, especially in the shipyards that lined the East River.

In 1843 Delano craved, first and foremost, a wife. After years of all-male carousing in the Factories and the illegal regattas on the Pearl River, he was ready to settle down in New York, even if the bustle and bawdiness of South Street seemed ten times worse to him than the chaos of Canton.[14] He had spent nine years without female companionship. By the standards of early-nineteenth-century America, when sixty-five was considered a ripe old age, he was a middle-aged bachelor. Men of relative affluence were usually married off in their early twenties. During Delano's years abroad, he appears to have been besieged by advice from home, much to his chagrin. "Many thanks to the 'modus operandi' of getting married," Delano had written his brother Franklin from China, "and it shall not be my fault if I do not give you an early opportunity to continuing your practice in the 'groomsman' line. The snubbing of noses by the two 'enamored' must be an interesting operation, and I suppose a large red nose would produce an effect sooner than a small and cold blue nose—I should in such case have an advantage over some folks."[15]

In a growing and vibrant city, Delano could have chosen from any number of eligible young ladies. Entrée into the world of New York society required an intricate knowledge of etiquette: when to make calls, how to use greeting cards, and what subjects were considered inappropriate for polite conversation. Women bore a special burden. "The eyes must be guarded, lest they mete out too much consideration to those who bear no stamp," sniffed one lady in *Sartain's Union Magazine of Literature and Art*. "The neck must be stiffened, lest it bend beyond the haughty angle of self-reservation . . . The mouth is bound to keep its portcullis ever ready to fall on a word which implies unaffected pleasure or surprise . . . Subjects of conversation must be any but those which naturally present themselves to the mind."[16]

Commerce could now pay for culture and leisure activities: private libraries, theaters, literary societies, and sporting events. There was even talk of building an opera house, financed by the Astor family, of course. In fact, the Astor Place Opera House would be completed in 1847. It opened with Giuseppe Verdi's *Ernani*, with hundreds of the city's richest residents preening in elegantly European-style evening finery.

There was a special haven for the city's upper-class men—the "Upper Tens," as they were called smugly by the *National Press* (later known as *Town & Country*) magazine founder Nathaniel Parker

Willis, an in-law of the Grinnells. The Union Club, founded in 1836, was located in the former mansion of John Jacob Astor's son William. A leisured gathering place designed for the city's "most distinguished citizens," it was explicitly patterned on "the great clubs of London, which give a tone and character to the society of the British metropolis."[17] The Union Club quickly became New York's premier social organization. Taverns and coffeehouses had become too public. Yet even the patrician tone of the Union Club was counterbalanced by the social reality that most of the founders were not idle members of a landed gentry as they were in London, but made their livings from the law, medicine, and shipping.[18] Even snob founding member Philip Hone was very much "in trade," having made his fortune as a commodities auctioneer.

As a member of the Union Club of Canton, Delano's partner Robert Bennet Forbes would certainly have approved of this establishment. One day Delano and his peers would seek an even greater degree of privacy, not just for themselves and their business but also for their families, in mansions well away from the faintest whiff of commerce or the scrutiny of fellow citizens, who were growing increasingly unhappy with the widening gulf between rich and poor.

The city could be downright dangerous: after dark, pickpockets and thieves prowled the streets, even around the aristocratic precincts of Bond Street and Washington Square. "This city is infested by gangs of hardened wretches," sniffed Philip Hone, who "patrol the streets making night hideous and insulting all who are not strong enough to defend themselves."[19] And then there were the prostitutes. Almost ten thousand of them brazenly walked the streets of New York or worked out of brothels, some which were fitted out as luxuriously as a prosperous merchant's private home. There was little the police could do. Many officers gleefully collected bribes from the madams and gang leaders, or extorted innocent citizens just as wantonly as the Bowery toughs. Flickering lamps fueled by New Bedford whale oil and coal gas did little to dispel the nocturnal gloom or fear.

There were those in these neighborhoods who resented the wealthy merchant class. Mike Walsh, an Irish-born politician and the publisher of the workingmen's publication *Subterranean*, fumed: "Demagogues will tell you that you are freemen. They lie; you are slaves . . . No working man is free to obtain one-fourth of the proceeds of his own labor; everything he buys, every step he turns, he is robbed indirectly by some worthless wealthy drone."[20]

What constituted being rich in New York, a city rapidly approaching a half million residents? According to *New York Sun* editor Moses Beach, who published biographies of the city's most prominent capitalists in 1845, it took a net worth of $100,000.[21] This was the minimum competence sought by Delano and his peers, but more was always welcome. Shipping barons such as Moses Grinnell and Robert Minturn had personal fortunes surpassing $200,000, making them extremely rich men by the standards of the 1840s. Some fifty to seventy men in New York City and Brooklyn were actually "millionaires," a new term coined by the novelist and future British prime minister Benjamin Disraeli.[22] To the typical New Yorker tradesman, who scraped by on only a few hundred dollars a year, a million dollars was a fortune of incomprehensible vastness, as distant and forbidden as the czar of Russia's riches. Among the American magnates were upstarts such as Cornelius Vanderbilt. The semiliterate ferry pilot turned riverboat king didn't give a hoot about civic virtue, and those in New York's business world made sure never to cross him. "The Commodore's word is as good as his bond," a contemporary wrote. "He is equally exact in fulfilling his threats."[23]

During his visit to New York, even the cool, skeptical Delano could not have been but impressed by the prosperity around him. He almost certainly went clothing shopping on Broadway—perhaps at the new Brooks Brothers store—so he could appear up-to-date and presentable at the many dinner parties, cotillions, and "sociables" that filled his calendar. The latest fashion for men was frock coats and colorful waistcoats, although the growing class of office workers now wore a so-called sack coat, which breathed much better than the stiff formal wear of the past. Women were wearing increasingly billowing petticoats and hoopskirts.[24]

The city's architecture was changing too. Delano, like others, marveled at the new LaGrange Terrace (known as "Colonnade Row"), a row of nine marble-clad townhouses whose procession of gleaming Corinthian columns formed a unified, elegant street front along Lafayette Place in the heart of the prestigious Bond Street neighborhood. A typical member of the Upper Tens group (which Delano's competence now allowed him to join) lived in a three-story brick townhouse twenty-five-feet wide and two rooms deep; these new five-story homes had an astonishing twenty-six rooms. They also upped the ante in terms of luxurious city living, with central coal heating, hot and cold running water, and indoor toilets.[25] The ceilings of the parlors and dining room were delicately molded plaster. Mantels were of solid marble; solid mahogany doors hung on solid silver hinges.[26] One day, Delano hoped, he would own one of these Colonnade Row mansions. As fate would have it, his brother Franklin would beat him to it.

For all that was exciting in the city, Delano did not stay long in New York. Perhaps he agreed with the New York physician's wife who complained of the ludicrous etiquette and expectations of high society. "I would rather be out of this fashionable society than in it," she decided.[27] Delano had not liked the aristocratic British expatriates in Canton; he may have disliked frivolous Gotham even more. Everyone in New York seemed to be wagering: prizefights and cockfights in the Bowery, whist games at the Union Club, and commodities prices at the Merchants' Exchange at 55 Wall Street.

So, after spending only a few weeks catching up on company affairs, Delano hightailed back to his native Massachusetts to pay respects to his parents in Fairhaven. His old hometown had changed along with the country. New business was springing up all along the banks of the Acushnet River, which separated Fairhaven and New Bedford. One of these companies would be run by Joseph Grinnell, younger brother of Moses, his brother Franklin's business partner. Retired from the family shipping business, Joseph had invested in a venture called the Wamsutta Mills. The long brick structure would house thousands of steam-powered spindles mechanically weaving cloth from southern cotton.

But manufacturing was never Delano's interest, and he had no intention of returning to his childhood home for good. Instead, Warren set out on a coach trip through the countryside. He breathed a bit easier at the sight of New England's farms and woods in the springtime.[28] His destination was Milton, Massachusetts, home of the Forbes clan. At a house party there, hosted by John Murray Forbes, he met Forbes cousin Judge Joseph Lyman, his wife, Anne, and their eighteen-year-old daughter. Catherine Lyman was a lovely and sweet-natured girl described by her mother as "never out of temper, and always ready to oblige to any extent that her friends could claim."[29] Yet as the years went by, it turned out that behind Catherine's placid exterior was a steely resolve to do what was best.

The Lymans, unlike their rich Forbes relatives, were not plutocrats, but they were prosperous enough, intellectual, and artistic at their core, counting philosopher Ralph Waldo Emerson among their friends. Invited to visit them in Northampton, Massachusetts, Delano must have found the Lyman home a welcome respite from the loneliness of Canton and the cutthroat competition of New York. As they gathered in the evening to play popular songs and classics on their parlor piano, Delano not only took to the Lymans, but also to Catherine.

Catherine's mother approved of the dashing China trader: "He has such a composed and dignified air for a man of business, and such a quiet, sensible mode of expressing his rational opinions," Anne wrote. She saw the "warm heart" that he had fought to keep reserved in Canton. To everyone ("where friendship is admissible," she qualified), he showed "every sort of kindness," prompting such reciprocation that "there is nothing but pleasure in his society."[30] Warren proposed to Catherine that summer, and she accepted. They were married on November 1, 1843.[31] Warren was now part of the Forbes's extended family, and his ties to the Russell & Company circle were strengthened further when Catherine's brother Edward married Abbot Low's sister Sarah and was taken in as a partner in Low's shipping firm.[32] The Canton brotherhood of siege days was drawing even closer.

But if the Lymans thought that their daughter was going to settle down with Delano in New York in domestic bliss, they were wrong. After only about six months in the United States, Delano announced that the best place he could serve Russell & Company was back in Canton. There, the company's vital China trade had effectively been in the control of Warren's bachelor brother Ned and his old boss Russell Sturgis. But Sturgis was selling out and planning to return to America—creating a vacuum that could jeopardize young Ned's role. For another Forbes contender had arrived in Canton: cousin Paul Siemen Forbes.

Months earlier, Warren Delano wrote his brother, with hope, "Mr. Forbes goes out without any great expectations and will of course never become a partner unless it is found for the interest of the House to admit him." But Delano was wrong. Paul Siemen Forbes was determined to advance himself aggressively, and felt— with some justification—that a fortune gained from the House of Russell was a Forbes family birthright.[33] To him, the Delanos were upstarts.

Warren Delano had once written that he did not trust the partners to manage the firm in his absence; clearly, he was still concerned.[34] The power struggle must have been especially awkward for a man who had just married into the Forbes clan. (It is unclear if Delano told Catherine and his prospective in-laws about his plans before the engagement.) Still, he had little choice: he would have to go to Canton for his family's future security. But Warren was not about to leave behind his young bride.

Catherine Delano must have been overwhelmed as they waited in New York for their ship, the year-old *Paul Jones*, to sail on December 4, 1843. At 628 tons, *Paul Jones* was a large ship for her day, built in Medford, Massachusetts, as the pride of the Russell & Company fleet. She was also equipped with something new: insulated storage space so that she could carry American ice to Asia. Ever the tinkerer, Robert Bennet Forbes had worked closely with Boston's "ice king" Frederic Tudor to pack blocks of ice in sawdust in her hold. The ship's ice cargo, claimed Forbes, would allow a previously unheard-of comfort for passengers on this trip: canvasback ducks and mutton, acquired off the Cape of Good Hope.[35] Warren Delano would not have wanted his young bride to suffer weeks of hardtack and salted pork on her first sea voyage.

Catherine was terrified of going to a strange country with a man she had known only for several months, but wealthy women of the time, no matter how well educated, were expected to be submissive to their husbands. And Catherine was—at least in public. "I feel that it is my duty to go," she wrote despairingly to a cousin, "but I do feel sad to think of the long separation from all my kind friends. When I think of my poor experience, it seems almost dangerous to undertake such a thing and I feel unhappy, and then if I stay home I should not be happy. I have determined to go and look on the bright side."[36] The prospect of a stormy winter passage must have made things look even bleaker for Catherine.

When the couple landed in China in the spring of 1844 after a 104-day passage, Ned Delano was there to greet them. In addition to the joy he felt at being reunited with his beloved older brother, Ned could not help but marvel at the culinary delights that came out of the ship's hold. "We had ice from the [*Paul Jones*]," wrote Ned. "Sent out for mint, and for the first time in China . . . mint juleps were concocted and drunk." There was enough ice left over to make "*ice creams*, things before unheard of in China."[37] Warren noticed his brother was lonely and growing quite fat.

Warren and Catherine settled into a mansion in Macao. They called it Arrowdale, and Warren sketched it for a scrapbook, most likely for the children that he and Catherine planned to have. In the same year, his brother Franklin scored a matrimonial coup of his own: marrying Laura Astor, John Jacob Astor's favorite grand-daughter. Although still employed by Grinnell, Minturn & Company, the thirty-one-year-old no longer had to sweat and strive like his brothers. Franklin's new grandfather-in-law gave the couple a house fit for American royalty: one of the Colonnade Row town-houses on Lafayette Place.

The Delanos on both sides of the world had arrived.

CHAPTER 5

MAZEPPA AND THE PROBLEM CHILD

The European navigator is prudent when venturing out to sea . . .
The American, neglecting such precautions, braves these dangers;
he sets sail when the storm is still rumbling by night as well as by
day; he spreads full sails to the wind; he repairs storm damage as he
goes; and when at last he draws near the end of his voyage, he flies
toward the coast as if he could already see the port.[1]

—Alexis de Tocqueville,
Democracy in America, 1835

Lord Byron wrote his poem "Mazeppa" in 1819, its main character a dashing Ukrainian Cossack who is quite the ladies' man. As
punishment for his affair with a beautiful young Polish countess,
her cuckolded husband orders Mazeppa strapped to the back of a
wild horse and set loose on a ride through the Polish countryside.
Somehow, Mazeppa survives his tortuous, galloping ordeal, and a
beautiful Cossack maid nurses him back to health.

For shipowner Abiel Abbot Low, thinking about it in the early
1840s, Mazeppa was a fitting name for a lithe, fast ship carrying illicit
cargo. His lightly built *Mazeppa* was only 150 tons, yet it was also
heavily armed with five brass 18-pounder guns and an Armstrong
68-pounder. The guns gleamed brilliantly in the sunlight upon the
ship's departure from New York in 1842, the orange-and-red Low

house flag fluttering proudly from her mainmast. The goal of this fast ship and her new kind was simple: control the opium trade with China, using vessels that would best the British opium clippers in speed and maneuverability.[2]

Robert Forbes of Russell & Company—A. A. Low & Brother's habitual business partner—almost certainly masterminded this initiative, along with his brother John Murray. They knew the opium trade, both its perils and its promise. Robert, who arrived back in New York from Canton in late 1840, had survived the siege of the Westerners' Factories earlier that year, when China tried to force an end to the opium trade. He had listened when the chief of the Chinese trade guild, Houqua, pleaded with his American protégés to get out of the opium business, and he had agreed. But, unlike some rivals, the Russell partners appear to have had few scruples about engaging in what they saw as a "fair and honorable" trade. And the Forbes brothers, as well as Abbot Low, had been following the ongoing news out of China: Britain's retaliatory naval blockade, its assaults on Canton and cities beyond, and its demand that China open to Western trade. The British would prevail—the Western world was confident of that. And the opium trade would boom again. Even at the risk of losing Houqua's patronage, Forbes and his partners appeared ready to break their gentleman's agreement in the name of making money.

Abbot Low, the former principal partner of Russell & Company, and, like Robert Forbes, also recently returned from the tumult of Canton, agreed. He had brought home a competence in the hundreds of thousands of dollars, just as his father, Seth, had hoped. He was rich, if not John Jacob Astor rich, but with money both to invest and to spend on a grand lifestyle. Shortly after his return in late 1841, the thirty-year-old bachelor had purchased a beautiful house in Brooklyn Heights, with a superb view of the Upper Bay.

Yet despite his newfound comfort, Abbot Low was restless. He did not want the Low family to coast on its past success, especially his own. Abbot set up offices for his new shipping company on Fletcher Street in Lower Manhattan, in the same building as his father's drug-import business. Above his desk, he hung a portrait of his adoptive Chinese father, Houqua, a daily reminder of what set him apart from all other American merchants. A relationship with Houqua was one that money alone could not buy.

Just as Colonel Thomas Perkins of Boston had done a generation earlier, Abbot resolved to send his relatives to Canton. He had several younger brothers coming of age who had a golden opportunity to follow in his footsteps and solidify the family's economic standing. Reading the incoming correspondence from China, Abbot saw two unknowns. The first: How long would Houqua live? The more Lows who got to know the Chinese merchant and benefit from his tutelage, the better. Houqua's relationship with Perkins and the Forbes cousins had proved fruitful indeed for the Boston Concern. The second unknown was when the Opium War would end. Until the British signed a treaty with the Chinese that ended hostilities, the risk to men and ships outweighed the profits.

Meanwhile, Abbot Low was working actively on his opium clipper project with Russell partner John Murray Forbes. Money was marrying money in the Canton alumni club. Forbes had wed Sarah Hathaway, a cousin of his old friend Francis Hathaway, one of the first New Bedford merchants to break into the China trade. Unlike his flashier New York friends, who were completely absorbed with making money and keeping up appearances, John Forbes loved intellectual pursuits such as reading poetry in the silence of his study. His wife's Quaker influence pervaded the Forbes family ethos: "cheerfulness, buoyancy, and simple mode of life," his daughter Sarah recalled.[3] Looking for peace and simplicity, Forbes decided to create a world of his own; a retreat from the congestion of Boston. In 1842 he purchased the island of Naushon from his wife's uncle. Located south of Cape Cod, Naushon was only seven square miles in size, and a wilderness of beech woods, sandy beaches, and marshes. Over the next decade, Forbes drained swamps, cleared trails, and built the first of a series of family houses on the north side of the island. He spent many days on horseback, trotting along sandy trails and gazing at his flocks of sheep. Forbes also raced small sailing yachts, making him one of the first of his set in Boston to engage in competitive racing for pleasure rather than profit. It was one of many diversions he and his friends had perfected in Canton.

"In smaller matters, his inability to enjoy the pleasant things in life without sharing them with others was a marked trait," his daughter Sarah wrote. "No sail in the yacht was perfect unless a party could be gathered to enjoy it, too. And the island friends, farmers, sailors, servants, and all, had one afternoon in the course of the summer, with supper served to them on the yacht."[4] Yet Forbes was not one to sit on his laurels. It was at the same time he purchased Naushon that Forbes began investing with his old friend Abbot Low in the new small opium schooners that they hoped would lead to even greater wealth. They were all heavily based on the "Baltimore clipper" model, only with less drag to their keels and less rake, or slant, to their ends.

Baltimore clippers were arguably the fastest type of ship on the high seas when the first generation of Yankees such as Captain Thomas Perkins entered the China trade. Conceived on the shores of the Chesapeake Bay, in the early nineteenth century, Baltimore clippers were rigged as two-masted topsail schooners with towering, strongly raked masts. Their fore-and-aft sails gave them the ability to sail close to the wind. The one or two square sails on their foremast gave them an extra bit of push, as the foresail and mainsail on their heavily raked masts resisted being sheeted out. The skilled shipbuilders who fashioned these lithe and elegant craft also defied design convention by giving these vessels a very sharp entry below the waterline and a sharp V-shaped hull that minimized drag. The keel angled below the typical horizontal line of earlier vessels. Taken together, most of these design changes had the effect of reducing wetted surface and thus minimizing drag relative to other ships of the day.

No single designer or builder had come up with the concept for this swift type of schooner. Rather, it was a slow evolution with roots in the early Bermudian, Caribbean, and Chesapeake sailing vessels. These had come to full flower during the War of 1812, when shipowners armed and outfitted the speedy and agile schooners as privateers to raid British merchant ships and deftly outmaneuver the slow, heavily armed behemoths of the Royal Navy. When peace resumed, the Baltimore clippers became popular as pilot vessels and revenue cutters. These rakish ships, which had more than a bit of a sinister cut to their silhouettes, were also a slave trader's dream, and were used to spirit their lucrative and shackled human cargoes across the Atlantic to the Caribbean and the American South at speeds fast enough to avoid coastal patrol vessels. As Howard Irving Chapelle, a historian, observed, "Illicit and desperate practices followed close in their wakes throughout their existence."[5]

One smart Baltimore merchant, Isaac McKim, built a full-rigged ship version of the Baltimore clipper in 1833 for the China trade, which he named after his wife Anna. As *Ann McKim* slid into the water from the shipyards at Fells Point, few observers could have imagined the influence she would have on future clipper ships. But certain sharp-eyed businessmen were watching, and not long after her launching, *Ann McKim* was purchased by New York merchant William Henry Aspinwall, partner in the shipping firm Howland & Aspinwall, who pressed her into the China trade.

Ann McKim cut an elegant figure in New York Harbor, and Aspinwall maintained her beautifully. She would eventually put in seven hard years of service. But the ship was more of a show horse than a workhorse; her design was too extreme, and she lacked the freight-carrying capacity that could make big money. "[T]he older merchants tended to view her unfavorably," historian Arthur Hamilton Clark wrote in retrospect.[6] Nonetheless, she captured the imagination of Aspinwall's peers, who thought that this type of fast vessel would be perfect as an opium hauler.

The new, small schooners on which Abbot Low and John Forbes placed their bets would be based on the Baltimore clipper model. *Mazeppa* and her later sister ships *Zephyr* and *Antelope*, along with *Brenda*, *Ariel*, and *Angola* were, in Clark's words, "formidable vessels, especially in light winds and calms, when they were propelled by long sweeps."[7]

Forbes and Low had a wonderful fleet in the making, and another Low would soon be instrumental in making it real. But for now, the teenage Charles Porter Low worried his entire family because he simply could not sit still.

At Brooklyn's Classical Hall, founded by his father, Seth, to cater to scions of transplanted New England families, young Charlie tormented his strict Yankee schoolmasters. Old Seth Low, an 1804 graduate of Harvard, had built a substantial business importing apothecary goods from Asia, and his firm thrived thanks to his brother William Henry I and son Abbot's ties with Russell & Company.[8] Young Charles, unlike his siblings, had no interest in growing the Low family's wealth. When put to work as an apprentice merchant in a New York firm (not his father's), Charlie complained that preparing remittances was "tiresome work, and I was always glad when it was over."[9]

South Street, home to the wharves, was what caught his attention. In his off-hours, Charlie wandered and explored, listening to the laborers sing as they hauled crates of fragrant tea and pungent peppers into the Low warehouse. "We had lots of fun and never did anything wicked, but we created a good deal of talk about the bad boys of Brooklyn," he recalled gleefully.[10] When the owner of a cart bearing a load of gum copal (a resin used for waterproofing) left it to carry out some business inside his father's store, Charlie jumped on the cart bench and started singing a family ditty: "Old Low! Old Low's son. Never saw so many Lows since the world begun." His singing startled the horse, and off they went, cart, horse, and Charlie, careening through the crowded streets until together they spun out of control on a sharp turn onto Platt Street. Charles flew out of the cart. "Both wheels had gone over me," he remembered. He was bedridden for the next six months. "I recovered," he remembered, "and went back to the store again and went to work on new plans for going to sea."

Charles spent time with an old sailor named Jan Jansen on his Uncle James's ship *Cabot*. "I learned from him all the running rigging," he recalled, "and, as it is the same on all ships, I was a good sailor, and I knew just where to find a rope when I first went to sea."[11] Here, on the deck of a ship, under Jansen's tutelage, Charles became intensely focused. He learned to lower the upper yards—the high spars, holding the sails—which had to come down fast to keep a ship stable in bad weather. Joining the two or three men who would scramble aloft to the very top of the mast, he would help furl the sail, secure it with gaskets, and then remove the yard from the mast; on deck below them, another two or three men would then slowly lower the yard, with its heavy furled sail, and secure it. He taught himself on the *Cabot* to get used to following orders, in a hurry, automatically, without regard to danger.

Charles took special pride in climbing *Cabot*'s main topgallant mast and helping the crew send down the royal yard, the highest of all. He knew that when he finally did join a ship, he would be singled out as the greenhorn* who had to risk this task.[12] As he balanced on the footropes, Charles must have sighed with joy as he beheld the city, the wharves, and the sparkling East River beneath him. He

---

* A first-time sailor.

imagined what it would be like to be in a gale as the mast swung in an arc over the boiling seas. Rather than freezing with fear, Charles wanted more.

His father, Seth, wanted Charlie's feet on the ground—and a quill in his hand—offering to take him into his prosperous drug importing firm as a partner, when he turned twenty, provided that he put in his time sitting in front of ledger books. "What my life would have been if I had accepted his offer I cannot say, but I refused it," Charles wrote. "I could not give up the sea. I loved it, and I was sure I should be unhappy on shore. At any rate, I felt I must try it."[13] He decided that if his family refused to let him go to sea, he wouldn't stay in his father's business; he would learn to farm, earn his own money for a sailor's suit, and then run away to sea. In earnest preparation, he read *Judd's Agriculturalist*.

Abbot Low, married recently to Ellen Dow, agreed with his father's misgivings. He hoped desperately that his wild kid brother would grow out of his childish fantasy. Not only was going to sea dangerous, but he considered it beneath the higher social station that his newly acquired wealth had entitled his family. Captains were only employees, after all, not company partners. And common sailors were considered scoundrels: hard-drinking, tattooed, foul-mouthed loafers, spotted instantly by their walk: a rolling gait that they used to stay steady on the deck of a rolling ship. True, Abbot's friend and Russell partner Robert Forbes was a master mariner who came from a prominent family, but Robert had not been the most prudent businessman.

Abbot probably thought that young Charles could go either of two ways: he could reform himself and become a proper merchant or become a frivolous wastrel and embarrassment to the family. The conflict between the brothers reached a flashpoint with *Mazeppa*. For Charlie Low, *Mazeppa* was a thing of beauty. "One of the handsomest vessels of the kind I ever saw," he remembered fondly.[14] For Abbot, it was an investment. As the steam tug towed *Mazeppa* out into the Upper Bay, Abbot and his brother Josiah Low bade the captain farewell and good luck on this treacherous run, and prepared to leave the ship. But to the fury of his brothers, seventeen-year-old Charles was nowhere to be found. After a ship-wide search, he was finally discovered hiding in a bread locker and was put aboard the tug to go back to the wharf.

After Charlie's attempt to stowaway on *Mazeppa*, Abbot and the rest of the Lows realized that their kid brother would never make a proper merchant. They allowed him to attend basic navigation classes and then got him signed on to the Grinnell, Minturn & Company ship *Horatio* as an apprentice, under the command of Captain William Howland, cousin of William Henry Aspinwall and owner Moses Grinnell.

Active and eager to learn, Charlie Low was unsure about this stern-faced, "aristocratic captain" who never went outside without slipping on a pair of kid gloves. A fine navigator but "not much of a sailor," Charlie thought of his new lord and master. Howland had achieved his rank by starting off "on the quarterdeck" instead of "before the mast"—meaning that he had started his career as an officer rather than moving up the ranks as a common sailor—and therefore had not received the practical experience that other captains of his generation had. Family connections and book knowledge almost certainly eased his way into the captain's cabin. Yet somehow he proved himself on the North Atlantic run, commanding a series of packet ships and gaining a reputation among his peers as being an "A-1 navigator and a gentleman."[15] Howland's wife accompanied him on his trips. When she gave birth to a daughter during one of their voyages, she named the baby after the ship: Horatia.

A captain's great power came with great responsibility. "The captain, in the first place, is lord paramount," wrote Richard Dana. "He stands no watch, comes and goes when he pleases, is accountable to no one, and must be obeyed in everything, without a question even from his chief officer." Such a man refrained from emotional intimacy, even with his chief mate, and when there were no family or passengers on board, "has no companion but his own dignity, and few pleasures, unless he differs from most of his kind, beyond the consciousness of possessing supreme power, and occasionally, the exercise of it." He had to be unknowable, feared rather than loved, to maintain power over her crew.[16]

On ship, Charlie would surely have matched Dana's description of a sailor of the day. Dana, the scion of a wealthy Boston family, shipped out himself after his freshman year at Harvard, in his father's hope that it would cure his frequent spells of ill health. In an 1840 memoir, *Two Years Before the Mast*, Dana wrote of the devil-may-care swagger that came with belonging to this fraternity of sorts. "A sailor has a peculiar cut about him," he observed, and went on to describe it: trousers, "tight around the hips, and thence hanging long and loose round the feet;" baggy checked shirt; and a "low-crowned, well-varnished black hat, worn on the back of the head, with half a fathom of black ribbon hanging over the left eye." These, "with sundry other minutiae" were in Dana's eyes the signs of a true sailor, "the want of which betrays the beginner at once."[17]

Dressed in his duck trousers and checked shirt, Charlie Low came aboard *Horatio* on November 5, 1842. His destination: Canton. News had reached America of the end to Anglo-Chinese hostilities with the signing of the Treaty of Nanking. It was time, Abbot and the other Yankee merchants felt, to act.

His official title on *Horatio* was ship's boy, which put him at the bottom of the onboard totem pole. As an apprentice, he was expected to learn from the other sailors. With luck, he would rise to become an able seaman and then mate. He got no wages, but did receive $30 in spending money from his father. He also got something more precious to him: "my freedom; that is, I was not to depend on him any further, but to make my own way in the world."

Yet big brother Abbot did not let Charlie set sail without family along: he also booked William Henry and Ann Low on the same trip. This was to be William Henry's second trip to Canton. He had returned to New York the previous year, safe but shaken by the Opium War—and with only partially filled pockets. Now that trade relations had resumed, he had little choice but to go back to China and try his luck again.

The steam tug pulled the sturdy wooden vessel out into the Upper Bay, and the guests on board *Horatio* debarked. The crew scrambled aloft, the sails came tumbling down, and off the ship sailed for China. "It being a fair wind, we did not stop work till all the studden-sails [*sic,* studding sails*] were set and we were nearly out of sight of land," Charlie recalled.[18] Then the first and second mate summoned all hands on deck and chose their watches, alternating until the crew was divided evenly into the two work crews that kept the ship fully operational twenty-four hours a day. The first mate was, in Dana's words, "the prime minister, the official organ, and the active superintending officer." Aboard *Horatio*, he supervised the larboard watch. Meanwhile, the other work crew, commanded by the second mate ("neither officer nor man . . . obliged to go aloft to reef and furl the topsails, and to put his hands in the tar and lush, with the rest") would take the starboard watch.

The two watches worked on an alternating daily schedule, also known as "larboard" and "starboard."[†] The larboard schedule went as follows: sail the ship from midnight to four in the morning (the dreary so-called middle watch); sleep from four to eight (with a short interlude for breakfast); sail the ship from eight until noon, lunch (known as "dinner") and leisure between noon and four; a two-hour "first dog watch" between four and six in the late afternoon; and

* Studding sails, whose booms slide outward from the yardarms of square-rigged vessels, are meant to increase a ship's sail area, and hence speed, in light winds.
† Larboard is synonymous with the port side, or the left side of the ship, when facing forward; *starboard* with the right side of the ship.

then two hours of cleaning, training, and repair from six to eight o'clock. Then they would go back on duty until midnight.

The starboard watch schedule went as follows: sleep between midnight and four in the morning. They would then sail the ship between four and eight o'clock, possibly overlapping for breakfast with the other watch about to go on duty. Eight until noon was their leisure time and dinner. They would go back to sailing the ship from noon to four, and then take off two hours for cleaning, training, and ship repair, as well as a quick supper. Then they would sail the ship between six and eight in the evening, or the "second dog watch," after which they could sleep from eight to midnight, and then go back on duty.

It was the use of two-hour "dog watches" that made the two schedules alternate each day.

The pace was grueling, and the schedule was not carved in stone. A skeleton crew had to run the ship during mealtimes, and in the case of bad weather ahead, the mate on watch would summon all hands on deck to take in sail and prepare the ship for the onslaught. A good mate knew that a group of idle sailors was a recipe for discontent. Repairing the rigging and polishing brightwork was done throughout the trip. Scrubbing the decks with large rectangular stones known as holystones because of their resemblance to Bibles was a tedious, much-hated task assigned toward the end of the voyage. The less time they had to talk among themselves, the better. "In no state prison are the convicts more regularly set to work, and more closely watched," Dana wrote of one particularly harsh master. "No conversation is allowed among the crew at their duty, and though they frequently do talk when aloft, or when near one another, yet they stop when an officer is nigh." The so-called Philadelphia Catechism was a common refrain among disgruntled sailors:

Six days shalt thou labor and do all thou art able
And on the seventh—holystone the deck and scrape the cable.[19]

* * *

As the *Horatio*'s voyage wore on, Charlie got his sea legs, absorbed the strict hierarchy, and steadily learned more seamanship: "slushing the masts and spars" (with galley grease), and "tarring the standing rigging," just as other men did who sailed "before the mast" had done.* He also learned the art of navigation, establishing the ship's position and plotting its course so it could make the fastest possible speed and avoid treacherous shoals, coastlines, and other hazards. Navigation in the nineteenth century required proficiency in basic arithmetic, a firm understanding of trigonometry, and the judgment that comes of experience. When clouds blotted out all of the celestial bodies in foul weather, the ship's position had to be determined by guessing the distance traveled since the last known fix. A good navigator meant the difference between life and death for all on board.

The first task was to calculate the ship's latitude, or position north or south of the equator. To accomplish this, Charlie had to look at the sun at noon through an instrument known as the sextant—invented in the 1750s—and then calculate its angle above the horizon. Such a procedure was known as "shooting the sun." To ensure that his reading found the sun at its highest altitude, or zenith, he would have to take several shots. The sextant altitude, as it was called, would then be corrected using published tables to create a "true altitude." This was subtracted from 90 degrees to reveal, finally, the vessel's latitude. This noon sight would be plotted on a chart map as a parallel horizontal line, giving a reasonable indication of the ship's latitude.

At night, Charlie would use the sextant again, this time to calculate lunar distances: discovering position lines from a combination

---

* "Before the mast" meant working as a sailor rather than as an officer, as sailors lived in the front of the ship (forecastle) while officers slept in the rear of the ship (in the afterhouse).

of stars or planets, chosen for their brightness, in both hemispheres. Star and planet shots were more difficult and time-consuming than shooting the sun. Clear twilight skies and a sharp horizon were a celestial navigator's best friends. Plotting stars and planets also required the precise time, taken from the ship's chronometer, as well as tables of exacting spherical trigonometry. After a good session, Charlie would have three or more stars tightly intersecting on his chart to form an exact position that provided both latitude and longitude.[20]

Calculating longitude—the ship's east-west location—had until relatively recently been a mix of guesswork by most mariners and complicated calculations by only the most skilled. The invention of the marine chronometer in the eighteenth century by the self-taught British carpenter and clock maker John Harrison resulted in a supremely reliable clock unaffected by changes in humidity and the ship's motion. Harrison's marine chronometer, which found its way onto most large merchant vessels, was set constantly at Greenwich Mean Time (GMT). Each day, when the celestial latitude was calculated by shooting the sun, the navigator would compare the ship's local time (the local hour angle) with the Greenwich time (the Greenwich hour angle), and, using published tables, be able to calculate the distance in degrees east or west from the Prime Meridian.*

Soon after the American Revolution, the United States made its own contribution to navigation, one, arguably, as important as Harrison's chronometer. This was *The New American Practical Navigator*, first published in 1802 by twenty-nine-year-old Nathaniel

---

* Before the chronometer, it had been done almost entirely by guesswork, otherwise known as "dead reckoning." British navigators and, later, American seamen used the longitudinal meridian running through the naval observatory at Greenwich, England, as the so-called Prime Meridian, at 0 degrees. An hour's difference from GMT equals 15 degrees in longitude, with each degree the equivalent of sixty nautical miles at the equator, a distance that decreased as the ship sailed northward or southward. But to know this required knowing the time.

Bowditch, a self-taught mathematician from Salem. The grammar school dropout had taken only one trip to Manila, serving as a super-cargo. But with typical Yankee dash and impudence, he noted every inconsistency in the calculations of the then-bible of navigation, John Hamilton Moore's *The Practical Navigator.* The result, an entirely new guide, became a massive best seller, was adopted by merchant captains and the US Navy as the gold standard for navigation, and has never gone out of print.

By the end of his first voyage, Charlie Low had shed his landlubber persona, as well as much of his childish impetuousness. He now had the air of one of the old hands that Dana memorialized; he walked with "a wide step, and a rolling gait," and swung "his bronzed and toughened hands athwart-ships, half-opened, as though just ready to grasp a rope."[21] Arriving safely in Canton in early 1843, Charles was summoned to dine with Houqua. The aging merchant was worn out from the difficulties of the past few years. Low noted that the merchant showed the Americans around his beautiful gardens and then offered them an "elaborate lunch;" Charlie thought the strange food was "very good indeed, though some did not please my fancy."[22]

The Chinese, caving to British demands when they signed the Treaty of Nanking, had effectively abolished the old Cohong system, rendering Houqua nearly irrelevant. Opium ships could now anchor and discharge their cargo free from Chinese interference—although, in truth, American opium traders had already been carrying illicit goods to closed ports. Britain allowed US merchants to set up shop on the island of Hong Kong, which had been ceded to the Crown, allowing them (and their families) to bypass the residential restrictions that had previously confined them to the Factories or to Macao. The ports of Xiamen, Shanghai, Fuzhou, and Ningbo were also opened to Western trade.

American merchants continued to shuttle between America and China, yet one in particular seemed dogged by bad luck. After only a few months in China, William Henry Low and his pregnant wife,

Ann, sailed home on *Paul Jones*. Ann almost certainly wanted to deliver their child in her native Brooklyn, away from the disease and heat of Hong Kong. Also, William Henry appeared to be floundering professionally again. For the second time, he had failed to make partner at Russell & Company. *Paul Jones,* the same ship that would carry Warren and Catherine from New York to China later that year, got the Lows home in 118 days—not a bad voyage, considering that 140 days was considered an average passage, but still not as swift as owner Robert Forbes had hoped.

It also seemed maddeningly slow to the ship's captain, Nathaniel Palmer, who must have been especially anxious to have his boss's brother and sister-in-law aboard.[23] The problem, to Palmer, seemed to be the shape of the ship. Although equipped with considerable "deadrise"—a sharp upward angle in the submerged sections of her hull—she still featured the bluff, apple-cheeked bow typical of older ships. The captain found himself tacking his fully loaded vessel awkwardly back and forth against the prevailing winds.

It was sometime during this voyage that Palmer went below to his cabin and picked up a stray block of wood. Using his practical experience with ships of all kinds, he whittled it into the shape of a vessel that he thought would be better suited for the tea trade.

Palmer showed his little whittled shape to William Henry Low, most likely at dinner in the main saloon of the *Paul Jones*. There, under the flickering oil lamps, feasting on the vegetables, meats, and fruits that the recently invented canning process had made possible on long voyages at sea, Low peered down at a uniquely different model ship. It had a sharp-ended hull—just like the little opium clippers that sped so efficiently, cutting through the waves rather than riding over them. Yet Palmer's model also had the flatter bottom sections of the cotton packets that sailed between New Orleans and New York, big cargo carriers that had proven to be surprisingly swift sailers.

Captain Nat knew that the small opium clippers had achieved some truly startling speeds. Now that the China market had been cracked open, why couldn't bigger, oceanic ships do the same? With luck, his refined clipper-type ship could approach the fourteen knots that the little opium runners had achieved. Palmer estimated that his new ship could bring fresh tea from China to New York in fewer than a hundred days, a faster voyage than the *Paul Jones* and other ships in her class.

The relatively flat-bottom contours of Palmer's prototype created the interior volume needed for greater carrying capacity. His new model would be ideal for hauling the maximum number of tea chests with the minimum amount of wasted space. And there was another factor at work. Some sailors on the China run had noticed how their ships sailed differently with a cargo of tea versus bulk goods. "A ship with a tea cargo is very buoyant and is not deep in the water and sails very well," the young sailor Charlie Low observed.[24] This enabled tea ships to make nine or ten knots sailing large in a quartering wind—compared with six or seven knots for merchant ships loaded with heavier cargo.[25] Imagine how fast a better-designed ship could be.

Such was the ship that Captain Nathaniel Palmer envisioned while slogging homeward on John Murray Forbes's brand-new *Paul Jones*. With luck, Palmer reasoned, a sharp-bowed ship could average twelve or thirteen knots in a fresh breeze—possibly even faster—when loaded with a full cargo of tea. The question was whether a ship with such sharp ends would lose crucial buoyancy and become unstable or structurally deficient in bad weather, especially when fully loaded with cargo.

Late in 1843, a newly disembarked William Henry Low turned up at the South Street offices of A. A. Low & Brother, sadly without the competence he had sought in China, but bearing Captain Nat's model ship. His brother Abbot controlled the family purse strings, and after careful examination and consultation with the East River shipbuilders Brown & Bell, he gave his approval for building this experimental craft. Captain Nat would design the new vessel and supervise her construction at the shipyard.

In the new economic landscape, with four new ports opened to American trade, Abbot knew there was no fortune to be made in being an ordinary commission house, simply taking a cut of every cargo of tea, opium, or Chinese luxury goods. To gain a competitive edge against both British and American rivals, a shipping firm had to offer a service that would command the highest freight rates: getting first to market. Working with Russell & Company, Low intended to dispatch China freight at maximum speed. In an age before electronic communication, swift ships also allowed crucial business correspondence and bills of exchange to travel faster between China and New York. Low wanted this business, too. But he knew his firm would have tough rivals: the Griswold brothers were already at work planning a fast ship, of course named *Panama*, to be built along the lines of an enlarged Baltimore clipper.

The Russell partners in China, including newly returned managing partner Warren Delano, were also aware of the need for speed. Although not trained as a mariner like his father, Delano knew what such ships would mean to the business. "[A] large ship can carry goods at cheaper rates of freights, particularly on long voyages, than small ones can do," he observed, "and in China, the port charges are about the same as small as on large vessels if they bring up rice." An ideal ship, he calculated, would be of 550 tons, be able to stow 1,300 to 1,400 tons of tea, and cost $35,000 to build and outfit. And the best captains, he advised, were ones "who will keep the vessel in good order—make short passages and spend but little money."[26] As Warren Delano kept track of opium chests coming in and tea chests going out in the company ledger book in Hong Kong, where the Russell & Company offices had moved, he scanned the Pearl River for the new class of ships that his friend Abiel Abbot Low had started building—ships that would make faster passages than the one he and his wife had endured.

*   *   *

The Lows could think of no better name for Captain Nat's dream ship: *Houqua*. What better way to honor their old friend than a portrait in wood and canvas, with his likeness as its figurehead?

The Lows trusted Captain Nat with more than a ship: he would be taking in their still-hyperactive, now-nineteen-year-old brother Charles, transforming him from apprentice sailor to ship's officer. For so many Yankees, business and family were one and the same. If a captain or merchant did not have a son to train in the ways of commerce, he would informally "adopt" the nephew or son of a close business associate as his apprentice. Captain Nat and his wife, Eliza, had no children of their own, and the Lows might as well have been family.

Abbot Low hoped to eventually sell *Houqua* to the Chinese government as a warship. The presence of a modern warship in the Chinese navy, as a counterweight to the Royal Navy, would make conditions safer for Americans trying to conduct business. China was still smarting from the humiliation of the recent conflict, and there was a strong chance that another conflict would erupt with the bellicose Great Britain.

The US government was also intent on looking after American interests in China. On the heels of the British Treaty of Nanking, American diplomat Caleb Cushing negotiated the Treaty of Wanghia, which would give American businessmen many of the protections and privileges they so desperately desired. Ratified by Congress and signed by President John Tyler, the 1844 treaty reaffirmed Americans access to the five ports now opened to foreigners, and specified:

> [T]he vessels of the United States being admitted to trade freely to and from the five ports of China open to foreign commerce, it is further agreed that in case at any time hereafter, China should be at war with any foreign nation whatever, and for that cause should exclude such nation from entering her ports, still the vessels of the United States shall not the less continue to pursue their commerce

in freedom and security, and to transport goods to and from the ports of the belligerent parties, full respect being paid to the neutrality of the flag of the United States.

The treaty also provided protections against the kind of violence merchants had experienced in 1841. If rioters burned or looted American buildings, the US consul was authorized to "immediately dispatch a military force to disperse the rioters, and will apprehend the guilty individuals and punish them with the utmost rigor of the law." The treaty also stipulated that only the US Consulate, not the Chinese courts, could administer punishment to Americans for crimes committed in the Celestial Kingdom; this extra-territoriality was much hated by the Chinese. There was one exception to this rule: any American "who shall trade in opium or any other contraband article of merchandize, shall be subject to be dealt with by the Chinese Government, without being entitled to any countenance or protection from that of the United States."[27]

Yet these provisions were almost entirely symbolic, a nod to the fact that opium trading still remained technically illegal in China. The American vice consul in Canton in 1844 was none other than Warren Delano II, partner of opium-dealing Russell & Company, so there was no real means of enforcing this opium ban. Delano himself dispatched a letter to the secretary of the navy urging America to send a fleet of ships that would give the Chinese "a sense of respect for the United States." Delano knew that a disruption of the opium trade by the Chinese would cause another war with England, one that the humbled Celestial Kingdom could not win.

So the "foreign mud" known as opium continued to flow into China.

CHAPTER 6

CAPTAIN NAT

Probably no one ever brought up so many young men who af-terward became successful shipmasters, while his character and example were an inspiration to many who never sailed with him.[1]
—CAPTAIN ARTHUR HAMILTON CLARK,
on Captain Nathaniel Brown Palmer

The man who in a fit of frustration carved the model of the ship that would become *Houqua* was Abbot Low's secret weapon. Captain Nathaniel Palmer was designer, master mariner, and adventurer, all packaged with a bearish yet calm exterior. Bearded and brawny, and standing six feet tall, forty-four-year-old "Captain Nat," as his friends called him, did not thrash his men or curse the bad weather. Rather, in a fit of pique, he threw his white beaver hat to the deck, stamped on it, and then retreated to his cabin to cool off. According to one fellow mariner, Captain Nat was "a man of great physical strength and endurance," and his "roughness was all on the outside; his heart was filled with kindness and sympathy for the joys and sorrows of others."[2] He was also a very gifted designer of ships, who had gained his knowledge through years of seafaring rather than by theoretical study or apprenticeship.

He was born in 1799, making him about a decade older than most of the recent Russell partners. A Yankee from the small Connecticut coastal town of Stonington, he grew up around his father's shipyard, which built fast, trim privateers of French-inspired design that were the scourge of the British during the War of 1812. According to one biographer, what distinguished ships built in and around the Connecticut River Valley was the native white oak, which "stood higher in the estimation of shipowners than any except the live oak of Hatteras Island and the coast of Florida."[3]

As he wandered the shipyard at his father's side, the young Palmer learned of the various types of American woods used in shipbuilding. Each one had a specific purpose. White oak, the gold standard of shipbuilding woods, was coarse grained and could be shaped into virtually any structural component: ribs that sprouted out from the keel; hull planking that covered the ribs; and hanging knees, triangular pieces bolted to ribs that supported the decks above. Its pores were infused with tyloses—occlusions of the tree's xylem cells—making it nearly waterproof. Other woods could be used based on price and availability. Some could be cut locally. Rock maple, a dense, tough wood that still was easy to utilize with iron tools, was often used for the keel, the backbone of the ship, and was rot resistant when immersed constantly in seawater. White pine, soft and also resistant to rot, was used for deck planking. Hackmatack, a species of larch found in eastern North America, was excellent for rough construction such as hanging knees. Other woods were harder to come by and had to be shipped to the yard from a distance, among them finely grained, imported satinwood and rosewood. These were used most often inside passengers' quarters and the captain's stateroom.[4]

The most prized wood for structural work was southern live oak, long reserved for American naval vessels, where price and transport were no object. Its most famous use was in the frigate USS *Constitution*, completed in 1797 in Charlestown, Massachusetts, and known as "Old Ironsides" because British cannonballs seemed to bounce off her hull during the War of 1812. Virtually impervious to rot, live oak provided bracing components for parts of the ship that were subjected to extreme stress. With a specific gravity of 0.88 out of 1.00 (an object with a specific gravity of 1.00 will be neutral in water; anything heavier than 1.00 will sink), it has the highest density of any American hardwood. In its "living" form, live oak trees, usually draped in languid Spanish moss, grew in bogs and bayous, and shaded the approaches to stately plantation houses such as Oak Alley in Louisiana.

Any shipyard apprentice who wanted to become a master shipbuilder had to become expert not only in the use of tools such as the adze and the saw, but also in the characteristics of all of the woods used in his craft. Unlike later ships built out of iron and steel, wooden ships were made out of living materials. The wood breathed, flexed, expanded, contracted, and, if not cared for, rotted away. Yet when seasoned and maintained properly, a high-quality wooden vessel could last just as long as a metal ship. Most importantly, wood was plentiful in the United States, unlike in Europe, which by the nineteenth century had decimated its stands of old growth timber. As a result, American shipbuilders continued to perfect the art of wood shipbuilding, while Europeans experimented with iron, first for use in the frames and then eventually for the entire hull.

As much as he loved prowling around his father's shipyard, Palmer did not stay in Stonington long. The channel leading out to Long Island Sound was only twelve feet deep, which severely limited the size of vessels that could be built there.[5] Nathaniel shipped out to sea at fourteen, just in time to miss the Royal Navy's 1814 bombardment of Stonington—one of the British assaults that seared itself into the memory of Warren Delano, then just five years old. While still in his teens, Palmer became captain of the small seal-hunting ship *Hero*. Sailing to South American sealing grounds, he became arguably the first Westerner to see the mysterious continent of Antarctica. Palmer's claim would be disputed in the years to come, but an Antarctic peninsula bears his name to this day. He later conducted his own Antarctic expedition, financed by wealthy Stonington businessmen.

Sealing ships were smaller versions of New Bedford whalers, filled with rough men who slaughtered mammals for their oil and skin, and Palmer soon decided to leave these "butcher ships adrift."[6,7] Yet, along with learning how to sail small but nimble craft in the open sea, the Antarctic voyages gave him a key advantage over other captains: an intimate understanding of the winds and currents around Cape Horn, that treacherous southern tip of South America that would one day prove to be the most feared obstacle on the sea route to the future boom town of San Francisco.

Leaving the bloody decks of the Stonington sealers behind, Nathaniel Palmer made a quick voyage to the West Indies to supply the Venezuelan revolutionary Simon Bolívar, then fighting for much of South America's independence from Spain. In a letter written to Abbot Low many years later, Palmer boasted that he'd crammed 175 sheep on the top deck.[8]

By the 1830s, Palmer was commanding flat-bottomed packets that carried bales of Deep South "King Cotton" between New Orleans and the cotton brokerages of New York. His boss was Edward Knight Collins, a colorful New York shipping entrepreneur who also ran a line of transatlantic packets. Although an excellent captain, Palmer knew when not to push his luck with the weather. According to one historian, "Palmer felt his way carefully to the extreme edge of safety and stayed there." The captain also demonstrated himself to be "something of a shrewd businessman besides, and something more than an average good ship designer."[9] He was especially impressed with the ship's flat floors, and thanks to his design suggestions, Collins's next packets proved to be extremely fast.

Soon Palmer was working for Collins's Dramatic Line's transatlantic packets. He set a new speed record from Liverpool to New York that October: an astonishing fifteen days, against the prevailing winds, when a more typical passage could last between six and eight weeks.[10] But he decided eventually that a year on the North Atlantic was more than enough. He might not have had the nastiness in his soul needed to keep his "packet rat" crews in line, especially on so punishing a schedule. "Packet rats they were called, and that was an insult to the rats!" snarled one North Atlantic packet captain. "Brawlers, sea lawyers, pimps, drunkards, no-goods all."[11] Unlike the navy, there was no court-martial system to enforce discipline on board. Punishment, just like the business itself, was at the mercy of the free market. Many masters and mates had to put down mutinies by resorting to fisticuffs and even pointed guns. This gnawing, constant fear of insurrection severely affected the personalities of many officers. Palmer's younger brother, Theodore, also a captain, was seen by one fellow mariner as a "harder man to get along with," as he had "been in Liverpool packets most of his life."[12]

So in 1840 Captain Nat bowed out of the transatlantic trade and signed on as a captain with A. A. Low & Brother. The timing was perfect. China packet crews were generally regarded as less stressful to command than their North Atlantic counterparts, for they tended to be less violent, desperate lots than the "packet rats." And the China passage, although still dangerous and much longer, could be relatively placid compared with the harsh North Atlantic.

As Captain Nat sailed the A. A. Low & Brother packets between New York and Canton, he thought back to his experience on the flat-floor cotton boats. Could he use that concept on a new generation of tea ships? He decided that he would want to be an owner—as well as the captain—of any ships he designed. He made his case known to A. A. Low & Brother, and the company accepted his conditions.[13] A $19,500 contract with Brown & Bell to build *Houqua* was signed on November 1, 1843.

All along New York's East River, wooden hulls were rising in the yards of Brown & Bell and competitors such as Smith & Dimon, and W. H. Webb. Since the Treaties of Nanking and Wanghia, other firms that previously did not do much business in China were challenging Russell's supremacy, a situation that greatly worried Abbot Low. "The China trade is passing into numerous hands," he wrote darkly in a letter to his brother Edward, "and will in all probability be attended with but little profit."[14] The word was out, and competition was growing stiff, as new companies shelled out for swift ships modeled on clipper designs.

The ship that attracted the most interest was being built for William Henry Aspinwall, who had once been one of Russell & Company's most valued commission clients but now competed against it in the China shipping business. Her designer was John Willis Griffiths, an eccentric, lowly draftsmen at Smith & Dimon who had somehow managed to sell Aspinwall on his own design.

Unlike Palmer, who was renowned for his seafaring exploits and expertise, Griffiths had a hazy past and appears never to have ventured on a blue-water voyage. In later life, he became something of a shameless self-promoter who claimed to have been the principal "inventor" of the American clipper ship. As one historian summed up, "John Willis Griffiths was considered a genius as a naval architect, although perhaps somewhat eccentric in his zeal to improve American naval architecture."[15] Griffith's aggressive salesmanship might have stemmed from an inferiority complex common to tradesmen at the time, who felt that their status in the increasingly mercantile nation was under threat. Shipbuilders were looked on as mechanics—highly skilled, perhaps, but people who worked with their hands, not their heads.

Griffiths, born in New York City, had trained as a shipwright under the watchful eye of one Isaac Webb at the Eckford yard. It appears that bad luck plagued the apprentice Griffiths at the yard. At seventeen, he cut himself in a shipyard accident, and Isaac Webb released him from his indenture. Despite his love of ships, Griffiths's head, one would surmise, was not in the right place.

Griffiths bounced around after his apprenticeship. He married and got a job at the United States Navy Yard in Portsmouth, Virginia. Here he absorbed military naval design practices, in which speed was paramount over cargo capacity, especially for frigates and other patrol craft. The US Navy recognized his talent; as a young man, Griffiths designed the hull of the fast frigate USS *Macedonian*, rebuilt from the keel of a British frigate captured during the War of 1812.[16] It was during this time that Griffiths grew more interested in shipbuilding theory and less in mere construction.

Finally, Griffiths landed a modest job at the Smith & Dimon yard back in New York. As a draftsman, he supervised the construction of half models for clients: wooden layer-cake-like miniatures that could be taken apart so that the shipwright could measure dimensions (sheer,* body, and half breadth), figures that would be expanded proportionally into full-size templates in wood three-quarters of an inch thick. Then they would go to the shipyard's wood stocks to see which types of wood were available for assembling the full-sized ship.[17]

How the Smith & Dimon draftsman Griffiths got the ear of someone as lofty as William Henry Aspinwall remains a mystery. Later in life, Griffiths claimed to have given a lecture at the American Institute of the City of New York—a civic association founded in 1829 that served as a forum for inventors seeking to promote their creations to capitalists—outlining his concept of a new China packet. Unlike Palmer, who advocated for sharp ends and a flat bottom, Griffiths believed that a V-shaped bottom (high deadrise) created a faster ship. Basically, the result would be an enlarged opium clipper. Griffiths maintained that the entire audience laughed at his presentation. Everyone except for William Henry Aspinwall, who was intrigued by the design and asked the young draftsman to prepare more elaborate plans. However, no record of Griffiths's lecture

---

* A measure of longitudinal deck curvature. The sheer forward is usually twice that of the sheer aft.

survives in the archives of the American Institute, and most of Aspinwall's papers have been destroyed.

A more likely story is that Aspinwall could not engage the new A. A. Low man, the respected Nat Palmer, and so he took a gamble by choosing Griffiths. The young draftsman may have been a radical, but his employer Smith & Dimon was one of New York's most respected shipyards, with a long track record of success. Aspinwall's aim was a larger version of a ship with which he was already intimately familiar: his own *Ann McKim,* built in 1833. Although it was the fastest ship in the China trade, it was too small and slim hulled to be profitable. He signed a contract with Smith & Dimon at almost exactly the same time that Palmer convinced A. A. Low & Brother to build his ship.

She was to be christened *Rainbow.*

Regardless of the competition, the Lows kept their eyes on the prize, and Palmer kept Brown & Bell on schedule.[18] At Russell & Co., Robert Bennet Forbes, although not directly invested in the ship, followed the construction closely. "Let me know a week before you launch so that I may go in her, your fine ship *Houqua,*" he scrawled eagerly to Palmer.[19] But she would not be ready for some time.

New York's East River was home to many other shipyards in addition to Brown & Bell. Employing thousands of men and boys, the yards built everything from China packets, to river steamers, to naval warships. Prior to the 1830s, there were no set hours for work. It took a number of strikes for the shipyard owners to concede to a series of short breaks throughout the day, marked by the ringing of the so-called Mechanic's Bell, set in a high wooden tower at the intersection of Lewis and Third Streets. Cast from hundreds of gold, silver, and copper coins donated by the shipyard workers, the Mechanic's Bell was an audible symbol of tradesman solidarity, its tolling a daily reminder to the bosses of the hard-won twelve-hour day.[20] The day started at six in the morning sharp. The men would pause for breakfast between eight and nine, and then continue on until noon. After an hour lunch break, the men would labor until the Mechanic's Bell tolled again at six in the evening.

The workers' attempt at forming a trade union proved futile. The best they could do was the so-called New-York Journeymen Shipwrights Society, which pooled member contributions into a fund to help workers debilitated by all-too-frequent accidents. The organization's charter forbade it from attempting to "control or fix the prices of carpenter's wages in the city of New York." Wages for skilled working-class shipyard workers, considered a good job at the time, seem shockingly low by today's standards. During the 1840s, a teenage apprentice might earn $2.50 a week, plus $40 a year "in lieu of meat, drink, washing, lodging, clothing, and other necessities." A master shipwright could expect to earn up to $1.75 per day. Such pitiful wages barely allowed these young men to survive in the big city.

Low wages aside, the highly skilled men of New York's shipyard were very proud of their craft, which demanded a combination of physical strength and extreme attention to detail. The first step in the actual construction of a ship such as *Houqua*—and all subsequent clippers—was laying the keel. This was the backbone of the ship; if the keel broke apart in rough seas or on the rocks, the ship had a "broken back" and was a total loss.

Keels were made of rock maple or another type of tough, rot-resistant wood. For maximum strength, a shipbuilder preferred to use a section of lumber from a single tree. Because *Houqua* was more than 130 feet in length, her keel probably had two or more sections made into a single unit by a so-called scarph joint. To make a scarph, the workers cut a diagonal at the ends of the two keel pieces and then linked together the pieces with wooden wedges, iron pins, or a combination of the two. On larger vessels, which required extreme strength for long ocean voyages, the keel might be composed of three vertical layers: the shoe (the bottom layer), followed by upper and lower tiers. The shoe was considered "sacrificial." Its main purpose was to protect the structural keel itself from damage from grounding, and hence it was constructed in short sections.[21] A crooked keel would wreak havoc on a ship's steering, so the shipwrights would carefully eyeball the sections to make sure they were straight. After that, the workers would then join the keel sections with pins and wedges. They would then use axe-like adzes to cut a groove into the keel known as a "rabbet." The garboards—or first range of planks— would be secured into this rabbet.

The keel defined the so-called centerline of the ship. With it in place, the shipwrights would then erect the ship's front and rear sections. Ideally, the front of the ship, known as the stem, would also be made of a single section of wood, usually white oak, with a grain that went with the curve of the bow. If made of two or more sections, the stem was scarphed together, just like the keel. The whole assembly was then joined by metal bolts (ranging in diameter from $7/8$ to $1 \frac{1}{2}$ inches) to the rest of the keel by a section of wood known as a filling piece. Ideally, rust-resistant copper bolts would be used for areas of the ship below the waterline, and iron or composition bolts for the areas above it. Copper was weaker than iron but much less likely to corrode than the ferrous metal. As for the iron bolts, corrosion (to a point) was a positive thing: when exposed to sea air, the iron bolts would expand in their holes, adding to the strength of the connection, something shipyard workers called "holding fast." Yet if they corroded too much, the entire ship would become "iron sick," in which continuous exposure of iron bolts to seawater would cause the ship to fall apart.[22]

A so-called false stem projected out from the front of the stemson—this was where the ship's bow met the water. The sternpost, which, projected upward from the rear of the keel, was never made from sections but rather from a single piece of wood, usually the lower section of a tree trunk. In the words of maritime historian William Crothers, "the chosen log had to be of unquestionable soundness in order to withstand the variable stresses imposed upon it by the rudder." It was secured to the keel by two additional massive wood pieces: a vertical inner sternpost and a stern "knee"—a piece of wood with one branch attached to the inner sternpost and the other joined to the keel.[23]

The next step was the framing, which spread out like ribs from the ship's keel and gave the ship structural rigidity. The angle of the frames from the keel would define how steeply the ship's sides rose upward, an angle known as deadrise. The higher the deadrise, the more closely the hull cross section resembled a V, while the lower the deadrise, the more closely it resembled a flat-bottomed barge.[24] The frames were assembled flat from a moving platform, and then raised into place and secured as a completed unit. The lowest frame section was known as the floor, followed upward by the first futtock, second futtock, and lastly the top timber, by which time the frames curved upward from horizontal to the vertical rail stanchion.[25] At the bow and stern, skilled carpenters crafted intricate framing for the "stern knuckle" and the "knightheads."

Above the keel, workers added additional timbers into an assembly known as the keelson. Usually made from hard pine, its purpose was to secure the ship's frame into the keel, as well as to provide additional longitudinal strength to the hull. For fine-hulled vessels such as *Houqua*, a strong keelson was critical to keep the ship's bow and stern from pulling downward (a process known as hogging) from the midship section. Naval designers realized that could be the stronger the keelson, the trimmer and more elegant a ship's lines. In the years to come, as clippers grew bigger and leaner, with less buoyancy fore and aft (in the bow and stern), the keelson would grow in size and complexity to compensate. The single keelson timber might have up to three "riders" on top, and three "sister riders" on each side. As Crothers observed, "If there was one structural feature proprietary to the clipper ship, it was the keelson." The beauty of the hull's exterior was made possible by the brute strength of the keelson timbers from within. Yet the increased size of the keelson had two negative size effects: severely diminished cargo capacity and increased weight.[26] The keelson also had to be strong because the masts were anchored to it, and it had to withstand the forces not just of the weight of the masts but also the immense force of wind pushing against thousands of square yards of canvas.

To support the decks, workers crafted beams that would be installed between five and seven feet apart, and then clamped to the vertical frames. What actually held the beams to the frames were knees, which performed the same function as the component that linked the keel with the sternpost. In Crothers's words, the knee's job was to provide a "mechanical connection between two parts that worked in different directions but were located in one plane."[27] Up to 1,500 such knees could go into the construction of a single ship, and, ideally, the natural grain of the wood would conform to the angle of the knee. As nineteenth-century production began to deplete American forests, there was an increasing shortage of tough woods such as hackmatack, and shipbuilders would start using wrought iron knees instead.

With the frame completed, the entire ship was planked with three- or four-inch thick boards, usually of white oak, that were steamed into shape and secured to the frames with wooden treenails. These one-inch wooden dowels, made from locust or other were hardy wood, hammered into bored holes with iron hammers. When in contact with water, the treenails swelled, tightening the connection between the frames and the planks.

Afterward, workers added sheets of copper to the hull below the waterline. The purpose of this expensive layer was to save money in the long run by stopping the *Teredo navalis*, or shipworm, a bivalve that gorges on submerged wood and wreaked havoc on hulls. The *Teredo* thrived in warm climates, making ships in the China trade particularly susceptible to destruction. After much experimentation, the Royal Navy had pioneered the use of copper sheathing in the mid-eighteenth century, which not only protected the hull from the *Teredo* but also impeded the growth of aquatic plants and barnacles. The practice soon spread to British and American merchant vessels. US merchants found another reason for the heavy initial outlay in coppering their ships' bottoms: increased speed.

After her bottom was coppered and her sides painted in lustrous black, *Houqua* was finally ready for her launch into the East River.

On July 1, 1844, under the command of her designer, Captain Nat, *Houqua* cast off and set sail from New York. Palmer ordered all hands to lay aloft and let loose the gaskets from the yards. The black-hulled little craft suddenly sprouted wings of billowing white canvas, which thundered downward and caught the wind with a deep rumble.

Compared with the hefty packets berthed around her at South Street, *Houqua* was a trim, fragile-looking vessel. As one reporter noted, the ship was the "prettiest and most rakish looking packet ever built in the civilized world . . . as sharp as a cutter—as symmetrical as a yacht—as rakish in her rig as a pirate—and as neat in her deck and cabin arrangements as a lady's boudoir."[28] Yet she was far from dainty: like the opium clippers on which she was modeled, Low and Palmer had built *Houqua* as an auxiliary warship, and mounted sixteen guns in case of an attack.

The ship carried a letter from Abbot Low to Warren Delano in Hong Kong, with Low writing that *Houqua*, if she "has not been unduly commended, ought to arrive in China in less than 100 days." Her cargo included four hundred tons of goods, "principally Domestics and chiefly outfreight," as well as an invoice of cotton goods worth $30,000 and a $15,000 letter of credit, most likely from Baring's bank. "Together these will yield as much as I shall wish to have sent home in the ship on my own account and Captain Palmer's," he continued, "so that there will be no need of calling upon you for an additional sum."[29]

The passenger list included perpetually cash-strapped William Henry Low, now on his third voyage to China, charged by his brother with making an "early disposition" of the ship's freight, especially if *Houqua* should make "a good passage and anticipate other vessels on the way." In the post–Opium War era, the Americans were now shipping lots of heavy freight for sale in Hong Kong, most likely to be sold to supply the new British colony. Common cargo included pig lead, cotton sheetings, and naval stores: pitch, tar, and turpentine.[30]

As she sailed out to sea, the partners of A. A. Low & Brother held their breaths, wondering if Palmer's experiment would capsize or plunge under at the first gale, taking their most valued captain, his crew, and passengers down with her. In addition to William Henry, another Low relative was on board: Francis Hillard, the youngest brother of Harriet Low's husband, John. Francis, according to Abbot Low, was "seeking a situation in some mercantile house and is furnished with good letters to your firm and others. He is a fine seaman & well qualified to act as a bookkeeper."[31] As for the third mate, Abbot knew that his cutup kid brother Charlie was in good hands under Captain Nat's rough but firm tutelage.

The voyage was smooth. In the ship's main saloon—adorned with rich wood paneling and plush upholstered sofas—the passengers whiled away the evenings by singing songs and telling long stories until the flickering whale oil lamps were extinguished at ten o'clock. Liquor was available to the captain, officers, and passengers, but not the crew. Food was ample if not varied. All ships carried a floating barnyard—pigs, chickens, geese, goats, and ducks—which were gradually slaughtered as the voyage continued.[32] Although fresh fruit and vegetables gave out within a few weeks, the ship carried tinned food. One China trade captain (not Palmer), famous for his malapropisms and proud of the spread that he could now have at dinner, told his passengers proudly, "Yes, gentlemen, those vegetables were put up in tin cans and *diametrically* sealed."[33] Little did the passengers know that tinned food was often contaminated with lead. What the sailors may have lacked in vegetables, they may have made up for in dearth of poison.

Captain Palmer would leave the dinner table as soon as a meal ended and either go to his stateroom or keep an eye over the ship's operations on the quarterdeck.[34] *Houqua* was living up to her designer's promise, sailing easily and consistently at around ten knots. As they approached the Dutch East Indies, Palmer spotted an English merchantman in the distance, and he prepared to hail it, firing one of *Houqua*'s guns and raising the Stars and Stripes. The English vessel suddenly reduced sail. Her captain, thinking *Houqua* was a warship and apparently believing that the United States and England might be at war again, prepared to surrender. As *Houqua* overtook the British merchantman, Palmer announced that there was no need to fear: this sleek Yankee craft was a merchant ship, not a warship. The British captain, Low remembered, "was mad as a hornet and would have nothing to say to us, but gave order to make sail again."[35]

Seventy-two days after departing New York, *Houqua* dropped anchor at Anjer in the Dutch East Indies, where the famished crew loaded new provisions: chickens, turtles, and fruit. Twelve days later, Captain Palmer brought her safe and sound into Hong Kong. "A splendid passage," young Low said.[36]

The merchant Houqua never got to see his namesake. He had died at age seventy-five the September before she sailed. However, during construction, Captain Palmer and Charles Low had sailed to Canton to pay him a visit at his grand mansion. There the Americans had presented their mentor with a model of the ship to be.

Shortly after their arrival in Hong Kong, William Low wrote Palmer about what to do with his cargo, which apparently included a cache of muskets.[37] It is not clear whether the guns were intended for the safety of the partners of Russell & Company or were being shipped on consignment. It does, however, appear that whatever their purpose, the guns would be smuggled ashore, as the first mate, Thomas Hunt, had already delivered a ship's manifesto for customs inspection at Whampoa.

Palmer had a letter of authorization from the Baring Brothers bank to bring back to New York up to £2,000 worth of British-owned "merchandise" on consignment. The merchandise remains a mystery—it was probably tea—but what is clear is that the British were now interested in using a fast American ship to sell their Chinese goods, hopefully at a higher price than could be fetched in London.[38]

Palmer, finding that the Chinese government had no interest in buying *Houqua* for its navy, loaded her with tea and turned the ship's bow down the Pearl River and out to sea, homeward bound. As she hurtled through the Indian Ocean toward the Cape of Good Hope, Third Mate Charles Low—by now tall and tan, his hands calloused and nails ringed with black tar—found that he could "turn a dead eye" and "clap on a seizing" as well as any. "I was getting great confidence in myself in regard to taking care of the ship," he boasted. "I kept the second mate's watch for more than six weeks."[39]

"A sailor can sleep anywhere—no sound of wind, water, canvas, rope, wood, or iron can keep him awake," Richard Dana observed in *Two Years Before the Mast*.[40] Charles snug in his bunk as the ship rolled toward home, dreamed that *Houqua* was in a race against Wetmore & Company's new clipper ship, *Montauk*, which he had seen arrive in Hong Kong on their heels. As the wind picked up, and the two ships surged ahead, he braced the yards once, twice, and three times, and *Houqua* gained the upper hand. Suddenly a squall hit the clipper with a terrific burst of wind and spray. The skies above darkened to charcoal black, and waves danced and rolled around the ship's hull.

"Let go the skysail and the royal halyards!" Low cried.

The winds howled and foaming waves smashed over the bow, and Captain Nat and First Mate Hunt ran out of their cabin in a panic. Then there was a great cracking sound, followed by the din of falling blocks, ripping canvas, and shrieking rope.

"It's not the main-topgallant mast; it can't be!" he yelled, and woke with a start in his bunk.

When he reported for duty, Low told the second mate about his dream and went on with his watch.

On a later voyage, Charles Low found himself atop the main-mast, hacking away the tangled wreckage of *Houqua*'s main top-gallant mast, which had collapsed during a race against Wetmore's *Montauk*.

"Well, Low, your dream has come true," the second mate said as Charles climbed down from aloft.[41]

Yet they had won the race.

CHAPTER 7

FAMILY PRESSURE UNDER SAIL

Oh, some there I know of now, in exile and captivity,
Disfriended of their lighted world and where it wanders, who
Would tramp that hall and raise their hands and shout the heighth
   and width of it:
"Give us the Clipper Ships, and then—we shall have Houqua
   too!"

—Benjamin R. C. Low,
grandson of William Henry Low II,
"*Houqua*, In Memoriam A.A.L.," (1893)[1]

While Third Mate Charlie Low was scrambling through the rigging on the homeward passage of the *Houqua*, his brother William Henry was locked in his cabin, listening to the waves thump against the sides of his family's ship. He was sad, alone, and feeling rather like the family failure. William was returning from his third stint in China. He had fallen ill there, likely from overwork, exhaustion, and Canton's hot and humid tropical climate. Yet something else was not right.

A third brother, Edward Allen Low, who had joined William in China at Abbot's behest, had written home worriedly some months before, shortly before the Christmas of 1844. William Henry, Edward noted, had not been able to carry out "some of the principal objects of his visit to Canton." And both merchant brothers were in the dark about their futures at Russell & Company. New and lucrative partnership slots would be decided within the coming year. Warren Delano, who had consolidated his power in the firm, was now in his second term as Russell's chief and had become its largest shareholder. In Edward's view, Delano was not one to give jobs to the younger Low brothers just because they were Old Seth Low's Sons.

William Henry Low's early departure hints that there was a succession problem and that Warren Delano was not eager to guarantee him a seat at the club table. "The partnership of R & Co. expires on 31st Decr. 1845, at which time a new one will be formed," Edward wrote to eldest brother Abbot soon after *Houqua* departed on her return voyage. "Who will retire and who will be admitted to the new concern, I have as yet no means of knowing. If William [Henry] had remained, it was my intention to have spoken to Mr. Delano some time in the fall of '45, and if I found there was no prospect of my being admitted for three years more, then I would join myself to William's Establishment and see what we could do on our own account . . . any suggestions or advice you can give me will go far in deciding my movements."[2]

Once aboard ship, headed for home, William Henry's spirits seemed to improve. He drank and laughed in the main saloon with Captain Nat and the other passengers, apparently ready to come home to his wife, Ann, and see his infant son for the first time. Yet behind the closed doors of his cabin, as *Houqua* bounded through the seas at close to twelve knots, William Henry seems to have lost all composure. Perhaps his visit to Canton without the calming influence of his wife was too much for him. The dissipation of his time in China—fueled by alcohol—may have gotten the better of him.

As *Houqua* approached New York, William Henry Low stepped out of his cabin and walked to the bow of the vessel. It was night, and the stars formed a flickering blanket over his head. The sails and the rigging strummed above him. Aft, he heard commands barked to the helmsman by the mate on watch. The sea curled beneath the ship's stem and figurehead—Houqua, his head crowned with a mandarin's cap; his painted eyes looking steadily ahead, just like the portrait in his brother Abbot's house.

Those on the night watch heard a splash. They ran to the rail, looking for a man overboard in the blackness of the Atlantic. They saw nothing. The ship sailed on; it was probably not for a few hours that the crew realized a passenger was missing. By then, the corpse had been taken by the sea.

William Henry Low was gone.[3]

William was the second member of the Low clan to die away from home. The first was his uncle, the first William Henry Low, the family pioneer who had established the Lows in the China business thirty years before and had also died, albeit from tuberculosis while on a homeward-bound ship. Abbot Low did not dwell on his brother's suicide, but correspondence reveals his shock and grief. "Poor William," he wrote their brother Edward in China. "His end was sudden, indeed, and all unexpected."[4]

Suicide, as well as mental illness, was a forbidden topic in nineteenth-century America, especially in rich families that expected great success from their members. The Low family maintained their Yankee reticence when writing later about their loss. In a letter to his shipping firm's representative in Canton, Abbot wrote, "It were more grateful to myself and kinder to you than devote these few lines to topics of a less painful nature." Abbot then proceeded to inquire about the cargo *Houqua* was loading in New York.

The ship's speed gave reason for measured confidence. *Houqua*'s voyage to New York from Canton, her cargo holds full of tea, had taken only ninety days. "The result, though not brilliant, is satisfactory," Abbot Low had written to Edward. "I think *Houqua*'s teas will yield a profit of 8% or 10% over and above commissions and charges."[5] He and Captain Nat set about building additional ships according to *Houqua*'s plan.

Yet *Houqua* was not the only ship making good time. "The vessels from China have come along in remarkably short passages," Abbot wrote Edward that April. "Such a course of winds has probably been never known before."[6] What alarmed Abbot the most: the old cotton packet ship *Natchez*, belonging to Howland & Aspinwall and under the command of Captain Robert Waterman, had made a "rapid passage" in "78 days!!!" Without this miraculous run in an old tub, he fumed, *Houqua* would have snagged the record by a margin of several days. "When would the world have heard the end of it?" Abbot wondered. "When?" The advent of all these fast, new ships, he reasoned, "must be regarded as having a bad effect upon our spring Tea market, and as 12 or 13 cargoes are yet to come along during the season and prior to June, I apprehend prices have not yet seen their lowest point by a good deal."[7]

What worried Abbot Low even more than older ships making quick passages was Howland & Aspinwall's new ship, *Rainbow*. Although her keel was laid before *Houqua*'s, construction delays followed, due apparently to William Henry Aspinwall's second thoughts about John Willis Griffiths's experimental design. Could a ship this slim and with so lofty a rig stay afloat in rough weather? And was her cargo capacity too limited to make a profit for her owners? One concern that Aspinwall might have heard at his dinner table from his fellow merchants was that his extremely sharp, V-shaped ship did not have sufficient buoyancy at the bow and stern to maintain structural integrity in rough seas, which would render the vessel a structural loss. Captain Nat's flat-floor design for *Houqua,* which gave his ship greater buoyancy, mitigated this problem somewhat, but in Griffiths's mind, the flat floor came at the expense of almighty speed.

Griffiths and Aspinwall wrangled about the final construction details until finally, in the words of clipper ship historian Captain Arthur Clark, "the ship was finished without the slightest alterations from the original plans."[8] (Although, according to one account,

Aspinwall did call in foreign experts—most likely British ones—to examine the placement of the masts.)[9] Contemporary observers mocked her "outside-in" look, but as Clark insisted a half century later, she was "designed and built with great care."[10]

It is hard to reconstruct a full picture of Aspinwall's thinking, but one thing remains clear: he was not one to shirk away from radical innovation. Timing was everything—more so now than ever, with a half dozen ships arriving from China each month. If going "extreme" meant getting an advantage over the more conservative Low, for example, why not take a radical approach first and modify later? Aspinwall had already taken a gamble on the swift but small *Ann McKim* several years earlier. Speed had previously been a matter of prestige in the China trade. Now Aspinwall felt the time was right to make speed truly pay.

On launch day, one newspaper announced that the ship "holds out a promise, we should judge by her model, of great speed."[11] Yet as beautiful as *Rainbow* was, she proved to be too extreme, too experimental. Only four days out of New York, as a howling Atlantic gale drove her ahead at full speed, Captain John Land heard a cracking sound, followed by the crash of tumbling spars and the shriek of ripping canvas. The ship careened out of control, as all three of her upper masts (topgallants) collapsed under the pressure. Land ordered all hands aloft to cut the wreckage free before the ship was driven under. Ironically, it had been Aspinwall's more traditional sail plan, not Griffiths's "inside-out hull," which had failed.

After battling more winter squalls, *Rainbow* limped into Hong Kong. Despite the troubles of the voyage, Warren Delano was still impressed with the ship's performance, writing home to his brother Franklin: "The *Rainbow* arrives at Hong Kong yesterday, 103 days from New York, of which one day was lost at Bally [*sic*] when she stopped for water. This passage is a good one—ranking with ours in the *Paul Jones*."[12] The following September, *Rainbow* returned to New York after 105 days at sea. It seems that Griffiths's extreme design needed a lot more tweaking, but Aspinwall didn't give up on the eccentric naval architect.

If Warren Delano inspected *Rainbow* as she lay anchored in Hong Kong harbor, he left no record of it—but given his inquisitive nature, he probably did. (Delano would eventually commission Griffiths to design a more refined sister ship.) He did, however, write home that market conditions demanded more of the fast ships, and urged his brother to get in on the clipper ship business so that he could ship more of Russell & Company's goods home in a hurry. "We are beginning to feel the want of the vessel of the class named in my letters," he wrote Franklin, "and I heard you will have acted promptly and that when this reaches you, a suitable ship may be on her way out to us."

But Franklin's employer, Grinnell, Minturn & Company, was not yet interested in investing in the new type of vessel, preferring to stick with its old-fashioned packet model and focus on the transatlantic trade rather than the tea business.

In Boston, Delano's old friend Robert Bennet Forbes had another idea for revolutionizing the China trade: *Midas,* a steam-powered ship built along clipper lines, which he hoped to use as a cargo ferry between Canton and Hong Kong. She made most of the trip between New York and China using her auxiliary sails, and proved leaky and unreliable. The vessel arrived with her machinery ruined by, as her mastermind remembered, "neglect and bad engineering, her reputation damned."[13]

Forbes later joked that *Midas* was "expected, like her prototype of old, to turn everything into gold."[14] Instead, she turned out to be a disastrous investment—although as a consolation, Forbes congratulated himself on being the first American to travel by steam east of the Cape of Good Hope. He tried the concept again the following year with the steam barque *Edith*, which he named after his daughter and hoped would be the first fast American steamer in the opium trade between Bombay and Canton. This ship, too, proved to be a mechanical nightmare. Delano, who greeted *Edith* when she arrived in Hong Kong, had nothing but harsh words for his brother Franklin back in New York:

> I must tell you confidentially that the clipper steam barque *Edith* is a failure. She has made two attempts to get up the East Coast against the monsoon and failed, while our *Eagle* performs triumphantly. She, the *Edith*, has not power enough to make head against wind and sea—and the immense weight of machinery and coals in the extremes of the vessel make her pitch and labor so heavily in a seaway that she goes ahead but slowly and then falls off to the leeward in a fearful way. If the new steam packet is built in the same way as the *Edith*—she must be a failure. All this weight could be amidships or the vessel cannot carry it. Upon the whole, the less we have to do with these experiments, the better.[15]

Warren, in Hong Kong, found the separation from his wife and infant daughters hard to bear—especially after the younger, Susie, died in the spring of 1846. With the loss of her child, Catherine's worst fears about the trip to China had been confirmed. She'd had only limited contact with Chinese culture during her three years there. Sequestered in a house in Macao while her husband conducted business in Hong Kong, surrounded by a coterie of other Western families, she lived as an alien *fanqui*, and it disturbed her. Far from home and her extended family, Catherine Delano sank into a deep depression, and Warren worried that she might actually commit suicide.

By the end of that year, the Delano family—now including a new daughter, Louise, as well as a Chinese manservant and a wet nurse—finally returned to America, this time, it seemed, for good.[16] Now possessing multiple competences, Warren finally had the means to purchase his dream house: one of the large mansions on Colonnade

Row, next door to his brother Franklin and his wife, Laura. Franklin enjoyed reminding his crotchety neighbor and new grandfather-in-law John Jacob Astor that in England, having a doorplate reading "Mr. Astor" designated a physician's office.[17] Old Astor probably couldn't have cared less—when he died in 1848, he was worth $20 million, making him by far the richest man in America.

But a grand house in the city wasn't enough. Warren Delano dreamed of creating a family retreat in the countryside. Even before leaving Canton, he had written Franklin about his intentions to build a home free from the worries and sadness of China, a haven on "2,000 or 3,000 acres of land . . . bought at a very low price." There would be "good fishing and good shooting—and sufficiently easy . . . access to New York or Boston." It would be impossible to put the hard years in Canton entirely out of mind; Louise would remain a sickly child, perhaps from exposure to tropical disease at an early age. But Warren's struggle to shield his growing family from the nature of his business—and from any unpleasantness associated with it—would continue for the rest of his life.

Warren kept his eyes open on properties for sale in the scenic Hudson Valley. Yet he was unable to find a place that suited his discerning taste. During the hot and steamy summer months, Catherine and the girls settled into a rented mansion in a section of Newburgh, New York, picturesquely called "the Danskammer" (from an old Dutch story about the "Devil's Dance Chamber"). Warren divided his time between his office in New York and Newburgh, commuting by train on the newly constructed Hudson River Railroad that skirted the east bank of America's Rhine.

During his trips to and from Newburgh, Delano's train roared past the writer Washington Irving's once idyllic Sunnyside estate in Tarrytown. The chuffing, spark-spewing steam locomotives infuriated the aging creator of Rip Van Winkle. Delano, too, wished to escape the noise and dirt of the iron horses and turned his search toward suitable properties farther north, with unspoiled views of the valley. But although Warren continued to dream of designing the perfect house for his growing family, his first big project after his return to America would be to build a ship.

Despite *Rainbow*'s lackluster first voyage, William Henry Aspinwall surveyed the damage and decided to repair the V-shaped clipper and send her on another trip. This time she performed according to plan, taking ninety-two days to reach Canton and eighty-eight to come home.[18] Thrilled with this success, Aspinwall commissioned John Willis Griffiths to design a larger and more refined version of the experimental craft. Her name would be *Sea Witch,* Griffiths's technical masterpiece.

To ensure greater stability than her predecessor, *Sea Witch* had a slightly less concave bow, as well as a diminished deadrise for a more flat-bottomed hull. She was still relatively small compared with transatlantic packet ships and narrow for her size, with a beam of only thirty-four feet. *Sea Witch* was the first ship of her type to do away with the old-fashioned beakhead bow and the latticework of braces underneath the bowsprit. Instead, her bow resembled that of an opium clipper schooner: angular, sharp, and free of ornamentation except for the dragon figurehead.*

Even Griffiths's employers, who had long considered him a mere draftsman, were impressed by the ship's novel design. "We have no hesitation recommending [Griffiths] as a 'Marine and Naval Architect' of the first order," wrote the partners of Smith & Dimon, "[a]

---

* According to drawings on page 282 of Howard L. Chapelle's *The History of American Sailing Ships* (published by W. W. Norton, 1935), *Rainbow* had a traditional packet ship beakhead bow, with the accompanying latticework under the bowsprit. Contemporary paintings of *Sea Witch* eliminate this feature, showing instead a stem shaped in a concave arch above the waterline.

gentleman who has reached an eminence in the line of his profession rarely attained, and whose skill in this branch of Mechanism we believe to be unsurpassed."[19]

Aspinwall selected as master of the *Sea Witch* the notorious "driver" Robert Waterman. In his mid-thirties, Waterman was charismatic, charming, and absolutely ruthless. He was the scion of an old Nantucket whaling family that had decided not to risk bombardment by the British during the War of 1812 and resettled in Hudson, New York—well up the Hudson River but with access to the Atlantic downriver. When Robert was just a toddler, his father was lost at sea, but despite his mother's pleadings, the son followed in his father's footsteps and entered the North Atlantic packet trade as a cabin boy. He quickly impressed the captains of the Black Ball Line with his daring. "[W]holly reckless of limb and life," one observer said of him.[20] The young Waterman greatly impressed Captain Charles H. Marshall of the packet *Britannia*, who was rarely impressed with anybody and who, according to one observer, "possessed an air of sternness about him that was somewhat repulsive to strangers."[21] Like many self-made men, Waterman had nothing but contempt for loafers and complainers. Going to sea was war, and he loved it.

As a captain, Waterman reveled in his reputation as a driver, making great speeds and great profits for his ship's owners. Though relatively short, he was lithe, brash, athletic, and something of a playboy while ashore. At the start of every trip, Waterman strutted aboard dressed in his finest-tailored clothes, which would include a topcoat with pearl buttons, a high beaver hat, tight gray pants, and a neatly tied cravat. He would then go below to his stateroom and emerge a few minutes later dressed in rough seafarers' garb. Striding over to the rail, he would hold a bundle over the side and shout with a maniacal grin: "Well, they will be out of fashion when we return!" He would then drop his fancy clothes into the swirling East River.[22]

New York's social set found Waterman irresistibly handsome and charming; in the words of Captain Arthur Clark, "a young captain of an unusually attractive personality," someone who was "regarded with pride and admiration" by his friends.[23] He was a dandy, a hero, someone who set records and made shipowners like Howland & Aspinwall money. He also had supposedly never lost a spar or thread of important rigging, and according to Captain Clark, "never called on the underwriters for one dollar of loss or damage."[24]

Few of his friends on land knew his dark side. Those who did whispered that he went too far as a driver captain; that he put padlocks on the topsail sheets and rackings on the topsail halyards* to make sure panicking sailors didn't reduce sail without his permission.[25] Waterman dismissed his critics as complainers and "sea lawyers."

As Waterman was making his record-breaking voyages to China—this was the man who had made the journey in Howland & Aspinwall's old cotton packet *Natchez* in an astonishing seventy-eight days—the German composer Richard Wagner premiered an opera based on the myth of the captain who made a deal with Satan. In exchange for impossibly fast trips and huge profits, the blasphemous captain and his ship would be condemned to wander the oceans forever. The spell would be lifted only if the captain could find a loving wife; every seven years, he would be thrown up on shore and given a chance.

Wagner based his darkly scored opera on a satirical novel by the poet Heinrich Heine, but the legend may have originated from a true story. Two hundred years before Wagner wrote *Der fliegende Holländer (The Flying Dutchman)*, Captain Bernard Fokke of the Dutch East India Company amazed his countrymen with his exceptionally fast trips from Amsterdam to Batavia—present-day Jakarta, Indonesia. At a time when a typical trip took six months, Fokke

---

* Ropes used to hoist flags, yards, and sails.

drove his ship to her destination in a mere three. He was such a hard driver that many whispered that the captain must have indeed made a deal with the devil.

If Waterman's journeys were less impossibly fast, he provoked no less awe in his contemporaries. In 1846, when Aspinwall hired him as captain and design consultant for his second experimental clipper, *Sea Witch*, Waterman was arguably more famous than Captain Nat Palmer. His contribution to the ship's design was a gigantic sail plan: five tiers of sails on each of her three masts. Taller than any other American merchant vessel on the high seas, her skysail yard would tower almost 150 feet above the main deck, only 50 feet less than her 192-foot overall length.[26] The daring sail plan, coupled with Griffiths's lithe, V-bottom hull, created a ship that was as skittish as a thoroughbred racehorse. The white oak hull rose rapidly on the stocks at Smith & Dimon, and she was scheduled for launching in December of that year.

Perhaps the curse of the Flying Dutchman had been broken, for come December, Waterman had a new bride at his side: the former Cordelia Sterling of Bridgeport, Connecticut. Like many captains' wives, Cordelia was forced to decide whether to stay at home on her own or accompany her new husband around the world. She decided to make the maiden voyage of *Sea Witch*.

The newlyweds arrived in the big city just as the Christmas social season was getting under way. By the 1840s, American Protestants had warmed to the idea of Christmas as a family holiday. Before that, Christmas was associated with Catholic—even pagan—revelry, in which the lower classes would ape and mock the mannerisms of the gentry. Following the example set by the German-born Albert, Queen Victoria's Prince Consort, a growing number of prosperous Americans—especially in the industrializing, congested cities—placed Christmas trees in their parlors and enthusiastically embraced the nostalgia evoked in New Yorker Clement Clarke Moore's poem "'Twas the Night Before Christmas."

Several years after the Panic of 1837, New York was more prosperous than ever. Shoppers thronged the chilly streets, peering into display cases at A. T. Stewart's white marble department store, which were stacked full of bonnets, hoopskirts, garters, vests, and beaver hats. As dusk fell, gas lamps flickered on in the windows of some homes, powered by the new mains that were starting to crisscross the city. New brownstone houses were replacing ones of brick.

On launch day, December 8, 1846, hundreds gathered at the Smith & Dimon yards to see Cordelia Waterman christen the ship. A reporter from the *New York Herald* was on hand for the ceremony, and his coverage must have caused both Waterman's and Griffiths's hearts to swell with pride. "The *Sea Witch* is, for a vessel of her size, the prettiest vessel we have seen," he wrote. "She is built of the best material, and, although presenting such a light appearance, is most strongly constructed." Observers could only imagine how *Sea Witch*'s white pyramid of canvas, once unfurled, would dwarf her skimpy, sleek black hull.

Just above Cordelia and the launch platform loomed a startling figurehead: a snarling, black Chinese dragon—"the symbol of the Chinese empire."[27] The imagery may have been in response to the rival *Houqua*'s figurehead, a battle between commerce and conquest.

Cordelia Waterman slammed the bottle of champagne against *Sea Witch*'s bow, the hull groaned, and the clipper slid into the East River.

Two weeks later, on December 23, *Sea Witch* sailed from New York. Like most ships of her era, she had no sea trials. Once finished, she was quickly loaded with cargo and dispatched for China. It was to be Cordelia's first and last voyage on one of her husband's vessels. She likely was seasick, a miserable affliction most new passengers and crew members battled the first few days out until they got their sea legs. Whenever she left the privacy of her stateroom, she found herself surrounded by men covered in tattoos, missing fingers and teeth, and speaking in a sailor's dialect no well-brought-up woman from Bridgeport could understand. Perhaps she saw personality traits in her husband that she never imagined while he was on shore.

Waterman piled on the canvas and drove *Sea Witch* southward through the bleak, wintry Atlantic toward Rio de Janeiro, Brazil, where she arrived after a twenty-five-day trip. After loading cargo and additional provisions at Africa's Cape of Good Hope, *Sea Witch* ran her easting down in the "Roaring Forties" (so-named because of the strong westerly winds between 40 degrees and 50 degrees south latitude) before heading northward into the tropical climes and light breezes of the Indian Ocean. Seventy-nine days after leaving South America, Waterman dropped anchor in the British port of Hong Kong.

Unlike her finicky predecessor *Rainbow*, *Sea Witch* behaved magnificently under Waterman's confident care. After picking up the usual cargo of tea, porcelain, and silks for Howland & Aspinwall, the captain tried to break his old seventy-eight-day record back home to New York. He missed by four days, arriving in port on July 25, 1847, but he surpassed other previous marks thought to be impossible to exceed. *Sea Witch* averaged 264 miles a day for ten days straight against the howling monsoon wind and rain; on her best sailing day, she traveled 302 nautical miles.[28] "Remarkably quick sailing!" the *Herald* declared breathlessly when Waterman departed for China again, this time leaving Cordelia behind.[29]

Waterman ultimately broke his old Canton-to-New York record in March 1849, when *Sea Witch* made the trip in an astonishing seventy-four days, with a best ten-day average of 11.10 knots.[30] Pleased with his creation, and no doubt feeling redeemed after *Rainbow*'s mixed performance, Griffiths would one day write proudly of his ship: "It will be entirely proper to add, that the model of the *Sea Witch* had more influence upon the subsequent configuration of fast vessels, than any other ship ever built in the United States."[31]

His boss probably agreed, but William Aspinwall had other irons in the fire. In addition to his clipper ships *Rainbow* and *Sea Witch*, he would order two steamers for his new Pacific Mail Steamship Company—the SS *California* and the SS *Panama*—to make the coastal run between the Isthmus of Panama and ports in the Alta California and Oregon territories. Exciting reports were filtering into East Coast cities about the discovery of gold.

Aspinwall had lobbied hard for a congressional subsidy to carry the mail to the West Coast, and it was this contract that made the steamship run a financially viable proposition. This venture would ultimately pay off in spades.[32]

CHAPTER 8

MEMNON: DELANO'S CALIFORNIA BET

My ship is sound, and wind and tempest proof.
Storm and adverse wind, in league,
Keep me away from the shore;
How long? How should I know it still,
When count I keep not any more?
I cannot tell the scenes I saw,
Nor name the ports I sought to reach;
The only scene I long to see,
I cannot find—my native beach!
And now, my friend, come take me home,
Give me shelter and give me rest.
My ship is freighted with treasures rare,
Choose thou the rarest, take the best—
Thy humble roof, oh, let me share!

—RICHARD WAGNER,
The Flying Dutchman, act 1, scene 3 (1843)[1]

For the rich, speed was becoming an addictive spectacle. When not seated at their desks or at home with their families, a growing number of New York's wealthiest men could be found speeding up and down city avenues in two-wheeled carts known as sulkies, pulled by a pair of fast-strutting horses. In the whitewashed taverns that lined Bloomingdale Road (later an extension of Broadway), the city's bankers, merchants, shipowners, and newspaper barons would challenge one another and place bets over jugs of pale brandy. "It would seem as if all New York had suddenly become owners of fast horses and were all out on Broadway on a grand trotting spree," noted the *New York Herald* of one such racing day.

Those with the time and money to maintain a stable and race in the afternoon would happily pay upward of $30,000 for a pair of winning horses. And few sulky drivers cut a more imposing figure than Cornelius Vanderbilt—the self-made steamship millionaire who drove his cart with a big cigar clenched between his teeth.

Crowds would gather along the course and cheer as he and other moguls sailed past at close to thirty miles per hour, their cravats whipping in the breeze, wire wheels whirling, horse hoofs pounding on the brown dirt. At the end of a race, they may have sung a catchy new minstrel tune by Stephen Foster:

> Camptown ladies sing this song,
> Doo-da, Doo-da
> The Camptown racetrack's five miles long
> Oh, doo-da day
> Goin' to run all night
> Goin' to run all day
> I bet my money on a bob-tailed nag
> Somebody bet on the bay.

Money changed hands, toasts were drunk, and plans were made for rematches. At the end of an afternoon of racing, the horse owners would go back to their staid townhouses and dress for dinner with their families, "thoroughly ventilated and in good condition for a comfortable supper and a sound sleep."[2]

But the China trade men were giving New Yorkers something

else to bet on: a race of wood and canvas spurred on not by pockets full of tin but pockets full of gold.

Abbot Low, not to be outdone by Aspinwall's 1846 *Sea Witch*, started construction in 1847 of a new masterpiece, an improved sister ship for *Houqua*, named after one of the American godfathers of the opium trade: *Samuel Russell*. Warren Delano was probably the man who suggested the name. In an undated letter, he wrote to Low: "If you built a ship, or buy her on the stocks, you may call her either the *Cushing* or the *Samuel Russell*, the latter jingles best to my ear."[3] Like *Houqua*, *Samuel Russell* was the product of Captain Nat's hand, boasting a similarly flat bottom and sharp ends—only this time she was somewhat larger than Low's graceful first clipper. For the comfort of her captain and passengers, as well as a bit of uncharacteristic whimsy, Palmer added a set of square gallery windows on her stern, a feature borrowed from the old British East India ships, although without their gilded decoration.

No doubt egged on by his old Canton friend, Warren Delano finally commissioned his own clipper ship the following year. Named *Memnon*, she would be the last clipper ship designed by the eccentric John Willis Griffiths. Perhaps Delano wanted to capture a whiff of the *Sea Witch*'s glory by trying an extreme design on the North Atlantic run, putting him in direct competition with Grinnell, Minturn & Company and other transatlantic packet lines. As it turned out, *Memnon* was a herald of things to come. Although built for the China trade, she would be the first ship to set a record in a new speed competition, one far more dangerous than the run to China. At 170 feet long, 36 feet wide, and 1,000 tons, *Memnon* was substantially larger than her predecessors, including Abbot Low's *Samuel Russell*. Griffiths appeared to have ignored the mounting evidence that Palmer's flat-floor concept produced a steady yet fast design—*Memnon* was a slightly larger version of *Sea Witch*, except that her sails were rigged as a barque with a fore-and-aft sail on the aftermost (rearmost) mast and square sails on the others. Delano named *Memnon* after the mythical ancient warrior king of Ethiopia who journeyed from afar to defend the city of Troy, and to whom the god Zeus granted immortality after Achilles stabbed him through the heart. Why Delano named his ship after a mythic African hero is a mystery, but according to one source, a figurehead depicting the monarch adorned the ship's sharp bow.[4]

On July 30, 1848, *Memnon* set sail from New York bound for Liverpool. The captain, Oliver Eldridge, a native of Cape Cod who "came from a hardy race of mariners," immediately expressed his distaste for the new ship: she was no *Sea Witch*.[5] On her first week out, the ship averaged a pitiful seventy-seven miles a day eastbound. Finally, after two weeks, she picked up speed. Captain Eldridge wrote: "I am now convinced this ship can sail." Still, compared with the new Cunard paddlewheel steamers that could cross the Atlantic in fourteen days, she made a mediocre first run—taking twenty-one days for the eastern crossing, and twenty-three days and seventeen hours to come home, "with much bad weather and much reefing."[6]

There is no record of what Griffiths thought about *Memnon*'s performance on the transatlantic run. In any case, the naval architect was already distracted by a new dream. Fueled perhaps by his newfound celebrity, he had decided he could make a living as a naval writer and theorist, giving lectures and publishing his shipbuilding magnum opus, *The Ship-Builder's Manual and Nautical Referee*. He also launched a serial publication entitled the *Monthly Nautical Magazine and Quarterly Review*. Its official mission was "cultivating marine architecture in the United States." Its unofficial one was to burnish Griffiths's reputation as the nation's foremost marine designer; the man who "invented" the clipper ship type and sold it to a disbelieving public.[7]

Ultimately, *Memnon* proved that the clipper type was not suited to the conditions of the North Atlantic passage. (Only one other, the 1851 *Staffordshire*, would be built specifically for the transatlantic run.) The vessels' slim lines and light construction made them ideal for ghosting along in light winds, and they sailed very well when loaded with crates of tea. But they simply did not have the cargo capacity to do battle economically with the more heavily built packet ships, nor could they guarantee the winds would keep them to a fixed schedule. With the recent advent of steamships, well-heeled passengers were now demanding to arrive as well as depart on time.

What Delano thought about *Memnon*'s initial performance is unknown, but he took a gamble by putting her on a new run. She might not have been able to compete with the big packets for freight or with the Cunard steamers for passengers, but perhaps she was strong enough to beat the gales of Cape Horn, bound for the Golden Gate.

Shortly before Delano's *Memnon* set sail for California in 1849, Captain Charles Low brought *Houqua* into New York after a ninety-seven-day passage from China. It was the twenty-four-year-old's first command. After proving himself as ship's boy and third officer, Low was told by Captain Nat that "I was just as capable of being master as I should be two years hence."[8] The young man was promptly promoted.

As *Houqua* came into view to the spectators on the Battery's shoreline promenade, it was clear to everyone watching that something was amiss with the ship. Her longboats were the wrong size, and the masts looked jury-rigged. Low must have trembled as he watched the bearish figure of Captain Palmer stride along the wharf to inspect the ship. The young captain had a report to make to his mentor about his ship's close brush with catastrophe some months before.

Sometime after passing the Cape of Good Hope, on January 15,

1848, *Houqua* was running along at night, all sails set, the light of a full moon shimmering down on the inky Indian Ocean. At twelve midnight, Captain Low felt a sudden chill in the air and went down below to look at the barometer. It was dropping rapidly. Returning to the quarterdeck, he ordered the watch to strike all the port studden sails,* as well as the jibs and spanker.† The ship continued along at full speed, the wind whistling through the remaining sails. Within a few hours, Low found he had no choice but to order his men aloft to take in all of the sails except for the main topsail and foresail; these he reefed, or drew in partially.

The ship kept moving as the waves grew higher, crashing over the bulwarks‡ and swirling around the deck. The wind blew out the remaining sails, yanked the furled ones from their gaskets, and carried them out into the sea. The barometer had plummeted to 27.50, indicating the onset of full storm conditions. "The sky was covered with dense masses of black, smoky clouds filled with thunder and lightning," Low recalled, "and all the mast-heads and yard-arms had composants, or balls of electricity, resting upon them, as low down as the lower yards." Low ordered the helmsman to turn the ship into the wind, heaving her to and bringing her to a near stop.

There was a brief lull in the ocean's fury, and the crew cut away the damaged rigging. But then something ominous appeared on the horizon: a solid wall of water, perhaps thirty feet high, bearing down on the clipper ship like an avalanche. Those on deck ducked under the bulwarks and held on to anything they could. At twenty-three, Captain Low was younger than most of the crew, yet he couldn't

---

* A sail attached to the side of another square sail, used to increase speed in light winds.

† The gaff-rigged fore-and-aft sail on the aftermost mast of a square-rigged ship.

‡ An extension of the ship's sides above the level of the deck, meant to protect the crew from heavy seas.

show his fear. "It is impossible to describe the roaring, howling, and shrieking of the wind," he said later. "Never did I imagine it. The stoutest and firmest man in the ship could not stand before any one of the ports, the spoondrift [spray] being driven through them with a force of a shot from a cannon."[9]

The rogue wave struck hard, as did successive ones, ramming the helpless vessel until finally *Houqua* lay over onto her side, and seawater began roaring into every door and hatch. Losing his grip, Low plummeted from the quarterdeck and into the ocean. Another wave crashed over the ship, and down he spun into the depths. "I never expected to see the ship again," he recalled. "I said my last prayer . . . Everything that I had done from my youth up came to my mind, and I wondered how long my relatives would look for me and never hear from me." Charles may have thought of his dead brother, who had jumped to his death from the very same ship. He was about to become the third member of his family to die at sea.

Then he shot to the surface. He pulled himself onto the weather rail, huddled alongside several other men. Somehow they got ahold of some axes and began cutting away the rigging that held two of the three half-submerged masts to the ship. Each one pulled away with a terrific groan, and slowly the ship righted herself. Yet more broke loose as the ship slowly pulled herself onto an even keel: away went the carpenter's shop and the galley (and its still-burning coal stove), all of the ship's boats, and the pen that was the home to all of the hens, cows, and pigs. The roar of the waves drowned out the cries of the animals as they plunged over the side.

With utmost care, Captain Low ventured below. Inside the ship, chaos reigned. Men were trapped as water continued to pour through the hatches. In an effort to escape, the Filipino cabin boy tried to smash his way through a skylight. He sliced his arms open, spilling blood everywhere. Low and others bandaged him up, along with a few other injured men. It was still blowing a full gale.

The holds were half full of seawater. The only way now to save the ship was to man the pumps. Working a manual pump—which operated like a railroad handcar—was backbreaking work even in fair weather. All wooden ships leaked; when driven hard, they might require an hour's pumping in each watch, work that "completely disheartened some of our best men," one observer wrote.[10] But on *Houqua* that night, Low and his men were in a race against time. The captain ordered both of the heavy iron pumps rigged, and set all hands to work. Did they sing to keep rhythm or stave off thoughts of death? When a shift of men tired, they lay down on the deck for rest, and another group took their place.

One exhausted man asked why the second mate wasn't helping out. Low waded into the main cabin and threw open a stateroom door. There, he saw the second mate on his knees, praying fervently, a "badly scared man." Low looked at him and said, "Hustle out of that quick and go to the pumps! God helps those who help themselves!"[11]

After hours of work, the water in the holds was holding steady. *Houqua* was no longer sinking. By the morning of January 17, some thirty-six hours after the storm had hit, the clouds faded away, and the sun shone down on the Indian Ocean. Two of *Houqua*'s three masts were gone, and her deck was covered in a tangled mass of ropes and wood, but her graceful hull was intact. Low breathed a sigh of relief.

Now was the time to use whatever spare spars were left to create a temporary rig on the remaining mast. "We had fine weather," the captain recalled, "and I sent the fore-yard and fore-topsail yard on deck to be refitted, which was a tedious job." Because the galley was gone, the men cut a coal cask in half, placed one end on deck, surrounded it with sand, and used it for boiling salt beef and pork. With a few tattered sails hanging from the foremast stump, *Houqua* sprung back to life, even if she looked like a badly wounded bird. Low made no mention of any lives lost in his later account of the near-disaster.

Houqua dropped anchor in Hong Kong on March 14, 131 days out of New York, 60 of them under the "jury rig." The cargo of cotton goods was almost completely ruined from water damage. Low abandoned the cargo to the insurance underwriters, who organized an auction of the cotton bales on the Hong Kong docks. Still eager to make a dollar, Low insisted on acting as the insurance company's agent for the sale. It was a smart move, at least as he remembered it: "Chinamen gathered in crowds and bid against one another, and the whole cargo was sold for cash for more than it would have brought in Shanghai if delivered in good order."[12]

Low then fired the second mate "for incompetency and drunkenness."

There was no dry dock in Hong Kong, so before rerigging the ship, Captain Low had to have *Houqua* careened onto her side so that workers could repair the hull. What he saw shocked him: the fallen masts had nearly punctured the ship's planking. If he and his men had not cut away the tangled mass, the ship definitely would have foundered with all hands lost.

After a series of repairs, which included mismatched longboats, *Houqua* sailed to Shanghai, now open to trade, with European and American "concessions" (foreign colonies) outside the city walls. After loading up with tea, *Houqua* returned to Hong Kong to take on additional cargo—which was when another typhoon struck the *Houqua* and all of the other ships riding at anchor at Hong Kong. Several other vessels, including one large English opium clipper, were either driven aground or sank in Hong Kong's harbor. "We rode out the typhoon in safety," Low recalled. "This was my third experience of hurricanes inside of a year, and I wanted no more, though as it would be the typhoon season for two months yet, I knew I might be favored with some more."

Houqua rode at anchor until November 1848, as her captain waited for more fresh tea pickings to arrive. News of the ship's near wreck had already reached home. Shortly before *Houqua* weighed anchor to set sail back to New York, Charlie received a letter from his father, Seth. Years before, Seth and Abbot Low had done everything possible, including offering Charles a desk job, to keep him from going to sea. Now the old man wrote: "The circumstance of your escaping from a watery grave is very striking . . . as I view the Providence of God, the fact that you were inspired by presence of mind, courage, resolution, fortitude, prudence, as well as blessed with health and strength to endure and meet the emergency of the occasion, were equally the gift of God, and should be cherished by you as continual causes of thanksgiving to Him."[13]

Charlie Low put the letter in his desk and kept it for the rest of his life. Presence of mind, courage, resolution, fortitude, prudence— the prodigal son had made good.

After Captain Low finished reporting on the harrowing voyage, Palmer looked at his battered creation. The old salt was notoriously cheap when it came to renewing his ship's rigging and other equipment. But he turned to the nervous Low and said, "Don't worry, you saved my ship and saved the insurance companies a lot of money, and they have got to make everything good, and I shall see to it that they do."

A few weeks later, Captain Palmer and Abbot Low presented Charlie with a wonderful gift: an eight-day ship's chronometer costing $800 from Negus & Company. It came with an engraved silver plate:

> Presented by the Atlantic, Sun, Mercantile and Union Mutual Insurance Companies of New York and the Insurance Company of North America of Philadelphia to Captain Charles Porter Low, late master of Ship *Houqua,* as a testimonial of their approbation of his good conduct in saving said ship and cargo, after having been thrown on her beam ends in the Indian Ocean on the 15th of Janu-

ary 1848 in a violent Typhoon, and nearly filled with water, but by the extraordinary exertions of the Master and crew was righted and subsequently taken by them to her port of destination which was 3,500 miles distant.[14]

There was a second surprise: the voyage home had made an accidental profit. Abbot took his battered brother aside and told him that if the voyage had gone as scheduled, the ship would have *lost* money; but since she had been delayed in Hong Kong, she had brought home the first of the year's tea, beating all other ships and clearing a profit of over $60,000.[15]

Soon Captain Low was pacing *Houqua*'s quarterdeck again, the ship back to her original glory, with the chronometer gleaming in her captain's quarters below.

Back when he had arrived in Hong Kong in March 1848, Charlie Low heard talk of gold having been discovered in the newly conquered territory of California. It was incredible news, and an opportunity not lost on the young captain. Now, in New York nearly a year later, Abbot confirmed that the gold was a reality, not a dream, and gave his brother new orders. Charles would leave *Houqua* for a new command: the brand-new *Samuel Russell*. He was to load up the *Russell* with manufactured goods and sail her around Cape Horn to California—right on the heels of Delano's *Memnon*.

President James K. Polk had officially announced the discovery of an "abundance of gold" in the California territory in his State of the Union address to Congress the previous December. "It was known that mines of the precious metals existed to a considerable extent in California at the time of its acquisition," Polk told the assembled legislators. "Recent discoveries render it probable that these mines are more extensive and valuable than was anticipated." After comparing the conquest of California with the purchase of Louisiana forty years earlier, the president predicted that "a great emporium will doubt-less speedily arise on the Californian coast which may be destined to rival in importance New Orleans itself."[16]

In the months following President Polk's address, 120,000 Americans dropped everything and headed for California. The vast majority were men. It was the largest migration yet in US history—much of it would be by sea.

In New York's saloons and boardinghouses, weary carpenters, shipwrights, and other tradesmen talked incessantly of the stories they heard about their comrades striking it rich three thousand miles away. A typical farmhand in New York State could expect to earn $11.50 a month, and even though tens of thousands of Americans were setting up new farmsteads in Illinois, Iowa, and Indiana, wages in the fertile prairie states were scarcely higher than those on the East Coast. In contrast, the wage of a typical farmhand in California was $60 per month.[17] Even if you didn't have the luck to strike gold, you could at least earn a decent living out West.

Some tried to get to the promised land by crossing the continent with horse-drawn wagons, traveling over the well-trod Oregon Trail, a treacherous trip over mountains and through desert that could take six months. So did the typical voyage by ship. That spring, it seemed that half the population of the Eastern Seaboard was heading to California on anything that floated. Old whaling ships, their holds still reeking of oil, were being hastily outfitted with makeshift bunks for would-be prospectors. So were countless coastal brigs, cotton packets, and fishing schooners. In 1849 about 750 vessels departed the East Coast for California, up from only 2 or 3 just a few years earlier. Many would never make it, lost in storms, often with all hands. And many of the battered ships that did make it to San Francisco Harbor never left, abandoned by their crews and left to sink into the mud of the bay.

Warren Delano's clipper ship *Memnon* was different from these old tubs: designed by the mastermind of *Sea Witch* and *Rainbow*, she was a lithe and elegant craft, painted to gleaming perfection, a black swan amidst the motley, broken-down fleet being readied in New York for the trip around the Horn. Delano had built her to compete on the transatlantic run to England but after one voyage decided to redeploy her on the new route.

What attracted the attention of Delano and other New York merchants were not the reports of California gold but the reports of California prices: a pair of boots selling for $50 (about $1,400 today); barrels of pork, flour, and beef for up to $60 ($1,600); whiskey for about the same; a drop of opium-based laudanum, $1 ($28).[18]

The best way to make money amidst the pandemonium, those in the China trade realized quickly, was not to dig for gold but to outfit and supply the hundreds of thousands of people who'd dropped everything and headed for the hills. Supposedly, a miner could earn up to $1,000 a day—money he would likely spend as well as save. Indeed, many would end up saving nothing at all.[19]

And despite the treacherous travel conditions, there were more new consumers than ever: San Francisco's population had jumped from less than a thousand to more than twenty thousand. The city was awash with money and lawlessness—gambling, prostitution, and gun violence were rampant. Joining the parade of Argonauts were thousands of Chinese, who found their way to America in hopes of work and to escape the once-proud Celestial Kingdom that Western opium had helped devastate.

As a result of California's growth, freight rates soared to heights that shattered even the records set for the freshest China tea. And in California, US merchants faced no foreign import duty.* It was all good, especially for the merchants who could make the trip the fastest. As the journalist Horace Greeley observed, "Experience has

---

* The following year, to the fury of southern politicians who dreamed of a plantation system that expanded westward into the territorial spoils won in the Mexican War, California was admitted to the union as a free state.

amply proved that all such products take the quickest rather than the cheapest route." He went on to theorize that if a transcontinental railroad connected New York and San Francisco, "twenty million dollars of costly or perishable merchandise would annually seek California overland . . . and that this amount would steadily and rapidly increase."[20] But such an overland route remained decades ahead; for now, goods would take to the seas.

Steam may have conquered the Atlantic, but the 3,100-mile voyage from New York to Liverpool pushed the absolute limits of Cunard's coal-driven ships. San Francisco via Cape Horn was still out of reach because the ships of the day could not carry enough fuel to make the voyage without frequent stops. And so, in a betting country gone mad about money and speed, the California clippers became an obsession. Americans of the time would bet on anything: cards, horses, trains, stocks, bonds. And Warren Delano was ready to gamble his earnings once again.

As he cast off from the East River pier in April 1849, *Memnon*'s master Joseph R. Gordon knew his would be a tough passage. Old Cape Horn had inspired fear among generations of mariners. The southernmost point of Chile, it marks the border of the Atlantic and Pacific Oceans. Navigators had feared this passage since the time of the Portuguese explorer Ferdinand Magellan in the sixteenth century because of its huge waves, icebergs, poor visibility, and strong currents. Ships attempting to make a westbound passage around Cape Horn frequently battled contrary winds that would leave them stranded and battered for days or weeks on end. Many a well-built ship had met her end in the waters of "Dead Man's Road." Yet Gordon also had a secret weapon on this historic trip: a new navigational manual, Lieutenant Matthew Fontaine Maury's *Winds and Currents Chart*, published around the same time that reports of gold started to trickle back to the East Coast.[21]

The timing was perfect. Forty-three years old in 1849, Matthew Fontaine Maury had been collecting data on the ocean's winds and currents for the past decade. This strenuous labor was born out of frustration. Ten years earlier, the promising young naval officer from Virginia had badly injured his leg in a carriage accident, ending his career at sea. To support himself and his family, he lobbied for a job as superintendent of the US Naval Observatory in Washington, DC. There he found stacks of old ship's logs from American naval vessels, piled helter-skelter in the archives. Among them were the records from the ill-fated US Exploratory Expedition, known by insiders as the "Ex Ex." During Ex Ex's circumnavigation of the globe, from 1838 to 1842, the small fleet had sailed around Cape Horn to explore the mouth of the Columbia River, as well as the sparsely populated bay that would one day be home to San Francisco. The ships then sailed south to Antarctica and island-hopped across the Pacific to Manila and Singapore.

Yet the expedition was plagued by mutiny against the expedition's volatile leader, Lieutenant Charles Wilkes, who used brutal methods such as "flogging around the fleet" to keep his men under control. It seemed, too, that wherever they landed, the Americans fought with the natives. By the time Wilkes arrived back in America, two of his six ships had been lost. Wilkes survived a court-martial, but his reputation was ruined.

Yet Ex Ex would leave behind 87,000 miles' worth of logs, as well as 180 charts of distant coastlines and islands.[22] No one seemed willing to comb through them except Maury, who had all the time in the world at his new desk job. And Maury was not content simply to organize the logs. Rather, he and a small group of assistants scanned thousands of dusty pages looking for patterns of the ocean's winds and currents. He published his findings in 1847: careful compilations of observations in the form of charts, providing recommendations to captains on the routes to follow to find ideal winds, avoid headwinds, and locate passages through the doldrums.

Maury himself called the Cape Horn passage from New York to California "the longest in the world . . . both as to time and distance."[23] *Memnon* would be the first clipper ship not only to travel this route, but also the first to use this crucial guide. The ship carried all the cargo that eager consignees could cram aboard: wheels of cheese, plate glass, tables, chairs, bolts of cloth, eggs, crockery, and brandy and other spirits. *Memnon*'s crew of about fifty men was also eager for its ship to get to California faster than anyone else—most of them planned to jump ship as soon as she tied up in San Francisco and head right for the gold fields.

These greenhorns were likely a mix of races and nationalities—Yankees, African Americans, Portuguese, Germans, and French—all of them in for a rude awakening about what they thought was a free passage. A clipper ship did not sail herself; her men did. What Charles Porter Low and other young apprentices had learned gradually over the course of years, the would-be prospectors would have to learn in a hurry, beginning as the steam tug guided the clipper through the New York Narrows and into the open Atlantic.

On deck, a sailor's only safeguard was the rope lifeline strung along the length of the ship, and "holding fast" to it so as not to be washed overboard if a freak wave struck. If they fell overboard, there was little to no chance of being saved; it was nearly impossible to stop a fast-moving clipper ship with all sails set, and most sailors could not swim. Small wonder that so many sailors had the letters spelling "Hold Fast" tattooed across their knuckles.

There was little room for sentiment following the death of a crewmate. According to one account, when a particular ship's African American cook died of disease, "no one was near him when he died. As soon as it was found out, he was sewn up in his blankets and hove overboard. No one thought anything of it. The men simply took off their hats. The captain didn't even come up on deck."[24] An auction might be held for the dead man's possessions, with the lucky bidders stowing away clothes they bought until their next time at sea.[25]

The devil-may-care swagger that sailors adopted was a survival mechanism, like laughing in the face of death. No one knew who might be next.

For Delano and other Russell men, California gold was a godsend. With little gold specie of her own, the United States relied heavily on the credit-backed bills of exchange provided by European institutions such as Baring Brothers and Rothschild's. After the collapse of the Second Bank of the United States in 1836, banknotes issued by state and local banks, usually backed by federal and state bonds, were dubious currency at best, backed more by a wing and a prayer than by specie.

The men of Russell & Company had an advantage: valuable access to the solid capital of London's Barings Brothers. British opium traders such as William Jardine and James Mattheson were more than happy to put in a good word for their American friends from Canton. The time spent in the Factories—rowing in the Canton Regatta, playing whist at the Union Club, working long hours at the countinghouse table, surviving Commissioner Lin's siege—was intense. Even Anglo-American rivalries could not tear these bonds. No outsider, no matter how talented or rich, could truly understand what bound these men together.

Still, the era's paper money was playing with fire. Many, such as Robert Forbes, had been burned in the past by currency subject to sudden devaluation, and knew others who had been ruined. Of course, a well-connected but suddenly impecunious former China trader like Forbes could simply go back to Canton and bring home another competence (assuming he made it there and back). But for men such as Forbes and Delano, the California trade offered another kind of opportunity: East Coast merchants could sell manufactured goods to western gold diggers for hard currency rather than for dubious paper notes. Soon shipments of gold bars and coins back east would skyrocket: from $4.9 million in 1849, to $27.7 million in 1850, and to $42.6 million in 1851.[26]

During a time in American history marked by extreme financial instability, the sudden infusion of California gold into the US economy promised two things. First, that Americans would be liberated from European banks, finally having their own source of stable, gold-backed currency. The second was that all Americans, regardless of their birth or circumstances, could go to California and earn a "competence" of their own. They did not have to be a Perkins, a Russell, or a Forbes to go to San Francisco and strike it rich. Nor did one need access to a haughty European bank to obtain a letter of credit. All one needed, theoretically, was a bag of gold dust. It was the classic risk-and-reward proposition, and Americans happily followed the prospect of money, even if it meant risking life and limb to make it to California to pan for gold, open a shop, or scrounge around in the dirt for golden flecks.

On July 28, 1849, the inhabitants of the sprawling shantytown of San Francisco saw a spectacular white-winged angel sail through the Golden Gate strait: it was Warren Delano's clipper ship *Memnon*, under Captain Gordon, completing her record-breaking 15,000-mile trip around Cape Horn in 123 sailing days. By dint of her sharp design and Captain Gordon's hard driving, *Memnon* had slashed the typical voyage around the tip of South America by almost 80 days and soundly beaten the six-month average it took a covered wagon train to trundle overland from Independence, Missouri to California. Her captain had followed Maury's advice by sailing eastward, almost entirely across the Atlantic, before turning back toward Brazil's Cape St. Roque—thus avoiding the calms of the Caribbean that he would have encountered had he followed a more southerly route.

When she tied up at her wharf, *Memnon* was undoubtedly the

most beautiful structure in this boisterous, dirty city. Her gleaming woodwork and jet-black hull contrasted sharply with the rest of the city's buildings, a hastily thrown together mass of boardinghouses, saloons, and casinos. Captain Gordon also had to pick his way through a maze of creaking, barnacle-ridden hulks that sat abandoned in the harbor; ghost ships left to rot when their crews had abandoned the sea for the gold fields. *Memnon* would not meet that fate: she was too new and valuable to be left behind.

Yet the voyage could have been much quicker. Soon after sailing south of the equator, *Memnon*'s greenhorn crew had had enough of Captain Gordon. His hard driving was terrifying. *Memnon* reeled off the miles, but only by keeping an excess of sail in gale force winds. To those who had never been to sea before, the prospect of climbing to the top of *Memnon*'s swaying masts to send down the royals* in an Atlantic gale was too much for them to handle. Gordon and his officers stopped the mutiny with fists and belaying pins,† and put into Montevideo, Uruguay, for a few days to rid the ship of the troublemakers and resupply the stores.

It would be another several months before a rickety wooden tower would be erected atop San Francisco's Loma Alta hill. The two semaphore wings atop this tower would signal to the citizenry what type of ship was coming into port: frigate, ship, sloop-of-war, barque, or side-wheel steamer. After seeing the signal, the merchants would send their representatives scrambling to the pier to find out what ship had arrived and what cargo she was carrying.[27] Eventually Loma Alta would have a new name: Telegraph Hill.

Delano's clipper ship *Memnon* was a sight to behold—and impressively swift—but she arrived in San Francisco on the heels of another intriguing new ship: the steamship SS *California*. In building

---

* A sail flown immediately above the topgallant sail on square-rigged ships.

† A wooden, pin-shaped device used to secure lines of running rigging.

her, William Henry Aspinwall, the owner of *Sea Witch*, had proved prescient again. Using a congressional mail subsidy of $200,000 for regular passenger and mail service between New York, Oregon, and the newly conquered California territory, he formed a steamship subsidiary of Howland & Aspinwall called the Panama Mail Steamship Company. The arrival of these two revolutionary vessels in San Francisco set a paradigm for the next decade. Subsidized steamships such as *California* were ideal for transporting passengers and mail to and from California on a regular schedule, while unsubsidized clipper ships like *Memnon* were perfectly suited for carrying bulk cargo at high speed around Cape Horn without having to either refuel or stop in port to unload and reload at the isthmus. Both types of vessels would earn their owners vast amounts of money in the years to come. Yet the steamers had one more advantage: with their ironclad strong rooms, they would carry California's gold bars back to New York and other financial centers: often as much as $1 million per trip. At 5 percent freight commission, this meant big profits.

SS *California* would soon be joined by sister ships SS *Oregon* and SS *Panama*. Operating with Congress's generous support, Aspinwall's Pacific Mail Line became the most reliable means of transport for passengers who could afford $300 for the comforts of cabin class—which included fresh horsehair mattresses and a well-stocked dining saloon—or $50 for the dreariness of salted pork and rude bunks in steerage. Whatever they paid, Aspinwall's steamship passengers still had to cross the Panama Isthmus to get to the next port of departure. The punishing trip through the mosquito-infested jungles by horse or mule proved fatal for many, with yellow fever killing the most. A canal would not be built across the isthmus for another six decades.

Other steamship operators were quick to invest in lower-risk alternatives. Cornelius Vanderbilt, flush with cash from his East Coast steamships, started a line that transported passengers and freight across Central America by floating them down the Chagres River.

And Aspinwall himself began planning the first transcontinental railroad in the Americas: a fifty-five-mile-long line spanning the Panama Isthmus that would allow his steamships to make regularly scheduled arrivals *and* departures. The Panama Railroad would be the crown jewel of his transportation empire.

In the meantime, Warren Delano's clipper business continued to succeed, despite competition from steam. Warren Delano Sr., the old sea captain, who had survived smuggling adventures and capture by the British, could not have been prouder of his son's achievements. "My Dear Son," began a letter sent from his Fairhaven home, "the beautiful *Memnon* has established her reputation."[28]

The Delanos were now global, riding the clipper ships all the way around the world. The exact profit Delano made from *Memnon*'s voyage has been lost to history, but it was certainly great enough to encourage others, including his own old business partner Abbot Low, to redeploy their clippers into the California trade. Within months, the lessons learned with these early China clippers would lead to the construction of a new type of vessel: the majestic "California" clipper. Bigger, faster, and stronger than their predecessors, they could circumnavigate the world in record time, able to earn more than $100,000 in a single successful voyage. For a brief period, the California clipper would be the envy of the seagoing world.

The benefits of Delano's successful investments were now there for all to see in New York. Warren and Catherine shed their Yankee reticence and threw themselves into New York's social whirl, hosting elegant parties at their Lafayette Place townhouse, its columned front room ablaze with flickering gaslight as couples danced to the strains of a small orchestra. To their young children, they were the picture of aristocratic grace and composure when they went out on one chilly evening, with Catherine wearing a silk dress under a flounced coat as she held Warren's arm.[29]

And a year after *Memnon*'s San Francisco voyage, Delano chose the site of his Hudson River country retreat.

*　　*　　*

Abbot Low may have been caught a bit off guard by his friend Delano's *Memnon*. But while he sent his brother Charlie off to California as captain of the *Samuel Russell* in *Memnon*'s wake, Low also started building a new clipper ship that could earn spectacular profits in a route that, until recently, had been legally impossible.

The year 1849 marked not only the start of the high-stakes California race but also the moment when America brought England to her knees in the China trade. Under pressure from British merchants demanding faster freight service, Parliament finally repealed the ancient Navigation Acts, which since the days of Oliver Cromwell, the seventeenth-century Puritan Lord Protector of the Commonwealth of Great Britain, had prevented foreign vessels carrying goods from Asia from trading in British ports. Originally meant to weaken the maritime supremacy of the Dutch, who controlled the spice and pepper markets of Indonesia, the old law had also hampered American traders eager to compete against the British East India Company monopoly. The East India Company's privileged position in the China trade had already collapsed in the 1830s, but the ships belonging to the British merchants who moved in to fill the massive hole were still slow compared with American vessels. Now the barrier to American competition was down.

Abbot Low jumped at the chance to beat every British ship to market and make a killing by selling the freshest cargoes of tea. A. A. Low & Brother's next clipper would not be named after a merchant but rather the trade that she was intended to dominate: *Oriental*. On September 14, 1849, *Oriental* set sail on her maiden voyage to Hong Kong under Captain Nat's command, arriving in a leisurely 109 days. But on her return run, with a full load of tea, Palmer pushed the ship's speed to the limit, arriving in New York only 81 days after departure, coming within just 7 days of beating the Faustian Captain Waterman's record in *Sea Witch*. After repairs and refitting, Palmer turned over command of his ship to his younger brother, Theodore Palmer, and booked passage in one of the ship's staterooms as a passenger. Although tired and happy to retire, the fifty-year-old master mariner could not bear to miss her next, history-making voyage: *Oriental* would be the first American clipper to deliver a cargo of tea from China to England.

The two brothers fought throughout the voyage. Compared with the cool, contained Nat—who believed that a happy, well-fed crew made for a happy, well-run ship—Ted Palmer was an irascible master. He had spent years in the rough North Atlantic packet service, where crews had a reputation for being drunks, loafers, and criminals, though many were probably men who simply had not had a fair shot at making their way in the world. That didn't matter: hard-to-handle or lazy sailors, Ted Palmer thought, should be lashed to the rigging and flogged. No excuses.

Bickering aside, the combination of Nat's design and Ted's driving led to a stunning outcome. *Oriental* sailed from Hong Kong to London in just 97 days, a new record, and months ahead of all British ships that had left at the same time.

On April 20, 1850, Captain Theodore Palmer nosed *Oriental* into London's historic West India Docks. When Delano's *Memnon* had sailed from New York to Liverpool the previous year, the British people had not paid her transatlantic passage much notice. Now, with government protections over the glamorous China trade lifted, *Oriental*'s arrival from Hong Kong represented foreign competition for all to see. For maximum effect, Ted Palmer had bedecked her with fluttering signal flags, and had her brightwork and brass polished to a radiant glow. On her mizzenmast* flew a giant American flag, as well as the red-and-yellow Low house flag embossed with a large *O*.

---

* The third mast from forward in a vessel having three or more masts.

The ship's early arrival meant her cargo of tea was the first of the season. It sold for $48,000, a sum equal to two-thirds of the cost of building the ship.[30] Stevedores unloaded the sweet-smelling cargo, bound for the silver services of London's wealthiest households, while crowds of the curious swarmed around the vessel. Compared with the stout, swell-sided British merchant ships on either side, there was not an ounce of superfluous flesh on the *Oriental*—she was lithe and sleek from stem to stern, and her raked white masts soared high above the quay. Rather than a ponderous figurehead, *Oriental*'s bow was adorned only with her name and a scrolled billethead, picked out in gold leaf.[31] For Captain Nat and other American ship designers, lavish nautical ornaments not only added unnecessary weight to the ship but also were contrary to republican simplicity. And her stern had no square gallery windows—they were superfluous to the ship's form and purpose, whatever palace-like comfort they provided officers and passengers. The purpose of the rounded counter stern was to provide extra lift in turbulent weather and compensate for her fine underwater lines.

Officials from the British Admiralty, the government branch responsible for the Royal Navy, boarded the ship, chatting with both Palmer brothers as they stood proudly on her pine decks, scrubbed to an ivory hue by the crew. The public might have been amazed, but the editors of the *London Times* were indignant: "We must run a race with our gigantic and unshackled rival," they wrote. "We must set our long-practiced skill, our steady industry, and our dogged determination against his youth, industry, and ardor."[32]

Oriental seemed a success. She *was* a success. Now Abbot Low needed to build a clipper strong enough to handle the fierce Cape Horn route from New York to California. It was becoming clear that the California trade was no passing fad, and he needed to make a few additions to his fleet to fully take advantage of this opportunity. Low had sent *Houqua* around Cape Horn once, with mediocre results; built to speed along in the light winds of the Indian Ocean, she was simply too small and finely built to handle the tumult of Dead Man's Road. A new ship was needed.

Unfortunately, Low could not look to Nat Palmer to build it. The New York–based captain, retired from the sea after his last *Oriental* captaincy, did hope to design one more ship. But New York shipyards were currently booked solid with a backlog of vessels being built for the Cape Horn passage. So, in 1850, Abbot took a chance and asked the yard of Samuel Hall in East Boston to design his new clipper. Low knew Hall's yard well: a decade earlier, he had launched a quartet of its loftily sparred, fleet-footed little opium clippers. The designer was a young man named Samuel Hartt Pook. Now he set out to design Low's new vessel: the *Surprise*. She would be the first of a great fleet of Boston-built clippers.

The port of Boston was still smarting from the meteoric rise of New York. It had been decades since the extended Perkins family of Boston Brahmins first made its wealth in the China trade; many of the leading merchants had since ended up in New York, and the city's East River shipyards had thrived. But the midcentury demand for clipper-type vessels gave Boston designers a new opportunity to show New York that they could compete in the lucrative trade.

Pook admired Palmer's flat-floor concept and adapted it to his design for *Surprise,* only this time giving her an even sharper bow than previous clippers. The result was the perfect California clipper: one that surpassed the ships that Griffiths had designed for Aspinwall and Delano in carrying capacity and also equaled—or perhaps even surpassed—them in speed. *Surprise* would be the biggest clipper in the Low fleet: 183 feet long, 38 feet wide, and of 1,262 tons.

At the new ship's launching on October 5, 1850, builder Samuel Hall had a surprise of his own for the thousands of people who had flocked to South Boston to watch. Up till then, sailing vessels were usually launched only partially rigged, without their topmasts and yards. Hall's *Surprise* was launched ready to sail. Watching from a festive tent pitched on the waterfront, feasting on a lavish spread that included raw oysters and German hock wine, Hall's special guests saw a ship that Boston could be proud of. Her skysail yards soared well over 150 feet above the deck. All the running rigging was in place. The ornamental carving on her bow glinted in the sun: an eagle's head, symbolizing America. On her stern were the arms of Low's New York City: a Dutch colonist and a Lenape Indian flanking a windmill, surmounted by yet another eagle.[33] The unusual launch went off without a hitch, and *Surprise* glided into Boston Harbor, where she was towed to an outfitting pier for final preparations.

The builder may have wanted to prove a point, but he had a practical reason as well. Low needed his ship as soon as possible, and rigging the ship before launch saved valuable time. Appreciating the quality of her construction, Abbot Low sent Hall a $2,500 bonus.[34]

Since Captain Nat Palmer had retired from the sea, Abbot Low decided he needed a similarly special man to command *Surprise*: opium-clipper veteran Philip Dumaresq, who had also worked with Pook on the design. *Surprise* left New York in December, flying the red-and-yellow A. A. Low & Brother ensign and carrying nearly $200,000 worth of cargo. Ninety-six days and fifteen hours later, she bounded into San Francisco Bay. Captain Dumaresq had taken Lieutenant Maury's advice and followed the *Winds and Currents* charts, avoiding the doldrums of the Tropic of Cancer by making a sharp "elbow turn" off the coast of Africa, back toward Brazil.[35] The San Francisco record now belonged to the House of Low.

Other New York firms were also cashing in on the California bonanza. Grinnell, Minturn & Company, which had specialized mostly in the transatlantic trade, commissioned its first clipper ship in 1850 when Moses Grinnell hired Charles Raynes of Portsmouth, New Hampshire, to build *Sea Serpent*. Unlike Low's yacht-like China clippers, *Sea Serpent* was a big, heavily constructed ship. At 212 feet long, 39 feet wide, and of 1,300 tons, she was beefier than any of A. A. Low's ships to date, able to take the battering of the westward passage around Cape Horn.[36] "To use a nautical phrase, 'Her model fills the eye like a full moon,' and her strength and workmanship are of the highest order," gushed the *Boston Atlas* on her launch day that November.[37] Under Captain William Howland, who also helped oversee her construction, *Sea Serpent* proved to be a reliable if not particularly fast clipper, taking 125 days to reach San Francisco from New York on her maiden voyage. For the rest of her career, she earned steady revenue for the company and would outlast almost all others of her type, sailing for another three decades before sinking in a North Atlantic storm in 1891.

But Robert Bowne Minturn, Grinnell's partner, did not share Grinnell's enthusiasm for the clipper ship type. He preferred investing his firm's capital in the transatlantic packet service—transporting Irish immigrants to America was a steadier source of income. The China trade was a side business and San Francisco too unsteady. One clipper was enough for him.

Overriding Minturn's objections, Moses Grinnell cast his gaze on a partially completed vessel in the Boston yard of the now-thriving Nova Scotian immigrant Donald McKay. Her name was *Flying Cloud*, her owner the merchant Enoch Train, McKay's principal client. Train operated a fleet of transatlantic packets plying between Boston and Liverpool and, like Grinnell's firm, made most of his money ferrying Irish emigrants to the New World.

Moses Grinnell apparently made Train an offer he could not refuse: $90,000 for the unfinished hull on the building ways. The arrival of *Flying Cloud* in New York in the spring of 1851 under the Grinnell, Minturn banner signaled a challenge to the supremacy of Low, Aspinwall, and Delano in the race to California. The year also marked the ascendancy of a new designer who had been carefully studying the work of Griffiths and Palmer for years and was ready to unleash his own clippers onto the oceans of the world.

CHAPTER 9

ENTER DONALD MCKAY

Yes, sir, and if there were any letter coming before A, or any figure standing higher than 1, the vessels of Donald McKay would be indicated by that letter and that figure.

—EDWARD EVERETT,
former secretary of state, US senator,
and fifteenth governor of Massachusetts,
"Launch of the *Defender*" (1855)[1]

Donald McKay's shipyard in the spring of 1851 was a popular sight-seeing destination for Bostonians. On a typical day, East Boston boys would play hide-and-go-seek amidst the piles of seasoning lumber. The shipbuilder saw no need to keep them out, as long as they weren't stealing. He knew or employed many of their fathers, anyway. The neighborhood of East Boston, located across the harbor from Beacon Hill, had only five thousand residents.[2] It was a workingman's town full of carpenters, rope makers, blacksmiths, coopers, and wagon drivers. Among them was a cooper named Patrick Kennedy—the progenitor of the Massachusetts political dynasty—who arrived from Ireland as an immigrant on the McKay-designed packet ship *Washington Irving*.[3]

Only a decade earlier, East Boston was known as Noddle's Is-land, little more than a tree-covered hill and smelly mudflats. Now it was one of the great shipbuilding centers of the world, having built nearly thirty thousand tons of shipping during the past decade.[4] That tonnage came from wood, a resource that mid-nineteenth-century American shipbuilders saw as virtually inexhaustible. The ships they built were nothing less than cathedrals of wood, both in their size and their structural complexity. Each ship required thousands of pieces of timber, each chosen according to its place and function in the vessel. According to historian William Crothers, "The most desirable product was a tree whose growth corresponded with the required configurations of the proposed finished piece. Laying out the piece so that its shape followed the natural sweep of the grain gave the component its greatest possible strength, which, in turn, guaranteed the greatest success of safety that could be built into a vessel. Such consideration was paramount, because at sea, small failures could become overwhelming disasters."[5]

Master woodworker Donald McKay was a tall man with calloused hands, rough fingernails, and wild, curly hair. Forty-one years old in 1851, he had a hands-on approach to operating his yard, which was very much a McKay family affair. His father, along with several of his brothers, worked for him at one time or another, including younger brothers Hugh and Lauchlan. His wife, Mary, managed the books.

As shipyard owner, Donald McKay was the charismatic leader of his workmen. His sympathies always lay with the mechanic rather than the business side of ship construction. According to one descendant, McKay was quick to lead by example, picking up a mallet and thudding treenails into planks to show his workers just how things should be done. Through force of personality, he transformed himself from a humble craftsman into the toast of his adopted hometown of Boston.

McKay had had to fight his way into the American shipbuilding world, and his manic drive reflected his outsider status. His was an immigrant success story, part of an exodus of Canadians who left the Maritime Provinces looking for work in the young, increasingly prosperous United States.

Born in Jordan Falls on the south shore of Nova Scotia in 1810, Donald was the eldest of eleven children. His father owned a sawmill and also built small wooden ships on the side. His paternal grandfather, also named Donald McKay, had been a Scottish sergeant in the British army regiment that had occupied New York during the Revolution. After the war, Sergeant McKay sailed for Nova Scotia, to claim the parcel of land promised to him by the Crown for his service. He ended up owning a swampy, hardscrabble farm by the sea, where the family eked out a living.

After learning rudimentary boatbuilding skills, his teenaged grandson and namesake left Nova Scotia for New York in 1825— the year before the opening of the Erie Canal—where he apprenticed himself to the shipbuilder Isaac Webb. There he worked alongside two other apprentices who would become famous clipper ship builders: Webb's own son William, and John Willis Griffiths. The three remained close for the rest of their lives, through changing times and fortunes.

Like Griffiths, Donald cut his apprenticeship short, though not because of injury. He was fed up with being an indentured servant. (It was he who described the apprenticeship system as slavocratic). Besides, he already had a job offer from Webb's rival firm, New York's Brown & Bell.

McKay also had another source of support: a young lady named Albenia Boole, the daughter of a successful New York shipbuilder, who, like himself was an immigrant from Nova Scotia. Unlike the impoverished McKays, the Booles had means, and Albenia's father had made sure that she was well educated, especially in mathematics. Albenia, in turn, must have sensed her beloved's insecurities about his lack of formal education, and spent countless hours tutoring him in the more theoretical aspects of ship design, such as physics and geometry.

In 1841 McKay finally got the chance he had longed for: run his own shipyard. He had married Albenia, and together they moved to Newburyport, Massachusetts, a coastal city long known for shipbuilding. There McKay built small ships and dreamed of doing something greater. Newburyport was in decline, as was nearby Salem, once the hub of the Yankee China trade. The trend affected shipyards in other New England towns that had once built packet ships but now were relegated to constructing coastal schooners and brigs.[6] Capital and access to it were moving away.

But Newburyport proved to be the stepping-stone McKay needed. When shipowner Enoch Train ordered a packet ship and McKay delivered the *Joshua Bates*, Train was so impressed with what he saw that he "grasped Donald McKay by the hand and said to him, *'Come to Boston; I want you!'* "[7]

Train was the patron McKay needed. The Boston merchant was an old hand in the transatlantic packet ship business. Owner of the White Diamond Line, which ran between Boston and Liverpool, he had spent much of his career trying to divert New York's immigrant traffic to his own city. Train had lots of money to invest. More important, Train, like McKay, had ambition. He wanted to show the world, in the words of the *Boston Atlas*, "that a Boston line of packets equal, if not superior, to any belonging to New York, could be built here." Such a task, of course, required "much discretion in selecting a suitable mechanic to carry out his views."[8]

Donald McKay, although no mere mechanic, was Train's man— and he delivered. His new shipyard on Border Street in East Boston was renowned for building tough, durable vessels for the North Atlantic trade. Between 1845 and 1850, McKay built Train five North Atlantic packets: *Washington Irving*, *Anglo-Saxon*, *Anglo-American*, *Daniel Webster*, and *Ocean Monarch*. They were built for strength and cargo capacity, and to be operated by hard-driving, often tyrannical captains who pushed them and their "packet rat" crews to the limit.

Yet McKay's designs also provided plush accommodations, considerably more luxurious than those of the rather grim Cunard steamships, Train's rivals in the Liverpool-to-Boston route. The rich woods, tufted sofas, cut-glass oil lamps, and marble tables of the Train Line packets were meant to make passengers feel as if they were aboard a fine hotel on shore, at least during calm conditions. (One Cunard partner snapped to a whining passenger, "Going to sea is a hardship. The company did not undertake to make anything else out of it.")[9] McKay and other American shipbuilders were unashamed to indulge their countrymen's taste for grandeur while at sea, even if it provided a mere momentary diversion from their discomfort. First-class passage on a crack packet ship was not cheap: $140 for a trip that could last anywhere from sixteen days to two months, depending on the season and the prevailing winds. Steerage was a different matter: an immigrant could purchase a berth in the airless, noxious hold of an Enoch Train packet for a mere $15.[10] However, Boston still remained a secondary destination, and there were signs that Cunard might change its mind about the location of its western terminus.

Word of McKay's shipbuilding prowess by this time was reaching New York. Before becoming third mate aboard *Houqua* in 1844, Charles Low had a stint as a sailor aboard the small coffee carrier *Courier*, which McKay had rigged with skysails and royal studding sails, unusual for a ship so small. On board, Charles Low noticed what a fine vessel she was: "The *Courier* was a small ship of about three hundred and fifty tons, very fast, and a beautiful seaboat." The voyage from New York to Rio and back, he recalled, was "one of the most pleasant I have ever made."[11]

McKay was raising the building of fast, clipper-type vessels from a commercial science to an American high art. The wellspring of rival Captain Nat's design inspiration came from his long career as a captain in the China trade; because tea was a light cargo, Palmer's clippers were relatively small and lightly built. Rival Griffiths was a theoretician who valued speed above all else, often at the expense of profitability. In contrast, although a supremely talented designer, McKay was more of a careful synthesizer than an innovator, his craftsmanship forged in the crucible of years of study and observation. Unlike up-and-coming New York builders, who were beginning to experiment with steam power and iron construction, he continued to place his faith in the power of wood and canvas. His packet ships were fast not just because they were sharp-hulled or heavily sparred, but also because they were built with the finest attention to detail in every possible way.

His shipyard was prospering, but tragedy struck the McKay family in December 1848, when Albenia died in childbirth. Stricken with grief, McKay buried his wife and stillborn daughter in Oak Hill Cemetery in Newburyport, where they had lived during the early part of their married life. By the time of Albenia's death, the couple had six rambunctious children, and in the fall of the following year, Donald married Mary Cressy Litchfield, the eighteen-year-old daughter of one of his shipyard's carpenters, who, like many another nineteenth-century second wife, would throw herself into caring for the family.[12]

Mary proved to be just as able as Albenia in helping her husband's career. Not only did she run the household, but also she served as his business manager. According to one descendant, she was a strong personality, "the type of person who stood up for what she believed in." In later life, she constantly lobbied local officials to ban the sale of alcohol at a local inn because there were so many young children in proximity.[13] Having been surrounded by rowdy shipyard workers her whole life, she knew the evils of demon rum all too well. Mary was also credited with giving her husband's clipper ships their melodious names.

McKay had no desire to conquer Beacon Hill society, and so East Boston made sense as a place to settle down with his growing family. As one of Boston's leading shipbuilders, he now made a good income, living in his Greek Revival mansion at the crest of the White Street hill. Out of pride for his adopted country, he added a veranda with thirteen columns, signifying each of the original colonies. As his grandson remembered, as much as the craftsman enjoying talking shop, "the charming qualities of his talented wife and his own interesting and attractive personality" made him a popular guest at parties.[14] On cold Boston winter nights, the windows of Eagle Hill would be aglow with the light of dozens of whale oil lamps, friends and family sending the sounds of stamping feet, laughter, and Scottish reels into the evening air. McKay loved playing the violin at these gatherings.[15] The famed Massachusetts politician Edward Everett declared of his friend Donald McKay's large family, "I wish to know, my friends, if you do not call that being a good citizen?"[16]

Built with his own hands and to his own design, McKay's house was only a short walk away from his shipyard on Border Street. There, on a typical day, Donald McKay worked alongside his men in the shipyard: hammering trunnels into frames, planing hull planks, and joining keel scarphs with iron pins.[17] Night watchmen swore that McKay would sometimes get up in the middle of the night, walk down to the yard, and caress the hulls of his vessels as they sat on the stocks.[18]

"My speech is rude and uncultivated, but my feelings, I trust, are warm and true," Donald McKay once said.[19] Yet while seemingly unambitious for social status, he remained hungry for professional recognition. His gift for self-promotion set him apart from equally skilled and capable designers. As his reputation grew, McKay cultivated a circle of journalists and politicians, letting them roam around the shipyard, especially at launchings. Senator Daniel Webster of Massachusetts was an admirer, as was Henry Wadsworth Longfellow, bard of the Brahmin establishment and author of "Paul Revere's Ride" and "The Song of Hiawatha." Longfellow was so impressed with what he saw at McKay's shipyard that when he returned home to Cambridge, he composed "The Building of a Ship," published in

1849. In it, he praised the shipbuilder Donald McKay as the "worthy Master." To Longfellow, a great sailing ship was analogous to the union, and the shipbuilder analogous to the Lord Almighty:

Thou, too, sail on, O Ship of State!
Sail on, O Union, strong and great!
Humanity with all its fears,
With all the hopes of future years,
Is hanging breathless on thy fate!
We know what Master laid thy keel,
What Workmen wrought thy ribs of steel,
Who made each mast, and sail, and rope,
What anvils rang, what hammers beat,
In what a forge and what a heat
Were shaped the anchors of thy hope![20]

Arguably no other American shipbuilder had such a powerful cultural advocate, something that mattered in the city that prided itself as being the "Athens of America."

McKay was also determined to sell a clipper ship to a big New York firm and prove his worth to the growing metropolis he had left twenty years earlier. His business arrangement with Train allowed him to build ships for other operators if he had the time. Above all, McKay was dying for the chance to build not just fast ships but also big ones—bigger and faster than any of the New York clippers that had been built for the tea trade but were now being pressed into service for the long haul to California.

Attract attention he did with his first ship of the clipper type: *Stag Hound*, in 1850. Her owners were George R. Sampson and Lewis W. Tappan, a formidable Boston team whose bread and butter was importing hemp from Manila. With their substantial backing, McKay could finally think big with the clipper type. He had built sharp ships before, small compared with the New York clippers, less than five hundred tons each. *Stag Hound*, on the other hand, was a monster, the biggest merchant ship in the world, and purpose-built for the San Francisco trade. McKay's genius was to take Nat Palmer's flat-floored China clipper model and enlarge it so that it could comfortably haul large amounts of heavy bulk cargo rather than light chests of tea. *Stag Hound* measured more than 1,500 tons, a third larger than Low's brand-new *Surprise*, and almost twice as large as the pioneering tea clippers *Houqua* and *Rainbow* of only five years earlier.

By building longer ships than the competition, McKay acted on a scientific principle that shipbuilders had known for more than a century: extending a ship's waterline length increases its maximum top speed. By 1850, soaring California freight rates had made the construction of such large, costly ships financially possible, and McKay decided to build wooden merchant ships longer—and stronger—than had ever been constructed before, even for the tea trade.[21] He also made a few adjustments to basic clipper ship design.

The first tweak was to a section of the bow known as the forefoot, or the place where the stem meets the keel. Rather than the typical curved forefoot found on clippers, McKay gave his ships a more pronounced rounded (or "arched") one, reducing water resistance against the already sleek hull shape. The second tweak was to give the prow* an even greater forward rake than earlier ships, further diminishing the impact of the sea against the hull at high speed. The third was giving the sternpost—upon which the rudder was hung—a slight rake aft, giving the stern more buoyancy as the ship surged ahead while under a full press of sail.[22] The more pronounced rake also reduced the wetted surface area of the vessel, cutting down on drag.

The launching of *Stag Hound* on December 7, 1850, was a major celebration for the people of Boston, just as the launching of *Surprise* had been a few months earlier. Only this time McKay proved

---

* The above-water portion of a ship's bow.

to be an even greater master of publicity than his neighbor Samuel Hall. The handsome, charismatic McKay reveled in the attention as he showed the reporters around the 226-foot-long *Stag Hound* resting on the stocks. The newsmen looked up in awe at the three masts, which when rigged with a full set of sails would carry 9,500 square yards of canvas—enough, it was hoped, to give her massive bulk sufficient headway in light winds and unbelievable power in a breeze.[23]

The morning of the launch, McKay's workers carefully greased the gently tilted ways* with tallow, so that the huge hull would slide smoothly into Boston Harbor. Snow drifted against the clapboard houses of East Boston, clumps of pack ice pushed onto the shoreline, and howling winds thrummed the standing rigging on *Stag Hound*'s partially erected masts. Even so, anywhere from ten thousand to fifteen thousand bundled-up spectators gathered around the ship, waiting eagerly for the signal to launch.

By noon, the tallow along the launching ways was starting to freeze, and McKay ordered a gang of workers to pour boiling whale oil onto the tracks. When the last of the supports were knocked away, *Stag Hound* suddenly groaned and raced stern first toward the water.

The startled foreman in charge of the christening shouted, "*Stag Hound*, you're [*sic*] name's *Stag Hound*!" He leaned over the platform railing and smashed a bottle of Medford rum just beneath the panting-dog figurehead as his hat tumbled onto the frozen mudflats below.[24]

McKay's wooing of the press had worked. Duncan McLean, a reporter from the *Boston Atlas,* was taken not only with the ship ("an original, and to our eye . . . perfection in her proportions") but also with the personality of her charming designer. "Mr. D. McKay, of East Boston," he rhapsodized, "designed, modeled, draughted, and

---

* The ramp upon which a ship is built.

built her; he also draughted her spars, and every other scientific detail about her. She is, therefore, his own production—as much as any ship can be the production of any single mind—and upon him alone, as before remarked, rests the responsibility of her success—always assuming that she will be properly managed at sea."[25]

Not everyone was so confident about *Stag Hound*'s prospects, however. A prominent Boston marine underwriter, looking at the extremely rakish vessel, told her captain, Josiah Richardson, "I should think you would be somewhat nervous in going so long a voyage in so sharp a ship, so heavily sparred."

"No, Mr. Jones," Captain Richardson snapped back. "I would not go in the ship at all if I thought for a moment she would be my coffin."[26]

Some Boston shipowners questioned McKay's "bigger is better" mentality. Speed and power were one thing, but what about operational costs? The bigger the ship and the greater the rig, the more expensive she was to crew up and operate. William Fletcher Weld, perhaps Boston's richest and most powerful shipping man, ordered several clippers of his own for his Black Horse Line, but they were of a more conservative cut than McKay's. Weld dismissed extreme California clippers as a flash in the pan, and a bad investment in the long run.[27]

After a short delivery tow to New York, *Stag Hound* sailed for San Francisco on February 1, 1851, with a hold full of over $70,000 of goods. Six days out, as the oversparred clipper surged through the Atlantic at nearly seventeen knots, Captain Richardson and those of the forty-six crew on watch heard a groaning sound aloft, followed by the sound of splintering timber. The main topmast—the highest third of the main mast—snapped off and careened into the ocean with a thunderous splash. As it fell, it also carried away the tops of the other two masts, fore and mizzen. Richardson barked for the men to climb aloft and hack away the loose rigging. Yet they could not heave to.* A gale

---

* Coming to a stop by turning into the wind and leaving the headsail backed.

struck, and the crippled ship continued to fly before the wind. Like Charles Low on *Houqua* a few years earlier, Richardson supervised rudimentary repairs to the ship using the spare spars. After fighting around Cape Horn, *Stag Hound* limped into Valparaiso, Chile.

Despite the accident, Richardson wrote to Sampson & Tappan from Valparaiso, "Your ship, *Stag Hound*, is at anchor in this harbor after a passage of 66 days, which, I believe, is the shortest but one ever made, and had it not been for the accident of losing some of our spars, I do not doubt it would have been the shortest . . . We lost at least 800 miles by the accident." He then added emphatically, "The ship has yet to be built to beat the *Stag Hound*."[28]

Donald McKay had ushered in the era of the so-called extreme clippers, enormous vessels with sharp lines and massive spreads of canvas. The age of the small, trim tea clipper was over.

By the early 1850s, rapid technological innovation had begun to affect the shipping business. Many of those who had made their fortunes in the China trade were taking themselves away from the world of adventure on the seas and turning toward the new world of railroads, mining, and communication. Even as he was building more clipper ships, Abbot Low was in talks with financier Cyrus Field about laying the first transatlantic cable, which would allow near-instant messaging of news and capital between the Old and New Worlds. Warren Delano's disgruntled brother Franklin was no longer involved with the Grinnell, Minturn & Company's partnership, satisfied to live off his wife's immense Astor fortune after her grandfather John Jacob's death. The Astor patriarch had died in 1848, leaving $20 million to his descendants.

His brother Warren Delano had also begun to retreat from the rigors of the shipping business. Although there is no surviving record of official day-to-day involvement, Delano was still heavily invested in the Low brothers' shipping company. Yet he deployed most of his hard-won fortune in new enterprises, specifically coal mines, copper mines, and railroads. Rather than accumulating new wealth in secretive adventures abroad, Warren now sought to invest his capital at home, using what he earned to maintain his family as comfortably and worry free as possible.

Indeed, the international oceanic commerce that created so much wealth since 1800 was now a *waning* sector of the American economy. A few years after McKay opened his shipyard, President Polk's secretary of the Treasury, R. J. Walker, noticed an ominous trend for deep-sea shipping: out of the country's estimated $3 billion gross domestic product, only $150 million (a mere 5 percent) was being shipped abroad, and that number was declining. In the analysis of maritime historians Alex Roland, W. Bolster, and Alexander Keyssar: "Beginning in 1820, America traded with itself more than it traded with the rest of the world. In 1830 world trade again exceeded domestic, but thereafter, with the two exceptions of the world wars of the twentieth century, the United States traded with itself more than others."[29] The California boom only accelerated this trend.

New York's and Boston's merchant elite sensed this transformation as well. Tea and spices were all well and good, but the growing agricultural and natural resources of the newly won western territories of Texas, California, and Oregon were even more appetizing. The California boom had provided a life-saving boost to Boston builders; with freight rates reaching $40 a ton, local merchants with long experience in the coastal, Caribbean, and South American trades threw their hats into the ring. The competition grew intense. John Murray Forbes's daughter Sarah remembered her father's battles with "box fever," after which he was laid up for days at his Naushon Island retreat with leeches on his head. "My mind was running on small boxes to fill up the chinks under the ship's decks," Forbes wrote later.[30]

The roster of clipper-type ships departing for California in 1850 was impressive. Boston-built ships included the Forbes brothers' little barque-rigged *Race Horse*, Low's *Surprise*, and Sampson & Tappan's *Stag Hound*. New York–built ships included Aspinwall's *Sea Witch*, Low's *Samuel Russell* and *Houqua*, Smith & Dimon's *Mandarin*, Bucklin & Crane's *Celestial*, and Delano's *Memnon*. According to Captain Arthur Clark, Boston's shipping community gathered in clubs, taverns, and hotels and wagered "large sums of money on the result, the four older ships, especially the *Sea Witch*, having established high reputations for speed."[31]

Aspinwall's *Sea Witch* handily beat both the Forbes brothers' *Race Horse* and the Lows' *Samuel Russell* by 12 days. But the Bostonians were redeemed early in 1851 when *Surprise* smashed *Sea Witch*'s record by arriving in San Francisco in a mere 96 days. Along with winning the record passage, *Surprise* sold her 1,800 tons of cargo for $200,000 on the San Francisco market.[32]

One by one, the slower ships came through the Golden Gate, freshly painted and polished by their crews so that they would look sharp for their grand entrances: *Memnon* in 123 days, *Celestial* in 104 days, *Race Horse* in 109 days, and then, finally *Mandarin* at 126 days.[33]

Following *Surprise*'s triumphant, record-breaking 96-day romp around Cape Horn, orders poured into Boston shipyards—both Samuel Hall's and Donald McKay's, only a stone's throw away from each other.[34] Even if Warren Delano might have lost money wagering on *Memnon*'s second voyage around the Horn, he could take comfort in the fact that he had been the first merchant to see the potential of the clipper ship in the California trade.

Only two years earlier, a passage of 180 days from New York to California via Cape Horn was considered respectable. By 1851, 100 days was the new standard for a fast run to San Francisco.

CHAPTER 10

GRINNELL GRABS THE *FLYING CLOUD*

Build me straight, O worthy Master!
Stanch and strong, a goodly vessel,
That shall laugh at all disaster,
And with wave and whirlwind wrestle!
The merchant's word
Delighted the Master heard;
For his heart was in his work, and the heart
Giveth grace unto every Art.

—HENRY WADSWORTH LONGFELLOW,
"The Building of the Ship," 1849[1]

When New York shipping magnate Moses Grinnell put a $90,000 offer on Donald McKay's second clipper ship in 1851, he was not making a blind bet. He was very familiar with McKay's work and trusted that the Boston builder could build him a ship that could beat his rival Abbot Low. Grinnell was forty-eight years old in 1851 and one of New York's most successful shipping merchants. The South Street house of Grinnell, Minturn & Company operated a fleet of fourteen ships and among packet owners long enjoyed a reputation as the outstanding firm.[2] Quipped one observer, "Everything that gets into their nets is fish."[3]

Like so many leaders of New York's shipping community, Grinnell was a New England transplant, a native of New Bedford, Massachusetts, and heir to one of the nation's greatest whaling fortunes. It was a fortune won by hard Yankee toil. Moses's father, Cornelius, had begun life as a hatter's apprentice in New Bedford. He went to sea in 1791 as the first mate aboard the *Rebecca*, the first American whaling vessel to round treacherous Cape Horn and hunt for prey in the Pacific Ocean. In 1815 old Cornelius quit the sea and started a shipping venture in New York with his friend, a fellow former whaling captain with the appropriately salty name of Preserved Fish. (Preserved was a relatively common New England name at the time, signifying being "preserved from sin.") Preserved ran the New York branch of Fish & Grinnell at 87 South Street, while Cornelius minded the New Bedford whaling operation. The firm flourished.[4]

If son Moses learned from his father's business savvy, he also learned from his mother's family ethos. A few years after the end of the Revolutionary War, Cornelius had married Sylvia, the sister of Cornelius Howland, a close friend and privateering partner.[5] Sylvia brought Cornelius wealth—and something more. The Howlands, from Dartmouth, Massachusetts, were staunch members of the Society of Friends. (They were also kin of *Sea Witch* owner William Henry Aspinwall.) The Quakers were a community that had drawn together in adversity, having been persecuted violently by the Puritan establishment in New England and, before that, the authorities in England. Their sin? Refusing to join the established church or recognize the supremacy of clergy—both acts seen as dangerously destabilizing to John Winthrop, founder of Massachusetts Bay Colony, the theocratic "City upon a Hill."

Through Sylvia Howland, the Grinnell family would enter the world of New England Quakers. Although Cornelius never became a full member of the Society of Friends, he nonetheless occupied a "rising seat" in his wife's meeting, and his nine children—Moses included—would become part of New England's tightknit Quaker network. The antiwar Christian sect's wealth was buoyed by a rising tide of whale oil and its ties were cemented by kinship. Cornelius never left the Unitarian Church, but perhaps to appease his wife's family, he dressed like a wealthy "plain" Quaker, wearing finely made but dull-hued broadcloth, knee breeches, and highly polished black shoes—a "quaint but tasteful costume."[6] (In due course, such Quaker frugality would find its most extreme manifestation in Cornelius's grandniece Hetty Green, a millionaire Wall Street speculator and legendary miser called the "Witch of Wall Street.")

Yet despite its stolid, prosperous façade, the New Bedford Quaker community was becoming a victim of its own financial success. As families like the Howlands grew wealthier, they became increasingly tempted by the worldly goods that their affluence afforded them but their religion forbade on principle: dancing lessons, luxurious carriages, square pianos, and brightly colored clothing. For a society that expelled members for owning keyboard instruments, keeping the flock on the straight and narrow path proved to be a real challenge. When the Grinnells and others moved to the booming, cosmopolitan city of New York, Gotham's all-too-worldly pleasures presented further temptations.

Cornelius's son Moses would grow up to be a New York Unitarian, yet he kept a lifelong spirit of Quaker community and responsibility. Wrote one admiring contemporary, "His liberality and enthusiasm in all good works, in all generous enterprises, and in all patriotic movements, inspired the sympathy and cooperation of others. There was irresistible magnetism in his voice and manner."[7]

Born in 1803, Moses Grinnell had not had to start off life the hard way by going to sea to slaughter and render whales in the Pacific Ocean. Following graduation from the Friends Academy in New Bedford, young Moses began his business career not in his father's firm in New York but in the countinghouse of his father's business associate William Rotch, one of the richest whaling magnates in town. His annual salary was a meager $100. During his teenage apprenticeship, Moses formed a close friendship with a young man named Joseph Anthony, who worked with him in the Rotch firm. At the same time, he became engaged to Susan Russell, the headstrong heiress to another New Bedford whaling fortune and the sister of Anthony's wife.

Like Delano, Moses soon left home as a shipowner's representative, but not to China. Rather, he sailed from New Bedford to Rio de Janeiro and then to Trieste, Italy, where he sold his cargo of coffee at a handsome profit. His friend Joseph Anthony apparently took his absence hard: "For the first time in my life," he wrote, "a tear moistened my eye on parting with a friend. For nearly five years, he has been my companion in the counting room and endeared himself to me so much that I can truly say that I felt for him all a brother's love."[8] Such grief was understandable, for there was certainly a chance Moses would not come home.

For the next year, Anthony kept a diary addressed to Moses, which apprised him of the business and social goings-on in New Bedford. At a time when letter delivery to friends and family abroad was sporadic at best and took months or even years, keeping a diary to be presented to the traveler upon his or her return home was a genuine gift. Even the most trivial news was treasured. "A cold day— very slippery—spent the evening at Cora's. Had some oysters and then took a sleigh ride around town," he wrote on January 6, 1823. Anthony also kept Moses informed about business: "Sunday—a pleasant day. The *Persia* commenced discharging her cargo, which made some stir being the first day of the week. Many considered it wicked."[9]

He also kept Moses in the loop about a scandal entangling his fiancée at Meeting. Apparently, Susan and her sister Mary were refusing to live the simple life. "The overseers of the meeting," Anthony wrote, "entered a regular complaint in the preparative meeting this day against Mary and Susan for not conforming to the Discipline in the all-important points of Dress, Address [possibly this refers to the polite use of "thee" and "thou"], attending disorderly marriages (viz. the marriage of Jere'h Winslow and mine), and frequenting places of public amusement. The girls have got their feelings a good deal excited, and will probably resign their membership."[10] Despite the complaint against her, Moses married Susan upon his return to New Bedford in 1824. Clearly, Joseph Anthony would not have cared—his own wedding was one of the "disorderly" ones that Susan attended. Yet Moses soon found himself out of a job at Rotch's. Was it because his wife would not conform to the Society of Friends's standards?

As an unemployed Moses wandered the New Bedford wharves, lined with barrels of whale oil, he ran into his father's business partner (and cousin): the cadaverous Preserved Fish. Fish had left the Quaker faith and become an Episcopalian, perhaps to align himself with New York's elite.

"You are out of work are you not, Moses?" Fish inquired.

"Yes sir," Moses responded dejectedly.

"You know the business," Fish said. "Will you take it over as a partner?"

Moses had a rich father, but he himself had no money. "But sir, I have no capital!" he protested.

"Nonsense!" barked Fish in his curt captain's voice. "You have all the capital I want: brains, youth, and ambition. Come now, no buts. Yes or no?"[11]

Moses packed up his belongings, moved to New York, and set up shop at Fish & Grinnell on South Street. His wife, Susan, must have been grateful to leave behind the ruckus about her conduct at the New Bedford Meeting.

Over the next few years, Fish & Grinnell would expand from whaling into an even more lucrative business: the transatlantic packet trade. This wing of its business became known as the Swallowtail Line, after the double-pointed red-and-white pennants that flew famously from its ships' mainmasts.

Another young man also joined Moses at the firm's New York countinghouse table: the sharp-faced, bewhiskered Robert Bowne Minturn. He, too, had family roots at sea—his grandfather had been a wealthy Rhode Island shipping magnate—but as a young man, he had hoped to go to Columbia College and become a physician. However, when Minturn was still a boy, his father died, leaving the family in poverty. To support his mother, Robert was forced to become an apprentice clerk at age fifteen. The work was so crushing that the despondent, fatherless boy contemplated suicide by jumping into the East River at the end of a long day at the countinghouse.

Only the thought of his mother's plight seems to have kept him going. "He felt deeply the restricted circumstances of his mother after she became a widow," a biographer wrote, "and this, no doubt nerved his arm for the battle of life upon which he so early entered." In 1831 Minturn became a partner of the firm following the retirement of Preserved Fish and Moses's father, Cornelius. Fish & Grinnell became Grinnell, Minturn & Company. At least one visitor was struck at how such a prominent firm was run by two men in their early thirties. According to one story, when a representative from London's Barings' Bank visited the firm, he asked if he could meet with Mr. Minturn.

"I am he," said Minturn.

"Not you—not you!" sputtered the Englishman. "But the old man."[12]

Four years after making partner, Minturn married Anna Mary Wendell, the daughter of a prominent attorney from Albany, New York. By then, he could more than provide for a family. Perhaps in deference to Anna, he left his family's Quaker persuasion and joined the Episcopal Church. A decade later, Robert Minturn was worth $200,000, thanks to his firm's booming transatlantic business.

His business partner's wealth was easily just as vast. As he grew richer, Moses Grinnell hankered for political office, perhaps as much to protect his shipping interests (under attack from Jacksonian populists) as by any desire to serve the public. Moses served one term in Congress as a Whig from 1839 to 1841. This was the party of the elite, which put Grinnell in opposition to President Andrew Jackson's Democrats, which was increasingly the party of working men— like the shipyard workers who built Grinnell's ships and the sailors who crewed them. After serving two years in Washington, Moses returned to the Grinnell, Minturn & Company countinghouse—to the satisfaction of many of his peers, who felt that politics was no place for a gentleman. "A 'popular candidate for office,'" opined one such person, "is equivalent to 'a vagabond who has no business of his own'; 'popularity' means 'the approbation of the mob.'"[13]

By the 1840s, the Grinnell, Minturn Swallowtail Line would receive a financial windfall, thanks to one of the greatest humanitarian crises of the nineteenth century: Ireland's Great Famine. Although Britain had abolished slavery by 1839, absentee aristocratic British estate holders kept millions of Irish peasants in a state of virtual serfdom as tenant farmers from whom they extracted a yearly quota of grain as rent. Often, Irish tenant farmers had little left to eat except potatoes. The famine began in 1845, when a fungus wiped out Ireland's entire potato crop. During the next few years, an estimated one million people starved to death, out of a total population of eight million. Another million and a half scraped together the money to immigrate to America, mostly aboard westbound packet ships to the New World. The passage could last anywhere from two weeks to three months.

After Irish emigrants had sold everything they owned except perhaps for a few treasured possessions, family and friends would gather for an "Emigrant Wake" that mimicked the wakes held for the departed. After an evening of dancing and drink, the sad reality sank in: they would never see those departing again. By crossing the North Atlantic, they might as well be crossing the River Styx. Leaving family, friends, and the graves of their loved ones behind, emigrants departed their decimated villages in Mayo, Donegal, and

Cork Counties, and headed to the coast by foot and horse cart, and then by ferry across the Irish Sea to Liverpool.

The "famine Irish" enriched Grinnell, Minturn & Company of New York and the White Diamond Line of Boston. As a result, the Irish population of both cities swelled during the 1850s, with the vast majority condemned to live in conditions of abysmal poverty. In a typical packet, more than a hundred passengers were shoved into the tween decks of the ship, spaces equipped with crude bunks and tables. Unlike cabin-class passengers, whose food was included in the fare, steerage passengers often had to bring their own provisions and bedding. Any food the company provided was little better than the lot of the crew: hardtack biscuits, salt pork and beef, and hash. Untold thousands died of sickness and accidents in so-called "coffin ships." Yet for these famine Irish, the terrifying journey was worth the risk. If they stayed behind, they would most likely starve.

As they raked in huge profits from the humanitarian disaster, packet shipowners took on a charitable face. The New York newspapers of the day repeatedly praised Grinnell and Minturn's altruism. Journalist and politician Thurlow Weed gushed that Grinnell "was so large-hearted that he desired to make everybody happy; he was generous to the last degree. Unlike many men situated in life as he was, he did not contribute to hospital or asylum funds at stated intervals only, but gave in charity every day. In fact, he was always giving either money or assistance of other kinds to the needy." He wrote similarly about Grinnell's business partner: "Indeed, no better man ever lived in New York than Robert B. Minturn."[14]

Not everyone appears to have shared this view. Fellow shipping man Abbot Low thought the Grinnell firm's profiteering from the famine distasteful. In a letter to a sibling, he wrote sarcastically: "Our friends, Grinnell, Minturn are heartbroken about the famine. They have a house dinner to celebrate the fortune it is bringing them, and dine on terrapin, salmon, peas, asparagus, strawberries—all out of season, of course—then Mr. Grinnell gives the famine fund $360, which he had lost on a bet with Mr. Wetmore [William S. Wetmore, founder of rival China trade firm Wetmore & Company]. That, my dear brother, does not remind me of the way Houqua used to do things."[15]* If this letter is authentic, Low conveniently forgot about the lavish spreads of Chinese delicacies at Houqua's Canton villa. To him, those who were involved in the immigrant packet trade were profiteers in human misery, while, as his old Canton partner Robert Bennet Forbes liked to say, those merchants involved in the opium-fueled China trade were "exponents of all that was honorable in trade."[16]

Ironically, Forbes joined the Irish humanitarian effort in 1847, commanding the naval vessel USS *Jamestown* on a transatlantic voyage to Ireland, her holds carrying eight thousand barrels of food. The local Protestant gentry feted Forbes and his forty-nine-man crew with a splendid feast, and the *Liverpool Herald* crowed that this American gesture came from "genuine concern for the plight of a starving nation. Also, the notion of an American ship of war going on an errand of mercy, at the height of the unpopular Mexican War, seems to have resonated with the American public."

Forbes was smart enough to see through the pomp and the publicity. Accompanied by a local priest, he saw enough in five minutes in the back alleys of Cork to horrify him: "hovels crowded with the sick and dying, without floors, without furniture, and with patches of dirty straw covered with still dirtier shreds and patches of humanity."[17] During his many years in China, Forbes might have seen similar scenes of despair had he walked the forbidden streets of

---

* This undated letter from Abbot Low to an unnamed sibling is cited by historian Helen Augur in her 1951 book *Tall Ships to Cathay*, a history of the Low family's involvement in the China trade and recommended as a source by Charles Low descendant E. Holland Low. There are no footnotes or citations in this book, but considering Augur's stature as a journalist in the 1950s, it is unlikely she made up this letter out of whole cloth.

Canton and peered into the numerous opium dens. He would boast later that "many of the children born about the time of our advent [in Ireland] were named 'Forbes,' 'Boston,' or 'James' [after the USS *Jamestown*]." Soon after his return to America, Forbes received from the city fathers of Cork "a splendid silver salver and other tokens of their regard—which my family hold in trust, hoping that the Treasury of the United States will, sooner or later, return the seventy-five dollars' duty exacted at the Boston Custom House, with compound interest, and a full apology for the grab!"[18]

The clannish Warren Delano probably respected Moses Grinnell— they were New Bedford boys, and he had a friendship with Grinnell partner Francis Hathaway that went back to their days in Canton. Besides, the Grinnell firm had helped make his brother Franklin rich. Yet it appears that Delano did not think much of Robert Bowne Minturn. "I note all that you say of RBM—in connection with your arrangements with GM&Co," Warren wrote Franklin about Minturn. "I am a bit surprised at his duplicity."[19] The feud seemed to stem from Minturn's wanting to bring someone into the firm as a partner who, in Warren's assessment, was "without expenses other than eating, sleeping, whittling, and smoking, and RBM might take a fancy to let him in, in your place."[20]

In the shipping business, good manners in no way affected tough competition or hard bargaining. Grinnell and Minturn were very different creatures from the Russell men, who had spent their formative years in China, raised on long-haul, long-term gambles, with big payoffs at the end—quite literally, when one's "ship came in." The availability of products to buy and markets for selling them dictated routes, cargoes, and seasons.

Grinnell, however, wanted to run his firm's vessels on a schedule. He was a man of the countinghouse who prided himself on providing regular service across the North Atlantic. His transatlantic packets made money several times a year, not once a year as on the China route. And, in fact, over the long haul, the transatlantic packet operators made more money with their ships than the China traders did. As one historian noted, "The packets traveled a bit more slowly, but they carried considerably more. Their shrewd operators resisted the 'bigger and better' temptations until the traffic was ready to support bigger and better ships."[21]

Moses Grinnell took a risk only when he could truly afford to lose what was at stake. Buying a California clipper ship was a huge gamble; he preferred to invest in ships and men with proven records. There was a Quaker conservatism about his firm's operations. According to one historian, "[T]hey achieved their success without the mean sharpness which marred the great house of Howland."[22] Such "mean sharpness" included Howland partner William Henry Aspinwall's ruthless pursuit of speed with *Sea Witch* under the controversial Captain "Bully Bob" Waterman.[23]

Compared with A. A. Low's concern, Grinnell, Minturn's stake in the China trade was relatively minor, and managed from the New Bedford offices of his business partner Francis Hathaway, whose specialty was importing tea, silk, and hemp from Canton and Manila.[24] The firm had interests in two older vessels plying the tea route: *Horatio*, in which the young Charles Low had gotten his start under Moses's cousin Captain William Howland, and *Oneida*, an aging former North Atlantic packet ship. Grinnell preferred to invest in the packet ship type, the sort of vessel with which he was most familiar, even if the Lows described his stubby old *Horatio* as a "pile driver." *Oneida* had made respectable if not spectacular runs from Canton to New York in the recent past but could not compete with the clippers.

It was probably Francis Hathaway who finally pressured Moses Grinnell to jump into the clipper business. He had spent time in China as the Grinnells' agent, and he knew Warren Delano and John Murray Forbes from their days in the Factories. A lifelong bachelor, he was a cousin of John Murray Forbes's wife, Sarah Hathaway, and of Warren Delano's wife, Catherine Lyman. He would have been well aware of the promise of his kinsmen's new, swift ships.

Or perhaps Moses Grinnell was simply tired of being bested on the high seas by the men of the Canton coterie. Whatever his motivation for belatedly joining his rivals in the clipper game, in 1850 Francis Hathaway wrote to Warren Delano's brother Franklin about a new sort of ship under construction for the firm. Hathaway did not hold back his opinions on the ship's design, writing, "I want nothing but a *fast*, the fastest large clipper."[25]

This clipper became *Sea Serpent* and was given over to Grinnell's cousin Captain William Howland, long master of the aging *Horatio*. But she proved not to be as fast as Hathaway had hoped, and so he may well have pushed Moses to go after another one for Captain Josiah Perkins Creesy of the antiquated *Oneida*. In 1851 the time finally seemed to Grinnell to be right. And he had a naval architect in mind: Donald McKay.

Grinnell was familiar with McKay's work. In between commissions for Enoch Train, McKay had designed Grinnell's most recent purchase: the transatlantic packet ship *Cornelius Grinnell*, named after the owner's seafaring father. *Cornelius Grinnell* had been built for strength rather than speed. Her bow was bluff and her stern square. The papers heralded her as "by all odds" the strongest ship of her size ever built in America. Nonetheless, she boasted an incredibly high rig, as lofty as any clipper ship's. *Cornelius Grinnell* broke no records in the transatlantic run but established a reputation for relatively regular arrival times in New York and Liverpool.

Yet the enormous clippers that McKay was now working on for Train were larger than anything in Grinnell's fleet. The larger of the two, *Staffordshire*, was a strange hybrid: a "clipper packet," designed for a regularly scheduled run rather than itinerant cargo service. Named after the famed pottery works in England, she was intended for the transatlantic trade, where, Train hoped, her great speed would allow the White Diamond Line to compete head-on with the Cunard steamships. A witch figurehead leered down from *Staffordshire*'s prow.

The other clipper on the stocks was slightly smaller than *Staffordshire*, registering at 1,782 tons and stretching 225 feet long, with a beam of 40 feet. She had a relatively flat bottom, inspired by Captain Nat's designs, which had proved their worth over the past several years. Duncan McLean wrote of her in the *Boston Daily Atlas*: "If great length, sharpness of ends, with proportionate breadth and depth, conduce to speed, the *Flying Cloud* must be uncommonly swift, for in all these she is great." She was to be Train's entry into the California trade, meant to compete with Sampson & Tappan's new (but yet unproven) *Stag Hound* and the crack vessels of Abbot Low's fleet.

This was the clipper on which Grinnell set his sights. The question was how much cash it would take for Train to part with *Flying Cloud*.

How Moses Grinnell was able to talk Enoch Train out of his *Flying Cloud* remains a mystery. But somehow the two men struck a deal: Train would keep *Staffordshire* for transatlantic service but sell *Flying Cloud* to Grinnell for use in the California trade. What part McKay had in this transaction, if any, is unknown. Most likely, the Nova Scotian was happy to see two of his most prominent clients, one from Boston and one from New York, get in a bidding war over one of his clipper ships.

George Francis Train, Enoch's unreliable, eccentric cousin who did a stint as partner at the White Diamond Line, would later not only claim responsibility for building *Flying Cloud*, but also for selling her to Moses Grinnell. "The proudest moment of my life," he wrote in his rather fantastical memoir *My Life in Many States and in Foreign Lands*, "up to that time, was when I received a check from Moses H. Grinnell, the New York head of the house, for $90,000."[26] George, who traveled the world to promote the Union Pacific Railroad after his time in the shipping business, would one day be imprisoned and nearly committed to an insane asylum after "publishing an obscene paper," the subject of which remains a mystery.[27] Whether he truly masterminded the sale of *Flying Cloud* is likewise unknown.

For his part, his much saner kinsman Enoch Train lamented later that selling *Flying Cloud* to Moses Grinnell for $90,000 was one of the great business mistakes of his career.[28]

Still, Grinnell, who hated taking risks, did not take on the entire risk of the clipper he bought from Train. Rather, he split up the ownership (and risk) of *Flying Cloud* into 32 shares and distributed them to partners. As lead partners, Grinnell and Minturn each held a 9/32 stake in the new vessel. Francis Hathaway, Henry Grinnell (brother of Moses), and a captain from Mystic, Connecticut, named John E. Williams each took a 4/32 stake. As an incentive for swift sailing and careful management of his *Flying Cloud*'s cargo and passengers, Captain Josiah Creesy received a 2/32 share.[29]

There was little question of Donald McKay taking a share: Boston builders mostly avoided investing in their own ships, which may well have contributed to their artistic success. As historian Henry Hall wrote: "Leaving to others the management of the ships . . . it is probable that the superior excellence of Boston vessels sprung from the particular fact that builders gave their whole attention to the art."[30] Why agonize over the ship you'd built piece by piece once it was out of your hands?

Besides, Donald McKay had no need to be in on his ships' future profits. Train's quick sale would soon prove to be his best business transaction.

Chapter 11

AT THE STARTING LINE

My sail-ships and steam-ships threading the archipelagoes,
My stars and stripes fluttering in the wind,
Commerce opening, the sleep of ages having done its work, races
reborn, refresh'd,
Lives, works resumed—the object I know not—but the old, the
Asiatic renew'd as it must be,
Commencing from this day surrounded by the world.

—Walt Whitman,
"A Broadway Pageant" (1860)

New York was all about clippers in early 1851.

Winter gave way to spring, and the melting ice drifted down the Hudson River and out into the salt-laced waters of the Upper Bay. Cargo sloops from Albany, their big white mainsails stretched taut in the breeze, passed passenger steamers heading upriver. In genteel Washington Square, well-dressed couples strolled along the winding footpaths under arching, freshly green trees. The Merchants' Exchange, a granite, Greek Revival fortress at 55 Wall Street, hummed with voices as the city's men of affairs met each morning to set prices for wheat, copper, and coal flooding into the city from the nation's heartland and for bales of cotton coming up from New Orleans. Among frequent attendees were clipper ship owners Warren Delano, Moses Grinnell, Abiel Abbot Low, and William Henry Aspinwall—who may have been professional rivals but behaved in public with complete civility. Mercantile, upper-class New York was a small, insular world, and members of this club had to act like gentlemen, above all else. Many of them were related to one another, in any case.

After a visit to the Exchange, the merchants would then go to their offices on South Street, where they would meet with shipbuilders to go over models for proposed clippers and with their clerks to review ledger books. They were eagerly awaiting the first shipments of tea from China and cash receipts from sales of dry goods in California. After winding down affairs at their offices around four o'clock, they would stroll home to dinner at their townhouses.

Yet the southern tip of Manhattan didn't sleep when the rich men left. As dusk fell on South Street, sailors, shopkeepers, and other denizens of working-class New York streamed out of their places of work. They headed to the saloons and downed ale and whiskey, although many had been drinking already throughout the workday. Garishly made-up streetwalkers flounced down the sidewalks, and members of the nativist "Bowery Boys" and Irish Catholic "Dead Rabbits" gangs wolf whistled as these women passed by. In the tenements, German and Irish immigrant families huddled around cast-iron stoves, cooking dinners of cabbage and porridge.

And with the coming of spring, the clippers from China and California were sailing home. The merchants were ready to count their bounty, the shipbuilders eager to learn of the latest records; the professional sailors were waiting to sign up, while thugs readied themselves to ensnare those unlucky enough to be at the wrong saloon at the wrong time.

New clippers, too, were rising in the shipyards on the banks of the East River, their skeletal hulls looming over the city streets. Refinements of earlier designs, they had longer hulls, sharper bows, and higher masts than the likes of *Houqua* or *Rainbow*, not even eight years old and already outclassed. For these new clippers, there was no time for sea trials or dry runs. Once completed, they would be sent on their way around Cape Horn to California. Time was too precious, and profits too great.

When Charlie Low arrived back in New York aboard *Samuel Russell* that spring of 1851, he had every reason to be happy. That is, until he heard, most likely at the bar of the Astor House Hotel, that the Low clipper *Surprise*—under the command of former opium runner Captain Philip Dumaresq—had bested his 109-day run from New York to San Francisco. Talk was that the latest Low clipper, *N. B. Palmer,* could lower the record once again on her upcoming maiden voyage. But the House of Low also awaited the challenge of the House of Grinnell, which had a new ship, *Flying Cloud*, looking to race around the Horn that spring. The fact was, the clipper field was getting crowded. More were nearing completion in Boston and New York, as well as in other yards in Maine, Pennsylvania, and New Jersey.

The first thing Charlie did on dry land was meet with his brother Edward to tour the Westervelt shipyard and inspect the partially completed *N. B. Palmer*. Edward asked Charles what he thought of the ship.

"The most beautiful vessel I have ever seen," his brother responded. "If I could have command of such a vessel, it would be the height of my ambition."

Edward must have smiled as he told Charles the good news: he should report to the shipyard the next morning and supervise her completion. After that, he would be her master on her maiden trip to California.

Content though Charles would have been to spend all his days supervising the construction of his latest dream ship, his brother Seth Haskell Low seems to have wanted his kid brother to get to work on finding a wife—preferably a New Englander—in his brief time ashore. At Haskell's urging, Charles took an overnight boat to Fall River, Massachusetts. After a quick visit to New Hampshire, he paused in Danvers, Massachusetts, just south of the old China trade port of Salem and recently connected to Boston by railroad.

Like others with deep ancestral ties to New England, the Lows looked for prospective mates among their fellow Yankees. Warren Delano had made a similar trip five years earlier and married Forbes cousin Catherine Lyman, who promptly sailed with him on his next trip to China. The reasons went deeper than simply marrying into families they already knew. After two centuries of making their livings from the sea, Yankee families were accustomed to long and dangerous separations. Rooftop balconies atop gabled waterfront houses—known as widow's walks—allowed the women of the house to watch for telltale masts and sails on the horizon. They knew that many of the captains and merchants who ventured to China or the Pacific whaling grounds never came home.

Perhaps the Lows also wanted Charles to avoid meeting the type of well-born New York girl who, in the scathing words of James Gordon Bennett's *New York Herald*, "are taught to sing, dance, flirt, laugh, and act French vaudevilles, but never learn one useful thing that will enable them to perform the part of a good wife and mother." The "finishing" of young women in such a continental manner, the editors concluded, would lead only to the finishing of a husband, and the practice was working "its way silently but surely to the complete revulsion in morals, manners, religion, philosophy, and finance of the whole community."[1]

Haskell Low had a woman in mind for Charlie, a "Miss D," but the sea captain was unimpressed when he finally met her, despite her beauty. "Night after night, I was invited to parties," Charles Low recalled of his time in Danvers, "but I was not carried away by any of the young ladies." Unlike the dandyish Captain Waterman, Charles was not a flirt. He wanted a companion who would travel with him rather than a socialite wife who would wait ashore for months on end.

Finally, at one party, the host asked the several young ladies there to sing. None stepped forward at first. "Each and every one had a cold—or something else was the matter—and wished to be excused," Low recalled. As one *Godey's Lady's Book* magazine writer smirked, a typical "young girl who sings" of the era had a "voice like that of a tin kettle if it could speak, and takes more pride in reaching a high D sharp than if she had reached the top of the pyramid of Cheops."[2] Nobody wanted to be judged so harshly, especially in front of potential suitors such as Charles, whose years at sea had left him with a round, sun-creased face, flashing blue eyes, and hardened hands.

Then a dark-haired, black-eyed girl stepped forward without a word, sat down at the piano, and started to play and sing. The song may have been one of the sentimental ballads of the era, which usually had to do with love and death. Went one popular song of the time:

> Thou have learned to love another,
> Thou hast broken every vow,
> We have parted from each other,
> And my heart is lonely now;
> I have taught my looks to shun thee
> When coldly we have met,
> For another's smile hath won thee,
> And thy voice I must forget.[3]

If she were highly skilled, she might have tried an aria such as those popularized by "Swedish Nightingale" Jenny Lind, who had made a sensational American concert tour the previous year. Lind's figure graced the prow of the clipper *Nightingale*, then under construction in Maine.

That night, Charles Low heard Sarah Tucker's voice soar above the pearly notes of the piano and thought to himself, "This is the girl for me." Unlike other women of her set, who sang "scientifically," Sarah must have sung with confidence and poise. What a contrast from the rough-hewn, lusty voices of men singing chanteys, like that about a captain named "Kickin' Jack Williams," or being paid a measly "dollar and a half a day." But even such singing meant something to Charles, for he boasted that he wouldn't hire a sailor if he couldn't sing.

Charles and Sarah sat and talked all night. Sarah was only eighteen and had recently lost her father. At the end of the evening, the couple cracked open a peanut, ate the two kernels, and promised each other a gift at their next meeting—a dating game known as a "philopena."

When the two of them met again, Charles gallantly drove a rented carriage up to the Tucker house.

"Philopena!" she exclaimed after she opened the front door.

A few days later, Charles and Sarah were engaged. Charles then hurried back to Manhattan to oversee the final fitting out of *N. B. Palmer*.

N. B. Palmer would be ready for her maiden voyage to California by May 1851, just in time for a race against Moses Grinnell's new *Flying Cloud*. There were more than just profits riding on this trip: the ship's reputation was being watched from England. That spring, an exquisite, fully rigged model of the *N. B. Palmer* had gone on display at London's Great Exhibition of 1851 (the first true world's fair), attracting much interest amidst the clanking steam-powered machinery and other curiosities on display in the vaulted cast-iron-and-glass halls of the Crystal Palace.[4] The model reminded visitors that a Yankee Low clipper still held the record on the prestigious tea route between Hong Kong and London.

Flying Cloud and *N. B. Palmer* were not the only ships that spring with a shot at setting a record on the San Francisco run. There was also a gigantic new vessel under construction on the East River, commissioned by Nathaniel and George Griswold. Perhaps acting on intelligence gleaned from the McKay yard, the Griswolds had charged shipbuilder William H. Webb to build the biggest clipper in the world, larger than *Flying Cloud* and *Staffordshire*. Named *Challenge*, she would tip the scales at over two thousand tons displacement and would be propelled by more than twelve thousand square yards of canvas. The mastermind of *Challenge*'s bold sail plan was none other than Captain Robert Waterman, whom the Griswolds had coaxed out of his sunny California retirement to serve as a design consultant—as well as to be the ship's master on her maiden voyage. The incentive: a $10,000 bonus if Waterman brought her through the Golden Gate in ninety days or less, handily breaking *Surprise*'s record run the previous year.

The prudent, conservative Webb—an old friend of McKay's and perhaps his foremost New York competitor—balked at the scope of the commission. *Challenge* was more than twice the size of his two previous clippers, the trim and elegant *Mandarin* and *Celestial*. He already had his hands full, building oceangoing steamships for the California trade, but he obliged—perhaps because the Griswolds forked over $150,000, almost twice the already high price Grinnell had paid for *Flying Cloud*.

Webb and Waterman bickered constantly during the design process, so much so that the Griswold firm had to mediate. Webb did not like Waterman's plan for more canvas. The designer was worried that such a huge spread of material pushed the practical limits of seamanship, making the ship too unstable and dangerous to operate. Ultimately, *Challenge*'s sail plan was somewhat reduced, which gave Webb some comfort. Yet her topmost yard still towered two hundred feet above the main deck.

A ship as large as *Challenge* was a severe test of wooden shipbuilding technology at the time: only the warship USS *Pennsylvania* was larger. *Challenge* would be the first clipper with three full decks rather than two. To ensure that the huge vessel did not come apart in bad weather, Webb added iron strapping that was bolted diagonally into the outer surface of the frames. This gave her greater longitudinal rigidity and, hence, resistance to hogging. She also had a sharp, V-shaped hull like earlier China clippers *Rainbow* and *Memnon*. But ultimately, the issues facing the giant *Challenge*'s quest for the record run to California were not structural, but human.

N. B. Palmer was the first of the big new clippers to sail from New York during the 1851 spring sailing season. As Captain Charles Low supervised the finishing touches to the sparkling new clipper, he was determined that his ship would break *Surprise*'s ninety-six-day record from the previous year, as well as fend off the rival clippers scheduled to sail for San Francisco: *Flying Cloud*, *Challenge*, and *Gazelle*. His older brother Abbot Low wanted the record to remain in Low family hands at all costs. Low's business now depended on quick voyages around the world: New York to California, California to China, and, finally, China to New York. In the public eye, the ocean voyage to San Francisco had outclassed the China run in glamor not only because it was so physically dangerous and financially risky, but also because it was a new and novel embodiment of America's Manifest Destiny and of quickly won riches.

For a shipowner, owning the fastest ship in the China trade was still a big feather in the cap, but by 1851, it was nothing compared with the profits that came with the fastest voyage to San Francisco.

Despite the lighthearted tone with which he relates this period in his memoir, the pressure on Charles must have been immense. The prospect of nearly a year apart from his bride-to-be, Sarah Tucker, bothered him enough to make him lose focus on supervising the fitting out of his brother's flagship.

200

Shortly before the May 6 sailing day, Captain Nat Palmer and Abbot Low noticed that the now-veteran clipper captain was looking sad and distracted. They pulled him aside.

"Charlie," Abbot said sharply, "you would like to go to South Danvers, would you not?"

Charles responded that yes, he would.

"Why should he not go?" Palmer asked gruffly.

Abbot relented. "You have time to catch the boat at five o'clock, but not much time to spare," he said. The usually businesslike merchant might have been sympathetic to his brother's emotional distress because of recent changes in his own personal life. His wife, Ellen, had died the previous January after giving birth to their fourth child: a son, Seth, who himself barely survived. Abbot had already taken in his brother William Henry's widow, Ann, and her young son following William Henry's suicide. After Ellen's death, Ann became a mother figure to Abbot's motherless young children, two girls and two boys.

Charles left the *N. B. Palmer*, packed his suitcases, and ran to catch the steamer *Bay State* up to Boston. "I only had a few days to spend with my betrothed," Low recalled, "and then back to the ship I went."[5]

On the sixth of May, as scheduled, *N. B. Palmer* left New York for San Francisco "with light winds from the southwest."[6] The crowds who gathered at the Battery to watch the departure heard a cacophony of sounds coming across the water: the clank of the windlass,* the creaking of yards as they were hoisted up the masts, the roaring commands of the first mate, and the bellowing of one of Captain Low's prized chanteymen as he sang out work songs to keep the men in rhythm as they hauled on the lines. The words, as one observer

---

* A device used for raising the anchor, consisting of a barrel turned by a crank or lever.

noted, sprung from "undeveloped intelligence," and the melodies had a "wild, inspiring ring" that took on a "pungent, briny odor and surging roar and rhythm of the ocean, and howling gales at sea."[7]

The chanteyman's lyrics about leaving ladies behind must have been especially poignant for Captain Low. As *N. B. Palmer* set her sails and headed out into the North Atlantic, he looked forward to a time when Sarah would be his wife and be able to accompany him on ship.

That same May, Josiah Creesy, master of the *Flying Cloud*, was loading up his ship on South Street. The veteran captain of the *Oneida* had finally received his dream commission, and, unlike Captain Charlie Low, he would not be sailing alone: his wife, Eleanor Prentiss Creesy, was a veteran of life at sea and a vital member of his crew. An accomplished mathematician, Eleanor (called Ellen by her husband) was so skilled in practical navigation that tough-hided Josiah trusted her with keeping his ship on course. Her finesse with a brass sextant and charts was unmatched, and Creesy encouraged his wife's talents. Ellen, for her part, moderated her husband's intense, competitive character.

Creesy, already grizzled at thirty-seven years old, was a native of Marblehead, Massachusetts, a fishing port north of Boston, where he had grown up racing small sailing boats. As a teenager, his idea of a good time was sailing all the way to Salem in a fishing dory to stare at the big China trade vessels, and, while still in his teens, Creesy shipped off to sea. By age twenty-three, he had become a captain.[8] Before long, Josiah would marry a woman from home, Eleanor Horton Prentiss.

Hers was a seafaring family: her father, a sea captain, died when Eleanor was only three; a few years later, her mother married his brother, a US Navy lieutenant. Unlike other well-brought-up girls of the day, Eleanor Creesy had no interest in the cult of domesticity that dictated a woman should stay out of the hurly-burly, male-dominated arena of commerce. Instead, she followed in the footsteps of staunch New England women such as Abigail Adams—the influential wife of America's second president, John Adams, and the mother of future chief executive John Quincy Adams—who defied the notion that women's education should be geared primarily to attract a husband, run a home, and charm people at parties. Eleanor had no desire to pace the widow's walk atop her Marblehead home, worrying like countless captains' wives before her whether her husband would return.

Although it was not uncommon for captains to bring their wives on long ocean voyages, Eleanor's role as a mariner set her apart from her peers. "It was the rare bride who knew how to 'work time' to calculate the ship's position," writes historian Joan Druett.[9] Not everyone was kind about wives on board; superstitious sailors derisively called such ships "hen frigates." But it seems Eleanor had a way with people as well as technology. According to one passenger, she was "social and gentle . . . such glorious eyes I never saw, large, liquid, and hazel, soft as a gazelle's and always beaming with kindness on somebody."[10]

Creesy did have a terrible temper and had no qualms about engaging in "belaying-pin and knuckle-duster" tactics with his crew.[11] His runs on the China trade were good but not spectacular, and he was also a "pencil sharpener"—suspected of fudging daily records for the sake of pleasing his bosses. The ambitious captain had long been hoping to get command of a faster vessel of the clipper type. With *Flying Cloud*, he had his chance.

While waiting to set sail, the Creesys stayed at the Astor House, New York's largest and most modern hotel and the crown jewel of the Astor family's real estate portfolio. The hotel boasted such modern amenities as running water, room service, and a bell system to summon servants to a guest's room. Gaslight, rather than whale oil or tallow candles, flickered in the crystal chandeliers and gilt sconces.[12] In the central courtyard, adorned with trees and splashing fountains, was a dark wood bar around which shipowners and captains loved to congregate, place bets, and spin yarns. Captain Creesy must have relished being the center of attention at the Astor House bar. He now commanded the largest merchant vessel in the world—and possibly the fastest, too.

In the weeks before *Flying Cloud*'s sailing, Moses Grinnell and Robert Bowne Minturn hosted a series of onboard receptions to market her to prospective passengers and to merchants looking to ship goods to California. The promotional effort worked wonders. After a tour, one New York reporter wrote, "Hundreds of people have visited this beautiful and unique ship . . . The *Flying Cloud* is just the kind of vehicle, whatever else it may be called, that a sensible man would choose for a ninety-day voyage."[13]

On June 2, 1851, flying the red-and-white swallowtail banner of Grinnell, Minturn & Company, *Flying Cloud* departed New York's South Street on her maiden voyage. Her holds contained about $50,000 worth of goods: 500 kegs of white lead, 100 cases of imperial black paint, lamp black, 100 cans of turpentine, 190 dozen brandied peaches, 100 dozen tomato and pepper sauces, 68 boxes of candles, and many casks of wine and spirits.[14] She was also carrying something even more precious: Moses Grinnell's ambition to break the monopoly of the old China hands on the speed record to California. He hoped, too, that his McKay-designed ship would be a worthy adversary to the Low ships on the race from China to New York.

There were twelve passengers on this maiden voyage: six men, five women (including an Irish maid), and one male child.[15] None of them appeared to be gold prospectors: the ticket price for passage on a clipper ship was way too high. Unlike passengers on the steamers, who were divided into two classes, there was only one class: the equivalent of modern-day first. Among the several passengers who boarded *Flying Cloud* with valises in tow were three Boston siblings:

Whitney, Sarah, and Ellen Lyon. Ellen was en route to San Francisco to marry Reuben Patrick Boise, a distinguished Oregon jurist. Her father had taken a Panama steamer and was scheduled to arrive ahead of his children. Why the three siblings decided to take *Flying Cloud* and not the more regularly scheduled steamship line is a mystery.[16] Sarah Lyon would not regret her choice.

But with the departure of *N. B. Palmer* just four weeks earlier, Captain Creesy was presented with a predicament: manpower. By the early 1850s, recruiting enough sailors—no matter how inexperienced—to sail a big clipper to California was becoming a problem. In the first few years after the discovery of gold at Sutter's Mill, captains had no problem signing on men to work on a sailing ship rounding Cape Horn to California. Gone now were those heady first months, when hordes of prospectors would happily board anything floating bound for San Francisco. The steamships of Pacific Mail and other lines had made the trip to California via the Panama Isthmus almost routine. Tickets were expensive, but most prospective travelers preferred to fork over the money rather than endure hellish conditions on a clipper as part of the crew. Yet despite the labor shortage, freight rates to California remained sky high. *Flying Cloud*'s maiden voyage cargo was worth the modern-day equivalent of many millions in California—and worthless if the ship didn't sail or sank en route.

By the last days of May, Creesy, like other captains, had to resort to shady, often brutal tactics to get the fifty or so men needed to crew up a ship like *Flying Cloud*. He hired "crimps," crew recruiters who were little more than thugs. The crimps made deals with the operators of New York's waterfront dive bars and brothels, who would drug unwitting patrons into a stupor with a few drops of opium. The crimps would then dump the unconscious men onto the deck of the waiting ship. When they awoke, the newly conscripted members of the crew not only found their pockets were empty but also that they were now contracted to sail the duration of the voyage. Worse still, three months' worth of their wages had been paid out to the crimps.[17]

Some of these men were experienced sailors who had been out on a spree the night before. For them, especially the packet rats, climbing aloft in a blinding gale to shorten sail was all in a day's work. Such brashness when faced with danger or uncertainty was all part of a sailor's lot. Others were unfortunates caught in the crimp's clutches: famine Irish, African American freedmen, and fugitive slaves, Portuguese, Italians, Finns, and many others in the wrong place at the wrong time. Even captains and officers could be targets. According to a New Orleans clergyman writing in an 1851 issue of the *Sailor's* magazine, "In one case, the captain of a ship who had unfortunately taken too much liquor was shipped as a common sailor and went down the river in that capacity, leaving his own ship on the levee."[18]

The year 1851 was a terrible one for deaths on board American merchant ships. According to one source, 103 men died from disease and shipboard injuries while on the job. The average age was only twenty-eight.[19] Few other records survive, but it is safe to say that the year's death toll on ships and in foreign ports was probably in the thousands. It came down to lack of training, insufficient manpower, profit-driven owners hell-bent on speed, and the dangers inherent to life at sea.

A month after Grinnell's *Flying Cloud* departed New York, a third and even bigger clipper, *Challenge,* set sail in pursuit. Not only was she the biggest merchant ship in the world, but also she was likely the most expensive, costing the Griswold brothers well over $150,000 to construct. Yet Captain Waterman had a problem: his rivals Creesy and Low had taken the best men from the New York waterfront. In charge of a much bigger ship with significantly larger sails than her rivals, Waterman needed at least sixty men to cast off for San Francisco. The crimps he hired delivered too few men; what's more, they were the absolute dregs of the waterfront. Seventeen were unfit for duty and lay moaning in the ship's sick bay. Only six of them had ever steered a ship before.

Waterman was so upset that he considered canceling the voyage. But with so much cargo in his hold, a giant clipper built to his specifications—and that $10,000 bonus from the Griswolds if he made the trip to California in less than ninety days—the captain decided to set sail.[20] First, though, he made a quick change in personnel. While riding at anchor off the Battery, he fired his first mate and replaced him with James Douglass, who had arrived in New York Harbor aboard the Black Star Line's transatlantic packet *Guy Mannering*. Waterman knew his reputation and felt Douglass was the only person who could whip his slovenly crew into shape. Douglass was the archetypal bucko mate: six feet tall and well over two hundred pounds, he was rough-hewn, belligerent, and had an almost maniacal love of beating his men. The word on the docks was that the new first mate "would rather have a knockdown fight with a lot of sailors than eat a good dinner."[21]

Waterman probably had another, more immediate reason to hire a big man like "Black Douglas": he was the ideal bouncer to have guarding the space between the fo'c'sle and the captain's cabin. Waterman was slight of build, with almost feminine features—and he was detested. On this trip, he needed not just a first mate but also a bodyguard.[22]

Before delivering his lecture to the crew, Waterman splashed his face with seawater, a ritual baptism he did before every voyage. A skilled sailor, he had supposedly never lost a spar and was not about to lose one on this voyage, either. He and Douglass went through the sailors' chests, collecting all pistols, personal knives, brass knuckles, and other weapons, and then threw them overboard. The only sharp objects the men could keep were their sailor's knives and marlinspikes, which were needed for unjamming halyards, cutting through damaged rope, and performing other essential tasks while aloft.[23] As one more precaution against violence, it wasn't uncommon for the first mate to break the sharp ends off these knives before returning them to their owners.

The stage was set for one of the most infamous voyages of the clipper ship era, one that would expose to the nation the human cost of speed and profit at any cost.

The Canton Factories, as depicted in 1805 by the artist William Daniell. Between 1685 and 1841 this was the only place where Westerners could conduct legal trade with the Celestial Kingdom. At the center of the painting is a British rowing gig, working its way through the junks and other traffic on the Pearl River. Warren Delano and his compatriots mixed with traders from many nations in the so-called "Golden Ghetto," and lived in a manner far grander than they were accustomed to in their native New England. *Alamy Images*

The merchant Wu Ping-Chien, known by his American friends as Houqua. With an estimated worth of $26 million, Houqua was one of the richest men in the world and served as a mentor to many American traders in Canton. Portraits of Houqua adorned the homes of his American "sons." This portrait by Lam Qua once hung at the Delano family's Algonac estate. *By permission of Frederic Delano Grant, Jr.*

Abiel Abbot Low, close friend and colleague of Warren Delano II and founder of the shipping firm A. A. Low & Brother. By the 1850s, Low operated the largest and most successful fleet of clipper ships in the China and California trades. Meticulous and shrewd, Low vastly expanded his fortune by investing in railroads and the transatlantic cable. He also used his influence to send his other brothers to China to earn their competences. *Courtesy of Nadeau's Auction Gallery*

Portrait of Captain Nathaniel Brown Palmer: Antarctic explorer, master mariner, and clipper ship designer. Palmer served as head design consultant for A. A. Low & Brother, supervising the construction of many of the company's clippers. Although a proponent of sharp lines, he favored the flat-bottomed hull-type used in New Orleans cotton packets, giving his vessels extra capacity and stability without sacrificing speed. *The Stonington Historical Society*

The early clipper ship *Houqua*. Designed by Captain Nathaniel Palmer, she boasted a sharp bow and a flat floor. Upon her completion in 1844, a newspaper reporter described her as the "prettiest and most rakish looking packet ever built in the civilized world . . . as sharp as a cutter—as symmetrical as a yacht—as rakish in her rig as a pirate—and as neat in her deck and cabin arrangements as a lady's boudoir." Her figurehead was a bust of the great Chinese merchant, mentor to her owner Abiel Abbot Low. *Courtesy of the Peabody Essex Museum*

A sketch of Algonac, the forty-room Italianate mansion designed by Andrew Jackson Downing for Warren and Catherine Delano at Newburgh, New York; the house was filled with mementos of the Delanos' years in China. This drawing is in the hand of either the architect or Warren Delano II, who appears to have been a talented amateur sketch artist. For generations of Delanos, "Algonac" was a code word for good news. Algonac burned down in 1916. *The Franklin D. Roosevelt Presidential Library*

Warren Delano II with his children Sara ("Sallie") and Warren III, in a daguerreotype taken in 1856. Three years later, the patriarch would leave the idyllic life he had created for his family at Algonac to rebuild his fortune trading opium and tea in China. *Sara Delano Perkins Collection*

Catherine Lyman Delano, wife of Warren Delano II, was noted for her beauty, intelligence, and calm demeanor. During the course of her marriage, she traveled to China three times and kept a detailed journal of the family's adventures with their eight surviving children. *The Franklin D. Roosevelt Presidential Library and Museum*

William Henry Aspinwall, owner of the early clipper ships *Rainbow* and *Sea Witch* and mastermind of the Panama Pacific Railroad. He had the foresight to take a gamble on John Willis Griffiths' revolutionary clipper ship designs, and put his trust in the aggressive sailing tactics of Captain Robert Waterman. Not part of the "Canton Coterie," Aspinwall had business interests as far afield as China, South America, and the Mediterranean. Despite running an aggressive shop, he was also known as someone who had "rare faith in the honesty of his fellow man." *Courtesy of the National Portrait Gallery, Smithsonian Institution*

John Willis Griffiths, the groundbreaking shipbuilder who designed the *Rainbow* and *Sea Witch* for William Henry Aspinwall and the *Memnon* for Warren Delano II. His revolutionary clipper ship hull designs called for a sharp bow entry and a V-shaped bottom. An eccentric self-promoter in his later years, Griffiths would claim that he presented his radical designs to a snickering audience at the American Institute of the City of New York before being hired by Aspinwall and vindicated. There is no proof this actually occurred. *Courtesy of Deborah Pearson*

Captain Robert "Bully Bob" Waterman, one of the most charismatic and feared captains under the American flag. He commanded Howland & Aspinwall's *Sea Witch* on her record-breaking seventy-four-day run from Hong Kong to New York in 1849, a record that still stands to this day. Despite his reputation for brutality and hard driving, no ship under Waterman's command ever lost a spar. *Alamy Images*

The clipper ship *Sea Witch*, John Willis Griffith's masterpiece for William Henry Aspinwall, with her figurehead of a snarling Chinese dragon. Captain Robert Waterman was the guiding force behind her spectacular performance at sea. *Courtesy of the Kelton Foundation, Los Angeles*

A photograph of San Francisco taken in 1850, showing the harbor full of ships riding at anchor, many of them left to rot by crews who had jumped ship looking for gold. During the heady years of the Gold Rush, eggs sold for $1 a piece, a pair of boots for $50, and a barrel of flour for $60. To cash in on the unprecedented demand for passengers and freight, East Coast shipping operators sent almost anything that floated on the treacherous voyage around Cape Horn. *Library of Congress*

Moses Grinnell, partner in the successful shipping firm of Grinnell, Minturn & Company. In 1851, the packet ship operator paid Enoch Train $90,000 for his unfinished clipper ship *Flying Cloud*, then under construction at Donald McKay's East Boston shipyard. Train later lamented that selling *Flying Cloud* to Grinnell was the worst business decision he had ever made. *The Union Club of the City of New York*

Captain Josiah Perkins Creesy, commander of the clipper ship *Flying Cloud* during her two record-breaking voyages from New York to California. *Flying Cloud* was his first clipper ship command, and he pushed the ship to her absolute limit. His wife Eleanor Prentiss Creesy, an expert navigator, always went to sea with her husband, whom she fondly referred to as "Perk." This photograph of Josiah Creesy dates from his Civil War naval service as master of the clipper *Ino*. Sadly, no image Eleanor Creesy survives. *Courtesy of the Peabody Essex Museum*

Captain Charles Porter Low, who defied his older brother Abbot's wishes and went to sea. The family troublemaker proved his worth, going on to command the clippers *Houqua, Samuel Russell, N. B. Palmer,* and *Jacob Bell. Public domain*

The clipper ship *Flying Cloud*, as depicted in a popular Currier and Ives engraving. Upon her return to New York after her record-breaking voyage from New York to San Francisco, Moses Grinnell ordered copies of Captain Creesy's log printed in gold letters on white silk and distributed them to his friends and associates. Composer Charles D'Albert even penned a "Flying Cloud Schottische" dance in the ship's honor. *Image courtesy of the Kelton Foundation, Los Angeles*

A painting of the elegant *N. B. Palmer*, anchored off Staten Island. This clipper, the final masterpiece of designer Captain Nathaniel Brown Palmer, was Captain Charles Porter Low's favorite and longest command. Low's wife Sarah gave birth to their son Charles Jr. aboard *N. B. Palmer* in 1852. *Courtesy of the Kelton Foundation, Los Angeles*

A formal portrait of the Nova Scotia–born shipbuilder Donald McKay. Possessing immense technical gifts and a strong immigrant's drive, McKay declared, "I never yet built a vessel that came up to my own ideal. I saw something in each ship which I desired to improve upon." As arguably America's most famous clipper ship builder, McKay was lionized by poets, journalists, and politicians in his adopted hometown of Boston. *Courtesy of The Metropolitan Museum of Art*

The clipper ship *Great Republic*, the masterpiece of Donald McKay. When completed in 1853, she was the largest merchant vessel in the world—until she was almost completely destroyed by a disastrous fire on the eve of her maiden voyage. This painting by James Edward Buttersworth shows *Great Republic* as she would have looked under sail had she not burned. *Courtesy of the Kelton Foundation, Los Angeles*

President Franklin Delano Roosevelt building a model of a clipper ship in his study at his Hudson River estate at Hyde Park, c.1935. As a politician, Franklin was fond of quoting his maternal grandfather's business dictum: never let your left hand know what your right hand is doing. *The Franklin D. Roosevelt Presidential Library and Museum*

CHAPTER 12

AROUND THE WORLD

To protect the cigars, I had a tin chest made & hope it will fetch a
profit above cost . . . I hope you will not part with the shipment of
butter without a full consideration, none can be better than per F.
Cloud which was new as you were informed.

—Francis S. Hathaway
to the Grinnell, Minturn & Company
office in San Francisco, May 30, 1851[1]

Leaving New York Harbor that June day in 1851, Captain Creesy
guided *Flying Cloud* on a southeast course across the Atlantic. He
was aiming to avoid the doldrums: the windless belt of equatorial air
that could trap sailing ships for days. To do so, Creesy first headed
the ship toward Africa. Then, not far from the coast, he turned and
tacked back southwest toward Brazil. Wife Eleanor was, as always,
his careful navigator as they plotted their way using the new charts
that Matthew Fontaine Maury had published only two years before.

Creesy's earlier command had been *Oneida*, a vessel half the size
of *Flying Cloud*, so getting a feel for a ship this large and skittish
was a tall order. Yet he would not let his crew see his anxiety about
his valuable command. Swapping yarns at the Astor House while
awaiting *Flying Cloud*'s launch, Josiah Creesy almost certainly heard
how McKay's earlier *Stag Hound* lost her top-hamper under a heavy

209

press of sail in gale conditions on her maiden voyage the year before. The accident had ruined Captain Josiah Richardson's chance of grabbing the record. Creesy hoped that his ship, only the second clipper built by McKay, did not have the same design flaw.

Three days out of New York, the wind freshened, but Creesy kept his speed and did not reduce canvas. The wind blew harder and harder. The shrouds creaked, and the ocean broke over the bow as *Flying Cloud* bounded through the waves. Ships such as *Flying Cloud* were pushing the absolute limits of wooden ship technology, especially when it came to the terrific forces exerted upon the masts by wind and the tremendous pounding of heavy seas on the hull. "They carry enormous cargoes, and the speed of these Leviathans, when sporting with the winds and the waves, is almost terrific," wrote a San Francisco journalist. "It is in fact so great, that could power enough be brought to bear on the hull of an old-fashioned ship, as to force her through the water at the same rate, it would crush her to pieces."[2]

Down below, most of Creesy's passengers were laid up in their staterooms, suffering from seasickness. Compounding their nausea was a pungent mix of odors: coal smoke from the galley, animal excrement, vomit from commodes and chamber pots. The ship's luxurious passenger quarters became a mockery as *Flying Cloud* heaved and lurched through the ocean. And then there was the strange cacophony of noises from up above: the creaking of yards and shrieking of ropes in their blocks, as well as the hoarse shouts of the first mate to the men on watch, followed by the pounding of bare feet on pine decks. Passenger Sarah Bowman was all too aware of the "immense amount of livestock on board." As she sat in her chair, staring out at the vast ocean, she felt it odd to hear "roosters crowing, hens cackling, turkeys gobbling, pigs grunting, and lambs bleating."[3]

When the passengers got their sea legs, the next challenge was finding ways to fill the days in the middle of the vast ocean, far away from all that was familiar. "Oh, how I should like the daily papers,"

Sarah yearned. "I want to know what is going on in Boston, and vicinity. I want to see all the folks at W., the Whitmans, the Silsbys, and hosts of others I shall always remember so pleasantly—shall I ever see their faces again? Yes,—*I will believe so*."[4]

By June 6, four days out, those passengers who had gotten over their nausea were eating their first full dinner when they heard a cracking and splintering from up above. The main and mizzen topgallant masts came crashing down, along with the main topsail yard. The broken masts and spars swung in the air from a mass of tangled rigging, as *Flying Cloud* flailed before the wind like a wounded beast. Down below, passengers noticed the ship break her forward motion. Her previously steady roll became uneven, as she leaned drunkenly to one side.

The easy thing for Creesy to have done was to order the crew to cut down the broken masts and spars, turn around, and proceed back to New York under reduced sail. Yet the old master refused. Ordering the crew to heave to, he held the ship in position and waited for the wind to die down. He was lucky. The weather turned.

The following day, the captain sent his crew aloft. Rather than cut away the damaged rigging, Creesy wanted the ship brought back to her original rig. There in the middle of the ocean, that's what the sailors did. Using the stock of extra spars stowed on deck, the crew repaired and replaced the damaged masts. Broken pieces from the originals were refashioned into smaller spars. Skilled hands led by example and repaired the rigging. The restoration of the ship at sea was altogether a heroic feat, one made possible by the remarkable stability *Flying Cloud* enjoyed—partly because of her relatively flat bottom, and partly because Creesy had probably made sure that cargo had been loaded carefully to preserve her center of gravity.[5]

Onward, *Flying Cloud* sailed for San Francisco, the crew watching the repaired masts for any danger signs. Passengers must have breathed a sigh of relief. Most were young—none was past his or her midthirties—and were generally affluent and well educated. Sarah

Bowman amused herself by reading poetry to Eleanor Creesy. She also took a strong interest in one of her fellow passengers, Laban Coffin from Baltimore, who was, she thought, a "finished, traveled gentleman, well bred—well read—posted up on every subject—fine looking to boot." Sarah was especially taken with Laban's travel stories: he claimed to have been around Cape Horn thirteen times and that this was his third trip to San Francisco. He may have been exaggerating to put Sarah and the other ocean novices at ease, but he did have plenty of sea experience. A scion of an old Nantucket whaling family, Laban was tall and well built ("rather inclined to be on the fleshy side," Sarah wrote). He had shipped to sea at fifteen and survived being crushed between a bobbing whale and the side of the ship as he tried to remove a harpoon from the dead beast's flank. After recovering from this near-fatal experience, he spent many years sailing between Baltimore and South America, trading hides for machinery.[6]

Captain Creesy liked the tough but gentlemanly Laban enough to play chess with him during his precious free time.[7]

Laban was also a lot of time with the Lyon siblings, and fellow passengers couldn't help but notice that he was especially attentive to Sarah Lyon.

But there was still trouble ahead for *Flying Cloud*. The ship's carpenter reported that her mainmast was badly sprung at the base and could crack if put under too much pressure. Word spread, and the passengers fretted. "It is a pity, of course, it would not do to crowd on sail, and we cannot make the voyage as soon as we otherwise should," wrote one passenger. "Besides, the Capt. Fears we may lose the mast in passing that dreaded 'world's corner,' Cape Horn." Creesy weighed his choices and decided to keep the ship under a full press of sail, all the while keeping a careful eye on the mast. His best hope was to trust that Lieutenant Maury's course would save them valuable time and that Cape Horn would not hit them with a western gale that would topple the mainmast.[8]

Within twenty-one days, *Flying Cloud* swept past the equator. "[P]assengers have been on deck watching the lovely sunset," Sarah Bowman wrote in her journal. "[L]ong before the rich colours have faded from the clouds, the stars were out and our gaze was turned [to] the southern cross—Ah! How strange it seems—We are now going at the rate of eleven knots an hour . . . great speed for this latitude."[9]

Flying Cloud continued sailing along Maury's recommended route for finding the most favorable winds and currents. The sprung mainmast held, as did the repaired rigging. Then the gentle, sunny balm of the tropics soon gave way to gray seas and lowering skies. The passengers, still worrying whether the mainmast would hold, distracted themselves by playing games and reading in the warmth of the main saloon.

On the Fourth of July, everyone dressed in his or her Sunday best for the festivities on deck: cravats and suits for men, hoopskirts and bonnets for women, and white duck trousers and black straw hats for the sailors. "Descend we to the richly furnished cabin," Bowman wrote. "I must name the 'goodies' that crowd our table: roast turkey and chickens with oyster sauce, roast pig, boiled ham, all kinds of vegetables, English plum pudding, tarts, Blanc Mange, walnuts, filberts, almonds, raisins, oranges, apples, champaigne [*sic*], and Madeira in abundance."[10]

The crew had none of these treats, except perhaps for leftovers. Typical fare was rice, beans, potatoes, hardtack biscuits, and dried codfish (known among sailors as "Cape Cod turkey").[11] For them, the best they could generally hope for on a holiday was a "duff," made by boiling a bag of flour with butter, eggs, molasses, and perhaps some figs or other dried fruit to add some sweetness. Holiday duff was a sailor's sacred prerogative, for special occasions seldom brought rest for them. "This day was Christmas, but it brought us no holiday," Richard Henry Dana had written of his experience going around Cape Horn a decade earlier. "The only change was that we

213

had a 'plum duff' for dinner, and the crew quarreled with the steward because he did not give us our usual allowance of molasses to eat with it. He thought the plums would be a substitute for the molasses, but we were not to be cheated out of our rights in that way."

Incidents like these snowballed into simmering feuds and grudges among the crew. Overworked, underfed, and sexually repressed, clipper ship crews quickly grew sick of one another, fueling a cycle of paranoia and resentment: "Little wars and rumors," wrote Dana, "reports of things said in the cabin, misunderstanding of words and looks, apparent abuses—brought us into a condition in which everything seemed to go wrong. Every encroachment upon time allowed for rest appeared unnecessary. Every shifting of the studden sails was only to 'haze' the crew."[12]

Aboard *Flying Cloud,* the chasm between the well-heeled passengers and the hardworking crew did not go unnoticed. Nor did Captain Creesy's split personality. "The Capt. is an able seaman, no doubt," observed Sarah Bowman, "but I will not wrong my conscience by calling him a gentleman. He is overbearing and jealous of every attention bestowed by the passenger upon the Mate."[13]

At least two crew members were sick of Captain Creesy as well. Sometime after the ship's top-hamper fell into the sea, one of them got an auger—probably stealing it from the ship's carpenter's shop—went to the fo'c'sle, and drilled two neat holes through *Flying Cloud*'s thick oak planking, three feet above the waterline, on the port side. The other took a marlinspike and joined the two holes into one opening. With each plunge that *Flying Cloud* took into the heavy seas, a plume of water spurted into the crew's quarters, and then trickled down into the hold below. It would only be a matter of time before damage was done to Creesy's precious cargo. The two men then went back to their duties as if nothing happened.[14]

As Creesy guided his ship toward Cape Horn, he and his Ellen wondered what sort of weather would greet them. The worst would be a westerly gale, preventing *Flying Cloud* from making headway past what sailors called "Cape Stiff." Such a gale could be so strong that captains would have to furl most sails and heave to for days, even weeks at a time. In that circumstance, speed, of course, went by the board. The captain's only responsibility was keeping his ship afloat, his cargo dry, and his passengers and crew alive.

After almost a month on board, Sarah Bowman was starting to find the once amusing quirks of her fellow passengers rather annoying. One passenger, Francesco Wadsworth from New York, sat in the lounge reading racy books ("questionable French novels")— although she noted that he wasn't all bad; he sang Italian opera arias in a "rich, mellow voice." Then there was J. D. Townsend, a fast-talking nineteen-year-old who claimed to have an income of $3,000 a year and "talks big of his fast horse, etc., drinks Claret, Champaigne [*sic*], and Cherry Bounce as if he loved it."[15]Bowman found this boor's company more off-putting than that potent concoction of cherries, whiskey, and sugar.

Yet all of these petty disputes among the passengers and crew were mere distractions from the tremendous danger the entire ship's company faced as they surged toward the southern tip of South America. During the California Gold Rush, many ships did not survive the journey around Cape Horn, swamped as they were by heavy seas, or capsized by a sudden squall, or dashed onto the rocks in blinding snowstorms. The Boston clipper *John Gilpin* sailed right into an iceberg and sank rapidly. Miraculously, the crew scrambled into the lifeboats, to be picked up by a passing vessel.[16] The vast majority of those shipwrecked off Cape Horn were not so lucky. They froze to death or drowned in the furious sea, their ships vanishing without a trace. In his 1850 novel *White-Jacket*, Herman Melville wrote of the feared maritime obstacle: "And now, through drizzling fogs and vapours, and under damp, double-reefed top-sails, our wet-decked frigate drew nearer and nearer to the squally Cape. Was the descent of Orpheus, Ulysses, or Dante into Hell, one whit more hardy and sublime than the first navigator's weathering of that terrible Cape?"[17]

Those aboard *Flying Cloud* wondered whether their brand-new ship, already weakened from the dismasting accident, could survive the worst of Cape Stiff.

Far ahead of *Flying Cloud* was *N. B. Palmer*, which had left New York a month earlier, captained by Charles Low. The clipper had not had an easy passage either, battling rough weather and pushing forward against contrary winds. Passing a dismasted brig, Low decided not to stop. The disabled ship was "evidently abandoned for some time," wrote Low, and "there was nothing to be gained" by *N. B. Palmer* slowing to investigate further.[18] A boarding in mid-ocean would also cost valuable time.

Low's ship made a mediocre twenty-eight days to reach the equator. He blamed this not on *Palmer*'s design but on the bad conditions. "It was no fault of the ship but of the weather, that the passage was so much longer than my previous two voyages," Low wrote. "[T]he ship was all I could wish for, and much faster than any other ship I had ever sailed in, and a splendid sea boat in heavy weather."[19]

On July 3 *N. B. Palmer* reached Argentina's Isla de los Estados, located just to the east of Tierra del Fuego at the very southern tip of South America. The island, as Richard Henry Dana remembered it, was a barren pile of "girt with rocks and ice, with here and there, between rocks and broken hillocks, a little stunted vegetation of shrubs."[20] It was in these waters that as a young man, Nathaniel Palmer had hunted for seals in his small brig *Hero*, and eventually sailed south to be among the first people (if not the first) to sight the Antarctic continent. Now, three decades later, Palmer's protégé Captain Low surged toward Cape Horn in his namesake clipper ship, one of the finest examples of American maritime technology on the high seas.

Three days later, *N. B. Palmer* rounded Cape Horn. It had now been sixty-one days since her departure from New York. In his memoir, Low did not note any particularly bad weather on this passage around notorious Cape Stiff. But, like his mentor, he did not keep too much of a press of sail in risky conditions.

Once in the warm waters of the Pacific, *N. B. Palmer* picked up speed and headed northward. Despite the ship's wonderful performance on this second half of her voyage, Low must have felt a tinge of sadness when, somewhere off the coast of Central America, he sat down in the captain's cabin and recorded the entry for day ninety-six of the voyage. They would not be breaking *Surprise*'s record time to the straits of the Golden Gate.

San Francisco in 1851 was still a rough-and-ready place, its wood frame buildings rising ever higher up the steep slopes of Telegraph Hill. Even though a catastrophic fire had ripped through the city that spring, new buildings sprouted up everywhere. Prospectors from as far away as France, England, Australia, and China descended on the city, hoping to strike it rich in the gold fields. Hot on their heels were prostitutes, loafers, and thieves. Gambling dens lined the waterfront, including the notorious Bella Union, sometimes thronged with as many as a thousand gamblers trying their hands at roulette and card games.[21] Lavish to the point of gaudiness, its interior glowed bright as day from hundreds of flickering candles and whale oil lamps. At midnight, servers brought out four heaping breakfast spreads. Piles of gold dust sat on the gaming tables, next to knives and revolvers.

The wharf district teemed with sailors just liberated from their duties and San Franciscans there to enjoy the activity and see the ships. The harbor was always full of steamers and small craft. But the arrival of the clipper ships in the late summer and early fall brought a special sense of excitement. The paddlewheel steamers of the Pacific Mail and US Mail generally arrived on schedule, traveling at the predictable speed of their coal-fueled engines. But the clipper ships out of New York and Boston were dependent on the winds and had no set time of arrival. When a clipper glided regally into San Francisco Harbor, crowds ran down to North Beach to see her come in.

The rapid pace of shipbuilding evolution over the past few years had not been lost on San Francisco's burgeoning community of journalists. "[T]he discovery of our golden sands has done more in four years toward improvement in the style of shipbuilding than would have occurred from other general causes in half a century," boasted the *Daily Alta California*. The old ships had been "huge washing-tubs" which traveled "about as fast sideways as in any other direction." The new ships were as "graceful in their motions as a swan on a summer lake, and fleet as the cloud which is blown by the gale."[22] As the gold continued to flow out of California's fields and streams, the clippers kept coming from the eastern shipyards by the dozen, each more beautiful and beautifully named than the last: *Herald of the Morning*, *Whirlwind*, *Sunny South*, *Coeur de Lion*, *Witch of the Wave*. Under enormous pressure from their demanding clients, the shipbuilders experimented with a variety of forms not only to make their vessels faster but also to distinguish them from the growing pack of three-masted beauties. Most clippers had straight keels, although a few designers experimented with the drag keel, in which the stern had a deeper draft (depth) than the bow, a form popular with the old Baltimore clippers in their privateering and slaving days. To slice through the water at high speeds, some designers used a bow with a straight, nearly vertical stem, while others relied on a curved, or arched, forefoot that harkened back to the older packet ships.

By the spring of 1851, San Franciscans had already been treated to a string of exciting new arrivals. Most thrilling of all had been *Surprise*, arriving that March after a record-breaking passage of 96 days. On May 17, another big clipper, the *Sea Serpent*, had arrived in San Francisco after 115 days at sea. It was not the result that owner Grinnell, Minturn & Co. had hoped for, but *Sea Serpent*'s passage had been marred by bad damage in storms off Cape Horn and, much to the kid-gloved Captain Howland's fury, had been forced to put in to Valparaiso, Chile, for repairs.

Now, in late summer, the San Francisco crowd gathered to watch yet another great clipper arrive. On August 21 the *N. B. Palmer* sailed through the Golden Gate, 107 days out of New York.

Even if the passage had not been everything he'd wished, Captain Charlie Low was able to end this leg of the ship's maiden voyage with a spectacular feat of seamanship. The trouble began when the harbor pilot who would guide the ship to the wharf refused to do the job until the next day. A frustrated Captain Low was rowed ashore to meet with A. A. Low & Brother's agent, a Nantucketer named Frederick Coleman Sanford, who demanded why the ship was still lying at anchor, three miles off shore.

"The pilot refused to bring her any closer," Captain Low responded, no doubt gesticulating to the clipper bobbing in the distance.

"The ship must come up to the wharf," Sanford said.

There was only one thing left to do. Low went back to the ship and ordered all sails set, "skysail and all."

A ship's captain was never supposed to take the ship to her dock. That was the prerogative of the harbor pilot, with his deep knowledge of local tidal and underwater conditions. In addition to breaking all protocol, Captain Low was taking a big risk to the ship's safety so that he could start unloading that day. Yet he was confident in his own abilities. "As soon as I got near enough, I backed the main yard* and went along the wharf so easily that there was hardly a jar," Low recalled. It came so close to other ships that her flying jib boom struck the wheelhouse of the steamer *Senator*, wrenching two planks loose. The crowd assembled on the pier groaned but then cheered

---

* The lowermost yard on the main mast (second mast back from the bow), supporting the main sail.

loudly when *N. B. Palmer*'s crew tossed the lines to the waiting stevedores to make her fast.

"Well done!" Sanford shouted in disbelief.

Low was quite pleased with himself. "The prettiest piece of seamanship ever done in San Francisco," he joked. The harbor pilot was furious.

The regular crewmen received their wages and promptly went ashore. It would be more than six weeks until *N. B. Palmer* went to sea again, continuing her maiden voyage on to China. She would be sailing across the Pacific with her holds almost empty, as aside from gold, California was not producing much of interest for the Chinese market. By October 7, the ship had been loaded with three hundred tons of ballast, and Low had hired enough crew at $25 per month to make the dash across the Pacific to Hong Kong, where he would fill his ship with a full load of tea. To earn some additional revenue, Low also took aboard seventy-five corpses—the mortal remains of Chinese migrants—in wooden caskets. Hearing about gold in "Californ," thousands of Chinese men had flocked to San Francisco in search of a better life. But prospecting was a dangerous business. The dead bodies on board were going home for burial, their trip paid for by family or friends. Some shipowners couldn't pass on the opportunity to make a handsome profit from this sad task. "At the time captains received an eighth of money paid for a passage," Low wrote, "but dead bodies were considered freight. So one smart captain, to secure his passage money, loaded his cabin with corpses and called them passengers."[23]

Four years into the Gold Rush, there were already twenty thousand Chinese residents in San Francisco. A few merchants, such as Charlie's brother Abbot, welcomed the arrival of the Chinese. "As gleaners in the gold fields which our own people had deserted," he said, "as agriculturalists and horticulturalists . . . they were proving their value and importance to the development of the country." New arrivals from China offered "an abundant supply of cheap manual labor" and "a boundless opportunity of that vigorous State to advance in the useful arts."[24]

Whites in San Francisco did not see the Chinese as an asset but rather as competition. A year before *N. B. Palmer*'s arrival in San Francisco, the California legislature passed the Foreign Miners Tax, which exacted a $20-per-month tax on all foreign miners and specifically targeted the Chinese.[25] Newspapers caricatured Chinese immigrants as opium-smoking, pig-tailed, dirty, bucktoothed, dishonest rascals. Violence and discrimination against the West Coast's growing Chinese population would eventually lead to the federal Chinese Exclusion Act of 1882, which ended all Chinese immigration to the United States for more than sixty years.

Some Americans saw both slavery and anti-immigrant sentiments as antithetical to American democracy, especially in a place like California, which had been admitted to the union in 1850 as a "free state." But the Know Nothing Party, a coalition of white Protestant nativists, was gaining support among working-class Americans who feared newcomers, the Irish and the Chinese among them. "As a nation, we began by declaring that 'all men are created equal,'" an up-and-coming Illinois lawyer named Abraham Lincoln wrote his friend Joshua Speed about the growing political crisis. "We now practically read it 'all men are created equal, except negroes.' When the Know Nothings get control, it will read 'all men are created equal, except negroes, and foreigners, and Catholics.' When it comes to this, I should prefer emigrating to some country where they make no pretence [*sic*] of loving liberty—to Russia, for instance, where despotism can be taken pure, and without the base alloy of hypocracy [*sic*]."[26]

Yet a clipper ship captain such as Charles Low did not have time to worry about the country's future. What mattered to him were profit and speed. With her human and other cargo, *N. B. Palmer* cast off and set off across the Pacific for Hong Kong. It would be left to the other two clippers in the running, *Flying Cloud* and *Challenge*, to smash the ninety-six-day record *Surprise* had set in May in her passage from New York to San Francisco.

Proceeding to Cape Horn in a bad storm, Captain Creesy couldn't understand why there was so much water in the hold. *Flying Cloud* was brand new, her seams newly caulked, yet she was heeling sickeningly while under full sail. When the ship's carpenter went below on July 12, he found himself up to his waist in water that reeked of filth. Her pumps couldn't handle this kind of inflow. Most of the ship's precious cargo was safe, stowed above the water in the bilge, but if the source of the leak couldn't be found, and quickly, all of it would be ruined, and the only hope of saving the vessel would be to come about and make straight for Rio de Janeiro.

Eventually the carpenter found the source: a small hole, near the crew bunks in the fo'c'sle, clearly drilled with an auger. Creesy couldn't believe it: the lives of seventy-eight people—not to mention cargo worth more than $50,000 and a ship valued at $90,000— had deliberately been put in jeopardy. But the last thing the captain needed was to cause a panic. He appears to have kept this sabotage secret from the passengers, as Sarah Bowman made no mention of the incident in her journal.

Fortunately for Creesy, the two culprits had not been especially bright. One had been seen leaving the fo'c'sle with an auger—not exactly standard sailor equipment. A shipmate pointed out the offender, who had drilled the hole above his own bunk. Crewmates then ratted out his accomplice. Both were placed in irons and confined to the brig.[27]

The carpenter plugged the hole in the fo'c'sle, the crew set to work pumping out the hold, and *Flying Cloud* resumed her normal course southward toward Cape Horn. Amazingly, despite storms and sabotage, the ship seemed to be making excellent time.

*   *   *

As *Flying Cloud* surged ever southward, Captain Waterman of the much bigger *Challenge* could barely keep his ship's company together as she beat along the Brazilian coast, headed for Cape Horn. That he was running into the doldrums only added to his frustration.

Challenge had left New York a month after the *Flying Cloud*, but both captains knew that *Challenge* did not have to catch up to win: the real race was which ship would make the trip to San Francisco in less time. Waterman's bonus depended on a talented, hardworking crew—but that wasn't what Waterman got.

"They [the crew] would fight amongst themselves, cut, gouge, bite, and kept in a continual row," Waterman recalled later.[28] Even First Mate Douglass's lash did little to keep these men in line. They refused to work. Worse still, about a dozen were still lying in the sick bay, the victims of venereal disease and other maladies. The crimps truly had given Waterman the worst possible crew.

For the men who had little to no experience going aloft, the experience was terrifying. Climbing up the windward shrouds had to be done one foot or one hand at a time. Going out onto the yards to unfurl or take in sail required grace and balance, especially in rough seas, where the mast swung through a wide arc and the wind tore at the men's faces and hands. One slip, and down a sailor would plunge into the heaving seas, never to be seen again, or worse, smack onto the white pine decks, a pile of broken, bloody limbs. There was little the ship's captain—who usually doubled as ship's surgeon—could do except bury the man at sea.

When the wind did pick up, Waterman realized that his dream ship was not all she was cracked up to be. Not only was he cursed with a bad crew and a nasty first mate, but it was now apparent that he and the Griswolds had made *Challenge* too extreme for her own good. Their desire for sharpness and size had overridden Webb's skill as a naval architect. *Challenge*'s waterline was too hollow, her bows too sharp. Whenever a good puff of wind came along, a huge wave rose from her bow, indicating too much water resistance. Worse still, she moved through the water with a snappy, rather jolty motion, not with the easy roll of more full-bodied vessels.[29]

As *Challenge* made her way along the Brazilian coast, a sailor complained to First Mate Douglass that his belongings had been stolen. In a rage, the first mate ordered the entire ship's company, including those in the sick bay, to line up on deck and open their duffel bags.

It was not a captain's duty to mete out discipline unless it was absolutely necessary. As Douglass conducted the search, Captain Waterman stood out on the quarterdeck, took out his sextant, and started to shoot the sun to get the ship's position.

He then heard a yell from forward.

"Murder!"

Several of the crew jumped Douglass and threw him to the deck. One grabbed his throat. Another man slashed at his leg.

Waterman ran to Douglass's aid, dropping his sextant on the quarterdeck and grabbing an iron belaying pin as he ran along the main deck. He smashed each of the men tackling his first mate on the head.[30] Two of them dropped dead, their skulls split open. Several others scampered away, leaving Douglass bleeding on the deck.

A big man, Douglass got up, felt the gash in his thigh, and smiled with sick pleasure. "God damn their souls," he said. "I'm so damned glad the row occurred. I can lick them as much as I like, and they can't do anything with me when I get to California."[31]

Waterman and Douglass tied to the rail those who didn't get away. They would be dealt with later. One of the conspirators finally confessed to everything: the crew had planned to kill both Waterman and Douglass and sail the ship to Rio de Janeiro.

His leg bandaged by the ship's surgeon, Douglass grabbed a rope and flayed the backs of each of the seven men splayed out on the ship's railing. Blood spattered all over the deck. A bucket of salt water was then thrown on their tattered backs, and they howled in agony. Confident that the mutiny was over, Douglass sent them to the sick bay. Locking them up in the brig was out of the question. *Challenge* was already shorthanded, and they would be needed later when the ship rounded Cape Horn.

Douglass recovered from his wound. For the rest of the voyage, he kept a knife at his waist.[32]

The mutiny's ringleader, a sailor named Fred Birkenshaw, remained missing. *Challenge* was a big ship, but there were only so many places a man could hide, especially if he was deprived of food and water. Waterman was determined to find him.

But the captain had more pressing concerns. His worst nightmare was to get driven backward in his attempt to round Cape Horn, away from the Pacific and toward the southern tip of Africa, by a driving gale. "Turned on her heel by a fierce West Wind," Herman Melville wrote in *White-Jacket*, "many an outward-bound ship has been driven across the Southern Ocean to the Cape of Good Hope."[33]

Yet when *Challenge* tried to round Cape Horn, fierce weather struck hard. The clipper wallowed in a westerly gale for eighteen days. The footropes and sails became crusted in rough, skin-ripping ice. Three men tumbled from aloft and into the raging ocean. Chances of them surviving in such a gale were nil.

Two sailors still refused to bend to Waterman's will. One was the agile smart aleck George Lessing, whom Waterman nicknamed "the Dancing Master" for his ability to avoid blows from his first mate. When Lessing refused to go aloft, claiming illness, Douglass grabbed the man by the hair and dunked him into the frigid water that surged across *Challenge*'s deck.

"I think we'll baptize him," Waterman supposedly told his first mate.[34]

Gasping for breath, Lessing said he was drowning, which only steeled Douglass's resolve to punish him more. Soaked and shivering, Lessing was carried to the sick bay, now crammed with almost twenty of the ship's sixty-four-man crew. He died a few days later.

Douglass's next victim was an Italian known only as "Pawpaw," who could barely speak English and didn't own a pair of shoes. Several days on, still in the midst of the gale, he refused to go aloft, spluttering in Italian and pointing to his bleeding feet. Douglass beat him senseless and then added a fist to the ribcage for good measure. According to one witness, Waterman took a bit of pity on the Italian and served him water and a glass of wine. Yet wine or no wine, Pawpaw also died. His shipmates sewed up Pawpaw's corpse in canvas and threw it over the side.

Like the captain of the fictional *Flying Dutchman*, Waterman had sold his soul to Satan in exchange for extraordinary passages. Now, in the fury of a Cape Horn gale, it seemed the $10,000 bonus for getting his ship into San Francisco in fewer than ninety days was slipping from his grasp.

The angels smiled upon *Flying Cloud* as she made her way around the southern tip of South America.

"I shall sleep better tonight than usual," passenger Sarah Bowman wrote in her journal as the ship rounded Cape Horn in heavy seas and driving sleet, but without incident. "In the distance, the snowy mountains and frost covered rocks look like turreted castle forts and battlements, a soft blue haze descends and gives really a charm to the scene."

The much-feared westerly gale, powerful enough to drive the *Flying Cloud* backward or force her captain to steer toward Antarctica in search of favorable winds, did not materialize. The lack of terrifying weather seemed nothing short of a miracle.

"The Capt. says we should have such luck once in five hundred times," Sarah wrote.[35]

Not that the rounding of the cape was completely idyllic. Captain

Creesy noted in his journal on July 23: "hard Gale with much rain and sleet. Ship shipping much water bad sea running." At eight in the evening, Creesy took out his spyglass and saw rocky Cape Horn itself rearing up out of a boiling sea. "The whole coast covered with snow," he wrote, "wild ducks very numerous."[36]

On July 30, a week after passing Cape Horn and heading to the North, the ship caught the southeastern trade winds. It was then that *Flying Cloud* finally got her first true burst of extreme speed. Captain Creesy ordered all sails set for the first time in days, including the winglike studden sails that projected out from the yards of all three masts. Pushed along her spread of lily-white canvas, the ship raced along.

"Fresh breezes fine Wr.," Creesy wrote in his log. "All sails set At 2 P.M. wind SE. At 6 squally in lower and Top Gallant studding sails 7 in Royals At 2 A.M. in the fore Top Mast Studding Sail Latter parts strong Gales & high seas running Ship very wet fore & aft . . . During the squalls 18 knots of line was not sufficient to measure her rate of speed Top Gallant sails set."[37]

Earlier clippers such as *Sea Witch* had achieved speeds of 15 knots in very short bursts. Now, only four years later, *Flying Cloud* was achieving that speed for days on end. Twenty-six days, in fact, averaging, according to Matthew Fontaine Maury's later calculations, "the enormous rate of 15-7/12 knots, or eighteen statute miles per hour."

The ship complained, the rigging shrieking under the strain of more than ten thousand square yards of taut canvas. Everyone on board hoped the sprung mainmast and the rigging repaired at sea would hold. They did, against all odds. On one remarkable day, *Flying Cloud* shattered all records for deep-sea sailing ships—at least according to Creesy's calculations—by sailing 374 nautical miles.

Just as *Flying Cloud* approached the California coast, the winds died, leaving the graceful clipper rolling in the long Pacific swells. "Baffling and unsteady winds," Captain Creesy wrote in his log. He was angry not just at the weather but also at his first mate, whom he'd suspended from duty a few weeks earlier for general incompetence and for "long neglect of duty." The passengers on *Flying Cloud* fretted as their ship lay dead in the water, her once-taut sails slatting in the feeble gusts. Yet the wind picked up again on August 29, and *Flying Cloud* moved onward toward San Francisco. Two days later, guided by Eleanor Creesy's calculations and Matthew Fontaine Maury's charts, *Flying Cloud* reached the Farallon Islands, a series of jagged rock outcroppings that guarded the entrance to San Francisco Bay. The night was pitch-black, and to avoid running aground, Creesy noted in his log, "hove the ship to for Day light at 6 made South Farrlones [*sic*] bearing N E ½ E."

At seven o'clock, as dawn broke over the red-and-green-dappled coastline, a schooner drew up alongside *Flying Cloud*, carrying a pilot who would guide the ship through the Golden Gate and into San Francisco Harbor.

For several weeks, as the ship sped along at full clip, the crew had been hard at work getting the *Flying Cloud* ready for her triumphant arrival. They painted her weather-beaten sides jet black, touched up the gold boot topping line that accented her hull, tarred her rigging, scrubbed the decks and polished the brass until it gleamed in the morning sun.

Now her moment had come. *Flying Cloud* sailed past the former Spanish fortress known as the Presidio, and then past the Marin headlands, and up the bay to the docks. The crew then unbent and stowed all sails before a steam tug assisted her to her berth. It was September 1, 1851. Captain Creesy's log entry for the day was as laconic as ever: "Anchored in San Francisco Harbor at 11h 30m A.M. after a passage of 89 days 21 hours."[38]

The operator of the semaphore tower atop Telegraph Hill cranked the two wooden arms to the signal for a "ship": one plank pointed diagonally upward; the other pointed diagonally downward, oriented to the right. Hundreds of people swarmed out of the homes, offices, warehouses, and saloons of the city and clustered along North Beach to watch the swan-like clipper arrive at her anchorage. Aboard ship, Sarah Bowman was exuberant about their safe and speedy arrival. "Everyone here is talking about our passage," she wrote, "the quickest ever known." A cavalcade of clerks was already stampeding toward the waterfront, eager to get their hands on the ship's cargo and sell it for high prices and great profit.

From the ship's mizzenmast flew a huge American flag marked with thirty stars. It was already out-of-date: Congress had adopted the thirty-one-star flag, welcoming Wisconsin into the union on July 4, which the passengers and crew of *Flying Cloud* had celebrated off the rainy coast of Brazil.

Flying Cloud docked next to the slightly smaller but no less elegant *N. B. Palmer*, which had arrived in San Francisco ten days earlier, and was still in port preparing for her leg-to-China run. Low made no mention of the *Cloud*'s record in his recollections of the *N. B. Palmer*'s stay in San Francisco. Perhaps the young captain was steeling himself to beat *Flying Cloud* across the Pacific.

Sarah, Whitney, and Ellen Lyon disembarked for a joyful reunion with their father, who had arrived via steamship and the Panama Isthmus a few weeks earlier. Sarah had wonderful news for her father: the dashing Laban Coffin had proposed to her on board the ship, and she had accepted.

Also waiting for them was Reuben Boise, who had traveled down from Oregon Territory to meet his fiancée Ellen, Sarah's sister. The sisters settled into their hotel rooms and then explored the burgeoning city. Wedding shopping proved daunting: $18 for a silk bonnet, $15 for a silk dress, $4 for garter boots. "Parisian elegance," Sarah sighed at the inventory of the San Francisco clothing stores. "It is a *fast* country."

Among their shopping companions was Eleanor Creesy. Sarah wrote that she "has been very kind to us; indeed, she has taken as much interest in us as if we had been her own sisters, helped us sew, been shopping with us; in fact, done everything for us that our own mother could have done."

Captain Josiah Creesy officiated at the marriage of Reuben Boise and Ellen Lyon on September 17. It took place on deck, under *Flying Cloud*'s swaying yards and rigging. Eleanor Creesy was there, of course. "I love her dearly," her sister Sarah wrote of *Flying Cloud*'s chief navigator, "and shall regret very much the day that calls us to part."[39] Laban Coffin and Sarah Lyon were also married aboard the ship, two weeks after Reuben and Ellen's ceremony.

Captain Creesy then approached Coffin with a strange request: given his extensive experience at sea, would he be willing to serve as his first mate for the rest of the voyage? Coffin accepted the offer from his old chess partner, and Sarah naturally decided to accompany him across the Pacific.

That day came on October 20, when Eleanor and her husband sailed for Hong Kong to pick up a cargo of tea for sale in New York. This leg of the voyage earned *Flying Cloud*'s owners $45,555.75 in freight fees.[40]

The news of *Flying Cloud*'s record-breaking passage reached New York via the paddlewheel steamer, as the first transcontinental telegraph would not be up and running for another ten years. The ship's owners were thrilled about the new record, a great selling point for *Flying Cloud*'s future voyages, but what they really wanted to know was the return on their investment. When Francis Hathaway, probably the principal advocate for adding clipper ships to the Grinnell, Minturn fleet, heard about *Flying Cloud*'s triumphant arrival, he anxiously wrote his agents in San Francisco about the condition of the cargo. Creesy had told his employers about the sabotage attempt and the partial flooding of the cargo hold. Incredibly, the only goods damaged by the sloshing seawater were a shipment of steel shovels, boxes of brandied peaches, and some spoiled casks of wine and brandy. The ship had even succeeded in bringing fresh butter, which was scarce in San Francisco. One newspaper raved about the spring butter produced by A. Vandyke of Roxbury, New York, calling it "sweet as a nut" and "from the hands of the milkmaid."

"You will feel the *Flying Cloud* has indeed 'walked the waters like a thing of life,'" wrote the giddy reporter.[41]

What shipbuilder Donald McKay thought about *Flying Cloud's* incredible performance is unrecorded. But he did once explain his design philosophy thus: "I never yet built a vessel that came up to my own ideal. I saw something in each ship which I desired to improve upon."[42] For him, then, *Flying Cloud* was not the perfect ship. She was only the beginning.

McKay was already hard at work constructing an extreme clipper ship bigger even than the 1,800-ton *Flying Cloud* or the 2,000-ton *Challenge*: *Flying Fish*, which would be ready for delivery to Sampson & Tappan (owners of McKay's first clipper, *Stag Hound*) by November. To make his ship stand out, McKay called for *Flying Fish* to be painted in green and gold rather than the customary black. Her skipper would be Bostonian Edward Nickels, who was famous for hosting lavish dinners when he was in port[43] and who boasted that no ship he commanded had ever been "crawled up to or passed."[44]

McKay's rival William Webb, who built the *Challenge*, was also busy with a new clipper: only half the size of Waterman's huge dream ship but far more economical to operate. Her name was *Swordfish*, and her commander would be David S. Babcock, a Stonington, Connecticut, boy who was also none other than Captain Nathaniel Palmer's brother-in-law.

Both the captains of *Flying Fish* and *Swordfish* were hoping to beat *Flying Cloud's* record.

But where was the *Challenge*?

* * *

Nine days after *Flying Cloud* set sail across the Pacific in October 1851, a gigantic clipper ship passed through the Golden Gate, flying a distress flag. When the harbor pilot came aboard, he saw eight men chained together on deck. Found deep in the hold was crew ringleader Fred Birkenshaw, surviving on scraps that his fellow sailors had passed along.

Perhaps the pilot's men spread the news of this cruelty to their mates. By the time the *Challenge* approached the quay, an unruly mob was waiting for Douglass and Captain Waterman. As the ship tied up and stevedores began unloading her cargo, Douglass jumped into one of *Challenge*'s launches, rowed through the mass of abandoned hulks anchored in the bay, and disappeared into the hills.

His flight failed. A local sheriff apprehended him within a few days. He was found drunk in a horse-drawn wagon bound for Monterey. "I whipped 'em and I'll whip 'em again," Douglass snarled. He also demanded that the sheriff's men kill him rather than lock him in jail. "Well, gentlemen, if you want to hang me, here's a pretty tree," he supposedly said. "Do it like men."[45] He was charged with murder.

Waterman felt he had no need to apologize for anything. He would face justice head-on. Tired and weather beaten, but still bright-eyed and defiant, he strode off the ship, down the gangway, and into the mob, which parted before him, surely taken aback by this little mariner's audacity. Waterman made his way to the Alsop Building, headquarters of the Griswold firm's agent. There he debriefed the representative on the terrible voyage. Although *Challenge* did not make it to San Francisco in less than ninety days, that Waterman had completed the trip in about the same time as Captain Low had done in *N. B. Palmer* a few months earlier—with a much more fractious, inexperienced, and sick crew—was a remarkable feat. Waterman did not shy away from telling the press that he was "not satisfied with the ship's record on this maiden voyage," and that this "noble sea boat . . . had no chance during the entire voyage to try her speed."[46]

The journalists who came aboard *Challenge* were horrified at the sight of so many sick and injured men. As soon as the crew members opened their mouths to tell stories of Waterman's brutality, the reporters also knew that this was fantastic copy. "The ship *Challenge* has arrived, and Capt. Waterman, her commander, has also. But where are nine of his crew?" asked the *California Courier*. "And where is he and his guilty mate? The accounts given of Captain Waterman toward his men, if true, make him one of the most inhumane monsters of this age."

Despite the undoubted protestations of the remaining officers, the reporters went into the ship's fo'c'sle and sick bay. There they found the most lurid, ghastly scenes of human suffering: "The scene at this time on board of the ship beggars all description," the *Courier* continued. "Five of them are mangled and bruised in the most shocking manner. One poor fellow died today, and five others, it is expected, will soon be in the embrace of death. One of the men now lying on his deathbed has been severely injured in his genitals, by a kick from this brute in human form. Had these poor men been put in a den with bears and panthers, they could not have been much more inhumanely and shockingly maimed."[47]

By the next day, when the papers hit the streets of San Francisco, what had happened aboard America's newest and biggest clipper ship had become the talk of the town. Within a month, thanks to William Henry Aspinwall's rapid mail steamship service between California and New York, the star-crossed voyage of the *Challenge* was national news. Not since the publication of Richard Henry Dana's *Two Years Before the Mast* twelve years earlier had the shipping business faced so much public scrutiny.

The concerned citizens needed a scapegoat. On November 1 two thousand angry men marched to the Griswold offices and demanded that Waterman come out from hiding. When the captain refused, the seething mob broke down the front door with crowbars and pickaxes. Waterman fled the office by climbing to the top floor and jumping to the roof of an adjoining building. The vigilante leaders promptly seized Captain John Land, *Challenge*'s new captain, who had commanded the revolutionary *Rainbow* on her maiden voyage six years before and hadn't even yet set foot aboard his next command.[48] Then, according to Captain Arthur Clark's version of events, they debated whether to "shoot, drown, or hang him in place of Captain Waterman."[49]

Next, the mayor of San Francisco, a tough-talking former Kentucky boatman named Charles Brenham, showed up with members of the Committee on Vigilance, the city's de facto police force. With dozens of armed men backing him up, Brenham ordered the mob to disperse. Otherwise, he supposedly yelled, "I will put every damned one of you in jail!"[50] The mob murmured angrily but then scattered. Still cornered, Robert Waterman turned himself over to the authorities for protective custody. He demanded a public trial to prove his innocence.

On December 1 the Griswold brothers saw their proud family name splashed across the pages of the *New York Times*. The paper reported that one month before, there had been a "serious disturbance which occurred at San Francisco immediately after the arrival of the *Challenge*, growing out of the severity and cruelty charged to have been exercised by the captain and mate towards the seamen." The paper then reprinted a section of the *Alta California*'s coverage of the *Challenge*'s arrival, noting that ten of the clipper's crew had been killed during the voyage and that "there were many rumors afloat respecting the above mentioned affair."[51]

The captains who met at New York's Astor House bar also discussed the possible fallout from Captain Waterman's trial. So did shipowners such as Moses Grinnell and Warren Delano, who surely spoke about it over brandy and cigars in their townhouses.

No one knows what the Griswold brothers thought.

Captain Creesy was happily oblivious to all of this, as his ship raced across the Pacific.

CHAPTER 13

FRIGHTFUL TO LOOK ALOFT:

SOVEREIGN OF THE SEAS

*No more beautiful sight can be imagined than a morning at sea,
with these magnificent vessels racing in mid-ocean, perhaps two or
three of them in sight at once; the sun rising amidst golden clouds;
the dark blue sea flecked with glistening white caps; long, low
black hulls cleaving a pathway of sparkling foam; towering masts,
and yards covered with snowy canvas which bellies to the crisp
morning breeze as if sculptured in marble; the officers alert and
keen for the contest.*[1]

—Captain Arthur Hamilton Clark

The trial of Robert Waterman and James Douglass took place at the
US District Courthouse in San Francisco, and lasted four months.
It was a media circus, with reporters and curious observers cram-
ming the balconies of the rickety structure. The witnesses gave con-
tradictory, tangled testimony about the entire voyage: the attempted
mutiny, the knife assault on Douglass, and the alleged beatings and
deaths of Pawpaw, Lessing "the Dancing Master," and other crew
members at the hands of the captain and first mate.

Amidst the storm and fury of the press, Waterman remained unrepentant. (Although he did send $500 to the widow of one of the

men who fell from aloft, along with a sympathy note.[2]) The whole affair, he insisted, had been whipped up out of nothing when *Challenge*'s crew spread "slanderous falsehoods and outlandish stories to the newspapers" as part of their scheme to cover up their own guilt in the mutiny. For him, as for all clipper captains, the primary job was to ensure the arrival of his employer's ship and cargo as quickly and safely as possible. In his mind, he had been dealt a lousy hand by the crimps, and had hired Douglass because such a bully was the only kind of officer able to whip a diseased, inexperienced, and surly group of men into shape. What bothered Waterman the most was that due to bad seamanship and uncooperative weather, *Challenge* never had a chance to show her true top speed. Although a rich man, the loss of the $10,000 bonus still stung.

In February 1852 Judge Ogden Hoffman Jr., a Columbia-educated jurist appointed by President Millard Fillmore to bring some semblance of judicial order to San Francisco, admonished the jury to "weigh carefully the portion of the testimony touching on the state of discipline and behavior of the crew at the time the offense is alleged to have been committed and whether under a consideration of all circumstances, as detailed by witnesses, a reasonable man would have cause to fear personal danger or be deprived of the command of the ship and whether this state of affairs warned the committal of an assault like the one charged in the indictment."[3]

The jury came back hopelessly deadlocked, and so Waterman emerged from the ordeal triumphant. He was effectively exonerated on all charges, save for the cruel treatment of one crew member, for which he was fined $400—a paltry sum for a man who was busy plowing his considerable personal wealth into California real estate. (Like Creesy, Waterman probably owned 3/32 of his ship.) As for Douglass, he was out $250 for the murder of Pawpaw and $50 for assaulting the ship's carpenter. The mutineers were set free.[4]

Waterman never went to sea again. He and his wife, Cordelia, settled permanently on a ranch in northern California's Suisun Valley, where they cultivated eucalyptus trees from seeds imported from Australia. The hope was that wood from the drought-resistant tree could be used for shipbuilding. "For a person who has some capital and is willing to wait for returns," touted one newspaper, "there is a pretty chance to make a fortune in the growing of gum trees."[5] Unfortunately for Waterman and other cultivators, the Australian wood proved too gnarly for any practical use and no match for the stands of white oak on the East Coast.

Although permanently "on the beach," Bully Bob Waterman still took pride in the fact that while he may have lost men, he had never lost a sail or a spar. And the record he set while in command of *Sea Witch* several years earlier—seventy-four days from Hong Kong to London—remained as yet unsurpassed.

There would be other major races between clippers in the next few years. In the fall of 1851, as news of *Flying Cloud*'s new eighty-nine-day, twenty-one-hour record trickled back east, Donald McKay and his New York rival William H. Webb unveiled their newest contenders for the dash to the Golden Gate.

If the contest among *N. B. Palmer*, *Flying Cloud*, and *Challenge* had been informal, the one between McKay's *Flying Fish* and Webb's *Swordfish* was a true race on the high seas: six days after *Flying Fish* sailed from Boston, *Swordfish* departed from New York in hot pursuit. By latitude 50 degrees south, just past the stormy tip of South America, *Swordfish* had romped past her Yankee rival, and on February 10, 1852, she reached San Francisco first. Yet to her captain's consternation, he had fallen short of *Flying Cloud*'s record, by a mere twenty-four hours. Ten days later, *Flying Fish* sailed through the Golden Gate.

In late 1852 *Flying Fish* raced again from New York to San Francisco, this time against the clippers *Wild Pigeon* and *Trade Wind*. To create as fair a race as possible, each master was provided with a copy of Matthew Fontaine Maury's *Explanations and Sailing Directions to Accompany the Wind and Current Charts*. Donald McKay's *Flying Fish*, again under the command of Edward M. Nickels, emerged victorious with a fantastic run of ninety-two days and four hours—but still fell three days short of *Flying Cloud*'s best run. If her captain had not disregarded Maury's advice to sail as close to Brazil's Cape St. Roque as possible to avoid the doldrums, he might have broken the old record.

From the safety of the US Naval Observatory in Washington, Maury rejoiced in these new feats of navigation. He estimated that his charts alone saved ships an average of thirty-five days in the journey from New York to California.[6]

Yet what American clipper ship owners were really hoping for was an international derby that pitted the Stars and Stripes against the Union Jack. Scarcely two years after the *London Times* declared, "We want fast vessels for the long voyages which otherwise will fall into American hands," the British were prepared to challenge their "gigantic, unshackled rival" with clipper ships of their own.[7]

In August 1851 Captain Joseph Gordon of Delano's *Memnon* knew his would be a special passage out of Hong Kong. Also departing Hong Kong for Liverpool that summer was one of Abbot Low's ships, the *Surprise*. Both clippers were aiming to beat the ninety-seven-day record set by Low's *Oriental* the previous year. They were sailing against the monsoon from China to London's West India Docks, to bring the season's first crop of tea to the British markets and sell it for the highest possible price.

Alongside the trim American clippers were their bulkier British cousins, still modeled on the full-bodied warships of the Royal Navy. Yet right in the American *Memnon*'s wake would sail a new creation completed by the Liverpool firm Taylor & Potter that same year. Her name was *Chrysolite*.

Word of the new American flyers had rattled British merchants even before *Oriental*'s first arrival at London's West India Docks in December 1850, after her record-breaking ninety-seven-day voyage from Canton. "British sea captains must have seen the American clipper ships in the ports of China," observed Captain Arthur Clark, "or perhaps an Indiaman in the lone southern ocean may have been lying almost becalmed on the long heaving swell, lurching and slatting the wind out of her baggy hemp sails, while her officers and crew watched an American clipper as she swept past, under a cloud of canvas, curling the foam along her keen, slender bow. But when these mariners returned home and related what they had seen, their yarns were doubtless greeted with a jolly, good-humored smile of British incredulity."[8]

British merchants could meet such tales with incredulity no more, and pride went hand-in-hand with profit. For her first trip to London, *Oriental*'s holds were packed with what A. A. Low & Brother loaded at a rate of six pounds sterling per ton, while the bulkier British ships that had ridden at anchor at Whampoa beside her got in later to London and were forced to settle for three pounds ten per ton.[9]

After taking off the *Oriental*'s lines while she was in dry dock, the British quickly built their own response. Compared with the big American clippers, *Chrysolite* was a small ship: 150 feet long, 26 feet wide, and only of 570 tons.[10] By August 1851, she had made her way to Hong Kong and was ready to sail for home. Her passage would make this seasonal run the first international tea race, a maritime contest between England and her "unshackled rival."

With a full cargo of tea, Delano's thoroughbred hurried through the South China Sea, as Captain Gordon did his best to outrun *Memnon*'s British foe. On either September 14 or 16 (accounts vary), *Memnon* passed through the Gaspar Strait, a two-mile stretch of water between the Dutch East Indies islands of Belitung and Bangka. Bounded by shoals on both sides, its five-knot current shifted with the monsoon, making it even more treacherous. Pirates lurked off shore in small boats, lying in wait for a wreck.

As she wended her way through the strait, *Memnon*'s crew could hear chattering birds and screeching monkeys coming from the jungles that were only a stone's throw away from their ship. According to one account, the first mate told Captain Gordon that his ship was getting perilously close to shore. Gordon snapped back that he knew what he was doing. Ten minutes later, *Memnon*'s coppered bottom crunched onto the rocks. The pirates pounced, rowing toward the listing clipper at full speed, bellowing in triumph as they drew near. As they clambered up one side of the ship, the crew—including Captain Gordon and his wife—escaped in the lifeboats on the other side, hoisted sail, and set a course for Singapore, three hundred miles away.[11]

Warren Delano's *Memnon*—the first clipper to sail around Cape Horn to California, and a brainchild of the great John Willis Griffiths—was stripped of her valuable cargo and fittings within hours. The broken hulk was left to disintegrate on the shores of the Dutch East Indies.

Gordon and his crew made it back safely to America, but *Memnon* was out of the race. Warren Delano would have to wait to see whether his friend Abbot Low could preserve America's pride. Luckily for him, *Memnon* was almost certainly insured.

It wasn't until January that the results were in. On January 3, 1852, the *London Illustrated News* crowed gleefully that the *Chrysolite* had reached Liverpool with a sailing time of 104 days.[12] *Oriental*'s ninety-seven-day Hong Kong-to-London record set two years before still remained untouched, but the British were catching up.

Delano must have smarted from the loss of his prized vessel, but he remained confident of the American clipper ship's superiority on the China route. It appears that he retained stakes in some of Low's clippers, for that same January, a group calling itself the American Navigation Club challenged all British clipper ship owners—including their old Canton colleagues at Jardine, Matheson & Company—to a formal race from London or Liverpool to China and back. The American syndicate was top-heavy with the old "Canton bachelors" who'd made their fortunes in China, including Delano, John Murray Forbes, and the Russell & Company patriarch Thomas Handasyd Perkins, now in his mideighties.

The challenge was publicly announced in the *London Illustrated News*, with the following conditions:

> One ship to be entered by each of the party [*sic*], and to be named within a week of the start. These ships to be modelled [*sic*], commanded, and officered entirely by citizens of the United States and Great Britain, respectively . . . The challenged party may name the size of the ships, not under 800 nor over 1,200 American registered tons; the weight and measurements which shall be carried each way; the allowance for short weight or oversize.[13]

As an imprimatur of the Navigation Society's credentials, the challenge ended with: "reference may be made to Messrs. Baring Bros. & Co. for further particulars." The timing of this announcement was probably more than coincidence. By then, the august bank had taken on its first American partner: none other than Russell Sturgis, Warren Delano's first boss in China, who had settled in London rather than return to Hong Kong.

The proposed blue-water derby, the first of its kind in history, would be regulated in the same manner as the races of the Royal Yacht Squadron—the prestigious British yacht club at Cowes Castle on the Isle of Wight—where the cream of the British aristocracy competed with one another in private, custom-built racing boats. The previous year, the schooner yacht *America*, built along clipper lines and owned by a syndicate of New York merchants, had arrived uninvited at Cowes. John Cox Stevens, one of *America*'s co-owners, challenged the gentlemen of the Royal Yacht Squadron to a £10,000 winner-take-all ($50,000) wager to any yacht that could beat his ship. After much hemming and hawing, Royal Yacht Squadron allowed *America* to race in the final competition of the season: a fifty-three-mile sprint around the Isle of Wight.

America swept past the finish line nearly twenty minutes ahead of *Aurora*, her closest competitor.

In disbelief, the British sailors in hot pursuit hollered, "Is the *America* first?"

"Yes," came the reply.

"What's second?"

"Nothing."[14]

The British were outraged.

The American Navigation Society hoped to repeat this victory, only this time with big clipper ships sailing from England to China and back. Confident of their vessels' superiority, the Delano-Perkins-Forbes syndicate gave the British clipper ship owners the option of having a fourteen-day head start. The *Flying Cloud* would be excluded from the competition, as she was six hundred tons over the limit, but the Low clippers could enter.

There was no response from the British shipowners. To entice them, the syndicate then upped its stakes from £10,000 to £20,000.

Eager for the keen public interest that such a race would generate, the *London Daily News* published an editorial urging the British to accept the challenge. Then in October, the British magazine *Bell's Life in London* ran its own piece about the proposed race: "The limit of time is now expiring, and it is with no little disappointment that a letter received from the head of the eminent banking house of Baring & Co. . . . had to report no inquiry as to the proposition." Clearly disappointed, the writer added, "The Americans want a match, and it reflects somewhat upon our chivalry not to accommodate them."[15] The race never occurred. No British ship came close to shattering *Oriental's* ninety-seven-day run from Canton to London. According to Captain Arthur Clark, "No reason was ever given for the nonacceptance of the challenge, though the inference seems obvious."[16]

The Americans were left to compete with themselves. And they did so with a vengeance during the summer of 1852, with bigger and more heavily sparred vessels operated by a growing number of shipping firms. Out of all of them, A. A. Low & Brother remained preeminent in terms of its profitability and global reach. However, no amount of size or speed could convince Abbot Low or his partners to buy a ship built by Donald McKay. Revolutionaries in the China trade, they were conservative when it came to the California Gold Rush. A Low-owned China clipper was no longer the fastest to San Francisco, but they were generally faster on the tea route from China to New York. As a business proposition, men such as Low felt that a big McKay clipper like *Flying Cloud*, no matter how fast, was too expensive to sail and maintain in the long-term.

Low and his friends had other uses for their hard-earned capital. They were ultimately proved right.

In the winter of 1852, Captain Creesy was cruising the Indian Ocean in *Flying Cloud*, heading home with a cargo full of China goods bound for the Grinnell, Minturn & Company warehouses. He and Eleanor spied another ship on the horizon and closed in. She turned out to be an outbound cargo vessel from Anjer in the Dutch East Indies, a port where fresh provisions were available. Creesy asked her captain for the latest newspapers in exchange for fresh vegetables, fruit, and fowl.

As *Flying Cloud* sailed on, hens and capons cackling in her chicken coop, Creesy opened one of the New York papers, by now several months old, and read the following announcement:

Captain Creesy of the ship *Flying Cloud*—it will be seen by the telegraph news in another column that the gallant sailor is no more.
Two days after sailing from San Francisco, bound to China, he
died, and the ship proceeded in charge of the mate. In every scene
of a sailor's life "with skill superior glowed his daring mind"—his
dauntless soul "rose with the storm and all its dangers shared." But
now he rests from his toils, regardless of his triumphs. Peace to his
manes.[17]

Flying Cloud made it from Canton to New York in a very respectable
ninety-four days. Many of those on the pier must have been startled
to see Captain Creesy step off the ship and head toward the Astor
House, looking quite the picture of health, his wife at his side.

Josiah and Eleanor Creesy were showered with honors upon
Flying Cloud's arrival in New York, her first time in the city since
setting the eighty-nine-day record to San Francisco six months before. An elated Moses Grinnell ordered copies of Captain Creesy's
log printed in gold letters on white silk and distributed them to
his friends and associates. Curious New Yorkers visiting the Astor
House got a chance to see a display of the *Flying Cloud*'s fids (the
square wooden blocks used to support the ship's topmast). They had
been reduced to such relics because they had been so badly mashed
by force of the Cape Horn winds—and Captain Creesy's ruthless
seamanship.[18]

On May 23, 1852, Captain Charlie Low sailed *N. B. Palmer* out
of New York on her second voyage around the world. This time he
was determined to beat *Flying Cloud,* which had departed several
days ahead of him on her second voyage to California. And now he,
too, had company at sea: his new wife, Sarah Maria Tucker Low.
Two hundred of Sarah's friends and family had attended the couple's
wedding two weeks earlier. The marriage had almost encountered
a legal hitch: "I was a little put out when my bride was about to
go downstairs," Low remembered, "for the minister then asked for

the marriage license. I was never married before, and knew nothing about licenses, and no one had informed me that it was necessary to have one." Charles tracked down the Salem town clerk, who, luckily, was at home and gave him the marriage license. Once that formality had been taken care of, Charlie found himself standing around for two hours, "shaking hands and receiving the good wishes and congratulations of the company."

Yet Charlie and Sarah Low were not off on a conventional honeymoon. It would be a working one, and his wife's introduction to life at sea. "The next day," Low wrote, "we left for Brooklyn to prepare for a wedding tour around the world."

Nineteen-year-old Sarah must have marveled at the luxurious quarters of *N. B. Palmer*, resplendent with gleaming exotic woods, tufted sofas, and shimmering crystal ware. As a young woman who had never been to sea, she, like Catherine Delano before her, would have been unnerved by the unfamiliar sounds: the shouts of the mate, the stomping of feet, the flapping of the sails, and the shrieking of ropes and blocks, as well as the odors wafting from the galley and the bilge. Yet by the time the deck started to sway under her feet, she demonstrated the same fearlessness on board the ship as she had when she got up to sing in front of her husband-to-be.

Charlie Low admitted that taking a wife to sea was a "great lottery."

"A wife may be seasick all the voyage," he wrote, "or she may be very timid and afraid of a squall or breeze of wind, which makes it very uncomfortable for the husband as well as her herself." And then there was possibility of violence or death: illness, a sailor falling from aloft, a man overboard, a flogging, or even a mutiny.

Sarah knew that a clipper was to be her home for the next year and made the best of it. She would have some company other than her husband: in addition to a regular crew of about fifty, *N. B. Palmer* sailed with twenty passengers bound for China. That first morning at sea, all the passengers remained in their bunks, seasick and miserable. Sarah and Charlie enjoyed their breakfast alone at the big, swaying table.

The following day, *N. B. Palmer* hit rough weather. A group of frightened passengers showed up at the captain's cabin. When asked if there was any danger, Sarah responded confidently, "I don't know. My husband is on deck."

"There was no other comfort from her," Charlie noted, "and it was a great comfort for me."

On July 1, as *N. B. Palmer* ran before the wind off the coast of South America, Captain Low climbed to the top of the mizzen, took out his spyglass, and spotted sails on the horizon. He figured it could only be *Flying Cloud*, the fastest clipper on the high seas—or at least around Cape Horn. Low had, in fact, beaten Creesy from China to New York by ten days the previous year, with *N. B. Palmer* taking eighty-four days and *Flying Cloud* taking ninety-four days.[19, 20] Low ordered his ship onto the wind so he could catch up with his rival.

The two ships drew up alongside each other. Captain Creesy hailed *N. B. Palmer* and asked how long she had been at sea.

"Ten days after you!" Low bellowed over the sounds of flogging sail.

"He was so mad, he would have nothing more to say," Low recalled.

Yet as *N. B. Palmer* tried to pull ahead of *Flying Cloud*, the wind shifted. Low told the mate on watch to take in the studding sails. The ship slowed down drastically, and *Flying Cloud* raced ahead. Skies continued to darken, and the sea grew gray and unsettled. Then came eight days of gales, snow, and hail.

The bad weather slowed the ship's progress, but it proved to be the least of Captain Low's problems as he approached Cape Horn. At midnight on June 10, as he was putting on his boots, preparing to go above for a last check on the watch, he heard a shot ring out above him, followed by a cry. Grabbing a musket—it wasn't loaded, but to Low, "It did not matter"—and leaving his startled wife behind him, Charlie Low ran up the companionway,* accompanied by the carpenter and the sailmaker.[21]

On deck, flickering oil lamps cast a shadowy, fitful light. Low saw two men down. First Mate Haines had been shot in the thigh, some ten inches above the knee. The second mate was clutching an injured, bleeding arm. Low saw no one else nearby; the crew on watch was hoisting the mizzen topsail.

The night scene was confused and uncertain. Low shouted for the crew to finish setting the sail. The second mate was mobile, and hurried below to tend to his arm, as the captain called the men on watch to line up. Low needed the attacker to be identified swiftly if the ship's authority and his control of the crew were to be maintained.

The wounded first mate was still prostrate, with blood oozing through his trousers and onto the white pine of the clipper's deck. Low asked him if any of these men had been the shooter. Groggy with pain, Haines pointed out "a big rascal" named Dublin Jack. It took no time for Low to have the accused sailor clapped in irons. The immediate crisis seemed to be over.

It was at this moment that a different sailor stepped forward to say, "I fired the shot."

Low knew he had to make a spot decision. Uncertainty, injustice—or both—could shake the whole crew's confidence in his leadership and risk spreading the violence. He raised his musket at the second sailor, known as Lemons, and asked where the gun was. Lemons responded that he had thrown the pistol overboard.

Guns were, of course, forbidden the crew. Had he stolen it from the ship's stores? Had he brought it on board in secret? To a poorly paid sailor, such a weapon would be expensive. Had he really discarded it?

---

* A set of stairs leading from one deck to another.

"Was it a revolver?" Low asked, as he thought through the implications. No, Lemons said; if it had been, neither the first mate nor Low would still be alive.

"You are mighty cool about it," Low responded. He ordered Lemons put in irons and taken below. Then he turned to the first suspect, Dublin Jack. The crew would need to see its falsely accused shipmate treated fairly. Low had Dublin Jack unbound and told him to go.

Still, Low was on guard. The charge against Dublin Jack had been dropped, but he told the sailor that he would be keeping an eye on him. "All right, keep it on me," Dublin Jack snapped back.

Two English surgeons on board were tending to First Mate Haines below deck. They found the bullet still lodged in his thigh. Fortunately, it had not struck a bone—a critical, even fatal injury in this pre-antibiotic age—and there would be no need for an amputation. The second mate's wound was also treatable; he emerged from below in a sling.

It was now that Low had a chance to ask the second mate for his version of events. What he heard confounded him. This mate responded that he'd been struck with a handspike, not shot. His assailant, he said, was Dublin Jack.

Captain Low was in a quandary and must have spoken with frustration: "I told him he should have let me know *before* I let Jack out of irons."

It was pitch black, and all of the men except the skeleton night crew had gone below. Low felt it best to administer punishment in the morning, in full view of the entire ship's company. He knew he had a possible mutiny on his hands—a danger not only to him and other officers but also to the passengers and to his young bride. "I had a crew of thirty able seamen, six ordinary, and four boys," he would later recall, "and placed as I was, with my mate laid up, my second and third mates incompetent, I felt that I must not show the least fear, "but must show that I was able to take care of my ship."

The next day, as *Flying Cloud* bounded through the ocean toward Cape Horn, Low determined the punishment for Lemons, the shooter: flogging at the mizzenmast.

Low tied a rope across the quarterdeck to section off the area where the lashing would take place and hold back the crew. He told the watching men that anyone who crossed the line would be shot instantly.

Dublin Jack put one foot across the rope, a deliberate action to test the measure of his captain, and Low responded—not with his pistol but with the physical force that his sailors would have respected. The captain jumped Dublin Jack, "caught him by the throat, carried him nearly fifty feet, and landed him on the quarterdeck, put him in irons quick as a flash, and lashed him to the mizzenmast."

One of the crew brought Lemons from below and lashed him to the mizzenmast as well. Captain Low ordered the second mate (probably still in his sling) to give each man four dozen lashes with a rope.

The mate demurred. He had never done such a thing.

"Neither had I," Low recalled, "but it was no time to falter." He grabbed the rope and thrashed the spread-eagled Lemons. "I was angry at him, and angry at the second mate for not supporting me." Lemons was cut down, and Low gave Dublin Jack his forty-eight lashes as well.

Captain Low would have known that flogging was increasingly unpopular with the public. Under intense pressure, Congress had recently outlawed flogging on American merchant ships and in the US Navy, but the bill signed into law by President Fillmore did not explicitly forbid other types of physical punishment.[22] Low had certainly acted in anger, not the cool resolution appropriate for his position of authority. But he was no sadistic Waterman; he had never before flogged anyone. For Captain Low, the matter was clear-cut: violent punishment of two insubordinate sailors had been essential.

The law of the sea and the law of the land were different. Keeping the peace on board, and keeping the ship properly manned and sailing, was a matter of life and death for all.

Without his first mate to keep watch, Low remained on the quarterdeck for the next eighteen days, curling up in a corner to catch a few hours of sleep, his clothes drenched with spray.

"I only went to my room to wind my chronometers and take the time," Low wrote, "and yet my wife in all those troublous times never gave a sign of fear, but was braver than any man in the cabin."

When *N. B. Palmer* arrived in Valparaiso, Chile, to reprovision, Low immediately turned over Lemons and Dublin Jack to the American consul for a double trial on the charge of attempted murder on the high seas. The consul promptly locked the two men in jail. "I was glad to be rid of them," Low said.

No account of the event survives from the sailors of the *N. B. Palmer*. But it is suggestive that in Valparaiso, twenty men jumped ship. The flogging they had been forced to witness would have been an ugly, bloody memory. Low was left to scour the waterfront dives for more crewmen. Over the past few decades, the Chilean port had become a dumping ground for scoundrels and mutineers. "A fine set of men they were," Low recalled. Still, only one was actually drunk when they came on board.

N. B. Palmer arrived in San Francisco on September 30, after a rather disappointing passage of 125 days, 23 days behind the Creesys' *Flying Cloud*.[23]

Sarah Low, however, had been a success. While the ship was being loaded for the journey back across the Pacific, the ship's carpenter went aft to ask if the "Old Man," namely Captain Low, was on board. He wasn't.

"Is the Old Woman on board?" the carpenter asked the steward.

Twenty-year-old Sarah Low overheard the remark. "She rather resented this," her husband joked, "though I had a hearty laugh when I heard of it."[24]

N. B. Palmer then sailed for Manila and China, in hot pursuit of the season's first tea pickings—and *Flying Cloud.*

N. B. Palmer called at Manila after a passage of forty-five days to load a cargo of hemp. There Captain Low recalled, "we lived off the fat of the land and made easy acquaintances." They continued on to Hong Kong, where the couple was put up in a suite of rooms at the Russell & Company headquarters, and Sarah Low got her first taste of life as a *fanqui.* She was now several months pregnant.

With his ship's holds loaded with hemp and tea—most likely all from Russell & Company's account—and a baby on the way, Low raised anchor from Hong Kong on January 15, 1853, and set a course for the Cape of Good Hope, and, from there, New York and home. Within ten days, *N. B. Palmer* approached the Gaspar Strait, where Warren Delano's clipper *Memnon* had run aground two years earlier. They approached the moonlit sandy beaches of North Watcher Island around midnight, and Low called his wife and other passengers out on deck to see the "splendid sight." At four the next morning, the captain went up to order the watch to prepare to tack the ship. He was on deck when *N. B. Palmer* shuddered to a stop. She had run hard upon a coral ledge.

Immediately, Low ordered the crew to lay back all the sails, the only way for a sailing ship to go in reverse. He then ordered a kedge anchor* dropped from the stern of the vessel, and all salted provisions stowed in the bow of the ship to be moved aft, reducing her forward draft. The sails filled, and, with a grinding sound, *N. B. Palmer* came off the reef. Low ordered his men to sound the ship† and start pumping. She had lost part of her bow, and was making seven inches

---

* A small anchor used to reposition the ship.
† Find out how much water was in the hold and assess the damage.

of water per hour. Low would have to make for the nearest port, or his ship would be lost on her second round-the-world voyage. The best bet was Batavia, the crown jewel of Holland's East Indies spice-trading empire, which was ninety miles away.

As his injured ship limped toward the anchorage, someone came up from below and said that Low had to come to his wife immediately. There, in the cabin, he found Sarah in labor. She gave birth to a healthy baby boy, whom the couple named Charles Porter Low Jr.

Soon enough, the ship was in safe harbor—although far from sound. "It was a hard time for me," Low recalled, "my ship being in an almost sinking condition, but thanks to our splendid nurse, I was able to go on shore and secure coolies to come off and keep the pumps going all night, and also to arrange for the discharging of cargo." The nurse was a Miss Hemenway, one of the passengers.

After laborers removed the ship's hundreds of tons of tea, hemp, and rock ballast, *N. B. Palmer* was towed to the Dutch navy yard. With no dry dock, she had to be "heaved down"—turned onto her side against a bank, exposing her underwater hull. There Low saw a two-foot-wide chunk of hard coral sticking out of the ship's copper-plated bottom. "If this had come out at sea," he wrote, "the ship would have gone down in less than an hour."

Luck had saved not just his ship but almost certainly his crew, his wife, and his newborn child.

As for his son, several Dutch colonists suggested to Captain Low that the boy be registered as a Dutch citizen, as he would "have great privileges when he grew up." Low refused. "He was born under the American flag," he responded, "and was and always would be an American citizen."

Six months later, on July 25, 1853, *N. B. Palmer* picked up her pilot outside of New York Harbor. She had been gone fourteen months. It must have been a tearful reunion for Captain Low and his family, who rejoiced in the new addition to the clan. Soon after unloading the cargo, Charlie and Sarah Low took the boat to Boston and, from there, the train to the ancestral family seat in Salem. As Low recalled, they were "joyfully received by my wife's mother and her other relationships and friends."

Charlie Low then had to ask his wife a very important question: Would she come with him again on his next voyage around the world? She said yes. But there would be a catch: her mother would be coming as well. Baby Charles Jr. would remain in Salem.[25]

The around-the-world voyages of Captain Creesy and others were reaping immense returns for shipowners. Most financial records for many of these firms have been lost, so exact figures are difficult to determine, but merchants, captains, and historians alike attest to the profits they earned: Captain Clark described *Surprise*, for example, as a "mine of wealth" for A. A. Low & Brother.[26] A typical clipper cost between $50,000 and $120,000 to construct, depending on the size of the vessel and the quality of materials used. If a ship arrived in San Francisco at the right time, its cargo of dry goods and supplies could be worth up to $100,000; that first voyage alone could easily pay off most if not all of the cost of building the ship.

Yet the economics of the business as a whole were increasingly in trouble. Fewer young American men were willing to put up with the terrible conditions and low wages ($25 a month on average, and often quite less) for a career at sea. Between 1849 and 1860, more than one million people traveled to California in search of a better life, ending up as shopkeepers, craftsmen, and farmers in a new and prosperous land. In previous generations, many of the single men who made the trek would have gone to sea. There was also the lure of the fertile prairies of the American Midwest, especially in Kansas Territory, where free-soil Northern farmers hoping to till their own land fought pitched battles against proslavery Southern settlers determined to extend the plantation system farther west.

By the 1850s, there was a labor mismatch: the big clipper ships required big crews, and there were simply not enough qualified sailors to man them properly. Rather than raise wages, the owners were forced to use crimps and other dubious tactics to crew up their vessels and keep down costs.

Despite the fine craftsmanship that went into the many dozens of extreme clipper ships launched between 1845 and 1853, there was without question a good amount of haste and sloppiness as well. The financial pressures to get the ships finished and loaded up for California no doubt contributed to the problem. Haphazard maintenance didn't help, either. Charles Low noted how reluctant Captain Nat was to replace worn out rigging on *Houqua* after three voyages.

The China trade was still strong, especially for Russell & Company and, by extension, the shipping companies associated with it, most notably A. A. Low & Brother. As Robert Bennet Forbes wrote, "The period from 1851 to 1858 was probably the culminating point of the firm as purely a commission house. Its reputation had been built up and well established by a long succession of laborious, shrewd, but conservative partners, who nearly always left the house greater than they found it, and certainly with undiminished reputation." The secret to its success was access to capital. As each new Chinese port was opened to Western trade, Russell & Company established itself as the "exchange bankers of the place, by virtue of the currency of its sterling bills in India," and thus was able to ship superior teas to England and America.[27] Because of its special relationship with Baring Brothers, Russell & Company had easy access to specie-backed British currency, and British opium dealers in India appreciated this American house's ability to complete transactions in pounds sterling.

As the 1850s wore on, there were strong signs that the boom times in California were coming to an end. San Francisco was developing its own manufacturing and agricultural infrastructure, pushing down commodity prices. Declining freight rates for East Coast imports cut into the ability of shipping companies to pay crews of up to sixty men to operate an extreme clipper ship.

The reaction of New York's and Boston's shipping communities was to cut back on orders for clippers of the "extreme type," in which speed trumped all other design considerations. Captain Nat's time-tested design principles still ruled the day for the China tea business, which showed no signs of slowing down. As he listened to his younger brother Charles's account of racing against *Flying Cloud*, Abbot Low must have beamed. He then commissioned another extreme clipper to round out their San Francisco–China operations. With the addition of this ship, A. A. Low & Brother had one of the largest and most profitable fleet of deep-water tall ships under the US flag. None of these ships was above 1,500 tons. With *N. B. Palmer*, Low felt that he had achieved the ideal balance of size and speed.

In the years to come, the quest to build new ships to beat *Flying Cloud*'s record became the domain of less-established ship operators. It proved to be a futile enterprise. More seasoned shippers opted to build ships that were less expensive to operate and could carry more freight than the extreme clippers. These ships, called medium clippers, would still have relatively sharp lines but would carry much less sail, to balance reasonable speed with economy.

The first of this type was completed in Boston in 1851. She was named *Antelope*, and the *Boston Daily Atlas* noted that the deep-keeled, flat-floored vessel was "expected to hold as good a wind as most of the sharp-bottomed clippers of the same register. The design of her model was to combine large stowage capacity with good sailing qualities."[28] *Antelope* proved to be a lousy sailor compared with her sharper, more heavily sparred competitors, taking a leisurely 149 days to sail from Boston to San Francisco. But more medium clippers would follow her, ships that were able to make the Cape Horn trip in 110 to 120 days, carrying more freight and requiring less crew than their extreme cousins.

Brilliant a designer as he was, Donald McKay was not immune from changing times. Yet his reaction to the glut of clipper ships sliding down the ways was not to build slower and fuller but rather even bigger and even faster than ever before. And McKay did not have much interest in building deep-ocean steamships. Clippers were the ships he could build and wanted to build. And why should he not do as he pleased? Unlike his main rival—the more modest William H. Webb, who eagerly built steamships—McKay had become a bona fide national celebrity, courted by the press and toasted by Boston's high society. He was the mechanic and craftsman as American hero, one who could stand as the social equal of his august clients. Or so he thought.

Even if success had gotten to his head, McKay had every reason to feel that he could vanquish all competing shipbuilders with a grand gesture. By building bigger and more extreme clipper ships than his rivals, he figured, he would create his own market rather than conform to the current one, and prove the naysayers wrong. What's more, he had also grown quite prosperous in his own right, unlike the perpetually struggling John Willis Griffiths, who, by the 1850s, was having a very hard time making a living as a traveling lecturer and engineering consultant.

In 1852, following *Flying Fish*'s loss to Webb's *Swordfish* in an eagerly anticipated race to California, McKay had started construction of a new extreme clipper ship, the biggest in the world by far. He was at the peak of his creative powers. In May of that year, the *Boston Daily Atlas* announced that Donald McKay was naming his giantess *Enoch Train*, in honor of his first major patron.[29] Records are scanty, but it can be surmised that McKay was building her on commission from Train as a replacement for the *Flying Cloud*.

Yet it appears that Enoch Train walked away from the new clipper. If so, McKay was not going to let himself be embarrassed by dismantling the partially completed masterpiece at his yard. As the launching date approached and the timbers kept rising on the shores of East Boston, the papers announced that the ship's name was now *Sovereign of the Seas*—and that McKay was building the ship not on a shipping firm's commission but on his own account.

Even his most dedicated supporters must have shaken their heads at such hubris. McKay had taken on the financial risks of a massive project. And he had unapologetically given his ship the same name as a 1637 British warship that had boasted so many cannons and gilded decorations that England's enemies nicknamed her the "Golden Devil."

But unlike the ponderous flagship of King Charles I's navy, McKay's American *Sovereign of the Seas* would be trim and elegant in profile, even though she measured more than 2,400 tons and stretched 252 feet in length. She dwarfed every clipper that came before her, including *Flying Cloud.* Her figurehead was not a king on horseback but rather a half-man, half-fish figure blowing a conch shell. Boston reporter Duncan McLean was at no loss for words when comparing the American ship with her British predecessor. How strange that "uncouth hulk" would look against her namesake, he wrote: "Behold the modern *Sovereign of the Seas*, the longest, sharpest, the most beautiful merchant ship in the world, designed to sail at least twenty miles an hour with a whole-sail breeze. See her in the beauty of her strength, the simplicity and neatness of her rig, flying before the gale, and laughing at the rising sea; and then imagine her cumbrous ancestor, wallowing from side to side, tearing up the ocean into whitened foam, and drifting perhaps seven miles an hour; yet she was the finest ship of her day."

McLean summed up: "Imagine all this, and even a landsman can comprehend the wonderful progress of naval architecture." The hero of the story, of course, was Donald McKay, who "alone is responsible for her success as a sea-boat."[30]

The journalist might have swooned, and the public may have gawked as the ship neared completion. But at least a few visitors to the East Boston yard must have wondered if McKay had gone mad. One observer noted that he "had invested all he was worth [financially] in the ship" and that "he had built her in opposition to the advice of his best friends."[31] Valued clients had no interest in buying the ship. Not George Upton, owner of McKay's latest California clipper, *Romance of the Seas*; or Sampson & Tappan, owner of *Stag Hound*; or Moses Grinnell, proud owner of *Flying Cloud*. Two vessels of the extreme clipper type (Grinnell had commissioned *Sea Serpent*, too) were enough for the Swallowtail Line. Grinnell knew that the real money for his firm remained in the transatlantic packet business, a run for which clippers were wholly unsuited, especially when pitted against a new generation of paddlewheel steamers that could plow through the waves at more than thirteen knots, irrespective of winds and currents.

Other shipowners, still wedded to the more traditional clipper ships, kept their distance from *Sovereign of the Seas*. Abbot Low had yet to be won over by McKay's work. For the old China hands, it was a matter of wait and see.

By summer, salvation for Donald McKay had appeared in the form of New York shipowner Andrew F. Meinke, partner in the German firm Funch, Meinke & Wendt. Meinke's origins remain obscure, and he purchased *Sovereign of the Seas* for $150,000. Then, it appears, Moses Grinnell stepped in and offered Meinke his company's services as ship's agent—supervising the procurement and loading of $84,000 worth of cargo bound for San Francisco. The best part of the deal, it may have seemed to McKay's family, was that Donald's brother and trusted right-hand man Lauchlan became her first master.[32] Trained as a shipbuilder like his brother, Lauchlan had moved to the quarterdeck in the mid-1840s, captaining the barque *Jenny Lind* on several fast transatlantic voyages.[33] "No swearing, no bustle, nor even imperious language," one person remembered of Captain McKay's style on board ship.

Sovereign's designer would later claim to regret this act of nepotism.

On August 4 all of New York watched with awe as *Sovereign of the Seas* spread her twelve thousand yards of canvas and bounded out into the North Atlantic, headed for San Francisco. "With a good chance, we expect he will make the shortest passage on record," the *Boston Daily Atlas* said of the captain's prospects.[34] On board was the largest crew ever assembled on an American merchant vessel: 105 men and boys. Tucked away safely in Captain McKay's cabin was a set of newly drawn and updated *Winds and Currents* charts that Lieutenant Maury had donated to him personally. Maury wrote Captain McKay that if he followed his course, *Sovereign of the Seas* would reach her destination in 103 days. Her designer certainly hoped that the *Boston Atlas* would be proved right and Maury proved wrong, and that this new ship would beat *Flying Cloud*'s eighty-nine-day record.

Donald McKay's design instincts (and daring) proved right: bigger still meant faster for a clipper ship. *Sovereign* flew before the wind as no other ship had before her. "The noble ship," a crew member known only as Faulkner wrote of her departure from New York Harbor, "clawed off shore like a pilot boat, carrying whole topsails, courses, jib, and spanker. Next morning, the wind favored us a little, and we were soon under all sail, close hauled, walking to the eastward at the rate of 15 miles an hour, and long before sunset were out of sight of land."[35] She passed the equator in twenty-five days and continued forward at full clip.

As the seas worsened toward Cape Horn, Captain McKay made sure that his crew was comfortable and well fed, something lost on many other masters (with the exception of old Captain Nat). "He had stoves in their quarters, and continually had one or more of the boys to attend the fires, and at the same time dry the sailors' clothes," Faulkner wrote home, "had warm coffee, and tea, and provisions served out during the night as well as the day, and never exposed the men more than was absolutely necessary."[36]

Yet kindness to the sailors did not mean that Lauchlan McKay was easy on his brother's dream ship. Rather, he hoisted full sail and pushed her to the absolute limit. "He carried on sail so as to make it truly frightful to look aloft," Faulkner wrote.[37] *Sovereign of the Seas* rounded the cape without incident and then beat up the Chilean coast, battling gales and headwinds all the way.

Then, on the night of October 12, disaster struck. While carrying a full press of canvas, the backstays holding up the mainmast slackened under the strain of wind and rain. The main-topmast came crashing down, taking with it the top portion of the foremast. The entire fore-topmast was hanging over the side in a tangled mess, making the situation far worse than on *Stag Hound* or *Flying Cloud*. Huge plumes of seawater shot up from the tangled wreckage, and the once-graceful ship came to a halt. The mast was acting like a gigantic anchor, pulling the ship down to one side.

She was the third of Donald McKay's clippers to be dismasted on her first voyage. Captain McKay ordered, "Nothing must be cut!"

"Impossible, sir," the mate protested. "We must cut the wreck adrift."

McKay refused to give in. "Nothing shall be cut," he repeated, even as the wreckage threatened to cause mortal damage to the vessel's hull and rig. He then supposedly tossed in a quote from the revolutionary Lajos Kossuth, who had recently fled to the United States after his unsuccessful attempt to win Hungary's independence from Austria: "Boys, remember Kossuth's motto: nothing is impossible to him that *wills!* I *will* that everything shall be saved; now go to work like Trojans."[38]

Miraculously, the sea and wind abated, giving the men time to do emergency repairs. Over the next several days, the crew used blocks and tackles to pull much of the wreckage out of the water and secured to the deck. Captain McKay barely slept: "now setting a sailmaker's gang to work repairing sails, next a carpenter's gang to making and fitting masts and yards, and the sailors generally to clearing the rigging, getting down the stumps of the topmasts." In twelve days, Faulkner noted, the ship was once again "a-tanto, as complete aloft as if nothing had happened."[39] Aside from saving the ship's reputation, there was another good reason why Captain McKay refused to put in to Valparaiso or another nearby port for repairs: it would have cost about $25,000 to rerig the ship. Since the 2,950 tons of cargo on board were worth an estimated $85,000, this would have deeply cut into the ship's profit margin.[40]

Repaired and freshly painted, *Sovereign of the Seas* arrived in San Francisco in November after a passage of 103 days from New York. If she hadn't been dismasted off Chile, she probably would have finished her voyage at least 10 days earlier—tantalizingly close to *Flying Cloud*'s eighty-nine-day record passage the previous year.

For Lauchlan McKay's bravery off the coast of Chile, the New York Board of Marine Underwriters would eventually present him with a silver dinner service. *Sovereign of the Seas* then sailed in ballast (devoid of cargo) to Honolulu, where she was loaded with 8,000 barrels of whale oil. Rather than continue on to China, Captain McKay sailed her directly to New York, where she arrived 82 days later. During this run, *Sovereign of the Seas* showed her true speed, clocking 421 miles in a single day, or an astonishing average speed of 17.5 knots.[41]

In June 1853, with Lauchlan McKay still in command, *Sovereign of the Seas* set sail to Liverpool. Her mission: carry prospectors and supplies to England, and then on to a new gold rush, this one in Australia. In the past, Donald McKay had avoided making passages on his own clippers. Yet on *Sovereign of the Seas*'s run across the Atlantic, he booked passage with his wife, Mary.[42] That same day, the Cunard paddlewheel steamer SS *Canada* departed Boston with a full load of passengers. It was a state-of-the-art ocean liner, equipped with navigation lights for safety and able to maintain a steady speed of 10 knots in almost any wind and weather.[43]

Despite bad weather and rough seas, *Sovereign of the Seas* flew past the SS *Canada* in mid-ocean; on one day, she even logged an astounding 340 nautical miles. But wind failed the clipper toward the end, and *Canada* thrashed ahead. The steamship cruised into Liverpool two days ahead of her American rival—foreshadowing the growing capability of steam and the increasing irrelevance of sail.

Nonetheless, *Sovereign of the Seas* had outperformed any other sailing ship on the Atlantic run, making the 3,100-mile passage in 13 days, 22 hours, and 50 minutes, beating the old Black Ball packet ship *Yorkshire*'s best transatlantic time (on the harder westbound route) by 3 days.[44, 45] In triumph, the crew raised a big white banner from the ship's mast that read in black letters:

Sovereign of the Seas
Fastest Ship in the World
Sailed New York to Liverpool
Record Time—13 days, 22 hours[46]

According to Donald McKay's grandson Richard, the crowds on the Liverpool docks were greeted with the following chantey, sung lustily by the *Sovereign*'s crew:

O, Susannah, darling, take your ease
For we have beat the clipper fleet,
The *Sovereign of the Seas*![47]

The braggadocio worked. Impressed by the ship's performance, the British shipping firm James Baines & Company chartered *Sovereign of the Seas* for the continuing trip to Australia. There would be no competition from a steamship this time; its emerging technology didn't permit it the range for such a long voyage.

The clipper departed Liverpool for Melbourne on September 7, carrying sixty-four passengers and $1 million worth of cargo.[48] She reached her destination in a record-setting seventy-seven days, beating even the new steamship *Great Britain*, designed by the master engineer Isambard Kingdom Brunel. James Baines was so pleased with *Sovereign*'s performance that he commissioned four new extreme clipper ships from McKay. All would be purpose-built for the Australia trade.

Donald McKay felt that he had proven the naysayers wrong, bucking the conventional Boston wisdom that shipbuilders should not be ship operators. Cash in hand, he set about building something even more monumental.

Back in Boston, Enoch Train, a bit surprised that his former namesake ship had made such a splash, supposedly asked Donald McKay what he thought *of Sovereign of the Seas.*

"Well, she appears to be a pretty good ship," McKay responded, "but I think I can build one to beat her."[49]

She would be his magnum opus. But neither Train nor any other shipowner made an offer. McKay would have to build this one on spec, as well.

CHAPTER 14

GREAT REPUBLIC

Such is the Great Republic—*the ship of ships. She is a monument
of the skill and genius of her builder, and an honor to our common
country.*

—*Boston Post*, October 5, 1853[1]

October 4, 1853, was launch day for McKay's *Great Republic*. Boston's mayor Benjamin Seaver had declared a civic holiday: schools
and shops were closed. Thousands of people from Boston and beyond came by train, coach, and on foot to East Boston to marvel at
the huge ship on the ways.

At his big house on White Street, Donald McKay rose early as always and walked down to his shipyard, this time accompanied by his
wife, Mary, and his children. He may have noticed that his sixteen-year-old son, Cornelius, was not looking well at all. He learned the
reason as soon as he arrived at the yard. The night before, Cornelius
and his friends had broken into the champagne stores, consuming
everything, including the bottle to be used at *Great Republic*'s christening.

Everyone at the shipyard knew that it would be bad luck to
launch the ship without a proper christening. With everything else
they had to do that day, they would have to find a substitute.

As the shipyard prepared for the launch, Donald McKay paced

Great Republic's pine decks. The breeze from the harbor ruffled his coat and black bow tie. The aroma of timber and sawdust filled his nostrils, as did the tang of the salt air and hot pitch. His calloused hands tested the hemp shrouds. All seemed secure. He glanced over the woodwork of the upper deck, looking for imperfections, and then leaned over the bulwarks and called out orders to his men far below. McKay's workers yelled and scurried in response. Swinging heavy iron mallets, they knocked out the last of the timber props supporting the hull. One by one, the props thudded onto the muddy ground. Above the din of machinery and the neighing of horses, McKay also heard another sound: the growing murmur of the spectators who were streaming in through the Border Street gates.

"Visitors were in town from the back country and from all along the coast to witness the launch," a reporter from the *Boston Post* observed, "particularly from Cape Cod, delegations from which arrived by the morning train. The wharves on both sides of the stream where a view was obtainable were thronged with people; men, women and children vied in interest to get a look, and boys and men clung like spiders to the rigging of the ship, and the sides and roofs of the stores and houses, to get a glance at the sublime spectacle."[2]

All of Boston seemed afoot or afloat, all moving toward the slumbering giant. Her copper hull sheathing and jet-black topsides glinted in the sunlight. Across the harbor, the gold-leafed dome of the statehouse glowed in reply.

The year had begun with Donald McKay's ambition burning as bright as ever. After having sold *Sovereign of the Seas* for a handsome profit, he plowed his fortune into the construction of an even grander ship. Obsessed as always with the idea that bigger was better, he pushed the limits of ship design to create the ultimate clipper. *Great Republic* would have a designed displacement of 4,555 tons, making her the largest merchant ship in the world, bigger than any transatlantic steamship. In his model shop, McKay had laid out the hull for a true titan of the seas: stretching 335 feet in length—more than 80 feet longer than *Sovereign of the Seas*—longer than a modern football field. Previous ships of her type had three masts. *Great Republic* would be rigged as a four-masted barque: foremast, main, mizzen, and jigger. The first three masts would carry square sails, while the last one would have a fore-and-aft spanker (the trapezoidal sail meant to assist with tacking the ship). Her main course yard (which carried the main sail) was 120 feet in length, almost the length of earlier tea clippers such as *Houqua*.[3] She would have four complete decks, soon to be outfitted with luxurious staterooms for 50 paying passengers, and bunks for 150 sailors, officers, and cadets.

Even so, McKay had given the enormous vessel the graceful lines of a racing yacht. The plentitude and scale of her construction was a testament to the rich resources of the North American continent: 1.5 million feet of Southern hard pine, more than 2,000 tons of white oak, 336 tons of iron bolts and fastenings, and 56 tons of copper hull plating.[4]

Great Republic was McKay's canvas-draped reply to the large, coal-guzzling transatlantic steamers that were the talk of the shipping world. She was almost twice the tonnage of the two great ships of the Collins Line, SS *Pacific* and SS *Arctic*, which had cost $700,000 each to build and had attracted a generous $385,000 annual mail subsidy from Congress. In 1853 no one had any way to know that Edward Knight Collins's subsidy would eventually be revoked and his company would fold after two terrible disasters: the sinking of SS *Arctic* in 1854, killing 300 of the 400 people on board (including Collins's wife and two of his children), and the disappearance at sea of SS *Pacific* in 1856, with a loss of 186 lives. For now, these steam vessels posed a formidable threat to their rivals. Yet for his part, supremely confident in his new ship's success, McKay felt he had no need for government assistance. Sail, he felt, was still the only efficient way to make sustainable profits on long-haul voyages.

Indeed, McKay had become nationally and internationally famous as the shipbuilder with the Midas touch. For the first time in history, thanks to relaxed trade policies, English shipowners could now place orders with American builders, and to charter American vessels for long runs to the port cities of the far-flung British empire. McKay would soon begin work on a lucrative order from the British shipowner James Baines, who had shunned his country's yards and turned to him to build a quartet of California-style clippers for his line to Australia. All would fly the Union Jack. McKay was also building two American clippers based on *Sovereign*'s design: *Romance of the Seas* (purchased while on the stocks by a Baltimore shipping firm for $125,000) and *Empress of the Seas* (built for George Upton, owner of *Stag Hound*).

And so Donald McKay—for perhaps the first time in his life— was flush with cash. McKay had always reinvested his profits only in his ships and yard, in contrast to his rival William Webb, who invested his profits in a variety of enterprises, including the Panama-Pacific Railroad. As a result, Webb's net worth was approaching a half million dollars, making him a very rich man in 1850s America, almost in the same league as the Delanos and the Forbes brothers. McKay's personal wealth lagged considerably behind. Although, during his eight years in business, he had paid an estimated $2 million to his East Boston shipyard workers and suppliers, he himself was not worth even close to six figures.[5] McKay once said proudly that he had "done over five millions worth of business since I have been in East Boston, yet I have cheated no one."[6] As a craftsman and artist, his work was superlative; as an honest employer, he seems to have had reason for pride; but as a financial manager, his judgment was more than questionable.

Yet rather than set some of this sudden windfall aside for a rainy day or diversify his investments in some way, McKay plowed all of the proceeds from the sale of *Sovereign of the Seas*, as well as the advance funds from the construction of the other vessels, into *Great Republic*. He could boast that *Sovereign of the Seas* had earned about

$200,000 during her first eleven months under Funch, Meinke & Wendt's ownership. McKay himself netted $150,000 from her sale.[7] This may have fed his belief that *Great Republic* could be profitable too. If the behemoth vessel did not perform as expected, McKay would be ruined.

When construction started on *Great Republic*, no buyer stepped forward for the massive vessel. McKay was unfazed. He had built on speculation before, and he would do so again, selling his ship after she proved herself on the high seas. Rather than sending *Great Republic* to California, McKay planned to have his brother Captain Lauchlan McKay sail her to London to pick up passengers and cargo, and then go on to Australia.

McKay was still chasing gold dust. Prospector Edward Hargraves—who had cut his teeth in the California gold fields—had hit pay dirt in the town of Orange in New South Wales in 1851, two years before. Hargraves's discovery prompted a stampede of emigrants just as in California Gold Rush days, now in search of riches Down Under. Australia's days as a feared convict colony were over. During the next decade, almost three hundred thousand English emigrants set sail to start a new life in Australia. About eighteen thousand Americans joined them. They were followed by the usual witch's brew of gamblers, conmen, criminals, prostitutes—and merchants eager to sell wares at inflated prices. As the *Sydney Morning Herald* noted gleefully: "The discovery of the Victorian Goldfields has converted a remote dependency into a country of worldwide fame; it has attracted a population, extraordinary in number, with unprecedented rapidity; it has enhanced the value of property to an enormous extent; it has made this the richest country in the world; and, in less than three years, it has done for this colony the work of an age, and made its impulses felt in the most distant regions of the earth."[8]

McKay hoped to tap this new source of business. And former China merchant Robert Forbes, now comfortably rich from his opium dealings and his brother John's savvy investments, followed the construction of McKay's huge new vessel with great interest. Forbes and McKay had become friendly over the past few years, and, perhaps as a nod to the old salt's influence in Boston society, McKay rigged *Great Republic* with Forbes's new invention of a double-topsail rig.

The Forbes rig was indeed a blessing to the men who would climb aloft and work her sails. By splitting the traditionally large topsail in two, the dangerous task of reefing (partially furling the sail in strong winds) was a thing of the past, and furling sails in a hurry could be done in a much safer way than before.[9] As *Great Republic* was being constructed, Captain Forbes's rig proved its worth speeding the Canton–New York voyage of the small clipper barque *Mermaid*. "This rig is working its way slowly into favor with shipowners," noted one publication, "and when its advantages are known, it will soon be universally adopted. It is the proper rig for large clippers. The *Mermaid* has tested it in a voyage around the world, and like other vessels with it, has sailed with less men, than if she had been rigged in the usual style."[10]

The Forbes rig, with its split topsails, was especially promising for *Great Republic*, the crew of which would have to handle fifteen thousand square yards of canvas under full sail—more than any other clipper. Also perched on deck was a fifteen-horsepower steam engine, which in an emergency would help hoist the yards, as well as help load cargo into her hull. Donald McKay was resistant to using steam power for propulsion, but he was more than happy to give the crew a steam engine to help them work a sailing vessel.

As construction proceeded, Donald put his brother Lauchlan in charge of outfitting the vessel. He grew worried as Lauchlan, flush with confidence after his success with *Sovereign of the Seas*, went way over budget. He complained to Lauchlan about "the extravagance of the expenses you lavished on her" and "the stupid increase in her spars." Donald McKay had insured the vessel for $235,000, but her construction costs now ballooned up to $300,000.

Even before launch, visitors gathered to gawk at the massive ship rising in McKay's East Boston yard. A devotee of sailor-related charities, Robert Forbes wrote McKay to propose charging a small fee for a tour, proceeds which could then be given to the Sailors' Snug Harbor of Boston, a boardinghouse for retired seamen:

> As your ship, the *Great Republic*, is likely to be visited by
> thousands of admirers, I suggest that you make her the medium
> of doing a great service to an institution which is about going into
> operation, and of which I am, for want of a better, the presiding
> officer. The "Sailors' Snug Harbor of Boston" has the sympathy of
> all those who take an interest in ships, and they would willingly
> pay a "York shilling" to see your ship and at the same time serve a
> benevolent object. If you approve of the suggestion, I will carry it
> out at once by sending a competent agent on board, and if any one
> should by mistake drop a dollar in the purse, I will give him credit
> for it.
>
> I am a very truly
> Your friend and servant,
> (signed) R. B. Forbes[11]

McKay's response to the old China trader:

> Dear Sir:
>
> Yours requesting my concurrence in your very benevolent
> suggestion, that of having the privilege of collecting a small
> sum from the visitors to the *Great Republic* for the benefit of the
> "Sailors' of Snug Harbor" in Boston, has been received. I assure
> you that nothing will give me more pleasure than to afford
> you such an opportunity. This class of men have too long been
> neglected: they do the labor, they sail the clippers of which we

boast as a nation; and any little reward that they may be able to collect along this way, will be highly pleasing to me. And I hope the public will contribute in this way, and feel it to be a privilege to be able to build up a bulwark to shelter the weather-beaten sailor, now no longer able to earn his bread by his perilous profession.

I am, dear sir, yours truly
(signed) Donald McKay[12]

As midday approached on October 4, some fifty thousand men, women, and children spread out before Donald McKay and his ship. *Great Republic* perched at an incline on the tallow-greased ways, ready to slide into the water stern first. She was held back only by means of a tenon-and-timber* plank that would be sawed at the launch.[13] At her prow was a five-foot-long eagle figurehead—tongue flaring and eyes glaring—fashioned out of white pine. On her stern was another gilded eagle—this one complete with body and wings—talons grasping an American shield painted in red, white, and blue. Below, gilded letters spelled out *"Great Republic"* and *"New York,"* her port of registry.

At the stroke of noon, shipyard supervisor Captain Alden Gifford stood in front of *Great Republic*'s prow, her bowsprit and screaming eagle figurehead looming up in front of him. From her main truck flew a blue coach whip pennant, as well as a white flag bearing the arms of the United States. An American flag adorned each of her other masts. To complete the festive ensemble, a Union Jack streamed from a staff mounted on her bowsprit.[14]

Henry Wadsworth Longfellow, Boston's most celebrated poet,

---

* A tenon is a projecting piece of wood that is inserted into a hole known as the mortise to form a joint.

then read aloud his poem "The Building of a Ship" to the assembled crowd. It closed with the following stanzas:

> Sail on, nor fear to breast the sea
> Our hearts, our hopes, are all with thee,
> Our hearts, our hopes, our prayers, our tears,
> Our faith triumphant o'er our fears,
> Are all with thee, are all with thee!

Captain Gifford then picked up a glass bottle—now filled with Lake Cochituate water piped down to Boston via a new aqueduct—and smashed it against the hull.

The glass shattered, and the exploding water flashed in the sunlight.

On board, McKay felt a jolt, and the horizon started to move. The tallowed launching ways began to smoke as *Great Republic* picked up speed and hit the water. A huge wave crested up and broke onto the shore. Finally, the ship came to a halt, held back by a web of hemp cords.

The crowds cheered, and cannons boomed across Boston Harbor. *Great Republic* was afloat.

"*Great Republic* launched at 12 o clock, which was successfully and beautifully done," Robert Bennet Forbes proudly noted in his diary. "This ship has the Forbes Rig and is about 4000 tons measurement."[15]

Two months of work remained before *Great Republic* was ready to be towed to New York. There were masts and spars to be raised, rigging to be hung, and lavish interiors to be fitted out. The ship's thirty-eight-foot beam gave McKay's interior designers a generous floor plate to create a true floating palace that matched the finest Collins transatlantic steamers in luxury. Visitors who came aboard marveled at the gleaming mahogany paneling and wainscoting in the main saloon. Tufted velvet sofas and stained glass adorned the public

273

rooms and passenger staterooms. For the crew, the nasty, cramped fo'c'sle was a thing of the past. There was enough room on board for a crew library, stocked with books on seamanship.

Prominent visitors streamed into the shipyard to see the beautiful and imposing clipper at her fitting-out berth, as her four masts rose one by one. Forbes returned to the shipyard, this time with his children, among them sixteen-year-old Robert Jr., whom he had left behind as an infant during his 1838–40 trip to Canton. Shipbuilding had progressed by leaps and bounds in the past two decades, and *Great Republic* was the shining exemplar of America's role in a technological revolution. As for Donald McKay, he was anticipating the day when he would stand on her quarterdeck and see his company's black eagle ensign flapping overhead as his masterpiece barreled ahead under full press of sail past the gates of New York Harbor, into the great Atlantic beyond.

Captain Nathaniel Palmer journeyed down from his native Stonington, Connecticut, to take a look at McKay's maritime marvel. In the two years since his well-earned retirement, Captain Nat had been living the life of a gentleman yachtsman. From a white Italianate mansion on Long Island Sound, he spent his time racing a series of swift boats for pleasure rather than profit. Now, gazing up at *Great Republic*'s vast bulk, Palmer was nonplussed. The old man grunted that McKay was a brilliant artist but had a poor understanding of maritime economics.

The great China merchant Abbot Low joined Palmer in inspecting the ship. "She's beautiful enough to burst your heart," Palmer reportedly told Low. "But there aren't winds enough on this planet for her. What was this farmer's lad from Nova Scotia thinking of—sailing her to the moon?"[16] It was estimated—perhaps by Palmer—that *Great Republic* would cost an astounding $10,000 a month to operate.[17]

Little did Nathaniel Palmer and Low know that before long, they would be the proud owners of this greatest ship in the world.

*　　*　　*

All had not gone well during construction. McKay and his brother Lauchlan apparently clashed over the amount of sail the massive ship would be carrying. Still, after several weeks of fitting out, the steam tugboat *R. B. Forbes* towed *Great Republic* out of Boston Harbor. Her destination: Peck's Slip at the foot of South Street, in New York. The great ship's sails remained tightly furled.

Over the next several days, *Great Republic* was loaded with thousands of tons of grain, as well as tools, provisions, and dry goods—worth a grand total of about $350,000. The governor of New York came aboard to marvel at McKay's latest creation, as did politicians, prominent businessmen, and thousands of ordinary New Yorkers. Captain Lauchlan McKay's orders: sail *Great Republic* to Liverpool under the McKay house flag. There, Donald McKay hoped, he could sell her—and her cargo—to a British shipping company. Yet apparently it was clear that even when fully loaded with cargo and provisions, she could not carry all of her sails and spars (full rig) as designed. "I saw with regret," Captain McKay wrote his brother, "when too late, that the ship could not carry her top-gallants aloft when laden."[18] Less sail area almost certainly meant a reduction in speed.

A few days before her scheduled departure, a buyer stepped forward and offered McKay the unprecedented sum of $280,000 for the ship.[19] The offer may have raised McKay's confidence in the value of *Great Republic*, yet the sum would still represent a loss of an estimated $20,000 from his cost of building the ship. He turned it down.

The day after Christmas 1853, final preparations were made. The crew climbed aloft and unfurled all of her sails below the royals. *Great Republic* strained hard at her lines in the breeze, ready to break free.

Meanwhile, New Yorkers enjoyed a day of rest. Uptown in Bryant Park, at the intersection of Sixth Avenue and Forty-Second Street, visitors strolled through the glass-and-cast-iron concourse of New York's own Crystal Palace (inspired by the one built a few years before in London), poking amidst the exhibits and curiosities brought in for a new World's Fair, the "Exhibition of the Industry of All Nations," earlier in the year. These included clocks, daguerreotype cameras, printing presses, and an early Singer sewing machine.[20] The exhibition's most important display, the "hoist machine," would not be ready for several months: a young inventor named Elisha Otis would manipulate a series of levers—connected to a cable and a set of wheels—to raise a platform up and down. If the cable broke, a spring mechanism would prevent the platform from plunging to the ground. It was to become the world's first safe and practical elevator.

Those who wanted to take in a play could go to the National Theater and watch a staged production of *Uncle Tom's Cabin*, based on Harriet Beecher Stowe's provocative abolitionist novel. Those seeking something less controversial could stroll over to Barnum's American Museum, on Broadway, ostensibly to be educated but more likely to be amused by novelties such as a flea circus or disgusted by the much-ballyhooed Feejee Mermaid (a fishtail sewed to the mummified torso of a monkey). Among the living curiosities Phineas Taylor Barnum advertised that day included giraffes and the Bearded Lady, which could be viewed "without extra charge." Singing and dancing acts such as "Hot Corn," "Faint Heart," and "Major Jones" had been "singularly adapted to the current holidays."[21]

As the temperature plummeted, homeowners stoked their hearths and stoves. The acrid bite of coal and wood smoke filled the chilly winter air. That day, E. Merriam of the *New York Daily Tribune* also warned all firemen: "The cold has come and may be severe, and during its continuance fires may break out and a difficulty may be found in the use of leather hose from the actions of the frost." The best solution to this problem, Merriam continued, was for the fire department to provide barrels of brine.[22] Two decades earlier, most of New York's commercial district had been wiped out in a devastating fire on a night that the temperature fell to seventeen degrees below zero. Five hundred buildings were destroyed in the blaze, including the New York Stock Exchange, and in response to this disaster, the city had built arguably the most advanced municipal water system in the world.[23] Yet despite this measure, cold weather still remained the New York water system's Achilles heel, and on this night, the fire department failed to place any barrels of brine on the street corners.

Fires were a common occurrence in a city heated by open fires and lit by tallow candles and whale oil lamps. Usually, they were put out by a few pails of water or by tossing the burning furniture into the street. Otherwise the alarm was sounded, and volunteer firefighters—wearing their colorful uniforms—raced to the scene in their gaudy red horse-drawn engines.

Night fell, and the temperature dropped below freezing. Aboard *Great Republic*, the crew members slumbered in their bunks, resting up for one last day of work before sailing. A potbellied coal stove in the fo'c'sle kept them warm. Up on deck, the night watchman paced the vast ship's empty decks, his oil lantern flickering on the white pine planking. Moonlight streamed into darkened saloons and staterooms, ready to receive the ship's first passengers. Thousands of sacks of American grain, most of it floated down the Erie Canal from the nation's fertile interior, sat in her holds. All of this bounty was bound for Australia to feed hungry prospectors searching for gold.

Just after midnight, on December 27, flames leapt out the windows of the E. Treadwell & Sons Novelty Bakery at 242 Front Street, far downtown.[24] The fire was most likely caused by an unattended oven. A gale blowing from the northwest fanned the flames until they consumed the entire structure. Then, pushed on by the bitterly cold winds, the blaze jumped from one building to the next, heading straight toward the warehouses and piers of South Street.

A reporter from the *New York Times* arrived on the scene, as did firefighters from several volunteer companies in the area. "The flames were still extending in every direction," the journalist wrote in his first dispatch, "all efforts to get it under way having failed. A general alarm is now being sounded, and engines from all quarters of the City are hastening to the scene of the disaster." Their efforts were in vain. The horses pulling the fire engines skidded on the icy cobblestones. The water froze in the leather hoses. The conflagration devoured a provisions store, a coppersmith and bell foundry, a clothing store, the Fourth Ward political headquarters, and a boardinghouse "occupied by a large number of poor families." The reporter then looked toward the East River and saw something even more terrifying: one by one, the masts of the ships docked on South Street were catching fire. Sparks from the burning buildings had landed on the hemp ropes and furled canvas sails of the packet ship *Joseph Walker* and the clipper ships *Red Rover* and *White Squall*, setting them ablaze. Soon each ship had become a fiery torch, their burning masts and spars towering a hundred or more feet in the air, lighting up the night sky with a bright orange glow.

"A ship on fire is at any time a grand scene," the *Times* wrote, "but the appearance is remarkable when contrasted with the dark sky of early morning."[25]

The crowd milling around the waterfront then turned their eyes to the biggest ship of all: Donald McKay's *Great Republic*. Her mainmast was one of the tallest objects in Manhattan: towering 215 feet (about twenty stories) above the main deck. One by one, each of her four masts caught fire, dropping flaming canvas and hemp onto her decks. Captain Lauchlan McKay rushed out of his cabin, looked up at the conflagration, and realized that the only way to save the ship was to cut down the masts so that they landed in the water. Then, somehow, he had to get a steam-powered vessel to tow her out into the East River, away from South Street.

The spray of the fire engines could barely reach the main yards of *Great Republic*. No firefighter volunteered to climb up into the rigging. It would be suicide. Captain McKay quickly consulted with one of the ship's underwriters, who had rushed to the scene. He then ordered the crew to hack away at the stays that secured each of the four masts. First the foremast and foretopmasts came crashing down like blazing trees, sending up clouds of hissing steam as they toppled into the East River. Then came the main and jigger masts.

Yet McKay had miscalculated: a tangled mass of burning spars missed the water and fell onto the ship itself, flattening deckhouses, smashing the steam engine, piercing three decks, and igniting a fire in the hold. Clouds of thick smoke began to billow from its cargo hatches. Those still on board ran for their lives.

"The fire still raging with unabated violence," the *Times* correspondent wrote at three o'clock in the morning. "The sparks and burning cinders are falling in showers upon the Piers between Peck slip and Catherine Ferry. The mammoth clipper, the *Great Republic*, is on fire, and will in all probability be totally destroyed!"[26] There was only one thing left to do: Captain McKay ordered *Great Republic* deliberately sunk at her berth. Blazing from end to end, the giantess sank ten feet into the swirling East River.

The winter dawn revealed the smoldering hulks of dozens of burned-out buildings, their brick sides caked with ice from the futile efforts of the firefighters. *Great Republic* continued to burn for two days until the river quenched the flames. Miraculously, the great eagle figurehead, with blazing eyes and protruding tongue, survived the conflagration. It poked grotesquely above the lapping waters, just beneath the blackened stump of the bowsprit.

A telegraph line had linked Boston and New York for the past five years, so Donald McKay received news of the disaster by the early morning of December 27. Numb with shock, he paced the halls of his Eagle Hill home at sunrise, holding the telegram in his hands. His masterpiece was being consumed. Donald and Mary McKay were already in mourning this Christmas season: their two-year-old son, Lauchlan had died from meningitis only a few months earlier.[27] Now, in the darkest hours of his career, Donald McKay must have taken some comfort in his wife's love and support, even if he didn't express it at the time.

The following day, McKay took the boat to New York, where he viewed the smoldering wreckage of *Great Republic*. There, according to grandson Richard, "he realized that all possible had been done to save his ship." Donald returned to Boston to work on the Australian clippers commissioned by James Baines in Liverpool, "determined not to be idle, despite the calamity which had befallen him."[28]

The underwriters met and awarded Donald McKay $235,000 for the lost ship. As part of his gamble, and to save money on underwriting fees, he had insured *Great Republic* for $65,000 less than she was worth. He had no choice but to accept the judgment. Neither did he have much interest in rebuilding the ship.

The underwriters put the wreck of the giantess up for sale to the highest bidder. Conservative to the end, Abiel Abbot Low saw his chance for a bargain: he purchased *Great Republic* where she lay. He then called Captain Nathaniel Palmer out of retirement for the biggest challenge of his career: rebuilding *Great Republic* into the finest and fastest vessel flying the flag of the House of Low.

On January 25, 1854, *Flying Cloud*, which had been in the port of New York but had escaped the blaze that consumed *Great Republic*, set sail on her third voyage to San Francisco via Cape Horn. Captain Creesy was still in command; his wife, Eleanor, still his trusted navigator.

What Josiah Creesy thought as his ship passed the blackened, half-sunk wreck of *Great Republic* is unknown, but his competitive instinct remained as strong as ever. His previous San Francisco dash in the *Flying Cloud* was a respectable 105 days. Yet it rankled him that Captain Low in the *N. B. Palmer* had outsailed him yet again on his recent China to New York run. Creesy was determined to set a record on this next San Francisco passage, even if the record to beat was his own. Battling fierce winter gales, Creesy followed a course plotted by Eleanor, using Matthew Fontaine Maury's newest version of *Winds and Currents* charts. On April 20, *Flying Cloud* sailed triumphantly into San Francisco Harbor. Her sailing time had been 89 days and 8 hours anchor to anchor: 13 hours faster than the record she had set three years before.

Flying Cloud's record trip around Cape Horn under sail would stand for another 140 years. It was also the last time McKay's beautiful *Flying Cloud* would display such a remarkable burst of speed. Her principal owners—Moses Grinnell and Robert Bowne Minturn—felt that maintaining the vessel to run at such a clip was no longer a profitable investment. Freight rates were dropping, big crews were harder to come by, and the strain on the ships was too great.

Josiah and Eleanor Creesy decided the time was right to retire from the sea. Their next trip would be their last.

CHAPTER 15

HILL AND RIVER

The shores are cultivated by the water's edge, and lean up in grace-
ful, rather than bold elevations; the eminences around are crested
with the villas of the wealthy inhabitants of the metropolis: sum-
mer houses, belvideres, and watersteps give an air of refreshments
to the banks.

—NATHANIEL PARKER WILLIS,
American Scenery (1840)[1]

The 1850s was a golden age of gardening in America, and the Delano's family estate Algonac was one of the horticultural crown jew-
els of the northeastern United States. Influenced by the grounds of
aristocratic English estates designed in the seventeen hundreds by
Lancelot "Capability" Brown, Algonac's landscape blurred the line
between natural and manmade. There were apple orchards, spruce
groves, formal flowerbeds, and a kitchen garden that supplied produce for the table. Like many large houses of its era, Algonac had
greenhouses for cultivating fresh flowers—such as exotic and fashionable orchids—year-round. Warren Delano's son Frederic wrote
admiringly of landscaper Andrew Jackson Downing's skill with Algonac's plantings. "[E]mphasis was naturally placed on adaptability
to every season," he wrote of his childhood home, "thus evergreens
(Norway Spruces, Hemlocks, and Pines); Sugar Maples, Elms, Ashes,

Beeches; Locusts, Nut Trees, and Oaks for other seasons, not to mention other less familiar shrubs and the like."[2]

In the middle of one summer night, Warren Delano awakened his entire family, including little Sara, to see something special in the garden. Warren wrapped Sara in his strong arms and led his brood outside into the moonlit grounds, the Hudson River glimmering in the distance. There, in front of them, was a night-blooming cereus, a species of cactus whose luminous white and gold flowers appear only once a year.

Native to China, cereuses were expensive and difficult to grow outside of the tropics. Those who could afford to cultivate them often hosted parties to celebrate their blooming. Sara and her siblings never forgot the flower's magical bloom, as well as its rich fragrance.

By dawn, the cereus flower had withered away. But the enchantment of Algonac to the Delano children grew with each passing year. As one of them wrote, "As the years rolled on, the family increased in numbers, the trees grew, and it became more and more truly a home."[3] There were family accidents, of course. One day little Sara tripped and hit her head against a cabinet in the drawing room. Rather than call a doctor, Warren grabbed a needle and thread and sewed up the wound himself.[4]

Delano also sponsored the construction of a Unitarian church in nearby Newburgh. As a devout, minimalist Calvinist, Delano could not bear to expose his family to a whiff of the "high church" Anglicanism that was sweeping New York society. However luxurious their estates, the Puritan values of New England remained strong among the clipper ship magnates. "There is no standing room for any creed between our Unitarian faith and the papal church," Delano declared.[5]

Commerce was visible all the time from Algonac's windows, but it never came calling on the Delano family in their quiet home on the west bank of the Hudson River. Occasionally a paddlewheel steamer belonging to Cornelius Vanderbilt—its decks cluttered with sightseers—would chuff past on its way to Albany. Tall sloops carrying cargo bound for New York from the Erie Canal glided silently in the other direction, their trapezoid sails billowing in the wind. Delano could hear the roar of locomotives on the opposite bank.

Here at Algonac—named for the Algonquin word for "hill and river"—the patriarch hoped, his Yankee Delano clan would reside for generations to come. It was a serene, semifeudal existence on America's Rhine.

Warren was now one of America's few dozen millionaires. He had earned the $100,000 competence he had sought as a youth—enough to make one a member of the American upper strata—and, on his second trip to China in his middle years, he'd made far more, with his bride and young daughters at his side. His fortune was diversified in a variety of sectors, a strategy that seemed to insulate his family from the economic panics that shook the American economy every ten years or so. By the 1850s, according to family sources, Warren Delano and his brothers had ownership stakes in at least eight clippers. Although the records have been lost, it can be surmised that these included all swift ships flying his good friend's Abbot Low's house flag: *Houqua, Samuel Russell, Oriental, Surprise, N. B. Palmer, Contest, Jacob Bell,* and the recently salvaged *Great Republic.*[6] He had additional holdings in Maryland copper mines, Pennsylvania coal mines, and Manhattan real estate.[7] The Delano fortune seemed self-sustaining, generating enough income through dividends to allow Warren, Catherine, and their growing brood of children to live in halcyon splendor, secluded from the rest of the world.

In an age when the average life expectancy was between just thirty-eight and forty-four years, Warren had waited until his thirties to get married, all because he had sacrificed so many of his prime years in China making money. This delay no doubt magnified Warren's fervid obsession with family. He did not let the cares of business intrude into the pages of the "Algonac Diaries," nor did he talk about his business accomplishments. According to one family member, "There was an inhibition handed down from father to son, and common in New England as in old England: 'Don't brag: it's a man's job to do things, but men of action should not talk of their exploits.'" Another side to the Delano ethos was that one should never burden people with your problems. Life was uncertain enough as it was, even in the grandeur of Algonac. Whining was never acceptable, especially in public.

The Delanos occasionally paid visits to other stately homes, including the Staten Island, New York, summer retreat of William Henry Aspinwall—remembered in the family as a good friend of Warren's. There he could view an art collection that included works by Spanish old masters Bartolomé Esteban Murillo and Diego Velázquez (one of which, according to Delano family biographer Rita Halle Kleeman, was purchased from the Dutch royal family "for what was said to have been a fabulous sum").[8] Aspinwall may have visited the Delanos at Algonac, as his sister Mary Rebecca had recently married a nearby squire, the reclusive physician Isaac Roosevelt, whose Rosedale estate was just across the Hudson. Of this alliance of old Dutch pedigree and Yankee shipping money, Isaac's grandson Franklin would write one day, "Thus the stock kept virile and abreast of the time."[9]

When in New York for the winter season, Warren and Catherine attended lectures by the transcendentalist philosopher Ralph Waldo Emerson, who preached the values of "self-reliance" to adoring audiences. Although also a committed abolitionist, Emerson was afraid to attack slavery in public for fear of mob violence. In writing, however, he was explicit: if slavery continued, "the name of this nation, hitherto the sweet omen of religion and liberty, will stink to the world."[10] By the 1850s, the Yankee poet was firmly in the patronage of the circle of merchants from his old Canton days, and his daughter, Edith, had married into the family: her husband was William Hathaway Forbes, son of John Murray Forbes.

Of his daughter's father-in-law, Emerson wrote: "Never was such force, good meaning, good sense, good action, combined with such domestic lovely behavior, such modesty and persistent preference for others. Wherever he moved, he was the benefactor." In the nineteenth century, literary snobs looked down upon men in trade as uncultured; Emerson firmly removed Forbes from such a view because he believed the great China merchant had a holistic perspective regarding art, philosophy, and commerce: "How little this man suspects, with his sympathy for men and his respect for lettered and scientific people, that he is not likely, in any company, to meet a man superior to himself."[11]

Warren and Catherine Delano would have nodded in approval. Catherine was, after all, a Forbes cousin. On the matter of race and slavery, Warren Delano was as adamant as Emerson: "just laws for the Colored man as well as the White man," he wrote to his brother Franklin, now retired from Grinnell, Minturn & Company and living across the Hudson with his wife, Laura.[12]

Like Delano, John Murray Forbes detested chattel slavery. Although he never became a full-fledged abolitionist, he called for slavery's restriction in the western territories and once entertained the fire-eating activist John Brown at tea. Many of their peers in Boston and New York—scions of the powerful Lowell, Appleton, and Lawrence families—were proslavery because of their huge stakes in New England's textile mills. Abolishing slavery would disrupt the supply chain that funneled cheap cotton picked by enslaved African-Americans to the northern brokerages and then onward to the looms of New Bedford, Providence, Waltham, and Lowell. Many shipowners, if not openly proslavery, felt quite conflicted about the South's "peculiar institution" for the same reason.

Forbes, Delano, and other skeptics of slavery saw no contradiction in their being antislavery owners of fast clipper ships—the profits of which depended on crimps to forcibly round up crews, captains flogging their men for discipline, and paltry wages for the crew. Shipping fit neatly into the northern "free labor" system, in which sailors, unlike slaves, were paid (in the minds of the shipowners, fairly) for their work but still had no collective bargaining power or ownership rights. The same paternalistic mind-set carried over into their other enterprises such as mining and railroads. The best economic laws were "natural laws": if new groups, especially immigrants, were willing to work for less and improve the company's bottom line, so be it. "I cannot and will not pay any man more than $1.50 a day for ten hours' work," Warren Delano complained. He saw immigrants as a "new element that knows the value of shelter, food & clothing,"[13] and felt no animosity toward them—although he felt little sympathy, either. Like the opium business, human suffering could be justified in the name of respectability, honor, and profit—for all the right people, especially one's family.

The Forbes and Delano families shared other views and ways. Forbes kept in regular touch with Warren and Catherine—after all, it was he who had brought the couple together in the first place, ten years before. And in business, the master of Naushon Island and the master of Algonac still worked closely together. Beyond their shared investments in various clippers, Forbes and Delano joined forces to invest in coal mining, the source of the main fuel powering the nation's locomotives, steamships, and iron furnaces.[14]

While Delano lavished his money on making Algonac beautiful, John Murray Forbes went for simple surroundings. The cottages of Naushon Island were spare and basic in decor. His daughter Sarah Forbes Hughes wrote, "In any building which he personally used, he wanted room, warmth, and convenience; he did not like showy coloring, inside or out, but there ended his interest."[15] The real attraction for him was the great outdoors: horseback riding, sailing, and picnicking on the beach. The Forbes family yachts had nonshowy names such as *Wild Duck*.[16] And he didn't put on aristocratic pretensions about his family's Scottish origins, joking that his ancestors were "probably a set of old cattle thieves."[17] Forbes himself, despite or perhaps because of his roots in the opium trade, donated generously to educational and cultural causes in the Boston area. His pet project was the reestablishment of Milton Academy, near his brother

Robert's home, as one of America's most prominent nonsectarian boarding schools.

The Delanos, although adopted New Yorkers, still made sure to give their children a good dose of New England values. They didn't have a private island like the Forbeses' Naushon, but they did have their historic homestead in Fairhaven, where the old salt Captain Warren had hung the Delano coat-of-arms above the door. Every summer, the Delano clan boarded a Fall River Line steamer in New York to spend a few weeks with Grandfather Warren. The old captain's first wife, Deborah, had died in 1827. Sara and the other grandchildren were told to call their grandfather's second wife, Elizabeth, "Mrs. Delano," not "Grandmother." They called her Grandmother anyway; Elizabeth and Captain Warren had been married for more than two decades. Sons Warren II, Franklin, and Ned gritted their teeth and barely tolerated their stepmother, perhaps because she, in their eyes, was an interloper in their Delano clan.

Now in his eighties, Grandfather Warren was still formidable, always wearing a black frock coat and clutching a gold-headed cane. He also sported a toupee that the family thought was laughable, but no one dared mention it. At the dinner table, he always made sure that his grandchildren got large slabs of butter on their plates.

"Grandpa, not so much butter," they would protest.

"Eat it, child, it's good for you," he'd growl.

Although the old captain didn't have the retinue of servants that his son's family enjoyed at Algonac, he and his wife still employed a butler, one of whose tasks was to unfold, shake out, and refold the contents of their houseguests' suitcases because, as granddaughter Sara remembered, her stepgrandmother "never know otherwise what might be brought into the house."[18]

For his part, Warren II made sure that his children never went to the public beach but rather swam by themselves in a secluded cove near their grandfather's house. It may have been snobbery, but it also may have been fear of waterborne diseases, including the much-dreaded polio. Catherine Delano kept to herself whatever opinions she may have had regarding the family's separation from the rest of the world.

Yet there were cracks in the cool, confident Delano family façade. Ned—still fat, still unmarried, and still living with his brother Warren's family at Algonac—worried that Warren's furious pace of high living and high-stakes investing was simply not sustainable. Warren was "heels & head in business," Ned wrote in his diary. "Mixing in all kinds. I fear he is branching out too much."[19]

Ned was right.

After a brief few years of trading supremacy on the high seas, the extreme clipper ships were no longer making profits on the long-haul cargo run around Cape Horn to California. Filling the gap were slower, more capacious vessels, the medium clippers, which required fewer crew and could carry more cargo than their faster, more heavily sparred predecessors. William Henry Webb supposedly remarked to the mate of extreme clipper *Young America* in 1853: "Take good care of her, Mister, because after she's gone, there will be no more like her."[20]

It was true. Webb built no extreme clippers after *Young America*, focusing instead on steam-powered vessels and fuller-bodied medium clippers.

Not that *Young America* was a financial disaster for her owner. Far from it. A few successful voyages to California repaid Webb's investment (more than $140,000, four times what it had cost to build the earliest clipper prototypes such as *Houqua* a decade earlier). But Webb, the most cautious and conservative of the core quartet of clipper ship builders, had seen what was coming. So had Captain Nathaniel Palmer, who would soon complete the nearly impossible task of rebuilding McKay's *Great Republic*, his final building effort. So, perhaps, had the brilliant but erratic naval designer John Willis Griffiths, who left the shipbuilding world altogether to become a financially struggling publisher and maritime theoretician. In the pages of his *Monthly Nautical Magazine and Quarterly Review,* Griffiths slid into obscurity as he sought to popularize concepts such as "wave line theory" and propeller "slip," and continued to insist against the evidence that his design ideas had kicked off the great clipper race.[21]

Donald McKay was faring somewhat better, even after the tragic loss of his masterpiece *Great Republic.* He had grudgingly diversified into constructing medium clippers to meet the demands of some of his Boston clients, churning out a series of shapely midsized ships such as *Defender* and *Daniel Webster.* Still, the Nova Scotian stubbornly held on to the dream of extreme sailing vessels. The four extreme clipper ships he built for the Liverpool merchant James Baines, for use in the Australia trade, were arguably his finest work. *Lightning,* *James Baines, Champion of the Seas,* and *Donald McKay* were refined versions of the *Sovereign of the Seas*: three masts, flat bottoms, and rated at around two thousand tons each. His old friend John Willis Griffiths sang *Lightning*'s praises in his magazine: "No timid hand or hesitating brain gave form and dimensions to the *Lightning.* Very great stability; acute extremities; full, short midship body; comparatively [*sic*] small deadrise, and the longest end forward, are points in the excellence of this ship."[22] She proved to be yet another thoroughbred masterpiece. During her delivery run from New York to Liverpool in 1854, *Lightning* achieved speeds approaching 18.5 knots, and made 436 miles in a single day.

McKay's British clients did not understand or feel comfortable with the American clipper concept. *Lightning*'s new captain took one look at her hollow bows and ordered the company shipwrights to add additional planking for buoyancy. McKay was furious, calling them the "wood butchers of Liverpool." Nonetheless, each of the four clippers proved to be fantastic vessels, breaking records and making huge amounts of money for Baines.

These were the last of the true American-built extreme clippers. Despite their successes, there would be no more buyers for McKay's vessels.

His prestige and his records would remain. But fame had not bought financial stability for Donald McKay. By the mid-1850s, he was in a precarious position. Although he remained the heroic shipbuilder in public, in private he despaired at his financial distress. He reserved special ire for his younger brother Lauchlan, whom he accused of putting his grandiose dreams of being a great businessman ahead of his nautical craft: "As a boy, I knew you to be mean and selfish; but as a man, I forgot those early traits of character, and loved you affectionately as a brother," Donald snarled at Lauchlan.[23] The two brothers sued each other over what appears to have been real estate that they owned jointly in the Boston area ("You promised to send me $220,000 but only sent me $180,000"), though it seems that the conflict was more visceral than financial.

Donald McKay was proud of being a craftsman, but he was clearly very sensitive to slights of his status as a businessman and a naval architect. It was hard to blame him; he was still smarting financially and emotionally from the loss of *Great Republic*, and he knew that he could never build a ship like her again. Frustrated and angry, McKay wrote another letter to Lauchlan, accusing him of general incompetence as a captain, embezzling funds from his voyages as master of *Sovereign of the Seas*, and taking up with a prostitute. Above all, McKay was furious that his brother was going around telling people that the great shipbuilder was "*insane*, a mere '*woodchopper*,' void of all 'business talent.'"

"My ships are monuments on the ocean, and they float triumphantly on every sea," Donald wrote his brother in retort.[24]

Sadly, Lauchlan might have had a point. Donald McKay's net worth at the time was only about $15,000—substantial for a tradesman but poor for the nation's arguably most preeminent shipwright. In the high-stakes shipping game, McKay had dreamed large, built big, and triumphed in the quest for speed, but he'd lost in the race for riches.

* * *

One great McKay clipper flying the American flag was destined to make a bold second entrance onto the world stage. In the winter of 1855, a giant ship entered New York Harbor that made even the most hardened sailors turn their heads in awe. It was *Great Republic*, McKay's masterpiece destroyed by fire on that catastrophic Boxing Day of 1853. She was no longer nearly as mighty looking as she had once been. A simple scrolled billethead had replaced her screaming eagle figurehead. She still had four masts, but they had been reduced in height by seventeen feet. There were three decks now instead of four, and she measured 3,300 tons rather than her original 4,500. Yet she was still the largest merchant vessel in the world, sail or steam.

Captain Nat Palmer's restoration was a miracle. He had produced a leaner, less heavily sparred ship that was much more economical to operate: she needed a crew of only fifty to operate her rather than her original hundred. Let loose with sails unfurled, *Great Republic* sailed across the Atlantic in a mere nineteen days, and, in the words of her captain, "behaved nobly."[25] The following year, she sailed from New York to San Francisco in only ninety-two days, just three days short of *Flying Cloud*'s record. *Great Republic* would soon be sailing to different ports. Owner Abbot Low found that the most profitable use of his big ship was not the fragrant tea trade but hauling smelly guano out of South America for use as fertilizer.

The tragedy of *Great Republic* was that as beautiful as she was, she was only a shadow of what Donald McKay had meant her to be. She never got the chance to surge along under full sail—most likely smashing every record on the books.

Until his death, Donald McKay asserted that *Great Republic* would have beaten any other ship afloat. "Long cherished dreams were undoubtedly rent asunder," wrote his grandson, "for he built his mammoth clipper to conquer the wind and waves, as well as for financial gain and fame."[26]

The California clippers that had made McKay famous, those "monuments on the ocean," were now beautiful anachronisms.

California now had robust manufacturing and agricultural sectors, which enabled it to produce more of its own foodstuffs and consumer goods and sell them at lower prices than those shipped in haste from the East Coast. With the state increasingly self-sufficient, the public (and the merchants) demanded not sheer speed but also regular and reliable service. As a result, by the mid-1850s, steamships had conquered the passenger and mail routes. William Henry Aspinwall, perhaps the most aggressive and visionary of all New York ship operators, had leveraged government subsidies to achieve the dream of seamless, steam-powered passage between New York and San Francisco. The Panama-Pacific Railroad had opened with great fanfare in January 1855. The 46.7-mile railroad cost in excess of $8 million to build, eight times the original stock floated by Aspinwall and his business partners five years before. Six thousand men lost their lives in the undertaking, mostly from disease. Yet the railroad proved to be an extremely profitable investment for all concerned, cutting travel time across the isthmus from several days by mule to a mere four hours by locomotive.[27]

Among these investors was William Henry Webb, who had built so many of Aspinwall's steamships for the California trade. Webb's shrewd deployment of capital allowed the naval architect to weather the upcoming financial crisis in ways that his greatest rival, Donald McKay, could not. In fact, Webb's investment in the Panama railroad made him a very rich man. By the end of the decade, he had about $400,000 in the bank.[28]

Delano's old business partner Abbot Low was less diversified when it came to investing his China fortune. Rather than international railroads or Kentucky coal mines, Low put his opium-and-tea fortune in two projects that intimately involved his native Atlantic seaboard. Both revolutionized US commerce.

The first was the Baltimore & Ohio Railroad, which had been chartered in 1827 to connect the riches of the Midwestern heartland to the port city of Baltimore, much as the Erie Canal had done for

New York. By the 1850s, its dozens of steam-powered locomotives were hauling American coal, lumber, and grain for consumption in burgeoning American metropolises or for export to Europe.

Abbot wasn't alone among the Canton bachelors when it came to investing in American railroads. John Murray Forbes had long been involved in both the Chicago, Burlington, and Quincy Railroad and the Michigan Central Railroad Company, greatly expanding his family's fortune.[29] The railroads allowed both Forbes brothers, John Murray and Robert Bennet, to turn away from the sea as a means of commerce, although they continued to embrace it as a form of recreation. Both became avid yachtsmen, racing sleek sailing boats off their breezy Naushon Island compound. As John Murray's daughter Sarah remembered of her father, "All ships were deeply interesting to him, and dashing through the waves on a ship or yacht in a 'wholesail breeze' made his spirits rise."[30] Only this time it was in the safe confines of Buzzards Bay, not the rolling deep of the South China Sea or the treacherous eddies of the Pearl River.

But Low's second project was his real coup: an investment in an electrical marvel that proved faster than any clipper or steam-powered locomotive: the transatlantic cable. On August 16, 1858, after months of laying and splicing across more than two thousand miles of sea floor, engineers telegraphed the following message from Queen Victoria in Morse code: "The Queen is convinced that the President will join her in fervently hoping that the electric cable, which now connects Great Britain with the United States, will prove an additional link between the nations, whose friendship is founded upon their common interest and reciprocal esteem."

President James Buchanan cabled back: "May the Atlantic telegraph, under the blessing of Heaven, prove to be a bond of perpetual peace and friendship between the kindred nations, and an instrument destined by Divine Providence to diffuse religion, civilization, law, and liberty throughout the world."[31]

It would be another decade before the Atlantic cable was reliable, but its ramifications were enormous. News and financial transactions could be sent across the Atlantic electronically in a matter of seconds rather than two or more weeks by sailing packet or passenger steamer.

Just as Low's clippers allowed his tea to be the first to arrive in the marketplace, his transatlantic cable gave him a decided advantage when it came to financial information (and access to credit) from the Old World.

Yet despite his success in other ventures, Low did not remove himself entirely from clipper ships, his first expertise. He even built a series of small clipper barques for the Japanese trade to augment his bigger Chinese fleet.[32] That his younger brother Charlie still needed a job as a captain may have been a minor part of the equation. Miraculously, amidst the general slump in the shipping business, the House of Low had the financial acumen to keep its fleet of extreme clippers sailing profitably, mainly because of its continued business focus on China rather than on California. The American demand for tea was just as strong as it had been a decade earlier, and the opium trade was booming thanks to the terms of the Treaty of Nanking. Unlike the other operators, Abbot Low saw the San Francisco trade as a profitable but short-lived business opportunity. He didn't have much interest in building medium clippers to compete in the California trade.

The firm's ships were built to last for the long-term, and Low maintained them well. In 1856, while other owners were selling or laying up their clippers, Abbot Low purchased a second-hand extreme clipper, the three-year-old *Jacob Bell*, which at 1,300 tons was a reasonable-sized vessel but no *Sovereign of the Seas* or *Great Republic*. Captain Charlie Low commanded the ship (named after the New York shipwright who designed her) for one voyage. Used to the comfort and elegance of his custom-built *N. B. Palmer*, Low was circumspect about his new command, writing: "She was a fine ship, of the same size as the *N. B. Palmer*, but she did not have as fine accommodation."[33] Like many sailors, Low bonded with the ships that he sailed, but *Jacob Bell*, as fine a ship as she was, could never replace "the Yacht."

After an unremarkable 114-day trip from New York, *Jacob Bell* dropped anchor in Hong Kong harbor. After greeting all of the captains of the vessels in port, the thirty-six-year-old Captain Low experienced a shock: he was the oldest master in the China trade. For this, he was jovially appointed commodore of the fleet then in Hong Kong. Every morning at eight o'clock, he fired a gun from *Jacob Bell*, the sounds of which boomed and echoed off the bluffs of Hong Kong Island.

Yet among the forest of masts, Captain Low could not have helped but notice the growing number of funnels spewing coal smoke into the air, soiling the canvas of many a sailing ship. By the late 1850s, steamships finally had the range to make the opium run between India and China, although they had to pause for coal along the way. For now, the long, oceanic run between New York or London and China still seemed secure. But within a decade, Alfred Holt & Company (popularly known as the Blue Funnel Line) would launch the steamship *Agamemnon*, the first of three vessels that would sail regularly between Liverpool and Hong Kong, with a coaling stop at Mauritius, an island in the Indian Ocean. The voyage would take a mere fifty-eight days.

It was probably then that Captain Low realized that he was an old man in a young man's game, and that his days at sea were numbered. Besides, he missed his growing family, now safely ashore in Massachusetts. "Do you recollect," he wrote his wife, "how I drove you out last year along Boston Road [most likely in Billerica, Massachusetts], and we saw the children and young ladies coming home . . . driving down to Salem, stopping at Aunt Porter's and hurrying you away from ever [*sic*] place that I might be alone with you . . . I can imagine I hear the old bell ringing in Blubber Hollow as we drive past the Engine House at two o'clock homeward bound. Oh how I wish I was with you behind the old roan mare."[34]

What was especially troubling, however, as Captain Low looked over his professional shoulder, was the fewer and fewer young men who wanted to run away to sea, as he had twenty years before. When he scanned the ranks of his sailors, the captain was hard-pressed to spot a future commander among them. Finding a good first mate to execute a captain's orders and keep the men in line had become a problem, with or without the lash. Low's first mate aboard *Jacob Bell*, a New Bedford native who had come off a whaler, was "perfectly worthless on a merchant ship."[35] Low could have demoted the man. Instead, he fired him and left him in Hong Kong to find his own way home. Low then promoted his second mate to take the whaler's place.

The Hong Kong in which Low found himself in 1856 was not like the mysterious Canton he and his brothers had known. Gone was the sense of adventure and danger, of living on the edge of a vast and alien land. Rather than an outpost, it felt more like an extension of Great Britain. The opium trade, now conducted with near impunity, had attracted droves of fortune-seeking Englishmen (including relatives of the venerable China traders Robert Jardine and James Matheson) who sought to replicate the comforts of their home island while getting filthy rich. They bet on horses at the Happy Valley Racecourse. The midday meal, or tiffin, was a sacred ritual, as were evening feasts fit for Houqua's banquet hall, only with beef Wellington replacing plovers' eggs. "No lack of good dishes or of pleasant iced drinks at a Shanghai tiffin," noted a correspondent of the *London Times*. "Everyone is able, and is indeed obliged to have a lordly indifference to expense. They cannot control it, and they must let it go. There is no struggling or contriving to keep up appearances. The profits are large and the expenditure—laissez aller."[36] The *Times* reporter neglected to mention that the ice for the Englishmen's drinks came from frozen ponds in Low's native Massachusetts, courtesy of the Boston "ice king" Frederic Tudor.

Low sailed back to New York with a cargo of tea and resumed command of his beloved *N. B. Palmer.*

The rivalries between American and British houses, especially in the clipper trade, had subsided over the years, as American capital shifted away from the bitter sea and toward gold-flecked California and the agriculturally rich western territories. European investors, especially London-based Baring Brothers & Co., similarly funneled British capital into the railroads that stitched together the expanding United States. The old China trade had been about keeping it in the family, but in this new landscape of international investment, it was best to keep it within a tight-knit group of friends. The "special relationship" between the Americans and British in the Canton Factories—heralded years before by Robert Bennet Forbes as "*Union*—not merely political, not merely commercial, but the union of principle, the *union* of heart & soul"—had blossomed into a true gentlemen's agreement.[37] To the American and British international elites, it had become clear that cooperation in the China trade was much better for everyone than competition. In terms of wealth and taste, they realized that they had more in common with each other than with most of their own countrymen.

The formalized union of British and American high finance had come in 1851, when Baring Brothers—the London bank that had dealt with Houqua for decades—tapped Russell Sturgis to become its first non-British partner. The unflappable, courtly Sturgis, Warren Delano's first boss in Canton, took to British aristocratic life immediately and never returned to his native New England.

The relationship between Barings and the old Russell & Company coterie proved exceedingly powerful. From the European side of the Atlantic, Sturgis saw that France was experiencing a serious shortage of grain. So he wrote his old friend John Murray Forbes—president of the Michigan Central Railroad—to buy up fifty thousand barrels of wheat and ship it across the Atlantic. To prevent wheat prices from spiking, Forbes and Sturgis had to keep the huge transaction a complete secret, which they did. Both men knew that a bread shortage in France could lead to a revolution, so it was in their best interest to ship Emperor Napoléon III as much wheat as they could and profit immensely from the transaction.[38]

Another beneficiary of the "*union* of heart & soul" was Warren Delano, who had spent his childhood hating the British and had derided Canton as a "most stupid place." The once-thrifty whaler's son from Fairhaven was now raising his family in the style of the British nobility he had once mocked, in a country house stuffed with mementoes of China. Yet he was destined to return to the Middle Kingdom, not by choice but because of personal calamity. Unlike the "woodchopper" Donald McKay, who could make money only by building things, Warren Delano had access to a commodity that satisfied baser human needs.

CHAPTER 16

SURPRISE AND DANGER

I suppose it was altogether terrifying to my mother to give up her beautiful home and its peaceful security.

—SARA DELANO[1]

By the mid-1850s, many of the laid-up extreme clippers on New York's waterfront had been sold to foreign owners or had their rigs cut down drastically to save on crew costs. The saddest case of all was *Flying Cloud*. After her record-setting eighty-nine-day passage from New York to San Francisco in 1854, the ship had continued on its last, round-the-world voyage under the remarkable Captain Josiah Creesy and his navigator wife, Eleanor. Saved by Creesy after grounding on a reef in the South China Sea, the great ship had arrived back in New York in dire need of a refit. Instead, she was sent on to California under Captain William H. Reynard. The new captain seems not to have had the same chemistry as his predecessor, and the battered ship took a pathetic 186 days to reach port—although on one day, the ship reportedly showed a touch of her former speed by making 402 miles in 24 hours.[2] Upon her return, Moses Grinnell ordered *Flying Cloud* laid up.

Only six years old, her spars were rotten, her hull leaky, and her brass work corroded. Her owners had no interest in providing money for renewal. She had proved to be a profitable ship in her time, as well as fast, but the truth behind her sad condition was that Captain Creesy's hard driving had worn her out. Grinnell, Minturn's other clipper ship, *Sea Serpent*, never set records, but the company kept her in the China trade for another two decades. That Captain Howland was easier on her than Captain Creesy on *Flying Cloud* made her cheaper to operate.

Within a few years, Moses Grinnell sold his once-prized *Flying Cloud* to British interests, who cut down her rig and put her into the lumber trade.

Although sailing ships continued to make the Cape Horn route, steamships and railroads had created a seamless and reliable network between the two coasts. Then the unthinkable happened: a disaster at sea that would bring the American economy to its knees. On September 3, 1857, the paddlewheel steamship SS *Central America*—designed by William H. Webb—departed the port of Aspinwall, Panama (named for William Henry Aspinwall), bound for New York. The flagship of the United States Mail Steamship Company, she was only five years old; and at 2,100 tons, she was about the size of McKay's *Sovereign of the Seas*. On board were 477 passengers, 100 crew, and more than 9 tons of California gold coins and specie worth about $2 million. Six days after departing Panama, as she was steaming northward off the Carolinas, a hurricane struck the ship at full force. SS *Central America* was no match for the storm. Leaks flooded the boiler room, and the engines and the pumps ground to a halt.

Those on board reacted with disbelief; this was supposed to be a routine voyage. The ship was essentially a bigger, stronger version of a Hudson River steamer, equipped with powerful engines that eliminated the vagaries of winds and tides. Her sails were an auxiliary measure, there to give assistance in case of an engine breakdown or to provide an extra bit of power if sailing with the wind. But now, with power gone and rudimentary sails ripped to shreds, *Central America* was helpless in the tempest. Her captain's only hope was to fly her flag upside down, signaling distress to a passing vessel. The ship drifted farther and farther away from the American coast. As seas broke over her bulwarks, she slowly settled at the stern, despite the best efforts of an all-hands bucket brigade. The women and children aboard were rowed to a nearby ship that had emerged from the storm. On September 12, *Central America* sank to the bottom of the Atlantic, taking more than 420 male passengers and crew with her.

The sinking of the SS *Central America* was the worst passenger ship disaster in American history up to that time. And the loss of the ship's gold sent shudders through Wall Street. Bankers in New York, eagerly awaiting the specie from the ship, now found themselves staring at empty vaults and piles of devalued paper money. The American economy was already in trouble. A month before the sinking, the Ohio Life Insurance and Trust Company had collapsed. Worse still, land values in the western states had been falling throughout the summer, as European demand for American foodstuffs declined. Railroads, which had been eagerly building lines to service the new territories, found themselves unable to service their loans from the banks.

There was nothing the US Treasury Department could do to stem the panic; the North's economy was in free fall. Many rich men who had invested heavily in western lands and railroads were ruined. Among those hit by the crisis was Warren Delano. Although his pioneering clipper ship *Memnon* was a memory (stripped by pirates after running aground years before), he almost certainly still had a financial stake in A. A. Low & Brother, as well as holdings in mining and real estate. He was rich enough that he felt there was plenty of room to gamble. Yet as commodity prices dropped through the fall of 1857, so did the revenues coming from almost all of his far-flung speculative holdings. Those banks that survived the carnage refused to lend money. Coal was hit especially hard, as reduced demand from ironworks and other manufacturers wiped out once-fat profit margins.[3]

Delano's Midas touch had deserted him. His stock holdings had collapsed, and what dividends he did collect were not enough to maintain his family or his lifestyle. "The monetary situation from New York [is] worse than ever," Delano wrote in his diary, as Houqua's face loomed down at him from the portrait above his desk. "Stocks, bonds, and money tighter. Failures abundant and confidence diminishing. The *New York Times* reports further depression in stocks. I find if I had deferred settlement of my stock purchases, I would have paid over $900 more than I settled for."[4] As their financial prospects darkened, Warren and Catherine contemplated the shame of bankruptcy. Still, in the best of the Yankee tradition, they did their best to put on a good face in public. Even in front of family, Warren seems to have hidden the stress and sleepless nights caused by things gone out of his control. "Warren is looking as well as before the disasters to his fortunes," wrote one of his brothers, most likely Franklin, "and says he feels tolerably well and has a better appetite. He spoke of disastrous financial things in a general way, remarking that there had been a great change since I saw him."[5]

As his straits grew more dire, Delano noted that Abiel Abbot Low was still prospering in the China trade—Americans still craved tea, and the Chinese still craved opium. His stake in the Baltimore & Ohio continued to pay off handsomely. He could see that the situation in China was admittedly volatile. A Second Opium War had broken out in 1856, the year before the panic. This time traditional enemies Great Britain and France joined forces to strong-arm the Chinese government into legalizing the opium trade completely, opening all remaining Chinese ports to Western trade, and establishing diplomatic legations in the Chinese capital. After four years of fierce fighting and broken treaties, British and French forces would reach Peking, burning large portions of the city to the ground, including the emperor's summer palace.

For the Chinese, the defeat would be total. The once-mighty Celestial Kingdom would now be at the mercy of the Western powers. During the next fifty years, England, France, and others would carve up China's coast into "spheres of influence." While China never became a colonial possession like India, and its imperial family nominally remained in power, it was powerless to stop the settlement of its port cities by the reviled *fanqui* or to stem the still-growing addiction of its people to the "foreign mud."

As in the past, American traders had stepped aside to let Britain and France do the dirty work. The American men of Russell & Company spent the years of fighting huddled within the tightly guarded British island fortress of Hong Kong. This time their homes did not go up in flames, and they were allowed to resume trading immediately after each phase of the conflict ended.

America had, however, ventured into the imperialist arena—in Japan, in 1853, when it sent a fleet of steam-powered US Navy warships into Edo Harbor. Japan had coal, and the American government wanted a fueling station for its military vessels. Commodore Matthew Perry offered the Japanese government an ultimatum: open up to Western trade or face withering American cannonfire. The US shipping industry also had a special grudge against the closed, forbidden country: shipwrecked whalers who washed up on Japan's shores had long been subjected to imprisonment and death.

It was a strange echo of the British Royal Navy's appearance in Canton in 1842 to avenge the twenty thousand seized chests of opium. The Japanese, who had banned all white Christians (save for the nonmissionary Dutch) from their shores since the early seventeenth century, decided that the best course of action would be to open up to Western trade while preserving their sovereignty.

Matthew Perry returned to America triumphant, declaring in a speech that "Westward will the course of empire take its way . . . The people of America will, in some form or other, extend their dominion and their power until they shall have brought within their mighty embrace the islands of the great Pacific, and placed the Saxon race upon the eastern shores of Asia."[6]

Perry's speech proved darkly prescient, although Japan turned out to be a tougher nut to crack than China in opening itself to "spheres of influence," not to mention the opium trade. To get the Japanese to agree to sign a Treaty of Amity and Commerce in 1858, an American diplomat threatened to call upon the Royal Navy squadron stationed at Hong Kong to join in teaching the heathen Japanese a lesson. This time, however, there was no British navy involvement and no bloodshed. Within a few decades, the Japanese had modernized their military, especially their navy, to such an extent that any Western power would challenge them at its own peril, something the Russian czar would soon enough discover, when, at the Battle of Tsushima in 1905, the Imperial Japanese Navy obliterated his fleet.

En route to Japan, Perry's fleet dropped anchor in Hong Kong Harbor. While there, the commodore took shore leave in luxurious lodgings at the Russell & Company headquarters. The firm was still making money hand over fist in the drug trade, with the newest scions of the Perkins and Forbes families securely at the helm.

Abiel Abbot Low jumped at the new commercial opportunity in Japan, deploying some of his clippers, including the aging but still sprightly *Houqua*. Japanese tea and goods quickly became all the rage in America. "Being entirely free from dye," Low noted, the tea "preserves remarkable purity and delicacy of flavor." Not only was it delicious, but also his company had direct oversight of its production. "In Japan," he continued, "the uncolored leaf is brought to the warehouses of the foreign merchant and, under his supervision, fired, put in boxes, matted, strapped, and marked, ready to go on board ship."[7] Unlike in China, where fraud was rampant, there was no danger of the tea crates being stuffed with sticks, stones, and other plants to make weight.

*　　*　　*

Five years old in 1859, Sara Delano was too young to comprehend why her father wandered around the house looking worried. Warren Delano's fortunes had worsened since the panic two years before. With great regret, he had sold the family's townhouse on Colonnade Row. Yet the sale of the New York mansion provided only a temporary solution. The bills kept mounting for the household expenses to which the Delanos had been accustomed for so long: the wages for a small army of servants and gardeners, a fleet of coaches, a stable full of horses, and the best produce from the Hudson Valley. Warren Delano could shutter Algonac and move his growing family back to Fairhaven and his father's house. Or he could find a way to remake his fortune.

That fall, as word of Chinese defeats filtered back to New York, and tensions between the slaveholding South and the free-labor North increased, cash-strapped Warren Delano announced that he would be going again to the eastern shores of Asia to rebuild his fortune. How he would do it, only his closest business confidants knew: he would rejoin Russell & Company as a partner and return to the opium trade, not only shipping the drug into mainland China but also importing it into the United States for medical use.

Catherine, now pregnant with another child, was distraught at her husband's impending departure. The China trade was the domain of ambitious young bachelors, not middle-aged family men. But she worked to hide her anxiety, busying herself in cutting expenses and caring for the family's six children, with the help of her husband's cousin Nancy Church, who served as governess and tutor.

Warren could not have chosen a riskier time to leave the country. The political situation in the United States soured just as the economy had. Not only was the nation still mired in depression, with soaring unemployment, but tensions between North and South were reaching the breaking point. The South's cotton shipments slumped, as did England's demand for Northern goods. Many ships in the

Yankee commercial fleet lay idle. Shipyards saw their orders dry up. According to Arthur Clark, the total tonnage of ships built in the United States plummeted from 583,450 in 1855 to 378,000 just two years later.[8] Unable to fill their ships' holds, operators began selling their vessels at fire-sale prices, often to European interests.

Many of these once-proud vessels were pushed into the fertilizer trade, hauling bird manure from South America to ports around the world. Others were lost in accidents, sometimes with great losses of life. *Sea Witch* sank off Cuba in 1856, taking several hundred Chinese laborers with her. *Flying Fish* and *Oriental* were wrecked while leaving Chinese ports, their valuable tea cargoes disappearing too. *Staffordshire*'s end was especially violent: while on the return leg of a stormy transatlantic crossing, she ran aground and sank off the Canadian coast in December 1853, taking 170 of her 214 passengers and crew with her. Among the dead was Captain Josiah Richardson, former commander of Donald McKay's first clipper ship, the *Stag Hound*.[9] When news of the ship's sinking reached Boston, the editors of the *Boston Semi-Weekly Atlas* paid the following tribute to her captain: "We knew him personally and can say that he was modest, kind to his sailors, bold and manly in the discharge of his duty, and uniformly successful in all his undertakings. Peace to his manes, for a better sailor or a truer man never trod a ship's deck."[10] The financial and human cost of operating such big ships at high speeds, often without regular overhauls, was now a real concern.

In addition to mass unemployment, the matter of slavery came to the political fore. Despite the best efforts of those in Washington who sought to maintain the balance of power by admitting one slave state for every free state, Southern members of Congress, threatened by the power of the Northern transportation and industrial complex, cut off all subsidies for transatlantic steam travel, leaving the Collins Line to collapse into bankruptcy. Edward Knight Collins, once one of the most powerful and richest shipping magnates in America, never recovered from the blow.

In October 1859 an unsuccessful businessman and abolitionist named John Brown led a failed raid on the federal arsenal at Harpers Ferry, Virginia. Warren Delano took leave of Algonac around the same time as troops under the leadership of Colonel Robert E. Lee captured John Brown and quashed his attempt to incite and lead a slave insurrection.

As Catherine Delano worried that her husband's ship would sink in transit, the golden Hudson Valley autumn turned to silver winter, and a snowy calm settled down on Algonac. Huddled around the coal grate in the main parlor, the Delanos played games, wrote letters, and continued their school lessons as best they could. Several months after Warren left, Catherine gave birth to a baby girl whom she named Cassie. Sara, grieving with her siblings for their father now halfway around the world, called the baby the "posthumous child."[11] Warren had promised his children an absence of no more than two years.

Outside the gates of Algonac, the country edged toward war. In 1860 an unknown former congressman from Illinois named Abraham Lincoln, running as the candidate of the upstart Republican Party, was elected president of the United States with only 40 percent of the popular vote. Lincoln called for slavery's restriction "as with a chain of steel," and told one friend privately: "This is a world of compensations; and he who would *be* no slave, must consent to *have* no slave. Those who deny freedom to others, deserve it not for themselves; and, under a just God, cannot long retain it."[12, 13] After Lincoln's election, the country splintered, as eleven southern states seceded from the union and chose former Mississippi senator Jefferson Davis as their president. The Confederacy's vice president, Alexander Stephens declared, "Our new government is founded upon exactly the opposite idea; its foundations are laid, its cornerstone rests upon the great truth, that the negro is not equal to the white man; that slavery—subordination to the superior race—is his natural and normal condition."[14]

To antislavery businessmen such as Warren Delano, such statements were contemptible and further soured his already low opinion of Southern Democrats. In his experience, he said, "not all Democrats were horse thieves, but all horse thieves were Democrats."[15] By April 15 of the following year, when rebel forces shelled the union stronghold at Fort Sumter in Charleston, South Carolina, the United States of America and the Confederate States of America were at war. Almost as soon as hostilities broke out, the steam- and sail-powered ships of the Union navy blockaded the Confederacy's deep-water ports. President Lincoln's goal was to starve the rebels into submission.

To retaliate, the Confederacy contracted in secret with shipyards in Great Britain to build several fast steam-powered commerce raiders that would wreak havoc on the Yankees' fleet of clippers, transatlantic packets, and whalers. British politicians such as Prime Minister Palmerston turned a blind eye to this activity. What England couldn't destroy through commercial competition, she would destroy using the rebel government as a front. Also, a divided and weakened America was good for Great Britain's imperial ambitions. Better a subservient trading partner than a united economic competitor, on land and sea. Many British merchants were ardent supporters of the Confederacy, as they preferred an uninterrupted flow of Southern cotton to competing for Northern manufactured goods.

Yet the members of the old Canton coterie in England made sure that Britain's financial establishment did not declare economic war on the Northern economy. President Lincoln's minister to the Court of St. James's, Charles Francis Adams—son of President John Quincy Adams—worked fervently behind the scenes to make sure Great Britain stayed neutral in the conflict. At his side in London were John Murray Forbes and William Henry Aspinwall. Their mission was to try to purchase potential commerce raiders under construction in England that were "most likely to be used by the insurgents and to be dangerous in their hands."[16] The two shipping barons spent their time hobnobbing with British high society and defending the Union cause at dinner parties. They failed to purchase several ships that ultimately became notorious Confederate commerce raiders, yet they did successfully secure a $500,000 advance loan from Baring Brothers & Co. to the United States government on $4 million worth of bonds. Yet the deal came with a catch: if the United States government gave permission to American vessels to intercept British merchant vessels, the Treasury would have to return the advance. "The existing agitation of the public mind, both in and out of Parliament, rendered this condition a sine qua non," Forbes and Aspinwall wrote Treasury Secretary Salmon Chase, "and we may safely express our doubt if any other house would have undertaken to make the loan; certainly none on terms so liberal."[17] Russell Sturgis, Delano's old boss and the American-born Baring's partner, most likely smoothed the way for this deal to fund the Union war effort.

Yet other Yankee merchants couldn't resist colluding with the Confederacy, especially when it came to supplying the fledgling nation with slave labor. Using clippers for human trafficking was nothing new. Down-on-their-luck ocean greyhounds, most notably *Sea Witch*, had been used to transport Chinese indentured laborers to Cuba and Peru. Scarcely a week after Confederates fired on Fort Sumter, the Union patrol vessel USS *Saratoga* intercepted the clipper ship *Nightingale* off the coast of Africa. She had sailed from Boston with a cargo of grain, supposedly en route to Liverpool. Something, though, was amiss. The ship had no business being off the coast of Africa. *Saratoga*'s crew found no evidence of slaves on board *Nightingale*, at least not at first. But they didn't let her go. Rather, they waited until night and boarded again. There, in the ship's cargo holds and once-lavish staterooms, the Yankee officers found to their horror 961 captured Africans in chains, prostrate and terrified. The ship echoed with the cries of hundreds of captive human beings destined for Southern plantations. Sailing across the Atlantic in a week with a cargo of slaves was obviously more lucrative than sailing from China in three or more months with a hold full of tea. And when done in a ship able to outrun almost any naval vessel afloat, the enterprise was almost worth the risk. *Saratoga*'s captain seized the clipper from her shady owners, released the slaves, and sent her back to America under navy command. *Nightingale*'s captain, Francis Bowen, known as the "Prince of Slavers," jumped ship and escaped into the African wilderness.[18] *Saratoga*'s commander, Lieutenant John Julius Guthrie, may have allowed Bowen to escape because he himself was a Southern sympathizer.[19] Upon *Saratoga*'s return to Brooklyn, Guthrie resigned his commission and joined the fledgling Confederate navy.[20]

A strong supporter of the Union, Donald McKay quickly found his fortunes buoyed when the US Navy contracted with his yard to build new warships. To prepare for the real possibility that England would join forces with the Confederacy, the Canadian-born shipbuilder advocated that America's wooden warships should be armored with five-inch-thick "shellproof" iron plates. He also argued that America's underutilized fleet of extreme clippers, including *Great Republic*, could be armed, covered with iron armor, and converted into swift, steam-powered warships. This new, powerful fleet could then stand guard outside of Northern seaports, protecting them from the Royal Navy and from the Confederacy's own ironclad, which was then being constructed from the wreck of the scuttled steam frigate *Merrimac*.

"This fleet of about 2000 vessels of war . . . can be turned out in less time than four to six months, and it would be sufficient to protect our coast and meet the first storm," McKay argued in a public letter published by the *New York Times* in December 1861. "The times are gone when Europe could be frightened by thundering newspaper articles and the hollow brag of ambitious politicians; we have to show now that we know how to handle the engines of war, and to stand a hall [*sic*] of shells and balls. A powerful fleet is the best guarantee of peace for a great maritime nation."[21]

McKay proved prescient about the future of warships: in March

1862 the CSS *Merrimac* faced off against the Union ironclad USS *Monitor* off the coast of Virginia in a naval battle lasting several hours. The engagement, which ended in a draw, brought to a close the age of the wooden warship. Unfortunately, the Civil War—and ironclads— destroyed what was left of Donald McKay's finances. He had won the contract to build four ships for the US Navy, including the ironclad USS *Nausett*, which was to be put into action bombarding Confederate coastal defenses. Yet the navy did not issue finalized plans for the *Nausett* class before construction started, and, as a result, the first built exhibited severe design flaws, not the least of which being that her deck was only three inches above the waterline. The resulting design revisions meant huge cost overruns for McKay and other shipbuilders, whom the navy refused to compensate for their extra labor and materials. Faced with an additional $300,000 in debts, the desperate McKay was now in danger of losing his shipyard and would spend the rest of his life trying to claw back his losses from the American navy.[22]

It would take three decades for the McKay family to be made whole.

The Delanos, along with many other families that had made fortunes in the China trade, were committed to the cause of Lincoln and the preservation of the union. Catherine Delano made sure the children sang "The Battle Hymn of the Republic" with gusto when they worshipped at Newburgh's Unitarian Church, and Sara and her sisters learned how to sew so they could make shirts for Union soldiers. "Made by a little girl seven years old," said the label of one such garment that Sara made.[23]

Sunday was letter-writing day, and every week a batch of mail was sent by the family to their father a half world away in Hong Kong. For Warren Delano, at work in his old job at Russell & Company, the outbreak of the Civil War proved a huge boon. In addition to sending tea back to America, he took advantage of the huge market for opium-based drugs in the United States. Both sides in the conflict were using cutting-edge weapons far ahead of the Napoleonic tactics employed by the generals, and the carnage was awful. The rifled musket, the minié ball (a spin-stabilized bullet small enough to load through a barrel of a rifled long gun), the Gatling gun (a forerunner to the machine gun), and other killing machines led to thousands of casualties per day on the battlefields of Shiloh, Antietam, and Bull Run. At the Battle of Antietam, an estimated 22,717 men were killed, wounded, or captured in the single bloodiest day in US history.

Many who were not killed outright were disfigured by amputations and facial injuries. At the war's peak, there were over 135,000 filled hospital beds in the North. Pain, psychological as well as physical, had become a national epidemic, and opiate-based drugs such as morphine offered the only relief. Wrote Dr. Nathan Mayer, the regimental surgeon of the Sixteenth Connecticut Infantry: "In one pocket I carried quinine, in the other morphine, and whiskey in my canteen."[24]

Ultimately, opium proved just as addictive in America as it had in China. In addition to the nearly 700,000 dead, the Civil War left an estimated 281,881 injured on the Union side and 194,000 on the Confederate side.[25] Thousands more were left ravaged by disease. Besides being deprived of limbs, ears, and eyes, these men had to deal with the shame of no longer being fully productive members of society. An estimated 400,000 became opium addicts on both sides as a result of their morphine treatments.[26]

The use of opium was perfectly legal under American law. There were no state or federal agencies that regulated the use of opium-based painkillers, or any drug at all, for that matter. Charles and Abbot Low's father, Seth, had built his first fortune importing camphor and other exotic plants into the United States for use in patent medicines. A half century later, Warren Delano had no scruples about taking advantage of the huge opportunity to sell opium to the US government. For Delano, selling the drug to Americans rather than to Chinese was an "honorable business." As managing partner of Russell & Company, he contracted with the Medical Bureau of the US War Department to send large shipments of the drug to America.[27]

Some saw Delano's opium shipments from Hong Kong to New York as a tremendous humanitarian effort for the Union cause. Others weren't so sure. But for the family patriarch, there was little romance in business. It was a means to an end. He had a duty to save his family from financial embarrassment, not to mention to save Algonac for future generations. His interests were no longer merely making money but also protecting his family from the uncertainties of his youth: the British bombardment of New England during the War of 1812, the capture of his father by the Royal Navy, the decade of lonely bachelorhood in Canton, the siege of the Factories.

But as a husband and father, he could not bear to be so far away from those he loved. Warren Delano decided that if he could not go to the mountain, he would bring the mountain to him.

In the spring of 1862, as news of the Union defeats and colossal casualties filled the morning papers, the Delano family received a letter at Algonac. The letter itself has been lost, but it probably informed Catherine that things were going well in Hong Kong and he was making money, but not well enough for him to return within the year. He had therefore booked them passage aboard his friend Abbot Low's clipper ship *Surprise*. They were to pack their bags for its June sailing from New York, and then make the long ocean journey to rejoin the patriarch in Hong Kong.

Despite being twelve years old, *Surprise* was still in remarkably good condition and well maintained. After Captain Philip Dumaresq's then-record ninety-six-day run from New York to San Francisco in 1850, *Surprise* continued to make steady profits for the Low firm.[28] Unlike other clipper ships, her rig had not been cut down, allowing her to make consistently rapid and reliable passages. For the Delanos, it was as if Papa had chartered the mid-nineteenth-century equivalent of a Learjet for a trip halfway around the world. With good luck and fair weather, *Surprise* would carry the Delano family and their servants from New York to China in fewer than a hundred days.

On June 25, family and friends gathered in New York to see the Delanos off on their voyage to China. The traveling party consisted of a dozen people, including thirty-seven-year-old Catherine, sixteen-year-old Louise, fifteen-year-old Dora, thirteen-year-old Warren III, eight-year-old Sara, five-year-old Philippe, two-year-old Cassie, their thirty-five-year-old governess (and Delano cousin) Nancy Church, and two nurses named Davis and Ellen. Piled high on the deck of the steam tug that took the Delano party to the clipper ship anchored out in the Upper Bay were mountains of baggage from Algonac: changes of clothes, books, toys, and other souvenirs (and necessities) that the family would use over the coming months. Catherine Delano also carried a farewell gift for the children: a red notebook containing a children's story, written in longhand, by cousin Elizabeth Babcock.

"We need not say," Catherine wrote soon after *Surprise* headed out to sea, "it was sorrowful to leave our friends, but we must look forward to the happy meeting with our husband and Father at Hong-Kong."[29] The last time she had taken a long sea voyage, she was a young bride, nervous about leaving home for the first time but deeply in love with Warren. Now she was in her midthirties, with several children in tow, and driven there by loneliness and financial necessity.

The details of the arrangement between Abbot Low and Warren Delano are lost, but it is clear that in addition to giving the Delanos passage on *Surprise*, Low leased Algonac from the Delanos for the next five years, keeping it in tip-top condition. If Warren Delano succeeded in rebuilding his fortune within that time, his wife and children could look forward to returning home to the idyllic retreat they so loved. Houqua's protégés looked after one another: during the siege of the Factories, the bombardment of Canton, the years of wild speculating on clipper ships and railroads, financial ruin, and a Civil War.

There was another reason the Delanos booked passage on *Surprise*: her speed offered some measure of protection against a new threat in the offing. In June 1862, as *Surprise* prepared to slip out of New York Harbor, the shipyard of John Laird Sons & Company near Liverpool was putting the finishing touches on a new vessel that looked like any other large steam-powered merchant ship, equipped with a screw propeller and three masts. At 220 feet long and 1,000 tons, she was about the same size as an American clipper ship. Yet concealed behind *Enrica*'s graceful lines was a set of fearsome weaponry: six muzzle-loading thirty-two-pound smooth-bore guns (three per side) and two hundred-pound pivot guns at her bow and stern. She was paid for by a Liverpool shipping firm that had a lucrative business in selling Confederate cotton smuggled past the Union blockade of Southern ports.

The Southern diplomat who arranged for the construction and purchase of this new weapon was a Georgia aristocrat named James Dunwoody Bulloch. (His niece Martha, a staunch Confederate supporter, had married a New York merchant named Theodore Roosevelt Sr., and stopped her husband from joining the Union army—something their son Theodore Jr. would never forgive.) Soon after Bulloch's ship *Enrica* departed England, her new captain, Raphael Semmes, hoisted the Stars and Bars, and she was handed over to a Confederate crew. Under a new name, CSS *Alabama*, the ship took its orders from Richmond, Virginia, the capital of the Confederacy: loot, burn, and sink any Union vessels.

Armed and dangerous, the rechristened CSS *Alabama* began prowling the Atlantic sea-lanes for Yankee merchant ships that crossed her path. Able to steam at thirteen knots, she could outrace almost any merchant vessel, steam or sail, except possibly a China clipper such as *Surprise*. For Captain Semmes, a swift Yankee clipper ship was the ultimate war prize, and a family as prominent as the Delanos would be a fantastic diplomatic pawn if captured. Unfortunately for him, the *Surprise* was far gone by the time his ship was finished. Over the next several months, the Confederacy commissioned several more steam-powered commerce raiders from British yards. These vessels would ultimately wreak havoc on the Union's merchant marine, despite the best efforts of William Henry Aspinwall and John Murray Forbes to scope out and purchase such vessels.

The Delanos surely knew of the threats as they glided past the Narrows and out into the open Atlantic, their old lives fading away in *Surprise*'s wake. The cooing of the mourning doves in the trees of Algonac had been replaced by the calls of gulls soaring around the masts of *Surprise*.

For the first several days after sailing from New York, the Delano family lay in their bunks, miserably seasick. After the evening meal, Captain Charles Ranlett Jr. entertained those who could get up by playing the small pipe organ in the clipper's saloon. Probably among the tunes was a popular song from the 1843 opera *The Bohemian Girl* that would have made the Delano children homesick for Algonac:

> I dreamt that I dwelt in marble halls
> With vassals and serfs at my sight,
> And of all who assembled within these walls
> That I was the hope and the pride.
> I had riches too great to count
> Could boast of a high ancestral name,
> But I also dreamt, which pleased me most
> That you loved me most
> That you loved me still the same,
> That you loved me still the same.

Catherine was no stranger to travel, having been on two long ocean voyages to China and back, but the ship's strange motions and noises still bothered her. She wrote diligently in her diary, even if she could stomach only a few cups of rice gruel. Anything more would send her running for the water closet or the nearest leeward* rail. "Ship inclining to Leeward," she wrote. "Louise and Annie suffering a great deal from sea-sickness. Nancy has a bad head. Davis' head troubles her and Warren seasick. Dora not very bright and Sallie [Sara] uncomfortable." The young were sleepless, cranky, and often unwilling to do their lessons. "It took Sallie till noon to get dressed," a frustrated Catherine Delano wrote.

Sea travel limited the elaborate attire that women of Catherine's class were used to wearing, such as multiple layers of petticoats, fancy hats, and the so-called caged crinoline: a steel contraption that gave a dress a fashionable bell shape. The ideal look also called for pale skin and a delicate demeanor.[30] Now, Catherine lamented, "None of us present a very brilliant appearance."[31] Even if they wore more comfortable, simpler clothes aboard *Surprise*, all of the Delano women, including the little girls, almost certainly wore their laced corsets.[32] The only way to do laundry was by hand, either with seawater or rainwater collected in canvas bags. What with all the small children on board, the washing chores must have been onerous. The odors of dirty cloth diapers almost certainly added to the stench of sweat on board, compounding everyone's nausea.

Captain Ranlett did his best to make his miserable charges happy. He was a young man, and handling a big clipper ship was an overwhelming task without the distraction of important passengers. In addition to making sure the sails were trimmed and the *Surprise* remained on course, he fretted about those steam commerce raiders.

---

* The side of the ship sheltered from the wind.

"A large Eng. iron propeller passed near us bound South," he noted in his log.

Catherine, too, noticed the strange ship. "About ten o'clk a steamer was in sight to leeward of us, and the Captain was quite anxious about her, thinking she might be a privateer." By now a master of the Delano way of never showing fear, especially in front of the children, Catherine wrote that she was "perfectly cool and not at all frightened."[33] Fortunately, the English ship continued on its way. *Surprise* (and the Delanos) had dodged a bullet: soon iron-hulled, steam-powered ships flying the Stars and Bars would be terrorizing Yankee vessels around the globe. Whalers were favorite targets, especially when pointed into the wind as their crews harvested blubber strips from whale carcasses. The stinking black smoke from their flaming tryworks* could be spotted miles away.

Few, however, thought the fleet-footed clippers were at great risk—until 1863, when the raider CSS *Florida* gave chase to *Jacob Bell* on her way home from China with a cargo of tea and Chinese goods worth an estimated $300,000. *Jacob Bell*'s captain was lucky to have a strong wind astern, and the ship flew along at an astonishing clip, leaving the steam-powered Confederate vessel in her wake. The chase continued for four tense hours, the white-winged clipper surging ahead of the smoke-belching iron steamship. Then the winds died, and the magnificent clipper was left with her sails limp in the still air. CSS *Florida* steamed up to the wallowing *Jacob Bell*, raised the Stars and Bars, and fired two warning shots across the clipper's stern. The Confederates then boarded the ship, took the passengers and crew prisoner aboard the *Florida*, and then looted the cargo, which would fetch handsome prices in the blockaded South. They then set *Jacob Bell* afire, and CSS *Florida* steamed away in search of more Yankee prey.[34]

---

* An iron pot set upon a brick furnace, used for rendering whale blubber into oil.

Within a few weeks of sailing, the passengers and crew aboard *Surprise* had settled into their shipboard routines, and the days passed more pleasantly. On nights the family couldn't sleep, they could always go up on deck and experience an awesome sunrise at sea. As Richard Henry Dana Jr. observed in *Two Years Before the Mast*: "There is something in the first gray streaks stretching across the eastern horizon and throwing indirect light upon the face of the deep, which combines with the boundlessness and unknown depth of the sea around, and gives one a feeling of loneliness, of dread, and of melancholy foreboding, which nothing else in nature can."[35]

To the cloistered Delano children, who knew so little about the world beyond the gates of Algonac, the ship was an object of wonder, as were the sailors who worked on it. If Warren had been present, he likely would have forbidden them from mixing with the crew, just as he had forbidden them from mixing with the public at the beach in Fairhaven. It was a mind-set inherited not just from his father but also from his experience in the Canton Factories. Yet Catherine, no doubt exhausted, realized very quickly that keeping her family confined to the passengers' quarters was virtually impossible.

Catherine could not ignore the fact that her family was now living cheek by jowl with about forty men who worked for meager pay—men about whom she was almost as naïve as were her children. She saw the distribution of items from the slop chest as an act of charity on the part of the captain, not as deductions from their wages. "These sailors go to sea sometimes poorly provided, and were it not that the ship carries a chest of the needed articles, they would be poorly off," she wrote.[36] She also was likely ignorant of the fact that many of the crew had probably been recruited by the crimps who prowled New York's saloons and whorehouses.

Sara and her siblings found their way to the sailmaker's quarters and watched the leathery old man at work mending *Surprise*'s dozens of sails. Catherine didn't mind them passing the hours with him. She described the sailmaker as "decidedly a resource."[37] He told tall tales to the children, keeping them amused during the long days at sea. Yet what really captivated little Sara was how the sailmaker stuck pins and needles into a withered, useless thumb as he worked.[38]

Sometime during the voyage, the Delano family heard the cry of "Man overboard!" Captain Ranlett hove the ship to before it had traveled too far and, in the words of Catherine Delano, "hove a rope aft which the poor fellow caught hold of and was pulled in." The winds and seas must have been relatively calm, as a more aggressive captain, hell-bent on speed, would have given up the man for lost.

Surprise crossed the equator on July 25, and the season changed abruptly from summer to winter. Then Maury's charts failed them. The clipper lay becalmed for days in the Indian Ocean. The tropical sun beat down mercilessly on the stranded ship. Inside, the temperature of the cabin probably soared above 100 degrees. The ship's turkey and one of the Delano kittens, in Catherine's words, "departed this life and were thrown overboard."[39]

To keep his passengers cool, Captain Ranlett stretched a canvas tent above the main deck. There Catherine Delano passed the hours reading old copies of *Vanity Fair* magazine, as well as the latest novels by Nathaniel Hawthorne. Cousin Nancy Church and the two nurses did their best to keep the children focused on their lessons, as well as protected from the blazing sun. It was an impossible task. The children much preferred jumping from the bulwarks and paddling around the gently bobbing vessel to reciting their arithmetic tables or practicing the piano in the stifling cabin below. Sometimes sailors would take them out for a row in one of the ship's boats.

Finally, in mid-September, the winds picked up, and *Surprise*— two weeks behind schedule—sailed toward Java Head and the treacherous Strait of Sunda—not far from where Papa's *Memnon* had been looted by pirates so many years before. They desperately needed to stop for reprovisioning, or else the Delano party would be forced to eat the same salted beef and hardtack as the crew.

"The land, the trees and the shore look very refreshing," Catherine wrote as *Surprise* dropped anchor at Anjer in the Dutch East Indies. "There seems to be a perfect jungle."[40] All of the children got new sunhats, as well as a gaggle of pet birds. And there was exotic fare for the dinner table: tamarinds, bananas, cloves, and coconuts. The Delanos may even have sampled the spiky durian fruit, of which Captain Charlie Low said, "tastes like everything good mixed together," but only after he and his wife got over its "very offensive smell."[41]

It was on October 31, 1862—128 days after clearing New York Harbor—that the clipper ship dropped anchor in Hong Kong's Victoria Harbor. Compared with the clipper passages of the past, Captain Ranlett Jr.'s performance was mediocre at best. The ship's underwhelming speed over the nineteen-thousand-mile trip was a combination of a variety of factors: doldrums in the Indian Ocean, the age of the vessel (twelve years, old for an extreme clipper), and the cautious seamanship on the part of the young captain. Ranlett probably wanted to make sure that his passengers weren't exposed to the worst of a "driver" captain and a "bully mate." In her diary, Catherine Delano recorded no drawn daggers, flying lashes, or blood spattered on the decks.

The Hong Kong air was thick and humid. Looming above little Sara, her siblings, and her mother Catherine was the Peak, a lush, green mountain that soared more than 1,500 feet above the swirling waters of the Pearl River estuary. Whitewashed classical buildings, surrounded by palms and bedecked with ferns and awnings, were sprinkled like sugar cubes at the base of the mountain.

Below, riding at anchor in the recently renamed Victoria Harbor, were dozens of ships: Chinese junks, British and American clipper ships, and steamships emitting wisps of coal smoke. The Union Jack snapped from the masts of most of the vessels. The Civil War had ended US hopes of supremacy in the China trade. A greatly expanded (and improved) British clipper fleet had by now cornered the market in shipping tea from China to London. They had names such as *Fiery Cross*, *Robin Hood*, *Lord of the Isles*, and *Queen of Nations*. Unlike American clippers, which were built entirely of wood, British clippers were of composite construction: iron frames and wooden planking. These iron-framed ships not only were stronger and more fire resistant than wood ones, but also their structural components were thinner, giving them greater internal volume and carrying capacity.[42] They were harbingers of the all-metal shipbuilding practices to come, even if Americans were still generally skeptical of iron construction for deep-sea vessels. (According to one account, Captain Nathaniel Palmer bet an English shipbuilder that he could fire a musket ball through an iron plate. The shipbuilder called for a bet. Palmer grabbed an old gun, took aim, fired, and collected his money.[43])

A few old American clippers flying both the Stars and Stripes and the red-and-yellow A. A. Low house flag still fluttered on ships in the harbor. Among them was the *N. B. Palmer*, still under the command of Captain Charlie Low, who had recently sailed from Hong Kong with four hundred Chinese laborers as passengers, bound for San Francisco.[44] The valiant little *Houqua*, twenty years old and Captain Palmer's first true clipper, also showed up in the Pearl River from time to time. She still boasted the sad-eyed figurehead of the "adopted father" of Warren Delano and his comrades, whose carved mandarin cap and robes were weathered by years of salt air and pounding seas. Within a few years, *Houqua* would sail from Yokohama, Japan, and disappear at sea without a trace.

The Delano children had grown up with Houqua's face, which had gazed down on them as they played in their father's library at Algonac. They had known Houqua's villa, echoed in the construction and furnishing of their American mansion. The glittering treasures of China—colorful porcelain, silk wall hangings, green jade vases, and Buddhist temple bells—were everywhere. What's more, two of the Delanos' children had been born in China, and one had died there. Now the family was back.

The Delanos, like all foreigners, were no longer confined to the gilded seclusion of the Factories. They could go wherever they wished, so long as they kept to the Chinese port cities. Eighty miles upriver from the colony of Hong Kong beckoned the ancient city of Canton, where Warren Delano and his fellow "bachelors" had dined at Houqua's palace at Honam and hatched their plans for the first extreme clipper ships. In the twenty years since, Canton had gone from the single port of entry for Western trade into one of many. Hong Kong and Shanghai had surpassed it in trade volume years before.

In fact, almost all physical reminders of Warren Delano's youth in Canton were gone. Charlie Low had been shocked at the devastation when he traveled upriver a few years earlier. Scanning the Canton waterfront, he couldn't even tell where the colonnaded Factories once stood. The foundations had been "pulverized," the ground strewn with salt, and "whole acres of bare tumbling walls show the devastation made by fire and guns; it looks like the ruins you see in engravings." Charlie felt pangs of guilt at the devastation wrought by British guns. "How many worthy Chinamen have been driven from their homes where generation after generation have found a living in peace and quietness?" the veteran clipper captain wondered.[45] The one constant from the old Cohong days was opium, which flowed into the Middle Kingdom from Turkey and British India virtually unchecked.

From aboard the *Surprise*, the Delano children saw a sharp-bowed, many-oared vessel: a "fast crab," the type of boat used by smugglers to pick up crates of opium from the British and American storeships that anchored with impunity all along the Chinese coast. About a dozen Chinese men were pulling with all their might toward *Surprise*.

Captain Ranlett almost certainly lent the Delano children his spyglass to look more closely. Through its lens, they saw a tanned, handsome man clad in a snow-white linen suit, standing erect in the boat, whiskers blowing in the wind, eyes glowing with excitement.

"Papa!" they squealed as he climbed aboard *Surprise*, and showered him with hugs and kisses.

"I think Papa is a very nice man!" toddler Cassie shouted as she jumped up and down.

The Victoria's Peak section of Hong Kong was now thoroughly English, right down to the architecture of its buildings. Among them was a mansion called Rose Hill, a light-orange villa owned by Russell & Company, fully furnished, with ponderous English furniture in the parlors and straight-backed chairs in the schoolroom. This would be their new home, their Algonac on the Pearl River. A retinue of Chinese servants had already been hired, ready to draw the children's baths and cook their Western food.

Scattered among the whitewashed Western homes and shops were manicured cricket fields and horse race tracks. The tea and opium trade had caused Hong Kong's population to explode from a mere 8,000 in 1841 to almost 95,000 by 1860.[46] The British Crown enforced a rigid apartheid system: the colony's roughly 3,000 English and American residents lived on the east side of the island, while the Chinese were crammed onto the west.[47]

As Papa and Mama Delano and the children were whisked away in their sedan chairs, did little Sara Delano gaze back at the clipper ship *Surprise* at rest in Hong Kong's harbor? She would have seen an old lady, worn and tired from the long voyage, her oak and pine beams creaking from years of beating against the monsoon and around Cape Horn. Yet her bow was still sharp as a razor, masts raked and proud, looking every inch the revolutionary vessel that Delano and his partners had dreamed of so many years before.

CHAPTER 17

GLORY OF THE SEAS

In his later years, he endured misfortune and ingratitude with the same sturdy sweetness and equanimity that he had shown in the days when fortune smiled.

—CAPTAIN ARTHUR HAMILTON CLARK[1]

On a bright October day in 1869, Donald McKay—now in his late fifties—left his house on White Street in East Boston and strode down to his shipyard. He was still muscular and imposing but now was stooped slightly with age, his wavy, dark hair streaked with gray. He had made the walk from home to work for more than twenty years, during which time he had supervised the construction of thirteen extreme clippers, thirteen medium clippers, more than a dozen packet ships, and an assortment of schooners, barques, and other vessels—a monumental contribution not only to American shipbuilding but to the history of man and sea.[2] Now his firm, reorganized under the moniker of McKay & Aldus Iron Works, had transformed into a prominent manufacturer of railroad steam locomotives and engines for New England's burgeoning factories and textile mills. It was one of the most advanced yards in America. And it still built ships.

Shipbuilding work had declined severely since the Civil War. So had the number of American shipyards. McKay's old friend William Webb had just that year put his once-thriving New York shipyard up for sale. Grass was sprouting on the East River banks where Webb's yards once gave birth to clippers such as *Challenge* and *Swordfish*. Thanks to his extensive outside investments, Webb was far from penniless, yet his life's work, his passion, was a dying vocation. European shipyards were producing ships at lower cost, and fewer young Americans seemed interested in enduring years of "slavocratic" apprenticeships. When asked by the *New York Times* why he was getting out of the business, Webb not only noted the skyrocketing costs of materials but also complained about "the evident disposition of workmen to avoid accountability, the unwillingness of the rising generation to apprentice themselves to mechanical business, and the consequent and increasing difficulty of obtaining skilled labor."[3]

Donald McKay refused to go with the trends.

This day, he was headed for his yard's launching platform, where he would be joined by his wife, Mary, and the five McKay children still living at home. The newest addition to the family, one-year-old Wallace, was in a baby carriage.[4] Mary McKay had once again given her husband's newest ship a mellifluous name: *Glory of the Seas*. She was a medium clipper—at 2,100 tons and 240 feet, a compromise between speed and cargo capacity. Fuller bodied than McKay's 1850s speedsters *Flying Cloud* and *Lightning*, she lacked their rakish lines and sensuous grace. Looks no longer paid. But Donald McKay and his wife were still shameless about chasing publicity for his creations, and a friendly Boston newsman heralded the new vessel as "nearly perfect as a ship need be."[5] By naming her *Glory of the Seas*, McKay laid claim to his own glorious record as America's finest shipbuilder.

The serene, chiseled face of the ivory-hued figurehead stared down at the McKays and their guests as they gathered for her christening. The carving, set just below the bowsprit, was an expression of McKay's idea of female perfection: a seminude classical goddess striding forward, one arm holding her billowing robe above her left breast, the other thrown dramatically behind her right shoulder. Above the figurehead flew a big American flag.

As he stood on the platform, McKay must have remembered that he still owed wood-carver Herbert Gleason $362.35 for his masterful work.[6] There was nothing to do but put on a brave face.

As the crowd murmured with expectation, fifteen-year-old daughter Frances McKay swung the bottle of champagne and shouted, "I christen thee *Glory of the Seas*!"[7] Down she slid into Boston Harbor. The spectators cheered. Another McKay clipper was ready to conquer the seas.

She would prove to be his last.

Despite his reputation for honesty and fine workmanship, Donald McKay was struggling financially—again. The $300,000 loss from the US Navy contracts continued to cripple him despite his best efforts at a comeback. Lacking strong cash flow, McKay also owed banks and suppliers close to $250,000.[8] The past December, the *Boston Post* had informed the entire city about McKay's dire straits, something that must have caused tremendous anger at the Eagle Hill breakfast table.

"The journal understands that during the past week the officers of the firm have been investigated, and it is reported that the assets are considerably in excess of its list," the paper declared on December 5, 1868, hinting that McKay was hiding something from his creditors. "There is a general feeling of regret expressed that a firm doing so large a business and with such an excellent reputation for the machinery they make, should be obliged to suspend operations. It will be hard for the hundreds of machinists and laborers who are thrown out of employment at this inclement season by the stoppage of the works, and we hope for their sakes that some arrangements may be made to resume operations."[9]

The post–Civil War economic boom had left McKay high and dry, as it had others whose life was the sea. The war had devastated the Yankee merchant marine. Insurance rates for shipowners had skyrocketed, thanks to the havoc wrought by Confederate commerce raiders. To protect their ships and their cargoes, many Northern shipowners had registered their vessels under foreign flags. By the end of the war, most of the extreme clippers that had survived the 1850s had been sold to British concerns, among them the illustrious *Flying Cloud* and the star-crossed *Challenge*. In 1866, as a way of stimulating postwar American shipbuilding, Congress passed legislation banning ships such as these from being reregistered back under the Stars and Stripes. It was a shortsighted bill that had the opposite effect. Although domestic intercoastal trade remained healthy, American businessmen insisted it was cheaper to use foreign ships to send their goods out of the country than to invest the capital needed to rebuild the nation's merchant marine. As a consequence, US ships engaged in foreign trade plummeted from 1,388 in 1866 to only 817 ten years later.[10]

Congress did nothing to provide financial support for the American shipping industry, but it lavished millions of dollars on giveaways to railroads. As *Glory of the Seas* rose on the stocks, two beneficiaries of congressional largesse, the Union Pacific and the Central Pacific, were hard at work building the first transcontinental railroad, which would link San Francisco with the markets of the Midwest and the East. Congress backed the project by authorizing more than $100 million in government-backed bonds. Five months before *Glory of the Seas*'s October launch date, Leland Stanford, president of the Central Pacific Railroad, drove the ceremonial final spike of the transcontinental railroad at Promontory Point, Utah Territory. Cargo could now be shipped from New York to San Francisco in a consistent ten days, rather than a hundred days in an extreme clipper battling variable winds and currents.

Those few American clippers still braving the dangerous Cape Horn run were doomed when the hammer struck the spike that day. The old China trade was also dealt a fatal blow later that same year, when in November the Suez Canal opened for business after more than a decade of construction. The 121-mile-long canal, which linked the Mediterranean and Red Seas, eliminated the need for ships to sail around the southern tip of Africa to get to China, shaving 5,000 nautical miles from the trip.[11] Steamships could now sail economically to China and back on a regular schedule, with plenty of opportunities to refuel along the way. With the opening of the new Suez Canal trade route, even A. A. Low & Brother—the last American firm to successfully operate extreme clippers in the China trade—was squeezed to the breaking point.*

The British were now in possession of an overseas empire, with government backing and support at nearly every single port: from Suez, Egypt, to Bombay, India; from Singapore to Shanghai. To compete, American companies wanted their own government subsidies—but none was forthcoming. Instead, shipowners and builders complained about high taxation.[12] All of the nation's resources were being devoted to the debts of the Civil War.

The writing was on the wall. "I only know the English have always, in peace and war, manifested a determination to hold their supremacy on the ocean," Abbot Low had told the assembled crowd at the New York State Chamber of Commerce in 1867, "and the supremacy which they have acquired by arms in war they have in peace acquired by subsidies. They have deliberately driven and intentionally driven the Americans from the ocean by paying subsidies which they know our Congress would not pay."[13] Following the Civil War, British capital flowed into US railroads, steel, and manufacturing, but when it came to ocean commerce, Britannia made sure that she alone would rule the waves.

---

* Americans were not the only ones to take the hit. The timing could not have been worse for the owners of the newest and finest of the British tea clippers, *Cutty Sark*, built to beat the sixty-one-day Melbourne-to-London record from the rival British extreme clipper *Thermopylae*.

Low's own once-profitable ships were bleeding red ink. In 1866, a year after the end of the Civil War, he had sold off the grandest of his maritime assets, the giantess *Great Republic*, to Canadian owners. Even as rebuilt, she didn't really pay. This McKay masterpiece—her rig even further reduced—would ply the seas for six more years before foundering in a storm off Bermuda. The divestment of Low's ships would continue over the next decade—though his vast fortune remained intact thanks to his diversified holdings in railroads, real estate, and the transatlantic cable.

Donald McKay was caught in the crosswinds of these mighty shifts of the American and global economies. He was determined to keep the doors of McKay & Aldus open at all costs. With many mouths to feed at home, he still showed up at the yard at six thirty in the morning along with the rest of his employees. Although he was no longer as strong as he used to be, he did not hesitate to wield an adze or pick up a sledgehammer to drive the wooden dowels that bound hull planking to frames. He was a proud man, and the thought of burdening his family with his debts was simply too much to bear. His new ship had to live up to the standards of his previous triumphs, or he and his family would be ruined.

With *Glory of the Seas*, Donald McKay resorted to the same strategy that he had used for the acclaimed *Sovereign of the Seas* and the ill-fated *Great Republic*: he would build her on his own account, sail her on a successful maiden voyage to San Francisco, and, after she had proved her worth, sell her for a profit. It was the only way he knew how to make money. Friends probably told him he was a fool to try the same plan again, but the proud McKay was convinced that his masterpiece would pay if he spared no expense to create the finest sailing ship in the world.

Glory of the Seas was towed to New York for loading and departed on February 13, 1870, bound for San Francisco. She left three days after a survivor from the California Gold Rush days: Grinnell & Minturn's twenty-year-old clipper *Sea Serpent*, one of the very few ships of her type still making the punishing trip around Cape Horn. On board *Glory of the Seas* was an exhausted Donald McKay. He told the captain that he wanted the new ship to be driven just as hard as clippers were back in the days of the forty-niners.[14]

His beautiful vessel was now out in the open sea, slicing through the North Atlantic at fine speed. Yet the poetry of wind, sea, and sails did little to calm McKay's mind: he had been forced to take out two mortgages on the ship, with a Boston distiller and friend named Daniel Sortwell. One was made out for $100,000 at 9 percent per year—this was to pay back the angry creditors who showed up on McKay's doorstep every day. It was not enough. To finance the completion of the ship, he had to borrow another $70,000 from Sortwell, equal to the value of most of the freight carried on this trip. McKay was able to keep $12,000 in reserve to purchase cargo in San Francisco for a possible run across the Pacific to China.[15]

Glory of the Seas arrived in San Francisco on June 13, 1870, in 120 days, beating *Sea Serpent* to port by 3 days. It was a respectable time for a ship with fuller lines than her extreme predecessors, and a relieved Donald McKay was thrilled to stand on the deck of his masterpiece as she sailed through the Golden Gate, his blue eagle house flag flapping proudly in the wind. He had never sailed to San Francisco, the site of so many of his ships' triumphant arrivals. He gazed on the brown cliffs flecked with greenery, the bright-blue harbor, and at the forest of masts and funnels clustered at the foot of Telegraph Hill. The old shipbuilder could take pride in the fact that his *Glory of the Seas* was one of the largest sailing vessels flying the Stars and Stripes; she dwarfed everything else on the San Francisco waterfront.[16]

The newspapers rolled out the typical superlatives as they saw *Glory of the Seas* tie up at Cowell's Wharf. McKay, aided by his wife, may well have had a hand in the copy. "One of the finest specimens of naval architecture afloat," crowed the *San Francisco Bulletin*. The name Donald McKay was "a household word in nearly every American and English port of commerce—the vessels launched from his shipyard plow the seas wherever the white wing of commerce is known, and have earned a brilliant reputation among nautical men."[17]

However, once again fame did not bring fortune. McKay had sickening news in store for him the day after he stepped ashore: *Glory of the Seas* was no longer his ship to sell. A month before her arrival, while she was fighting her way around South America, Sortwell and other creditors had seized *Glory of the Seas* for unpaid debts. The legal notice beat the ship to San Francisco—most likely delivered by the new transcontinental telegraph (which, like the railroad, had benefited from a generous government subsidy).[18] Her new owners loaded her with California grain and dispatched her around Cape Horn to Queenstown, Ireland, where she arrived in only 112 days. *Glory of the Seas* would go on to have a long and profitable career, lasting until 1923, when she was burned for her scrap metal off Seattle, Washington.

McKay never saw a cent of her earnings. He returned to Boston in August and planned to sue Sortwell, when he learned of even more bad news: not only had they taken his ship, but also his creditors insisted on liquidating all of his assets. This meant selling the shipyard where he had worked side by side with his faithful men. He narrowly avoided losing his house, too. Eagle Hill, at least, he could save. He and Mary signed a legal document that put his entire life's work on the auction block: engine lathes, tools, lumber, steel standards, blocking, sliding ways, iron, coal, implements, grindstones, office furniture, pictures, and other personal property. He even lost the builder's model of *Glory of the Seas*, which was handed over to the contractor who had made the ship's spars.[19]

Still, within a few years of his financial catastrophe, Donald McKay decided that the grand house on White Street, the site of so many launching parties and family celebrations, was not worth keeping, either. Perhaps his partially dismantled, pitiful looking shipyard was too much to see from his windows. He had also begun to suffer from tuberculosis. He and Mary sold Eagle Hill and moved to a farm in Hamilton, Massachusetts, a rural community located north of Boston. It was the first time in his life Donald McKay had ever lived out of sight of salt water.[20]

As Donald McKay prepared to leave East Boston forever, his most famous ship finally met her end, in the waters near the place of her Canadian creator's birth. In June 1875 a group of torch-bearing men came aboard a ship that had lain wrecked in the harbor of Saint John, New Brunswick, for a year. *Flying Cloud* was more than twenty years old, worn out, paint peeling from her oak flanks. Her white pine decks had faded to moldy gray; her yards, masts, and rigging were a tangled mess swinging in the breeze coming off the Bay of Fundy. The sea flowed into her broken hull and over her splintered rock maple keel.

The three-masted sailing ship had been working for years as a humble lumber carrier between Canada and England, just one of many prosaic vessels that tramped around the world looking for freight. The most recent captain, a shadowy figure known in the Canadian Maritimes simply as "Wild Goose," had left Saint John on a routine crossing of the Atlantic.[21] Finding that he could not make headway against a horrific gale, he had turned around to try to return to port. He missed the channel and ran hard upon the beach. Hoping to refloat the ship, the crew unloaded the cargo of Canadian lumber—"deal timber" for house floors and coal mine ceiling supports in the Mother Country—but it was too late. She broke her back on the sandbar and was a total loss. Now, a year later, the people of Saint John decided that the ship had to go. The best way to get rid of her was to burn her and collect her metal parts from the smoldering wreckage: iron bolts, copper hull plates, and any leftover brass.

The flames rose higher and higher, consuming her masts and deckhouses. One by one, the three masts crashed into the ocean, followed by a hiss. Finally, the hull collapsed into itself, sending up great showers of sparks and embers. Within a few days, it was safe for salvagers to venture out to the blackened, charred pile and pick around for anything metal.

The farming life did not suit the great shipbuilder at all. As one descendant wrote of Donald McKay: "Farming was not his favorite pastime, but he made the most of it."[22] In the summer of 1880, the sixty-nine-year-old McKay was struck down by a paralytic stroke. After lingering for a few months, the greatest shipbuilder in America died on September 20, 1880, his second wife, Mary, and five of their ten surviving children: Lawrence, Anna, Nicholas, Guy, and Wallace, at his bedside.[23] His only legacy consisted of his Hamilton farm; a silver water urn, serving tray, teapot, coffee pot, and sugar bowl; two sets of silver forks; a diamond pin; a gold watch chain; assorted livestock and farm equipment; and several ship models and sets of blueprints. There was also the hope of future proceeds from a cash settlement with the US Navy over the ironclad USS *Nausett*, but the McKay heirs were probably resigned to the fact that they would never see any of the money.

To two of his sons, McKay had left nothing in his will because "they have already received as much of my property as is just."[24]

It would take another fifteen years of hard work by McKay's brother Nathaniel to win the family's settlement from the federal government. In March 1895, Congress finally passed a bill authorizing a payment of $101,592.73; according to a witness, Nathaniel McKay triumphantly carried the cash out of the Treasury Department in a hand satchel. The settlement was still only a third of what it had cost McKay to alter his ironclad design. When asked how he succeeded in getting the government to fork over the money, Nathaniel demonstrated the same persistence that had allowed his famous brother to succeed as an immigrant outsider in tight-knit Yankee New England: "Every time I received a rebuff, it always made me more zealous. There are hundreds of demagogues in Congress who think that if a man has a claim against the government, he wants to loot the treasury for his own benefit."[25]

The settlement allowed Donald's long-suffering widow Mary Cressy McKay to finally live in comfort. She died in 1923 at age ninety-one at her daughter Mary Bliss's house in the Boston suburb of Lexington, Massachusetts, attended by a nurse, chauffeur, and four servants.[26, 27]

Flying Cloud's record of eighty-nine days and eight hours from New York to San Francisco under sail would stand until 1989, when the sixty-foot yacht *Thursday's Child,* manned by a crew of three and captained by Warren Luhrs, bounded through the Golden Gate after eighty days on the high seas. Her sails and rigging were made of synthetic fiber, not the canvas of old. Satellites, not the sun and stars, guided her passage.[28] "Previous attempts to break the record have ended in disappointment or disaster," noted the *New York Times.* "Three sailboats in the last six years that tried to better *Flying Cloud*'s effort broke up or sank shortly after rounding Cape Horn, the perilous meeting point of the Atlantic and Pacific Oceans at the tip of South America."[29] Yet despite this triumph, *Thursday's Child* was a yacht, not a ship engaged in active commercial service. "The record that will probably be set by *Thursday's Child* and Mr. Luhrs may not stand as long as that of Captain Josiah Creesy and *Flying Cloud*," the *Times* noted.

To many diehard sailors, the immortal and forever beautiful clipper ship *Flying Cloud* still wears the Cape Horn crown.

CHAPTER 18

KEEPING IT IN THE FAMILY

These were our Gothic cathedrals, our Parthenon; but monuments carved from snow. For a few brief years, they flashed their splendor around the world, then disappeared with the finality of the wild pigeon.[1]

—Samuel Eliot Morison

As the Civil War at home played out at home, the Delano family continued life at Rose Hill as if they had never left the leafy sanctuary of Algonac. They had no exposure to Hong Kong's Chinese culture. Going out into the streets unsupervised was unthinkable and learning Chinese was forbidden. Warren and Catherine were terrified that the children might actually understand what the servants were saying about them behind their backs.

Warren furnished Rose Hill with the same acquisitive lavishness they had known back home. Household account books list velvet and silk wall hangings, sandalwood snuffboxes, and an ivory cross.[2] Warren also opened separate bank accounts for each of his children, ranging from $37.50 for his youngest children to $50 for his eldest, as well as one for his wife for $500.[3] For the Delano children, there were daily lessons from their strict tutor Aunt Nancy Church, boat rides on the Pearl River, occasional play dates with other expatriate children, and visits to the horse track that the British trading companies had constructed for their betting pleasure. A day at "Happy Valley" might as well have been at Ascot, except that the crowds wore cotton and linen instead of tweed to beat the tropical heat. The biggest thrill of the week was the so-called Chinese Scramble, in which untrained Chinese jockeys were paid by the *fanqui* to jump on horses and gallop around the track. More often than not, they fell off the saddles and crashed to the dirt, to the hoots and jeers of the white traders in the stands.[4] Warren also found the time to take his family on a trip across the East China Sea to the formerly forbidden land of Japan. According to one of Delano's associates, "Mr. Delano and his family have been north during the past three months, the young ladies having spent the greater portion of the time at Nagasaki, Japan, and have returned with a most glowing account of that beautiful country."[5] They surely sampled some of the fabled green teas that their father's friend Abbot Low was importing to the United States.

In 1865 Warren Delano decided that it was time for Sara, Warren III, and Philippe to go back home and continue their educations in America. By then, the Delanos had two new additions to the family: a boy named Frederic Adrian and a girl named Laura, both born at Rose Hill. And then there was the development that eighteen-year-old Dora Delano had fallen in love with William Forbes, a twenty-eight-year-old partner at Russell & Company. Will's father was Paul Sieman Forbes, a man with whom Warren Delano had quarreled twenty years before, angered that the Forbes's arrival in Canton might jeopardize his brother Ned's position with Russell & Company, and dismissed as "without any great expectations."[6] He now gave his blessing to the engagement. After all, Will Forbes had plenty of prospects: he was on the verge of being tapped to join the board of the newly formed Hongkong and Shanghai Banking Corporation, established by the British to finance the ever-expanding opium trade.

At the offices of Russell & Company, Warren was making money

once more. He had defied Confederate commerce raiders throughout the war to ship opium and tea back to the United States. He
made money in other things as well, sending thirty-eight bales of
silk, for example, to Boston merchant George Peabody aboard the
ship *Formosa*.[7]

Whether Delano knew it or not, Russell & Company, like other
shipping firms of its type, was doomed to fail within a few decades;
the once-mighty partnership was buckling under competition from
British shipping. But not before Warren Delano would be able to
wrest out one more competence, once again becoming a millionaire.
He would beat the naysayers, including his own brother Ned, who
had dismissed his scheme as ridiculous.

Yet Warren would continue working to permanently free his
family's fortunes from the caprices of the sea. And working with him
back in Boston was his old friend John Murray Forbes—long-time
fellow partner in Russell & Company; one-time denizen of the American Factory in Canton; his wife Catherine's cousin; and soon-to-be-
cousin-in-law (again) of his daughter Dora.

Shortly before he left China for the final time, Warren Delano committed a mysterious and risky act that gave him the potential to earn even more money in the years to come. In January
1867 Warren Delano appeared at the home of American consul,
Isaac Allen. There he met Wu Chongyao ("Young Houqua"), son
of the great merchant and heir to the fortune, a portion of which
had been under the management of John Murray Forbes. Delano
then signed a legal document granting him the power of "true and
lawful attorney, for me and in my name." Delano was given the
right "to ask, demand, sue for, recover and receive of and from the
same John M. Forbes" for any funds that the Wu family wanted
returned to China for their use. These family investments included
holdings in the Iowa Lands Trust, the Chicago, Burlington, and
Quincy Railroad, the Michigan Central Railroad, the Michigan
Pine Lands Association, and United States Treasury bonds. The

value of the Wu family's investment portfolio under John Murray Forbes's management was an astonishing $477,858.45, which had produced $26,915.89 in interest and dividends during the first half of the previous year.[8]

The enormous Houqua family trust was a crucial piece of one of the world's great family fortunes, and it had plenty of growth potential given its holdings in American transportation and land. The income thrown off by the trust would allow any Chinese or American family to live in opulence. As America emerged from the wreckage of the Civil War and became a global industrial powerhouse, these investments increased exponentially. Yet Houqua's son and his progeny lived in a troubled China, and had not inherited the Patriarch's business acumen. Despite the fine returns, they needed still more cash, as family expenses raced ahead of business income. "The demands of his family for increased allowances makes him anxious to take advantage of any favorable opportunity to add to his income," a Russell & Company officer wrote to John Murray Forbes of Young Houqua.[9]

As China was wracked by continued European incursions and civil unrest, Young Houqua and his family could rest assured that a substantial portion of their inheritance could be repatriated, if needed, by their shrewd American "cousin," Warren Delano II.

Had he found out about Delano's secret deal with the Wu family, his old friend John Murray Forbes would almost certainly have viewed it as a shocking betrayal. Delano's actions may have stemmed from jealousy of the substantial management fees that Forbes collected but he did not. Yet Delano appears never to have wielded his "power of attorney" to forcibly return funds to Houqua's descendants.[10] The US portion of the Houqua trust would remain under the aegis of John Murray Forbes and his firm for another decade, when the trust was formally dissolved and the proceeds dispersed to the Wu family.

By late 1867, the Delanos were reunited as a family in Paris, where Warren, rich enough from his own opium and tea earnings to live in grand style, rented an apartment on the fashionable Avenue L'Impératrice. While there, Warren Delano considered the idea of not going back to the Hudson Valley. "I have for some years had in mind a plan of European residence and education," he wrote to his lonely and loyal brother Ned. "Take the whole family down to the youngest to Europe (and) seek out a fine *old* country residence in a hilly country where woods abound and where saddle horses are good and cheap. I should want it to be a great degree if not entirely isolated from our countrymen or others who would speak English habitually, and I should want to organize my household as to combine the real comforts and proper luxuries of life with a system of studies, duties, exercise, and recreation." He had developed such a strong dislike for Americans of his social class that he wrote half-jokingly that he should do "what might be considered equally snobbish and in our retreat *sink* for the time being our name of Delano and write ourselves 'de la Noye.' "[11]

The draw of Algonac, though, was too strong. In 1868 Warren, Catherine, and the Delano children returned to New York—all except for Dora and her new husband, Will Forbes, who sailed back to Hong Kong after they were married in Paris. In 1870 the family took up residence again in the Hudson River mansion named for the Algonquin phrase for "hill and river." Everything remained in its place, including the big portrait of Houqua in the library. Frederic Adrian Delano, then only six, remembered the family's homecoming to the magical place that he had heard so much about: "There was snow on the ground and great drifts of it on the lawn. Laura and I, dressed alike in warm winter coats, were literally baptized by being thrown into a great snowdrift. It was a novel experience, but we thought it was grand. Then followed many golden years."[12]

The "Algonac Diaries" resumed right where they'd left off ten years before. "Stormy day and we all stayed home with books and work," Warren or Catherine wrote at the end of one winter's day. "Sallie and Cassie made caramels. Evening the Skeels came to see the *Magic Lantern*," an early image-projection device.[13]

For generations of future Delanos, the word *Algonac* was family code for good news.

Yet the origins of Delano fortune remained off-limits to discussion, especially in public. Sometime around 1880, the aging yet still ebullient Robert Bennet Forbes reached out to all of the surviving Russell & Company partners, asking for contributions for a company history. He wanted to memorialize the old days: the boat races in the Pearl River, the all-night whist games with the gentlemen of the Union Club of Canton, the siege of the Factories, the building of the first clipper ships, and the Yankee domination of the high seas during the golden years of the 1850s.

Warren Delano, by now blind in one eye and unable to walk without a cane, sent in a bland one-page summary of his time in China. He and Catherine had no interest in bringing up the opium demons of years past. They were more worried about the family's reputation. When one of his sons committed a prank while at boarding school, Warren wrote to the headmaster that if he could raise a second family, he "would seek a home among the Chinese, because in China the sons of the family could be depended on and honor their parents and live up to their standards."[14] For Delano, his family, not his memoir or his philanthropic activities, would be his most lasting accomplishment.

Robert's brother John Murray Forbes, now established as one of Boston's most generous philanthropists, also condemned the idea of a memoir. Robert Forbes published a rambling set of *Personal Reminiscences* anyway, but his younger brother intervened to make sure that nothing too negative got out, especially regarding opium. "I believe I have informed you that J. M. Forbes has bought the copyright of my memoir," Robert complained to Warren Delano, "not to destroy the plates as one would have suppose(d) who knows of his dead set against the printing of anything about Russell & Co. but in order to add a chapter on that renowned house. His only condition is that he may use scissors in cutting out what he calls irrelevant private matters."[15] Nonetheless, Robert Forbes, who never valued reticence, talked about opium in his book, justifying the trade as best he could.

In 1880, the twenty-six-year-old Sara Delano, now a regal and striking young woman, married fifty-three-year-old widower James Roosevelt, whose mother Rebecca had been the niece of William Henry Aspinwall. Tall and white-whiskered, "Squire" Roosevelt had promised Warren Delano that his bride would live in the utmost security and comfort at his own Hudson River estate at Hyde Park. The October wedding was held at Algonac. Some of the women present in the Delano parlor wept with sadness that "such a lovely girl should marry an old man."[16]

James and Sara Roosevelt's only child, Franklin Delano, was born on January 30, 1882. Sara and her son traveled frequently to Algonac, where he spent many pleasant days with the growing brood of Delano cousins. She also loved to sing him to sleep with her favorite sea chantey, one she'd heard the sailors sing as a little girl as they turned the capstans and hauled upon the lines of *Surprise*:

> Down by the river hauled a Yankee clipper,
> And it's blow my bully boys blow!
> She's a Yankee mate and a Yankee skipper,
> And it's blow, my bully boys, blow!

The China trading house of Russell & Company, the success of which had fueled the rise of the clipper ship and made the Delano clan so rich, failed in 1891 after Warren's son-in-law Will Forbes had over-speculated in silver. Daughter Dora Delano Forbes frantically sent telegrams from Hong Kong to New York, pleading for the old man to send money to save the business. "She, poor thing, was driven nearly mad with shame + chagrin," wrote one young Russell partner. Finally, Warren Delano decided to put up $30,000, but it was not enough to save the firm.[17]

Warren Delano II died in 1898 at the age of eighty-nine. The patriarch left each of his six surviving children $1.3 million, making him one of the few hundred richest men in America. The Delanos' fortune was secure, as was their place in the nation's ruling elite. A Unitarian clergyman said of the Yankee China trader: "This man seemed to have intuitions of right, justice, and equity in small matters, as in great. Dishonesty, pretense, chicanery, come how they might and in whom they would, felt themselves rebuked in his presence . . . His moral intensity and practical earnestness never relaxed their hold of what he felt to be good: the rest he left to God."[18]

Warren and Catherine's daughter Annie Delano Hitch and her husband, Fred, inherited Algonac. Blessed with deep pockets, they continued to run it in the grand manner that the patriarch knew. Over the years, the Delano siblings and their children united frequently at the family homestead, romping through the rooms cluttered with Chinese antiques and chasing one another around the fruit orchards.

Then, on a cold March afternoon in 1916, a fire broke out in the attic, caused either by a damaged flue or faulty electrical wiring. Annie Hitch smelled smoke, grabbed her fur coat, and ran outside. She watched in horror from the lawn as flames engulfed the upper floors of her father's house. "Thanks to neighbors from far and near, most of the books, furniture, pictures, and bric-a-brac on the first and second floors were saved," wrote her younger brother Frederic, who hurried from New York to the scene of the catastrophe, "but much was lost."[19]

The Lam Qua portrait of Houqua was one of the cherished family heirlooms that survived the conflagration. It remains in the possession of the Delano family.

Sara Delano, by now widowed, had brought other bits and pieces of the patriarch's Chinese collection across the Hudson to her husband's home at Hyde Park. She commissioned a complete renovation of the Roosevelt family estate so that it could house her son Franklin, his wife, Eleanor, and their six children.

Warren Delano's grandson went on to survive a debilitating case of waterborne polio at thirty-nine. In March 1933 he was sworn in as the thirty-second president of the United States. One day, while leading his country through the dark days of the Great Depression of the 1930s, he shared his grandfather Warren Delano's favorite bit of advice with his secretary of the Treasury, Henry Morgenthau: "Never let your left hand know what your right hand is doing."

"Which hand am I, Mr. President?" Morgenthau asked.

"My right hand," Franklin Delano Roosevelt responded with a smile, "but I keep my left hand under the table."[20]

The president kept a model of the clipper ship *Surprise* displayed prominently near his desk, one of more than two hundred models in his collection. He had built this *Surprise* himself.

In the spring of 1872, Captain Charles Porter Low sailed from New York for the last time aboard *N. B. Palmer*, the ship he had commanded for close to two decades. He was now forty-eight years old and had been at sea for most of his life. He was gray and balding, his face tanned and leathery, yet his crinkled eyes still burned the same bright blue of his youth.

His ship was also showing her age, one of the last American extreme clippers still sailing the high seas. Yet the ocean was still full of sailing ships, and would be for the next twenty years. They were American downeasters built of wood in Maine, or iron-hulled British windjammers built on the banks of Scotland's Clyde River. They were not as fast or as elegant as the clippers of the past, but they were sturdy and dependable on long-haul voyages.

Captain Low's wife, Sarah, who had finally tired of the sea, was back in Boston with their children. He was spending ten months or more away from shore each year and complained that he was "at home only some six weeks."[21] Sarah had more practical worries: out of all of the Low brothers, her husband Captain Charlie's career had been the most colorful, but he was also the least financially successful, save for ill-fated William Henry, now dead for more than thirty years. "We shall always be poor," the usually stoic Sarah lamented, "and will always be obliged to go to sea; for making money enough to stay at home is out of the question."[22]

Others in their family, and the larger family of the clipper era, had long ago come to land. Abbot Low was living comfortably in Brooklyn on the wealth he had amassed. "His name is associated with many good works," wrote an admiring journalist, "and his old age is a happy and honored one."[23] He died in 1893 as one of Brooklyn's richest men. Abbot's youngest son had used his father's standing to become a reform-minded mayor of Brooklyn, and then president of Columbia University, and would eventually become mayor of the newly consolidated City of New York. As president of Columbia, Seth Low would put a large chunk of his paternal inheritance toward the construction of the most lasting of the family's monuments: not a wooden clipper ship, but a marble library modeled on Rome's Pantheon, at the heart of Columbia's Upper Manhattan campus. He named it not after himself but after his opium-trading, clipper-ship-owning father, Abiel Abbot Low.

John Murray Forbes died in 1898—the same year as Warren Delano II—at the ripe old age of eighty-five. He was one of Boston's richest men, a premier railroad magnate and progenitor of a Boston Brahmin dynasty. His greatest legacy today is Milton Academy, a nondenominational preparatory school located near the Forbes family home. His son William Hathaway Forbes heeded his father's lessons in reinvesting capital in new technology. He became the first president of the American Telephone and Telegraph Company.

John Murray Forbes's oldest brother, Robert Bennet Forbes, lived out the rest of his days in the Greek Revival mansion he had originally built for their mother, Margaret, with his first fortune. He remained an active benefactor to the Sailors' Snug Harbor of Boston until his death in 1889 at the age of eighty-five.

Russell & Company finally failed in 1891, but the Canton bachelors had long since moved on. Some of the Russell fortune—passed down through Samuel's cousin William Huntington Russell—wound up at Yale University, where it funds the secret society Skull and Bones to this day.

Moses Grinnell, owner of McKay's *Flying Cloud*, was still residing in New York when he died in 1877. After retiring from Grinnell, Minturn & Company, he became active in Republican politics, campaigning on behalf of Abraham Lincoln. He also served as collector of the Port of New York and president of the Union Club of the City of New York. He is remembered today for his important role in creating and financing New York City's grandest ornament, Central Park, of which he served as a commissioner.

William Henry Aspinwall amassed one of the largest collections of European old-masters paintings in America. *Harper's Weekly* wrote of the collections of Titians, Van Dykes, and Veroneses: "Thus, as the foremost merchants of Florence, Venice, and Genoa became the greatest patrons of the arts in their day, so now we see many of the first men of our day following in their footsteps. This is the wise provision of Providence."[24] The president of the Panama Railroad and owner of the pioneering clipper *Sea Witch*, died in 1875. Aspinwall's railroad would remain a vital highway of commerce for decades to come, even after the opening of the Panama Canal in 1914.

The flamboyant and controversial Captain Robert Waterman, remembered both for commanding Aspinwall's *Sea Witch* and for the star-crossed voyage of *Challenge*, founded the town of Fairfield in California's Suisun Valley in 1856. It was named after his former home in Connecticut. In addition to running a gentleman's farm, he served as San Francisco's port warden and inspector of hulls. Captain Waterman died in 1884, a rich, unrepentant California squire.

The great Captain Josiah Perkins Creesy, hard-driving master of McKay's *Flying Cloud*, retired to a Massachusetts farm with his navigator and companion at sea, Eleanor. After serving his nation as a captain in the Union navy, the mariner who set the record from New York to California settled down to a comfortable life as an alderman and state legislator until being crippled by a stroke in 1868. He died in 1874 in Salem, Massachusetts, at the age of fifty-seven. Eleanor outlived him by twenty-six years, dying at their Salem home in 1900, aged eighty-five.[25] They left no children, and no account survives in their own hand of that history-making voyage in the legendary *Flying Cloud*, save for the terse log that Josiah kept between June and September 1851, which can be found in the archives of the Mystic Seaport Museum.

The great namesake of Captain Low's ship, his mentor Captain Nathaniel Palmer, would die in 1877 in his hometown of Stonington, Connecticut, long retired from commanding and designing ships. The tradition that he represented, of young American men braving the high seas for fame and fortune, was fast fading away. America was turning inward, away from the sea, and toward the Mississippi River Valley and California. Yet the sea would continue to call to Americans in history, literature, sailing, and song.

Charles Porter Low, the man who had tried to run away to sea aboard one of his brother's ships so many years before, would heed his wife's wishes and retire from the sea at age forty-eight. He moved his family to sunny Santa Barbara, California, dying there in 1913 at the age of eighty-eight.

He would always be a man in love with his life's calling and never forgot his last voyage as master of the clipper *N. B. Palmer* in 1872. He stood on the quarterdeck of his worn but still beautiful ship as she surged ahead, the trade winds swelling her white canvas sails that soared ten stories above his head. The sun glinted off the tarnished gilding on her stern, as well as the pitted brass compass and railings that the crew struggled to keep polished day in and day out. He glanced over at the helmsman and made sure he was on course, and then took out his sextant to shoot the sun at noon as he had done thousands of times before.

"One who loves the sailing of a ship is always watching for the wind to blow," Captain Low wrote, "and the wind is never in the same quarter for any length of time, and the sails have to be trimmed very often and the yards braced forwards or squared, to catch the veering winds. In the trade winds from Cape of Good Hope, you can run for weeks without altering the yards, in which time you can trice up all the running rigging clear of the rails, tar down all the standing rigging, scrape and oil the masts, paint the ship inside and out, holystone and oil the decks, and have her all ready to go into port in good shape; but in the variable winds, you must have everything ready for bad weather at any time."[26]

APPENDIX

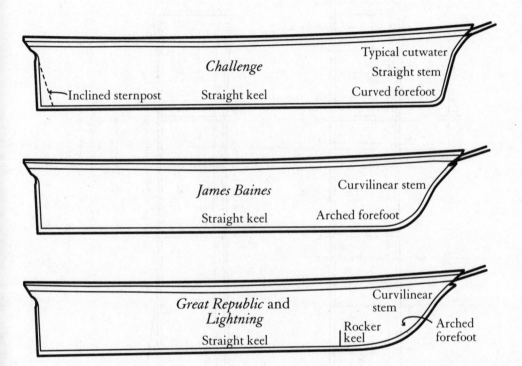

During the 1840s and 1850s, shipbuilders experimented with a variety of hull forms to maximize speed and cargo capacity while minimizing water resistance. William Henry Webb, designer of the *Challenge*, built clippers that, although fast, did not break China or Cape Horn records. Donald McKay, whose extreme clippers *Lightning* and *James Baines* achieved unprecedented speeds, gave his clippers a rounded (or arched) forefoot. The prows of his vessels also had a greater forward rake than earlier clippers, reducing the impact of the sea against the hull. The sternposts on his clippers had a slight rake aft, too, for greater buoyancy in that end of the vessel.

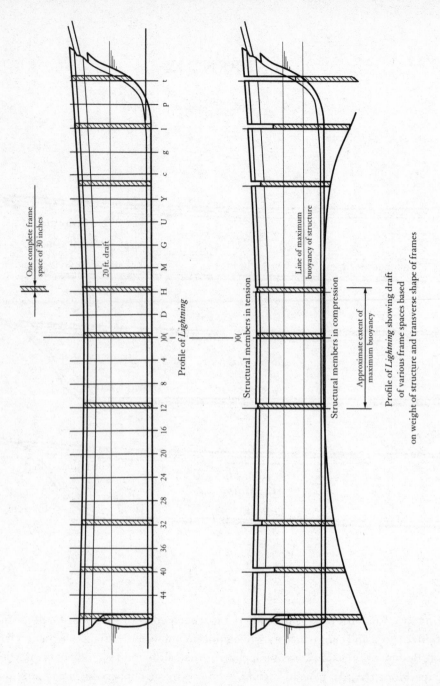

One complete frame space of 30 inches

20 ft. draft

Profile of *Lightning*

Structural members in tension

Line of maximum buoyancy of structure

Structural members in compression

Approximate extent of maximum buoyancy

Profile of *Lightning* showing draft of various frame spaces based on weight of structure and transverse shape of frames

The upper diagram demonstrates the numbering and lettering system that shipbuilders used to label frames during design and construction. The lower diagram indicates how, because of their sharp ends, clipper ships had less buoyancy in their bows and sterns than conventional vessels did. A strong keelson—an inside centerline structure that runs the length of the ship and holds together the frames—was critical to keeping the ship's bow and stern from pulling downward (a process known as hogging) from the midship section. The stronger the keelson, the trimmer and more elegant a ship's lines.

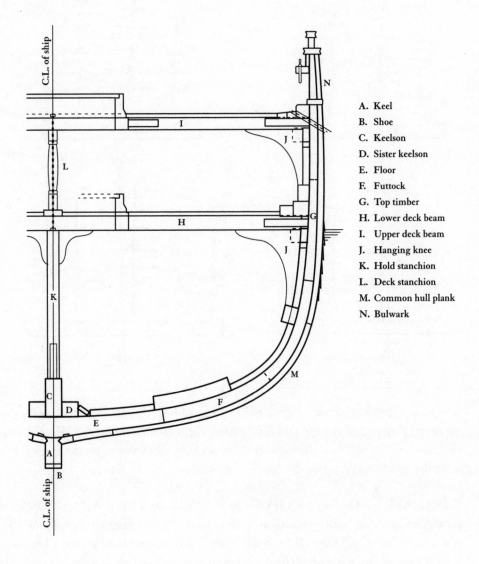

A. Keel
B. Shoe
C. Keelson
D. Sister keelson
E. Floor
F. Futtock
G. Top timber
H. Lower deck beam
I. Upper deck beam
J. Hanging knee
K. Hold stanchion
L. Deck stanchion
M. Common hull plank
N. Bulwark

C.L. of ship

This cutaway shows the key structural components of a clipper ship's hull. The keel (an outside centerline structure) was the backbone of the ship, while the hanging knees held together the ship's horizontal and vertical elements. The angle of the frames from the keel would define how steeply the ship's sides rose upward, an angle known as deadrise. The higher the deadrise, the more closely the hull cross section resembled a V, a form preferred by John Willis Griffiths. The lower the deadrise, the more closely the hull resembled a flat-bottomed barge, a form favored by Captain Nathaniel Palmer and Donald McKay.

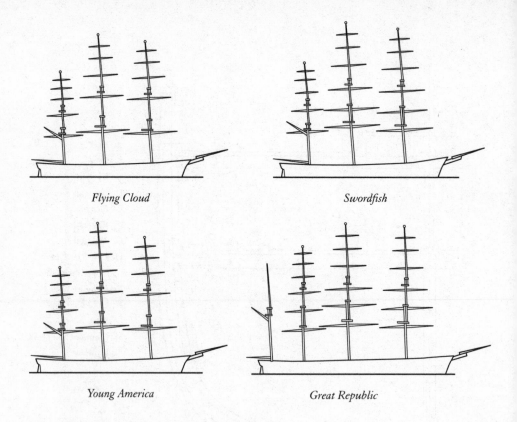

Flying Cloud

Swordfish

Young America

Great Republic

The record-breaking *Flying Cloud*, built by Donald McKay in 1851, had a fairly conventional ship rig, of the type used on earlier clippers such as the *Sea Witch*, *Houqua*, and *Samuel Russell*. What distinguished clipper ship rigs from more traditional vessels were the loftier masts and larger spreads of canvas.

Built to challenge Donald McKay's *Flying Fish*, William Henry Webb's *Swordfish* utilized the Forbes rig (split topsails) on her foremast (the first mast aft from the bow) and mainmast (the second mast aft from the bow). This arrangement, pioneered by Russell & Company partner Robert Bennet Forbes, made furling the sails much quicker and safer for the crew.

Young America, the 1853 extreme clipper masterpiece of William Henry Webb, had single topsails and a rare moonsail (set above the skysail) on her mainmast. The moonsail was usually set only in very light winds.

Great Republic as originally built by Donald McKay in 1853. She was a four-masted barque with a Forbes rig and skysails on her fore, main, and mizzen masts. She boasted fifteen thousand square yards of canvas. After she burned to the waterline just before her maiden voyage, Captain Nathaniel Palmer rebuilt *Great Republic* with a substantially reduced rig.

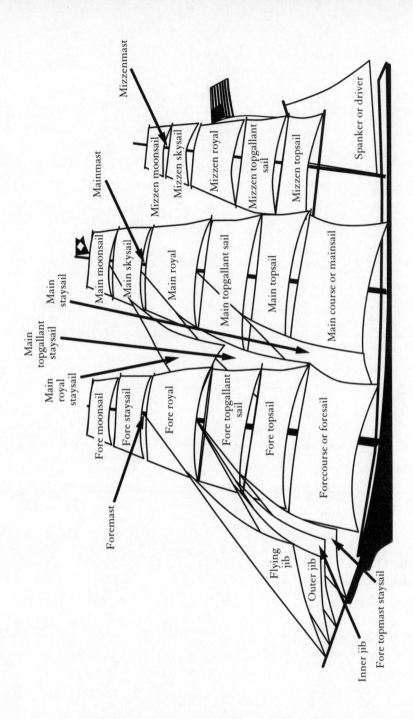

Most clippers were "full-rigged ships," meaning that they had square sails on all three of their masts. The topmost yard of the clipper ship *Challenge* soared more than two hundred feet above her main deck. When the crew went aloft, only the footropes and physical agility protected them from falling to their deaths. Some clippers, such as *Memnon*, were three-masted barques, meaning that their aftermast was rigged with a fore-and-aft sail only.

SOURCES AND ACKNOWLEDGMENTS

Sources on the clipper ship era are scattered, and careful detective work is required to separate fact from myth. The scores of mid-nineteenth-century American clipper ships that once sailed the seas are all gone—long since sunk, broken up, or burned for their metal parts. Yet their story is there to be told, in letters, diaries, published reminiscences, business contracts and receipts—not to mention in its enduring impact on American culture and history.

I have relied heavily on Captain Arthur Hamilton Clark's *The Clipper Ship Era*, published in 1910 and written by one of the great American experts on the sailing ship construction and handling. Clark knew many of the men who sailed the clippers of the 1850s, and he was also a friend of the great naval architect Donald McKay, who built more record-breaking clipper ships than any other shipbuilder of his time. Other invaluable secondary sources include the excellent work of Basil Lubbock, Carl C. Cutler, William C. Crothers, and Howard Irving Chapelle. And then there is Jacques Downs, who over the course of decades, studied the life and culture of the foreigners' community in Canton. The fruit of his lifetime obsession is the meticulously researched, colorfully written book *The Golden Ghetto*.

I am also indebted to the *Recollections* of Charles Porter Low, member of the historic Low family, who captained several of the great clippers whose stories are here told. Not written until 1906, fifty years after his glory years in the California and China trade, Low's recollections remain vivid, colorful, and full of self-deprecating humor. Like any memoir, especially a sailor's tale, the *Recollections* should be taken with a few grains of salt, but his specifics on dates and log entries indicate that although writing late in life, Low was working from actual references at his disposal.

The voices of the era's often-illiterate sailors survive in countless sea chanteys. To bring other lost voices to life, I have included descriptions of sailors and their craft from Richard Henry Dana's 1840 *Two Years Before the Mast*, the classic memoir of a Harvard-student-turned-sailor that remains arguably the most accurate and vivid account of life at sea aboard an American vessel during the golden age of sail.

Putting together the biographies of the men who designed and built the clipper ships involved a fair amount of educated guesswork. The naval architect most celebrated in legend, Donald McKay, also remains the greatest mystery. According to his descendant Richard Hamilton, most of his papers were destroyed in a flood many years ago, and many of the secondary sources on him are unreliable, including an account written by one of his grandsons in the 1920s. In this light, I've evaluated and cross-referenced stories carefully, and I'm grateful for Richard Hamilton's own recent research.

McKay's rival William Henry Webb was the subject of an in-depth commemorative 1987 biography by Edwin L. Dunbaugh and William duBarry Thomas, published by the Webb Institute. John Willis Griffiths, the builder of the early clippers *Rainbow* and *Sea Witch*, was not as fortunate. His life, too, remains shrouded in myth, and his own inflated accounts are not to be trusted. The most reliable character study comes from Dr. Larrie Ferreiro's biography published in the *Nautical Research Journal*.

Captain Nathaniel Palmer, designer of *Houqua* and other clippers for the Low family firm, is lovingly portrayed in Charles Low's *Recollections*, as well as in a few early-twentieth-century biographical sketches. The Palmer-Loper papers in the Library of Congress, however, do not reveal much in the way of personal thoughts.

The merchants who form the core of this story have left fascinating but widely scattered records. The Forbes brothers—John Murray and Robert Bennet—were prolific letter writers and diarists during their trading years in China and as shipowners and entrepreneurs in Boston. Their papers can be found in the Massachusetts Historical Society and in published memoirs. Robert Forbes, like his friend Charles Low, was a great yarn spinner and shameless self-promoter, yet he was a keen, colorful observer of the events of his time. John Murray Forbes, the soberer and steadier of the two brothers, was the bridge between the Chinese merchant elite and the Boston "Brahmin" aristocracy, both in matters of business and culture.

Warren Delano, progenitor of the presidential branch of his Yankee clan and a man whose life was full of adventure, was an inveterate letter writer, but many of his records were destroyed when the family mansion burned in 1916. My reconstruction of his life and personality comes from surviving correspondence at the Franklin D. Roosevelt Library & Museum at Hyde Park, New York, as well as from memoirs by his children and Geoffrey Ward's meticulously researched *Before the Trumpet: The Young Franklin Roosevelt*. Descendants Catherine (Nina) and Lyman Delano have been extremely helpful with family knowledge and lore, as has Sara Delano Perkins for allowing me use of some of her never-before-published collection of family photographs, and Frederic Delano Grant Jr. for solving the mystery of the portrait of Houqua that once hung at Algonac. It has been a real pleasure to get to know the Delanos over the past few years, and I deeply appreciate their enthusiasm and support.

William Henry Aspinwall was the most elusive personality of the shipowners, and I relied on the biography *The Aspinwall Empire* written by his descendant Colonel Duncan Somerville to shine some light on the man, his ships, and his character sketches of contemporaries. I faced a similar challenge with Moses Grinnell, part owner of the legendary *Flying Cloud*, whose stature loomed large in the New York merchant community but whose inner thoughts are lost to time. Finally, aside from one long letter written by Sarah Bowman on the *Flying Cloud*'s maiden voyage, as well as that vessel's log, there do not appear to be any deeply revelatory primary sources on Captain Josiah Perkins Creesy and his remarkable wife, Eleanor; I have had to base much of my knowledge of them on the detective work of the late A. B. C. Whipple.

James Grinnell of the New Bedford Whaling Museum has been extremely generous with his treasure trove of research documents and material. Thanks to his help, I have a much better grasp of the entire remarkable clan of Yankee capitalists and inventors. Many other wonderful institutions have shared their rich collections of primary and secondary sources, allowing me to stitch together the disparate strands of the story. These include the Mystic Seaport Museum and Library, Peabody Essex Museum, the New-York Historical Society, the Baker Library at the Harvard Business School, the New Bedford Whaling Museum, and the San Francisco Maritime Museum. Thanks also to Mary and Ian Lewis for being such generous hosts during my research stay in the Mystic area.

For me, the greatest living link between the clipper ship era and the present day is Llewellyn Howland III, a fellow Harvard alumnus and a book editor of the old school. Introduced to me by mutual friend Ed Kane, Louie is related to many of the old Yankee clipper ship families, including the Forbeses, and has a wealth of knowledge about the men who built, sailed, and owned the great and wondrous ships. It was he who urged me to write a book about New England family capitalism on the high seas and then devoted many precious hours of his time to help me do just that. I especially enjoyed his sailing stories. He's the real reason why it's wise to go sailing with someone who knows what he's doing. Thank you, Louie, for your encouragement, advice, and salty Yankee humor during our times in Gloucester.

Also much gratitude to William H. Bunting, one of the deans of American maritime history and author of *Live Yankees: The Sewalls and Their Ships,* for his input.

I would not have been able to complete this book without the assistance of many others, who have graciously given me their time and shared their resources so that I could complete the project.

Let me warmly thank Thomas LeBien, Brit Hvide, and Megan Hogan (who, it turns out, has a family connection to the Delanos), my editors at Simon & Schuster, for their extensive guidance and faith in the clipper ship project. With their extraordinary attention to detail and storytelling narrative, Simon & Schuster still publishes books the old-fashioned way. Jonathan Karp, publisher at S&S, has been a wonderful source of encouragement since 2007, and I'm grateful to him for giving me a chance at writing a second book under his aegis. Kudos to my agent Becky Sweren at Aevitas Creative for her tireless support and patience, as well as Vivien Ravdin for her expert narrative and editorial advice, which she had also provided in spades for my last book, *A Man and His Ship*.

In the fall of 2013, I spent seven weeks at the MacDowell Colony in Peterborough, New Hampshire. There amidst the autumnal splendor of New England, I wrote the initial draft of *Barons of the Sea*. Many revisions and rewrites followed, but I shall forever be grateful to my fellow artists at MacDowell, as well as its dedicated staff. Special thanks to Brent Watanabe, Alma Leiva, Riccardo Lorenz, Sutton Beres Culler, Anne Hayashi, and Blake Tewksbury for their friendship, and to the entire kitchen for their superlative culinary skill.

As with my previous book, I spent my summers writing at a special place on the South Shore of Massachusetts, where the sea is a constant source of inspiration, wonder, and reassurance. I'd like to thank the residents of this seaside colony, and recognize especially our long-time family friend Ramelle Adams, and her late brother, Peter Boylston Adams. It was through this community that I also met Richard Cadwalader, a graduate of Maine Maritime Academy and seasoned mariner who gave many great suggestions for the manuscript.

In the late summer of 2015, I was invited by my friend Stepha-

Sources and Acknowledgments

nie Speakman to sail around Martha's Vineyard aboard the clipper schooner *Shenandoah*. Aboard this reproduction of an 1850s sailing ship, the brainchild of the legendary Captain Bob Douglas, I was able to experience life at sea in a really vivid way. Although we passengers were not permitted to go aloft, we sang along with chanteyman Bill Schustik as we raised the sails and pumped the windlass to raise and lower the anchor. One of my favorite memories is of a night on the *Shenandoah* as she was anchored off Naushon Island (still the family retreat of the Forbes family), and I lay on deck, gazing at the Milky Way with Bill's bass rendition of "Lorena" wafting up from below.

The Union Club of New York was my home base when I traveled up from Philadelphia to do research in New York City. I spent many afternoons sitting in the library working on my manuscript and browsing the Club's excellent collection of history books. I'd especially like to thank fellow historians John Steele Gordon and David White for their counsel during the writing process, as well as fellow members E. Holland Low (direct descendant of Captain Charles Porter Low), Stephen Perkins (relative of Captain Josiah Perkins Creesy), John Train (kin of Enoch Train), and Lucius Palmer (relative of Captain Nathaniel Brown Palmer) for their insights into their family histories. I'd also like to thank Tielman Van Vleck for introducing me to the Delanos, and for offering me words of encouragement during the writing process.

While in New York, I also got to visit the *Stad Amsterdam*. This visiting Dutch-flagged clipper, completed in 2000, is the only square-rigged ship now plying the seas that is built according to original, extreme clipper principles. Despite a steel hull (rather than wood) and modern navigational and safety equipment, *Stad Amsterdam* illustrates the craft of her ancestors: the high rig, the sharp hull lines, and speeds exceeding fifteen knots. Her first officer Michaël Barbaix, was a wonderful resource for the art of seamanship on a square rigger. Thanks, Michaël, for keeping this body of knowledge alive into the twenty-first century.

My parents, Amy and Grant Ujifusa, have been wellsprings of support and love my entire life. They encouraged my love of ships and the sea as a boy, and have been wonderful artistic compasses during my entire writing career. I would especially like to thank my father, who brought his immense knowledge of the English language to bear on several iterations of *Barons of the Sea*, as well as to my mother for her rigorous proofreading.

Finally, I would like to thank my wife, Dr. Alexandra Vinograd, for her advice and support during so much of the writing and editing of *Barons of the Sea*. A writer needs a Rock of Gibraltar. She has been just that and so much more.

NOTES

Prologue: The Patriarch

1. Sara Delano Roosevelt, quoted in Geoffrey C. Ward, *Before the Trumpet: Young Franklin Roosevelt 1882–1905* (New York: Harper and Row, 1985), 87.
2. Ibid., 85.
3. *London Times*, 1850, quoted in A. B. C. Whipple, *The Seafarers: The Clipper Ships* (Amsterdam: Time-Life Books, 1980), 71.
4. J. D. B. DeBow, *Statistical View of the United States, Seventh Census* (Washington, DC: Beverley Tucker, Senate Printer, 1854), 164.
5. Andrew Jackson Downing, *The Architecture of Country Houses* (New York: Dover, 1969), preface, Kindle edition.
6. Rita Halle Kleeman, *Gracious Lady: The Life of Sara Delano Roosevelt* (New York: D. Appleton-Century, 1935), 27.
7. Reverend Henry Woude, *A Brief Memorial of Mr. Warren Delano, 1809–1898*, undated, Collection of the Historical Society of Newburgh and the Highlands.
8. Warren Delano II to Russell Sturgis, November 24, 1840, Papers of Warren Delano II, 5, General Correspondence, 1843–1891, Forbes, John Murray-Wood, Mrs. E. Wood, Franklin D. Roosevelt Library & Museum, Hyde Park, NY.
9. John Perkins Cushing, *Genealogy Finds: Documents with Ancestor's Names*, archives of Cynthia Owen Philip, Rhinecliff, NY, www.genealogyfinds .com/documents/bostoncushing.htm.
10. Sara Delano Roosevelt, quoted in Ward, *Before the Trumpet* (1985), 90.

Chapter 1: The Canton Silver Cup

1. John Murray Forbes, *Letters and Recollections of John Murray Forbes,* vol. 1, ed. Sarah Forbes Hughes (Boston: Houghton, Mifflin, 1899), 63–64.
2. Basil Lubbock, *The Opium Clippers* (Boston: Charles E. Lauriat, 1933), 147.
3. Amasa Delano, quoted in John Pomfret, *The Beautiful Country and the Middle Kingdom: America and China, 1776 to the Present* (New York: Henry Holt, 2016), 16.
4. Frederic Delano Grant Jr., "A Fair, Honorable, and Legitimate Trade," *American Heritage* 37, no. 5 (1986): www.americanheritage.com/content/"-fair-honorable-and-legitimate-trade"?page=7.
5. William C. Hunter, *Bits of Old China* (London: Kegan Paul, Trench, 1885), 279.
6. Warren Delano II to Robert Bennet Forbes, April 8, 1842, Delano Family Papers, II, Papers of Warren Delano II, 5, General Correspondence, Russell & Company—Wood, container 34A, FDR Library.
7. Warren Delano II to Franklin Hughes Delano, November 11, 1838, Delano Family Papers, FDR Library.
8. John Murray Forbes, *Letters and Recollections,* vol. 1, 83.
9. Jacques M. Downs, *The Golden Ghetto: The American Commercial Community at Canton and the Shaping of American China Policy, 1784–1844* (Bethlehem, PA: Lehigh University Press, Kindle edition, 1997), location 4721 of 13153.
10. Ibid.
11. Frederick W. Williams, *The Life and Letters of Samuel Wells Williams,* 170, quoted in Peter Ward Fay, *The Opium War, 1840–1842* (Chapel Hill: University of North Carolina Press, 1997), 21.
12. Downs, *Golden Ghetto* (Kindle edition, 1997), location 619 of 13153.
13. "Cohong," *Encyclopedia Britannica* online, www.britannica.com/topic/cohong.
14. John Wong, "Global Positioning: Houqua and His China Trade Partners in the Nineteenth Century" (doctoral dissertation, Harvard University, 2012), 119, http://nrs.harvard.edu/urn-3:HUL.InstRepos:9282867.
15. Abiel Abbot Low to William Henry Low II, November 12, 1837, Elma Loines, ed., *The China Trade Post-Bag of the Seth Low Family of Salem and New York, 1829–1873* (Manchester, ME: Falmouth, 1953), 64.

16. Grant Jr., "Fair, Honorable, and Legitimate Trade."

17. Downs, *Golden Ghetto* (Kindle edition, 1997), location 410 of 13153.

18. Charles Porter Low, *Some Recollections by Captain Charles P. Low, Commanding the Clipper Ships "Houqua," "Jacob Bell," "Samuel Russell," and "N.B. Palmer," in the China Trade, 1847–1873* (Boston: Geo. H. Ellis, 1906), 29.

19. Larrie Ferreiro and Alexander Pollara, "Clippers, Yachts, and the False Promise of the Wave Line," *Physics Today* 70, no. 7 (July 2017): 52, doi /10.1063/PT.3.3627.

20. Arthur Hamilton Clark, *The Clipper Ship Era* (New York: G.P. Putnam's Sons, 1910), 30.

21. Rosemarie W. N. Lamas, *Everything in Style: Harriet Low's Macau* (Hong Kong: Hong Kong University Press, 2006), 175–76.

22. Diana Rosen, "Teas of Yore: Bohea, Hyson, and Congou," Tea Muse, last modified October 1, 2003, www.teamuse.com/article_031001.html.

23. Eric Jay Dolin, *When America First Met China: An Exotic History of Tea, Drugs, and Money in the Age of Sail* (New York: W.W. Norton & Company, 2012), 8605.

24. Frank Shyong, "American Ginseng Has a Loyal Chinese Clientele," *Los Angeles Times* online, February 28, 2015, www.latimes.com/local/california /la-me-adv-ginseng-american-20150301-story.html.

25. Amasa Delano, *A Narrative of Voyages and Travels in the Northern and Southern Hemispheres* (Boston: E. G. House, 1817), 542.

26. James M. Lindgren, "'Let Us Idealize Old Types of Manhood': The New Bedford Whaling Museum, 1903–1941," *New England Quarterly* 72, no. 2 (June 1999): 165.

27. Charles Francis Adams, quoted in Lindgren, "'Let Us Idealize Old Types of Manhood,'" 165.

28. Frederic A. Delano, *Warren Delano (II) 1809–1898 and Catherine Robbins (Lyman) Delano 1825–1896* (Newburgh, NY: Collection of the Historical Society of Newburgh and the Highlands, 1928), 4.

29. Christopher J. Richard, "The Academy: Old Fairhaven's Civic Center," Fairhaven, MA, History, accessed November 16, 2015, http://fairhaven history.blogspot.com/2011/12/academy-old-fairhavens-civic-center.html. Original source: Charles A. Harris, Old-Time Fairhaven, vol. 3.

30. L. Elsa Loeber and Walter Barrett, "A Profile of Moses Hicks Grinnell," Grinnell Family Association of America, accessed April 11, 2016, www

.grinnellfamily.org/index.php?option=com_content&view=article&id=78&Itemid=68.

31. Joseph Alfred Scoville, *The Old Merchants of New York City* (New York: Geo. W. Carleton, 1862), 28.

32. Scott Reynolds Nelson, *A Nation of Deadbeats: An Uncommon History of America's Financial Disasters* (New York: Alfred A. Knopf, 2012), 15.

33. Ibid.

34. Joseph Alfred Scoville, quoted in Robert Greenhalgh Albion, *Square-Riggers on a Schedule: The New York Sailing Packets to England, France, and the Cotton Ports* (Princeton, NJ: Princeton University Press, 1938), 121.

35. Richard Henry Dana Jr., *Two Years Before the Mast* (Lexington, KY: Seven Treasures, 2008), 102.

36. Ralph Delahaye Paine, *The Old Merchant Marine: A Chronicle of Ships and Sailors* (New Haven, CT: Yale University Press, 1919), 161.

37. "Life on a Whaleship," New Bedford Whaling Museum, accessed November 14, 2016, www.whalingmuseum.org/learn/research-topics/overview -of-north-american-whaling/life-aboard.

38. Dana Jr., *Two Years Before the Mast*, 37.

39. Abiel Abbot Low to William Henry Low II, November 12, 1837, Loines, *China Trade Post-Bag*, 63.

40. Joseph Grinnell to Warren Delano, December 31, 1835, Delano Family Papers, II, Papers of Warren Delano II, 5, General Correspondence, Russell & Company—Wood, container 34A, FDR Library.

41. Downs, *Golden Ghetto* (Kindle edition, 1997), location 3786 of 13153.

42. Joseph Archer, February 12, 1838, quoted in Downs, *Golden Ghetto* (Kindle edition, 1997), location 3786 of 13153.

Chapter 2: Breaking Into the Family

1. Robert Bennet Forbes, *Personal Reminiscences* (Boston: Little, Brown, 1882), 145.

2. Thomas G. Cary, *Memoir of Thomas Handasyd Perkins* (Boston: Little, Brown and Company, 1856), 46.

3. Downs, *Golden Ghetto*, 85.

4. Lubbock, *Opium Clippers*, 33.

5. Ibid., 44.

6. Houqua to John Murray Forbes, August 10, 1838, as quoted in *John Murray Forbes, Letters and Recollections*, vol. 1, 99.

7. John Perkins Cushing to Margaret Forbes, c. 1819, quoted in Lubbock, *Opium Clippers*, 33.

8. John Murray Forbes, *Letters and Recollections*, vol. 1, 46.

9. Ibid., 40.

10. Ibid., 49.

11. Ibid., 72.

12. "History of J. M. Forbes & Co.," J. M. Forbes & Co., last modified December 2015, www.jmforbes.com/history.

13. Houqua to John Murray Forbes, August 10, 1838, quoted in John Murray Forbes, *Letters and Recollections*, 99.

14. "John Murray Forbes," *Spectator*, October 28, 1899, 18, http://archive.spectator.co.uk/article/28th-october-1899/18/john-murray-forbes.

15. Robert Bennet Forbes to Rose Forbes, October 16, 1839. Phyllis Forbes Kerr, *Letters from China: The Canton-Boston Correspondence of Robert Bennet Forbes, 1838–1840* (Mystic, CT: Mystic Seaport Museum, 1996), 63.

16. Ibid., 62.

17. Downs, *Golden Ghetto* (Kindle edition, 1997), location 9328 of 13153.

18. Ward, *Before the Trumpet: The Young Franklin Roosevelt, 1882–1905* (New York, NY: Perennial Library, 1986), 69.

19. Ibid.

20. Robert Bennet Forbes to Rose Forbes, October 16, 1839, Phyllis Forbes Kerr, *Letters from China*, 67.

21. *Other Merchants and Sea Captains of Old Boston* (Boston: State Street Trust, 1919), 18.

22. Cushing, *Genealogy Finds*.

23. Robert Bennet Forbes to Rose Forbes, October 16, 1839, Phyllis Forbes Kerr, *Letters from China*, 67.

24. Ibid., 69.

25. Lubbock, *Opium Clippers*, 147.

26. Ward, *Before the Trumpet* (1986), 71.

27. Abiel Abbot Low to William Henry Low II, November 12, 1837, Loines, *China Trade Post-Bag*, 63.

28. Harriet Low, quoted in Peter C. Perdue, "The Rise and Fall of the Canton Trade System II, Macau and Whampoa Anchorage," MIT Visualiz-

ing Cultures, accessed October 28, 2013, http://ocw.mit.edu/ans7870/21f /21f.027/rise_fall_canton_02/cw_essay02.html.

29. Helen Augur, *Tall Ships to Cathay* (Garden City, NY: Doubleday 1951), 91.

30. Lubbock, *Opium Clippers*, 33.

31. William C. Hunter, *Bits of Old China* (London: Kegan, Paul, Trench, 1885), 267.

32. Ibid., 38.

33. Robert Bennet Forbes to Rose Forbes, January 25, 1839, Phyllis Forbes Kerr, *Letters from China*, 87–90.

34. Ibid.

35. Warren Delano II, quoted in Ward, *Before the Trumpet* (1986), 69.

36. Hunter, *Bits of Old China*, 3, quoted in Ward, *Before the Trumpet* (1986), 69.

Chapter 3: Opium Hostages

1. Thomas De Quincey, *Confessions of an English Opium-Eater* (London, Walter Scott, 1821).

2. *Other Merchants and Sea Captains of Old Boston* (Boston: State Street Trust Company, 1919), 23.

3. Hall Gleason, *Old Ships and Ship-Building Days of Medford*, 1630–1873 (West Medford, MA: J. C. Miller Jr., 1936), 59. [[Source: Library of Congress.]]

4. Robert Bennet Forbes to Rose Forbes, March 10, 1839, Phyllis Forbes Kerr, *Letters from China*, 101.

5. William C. Hunter, *The "Fan Kwae" at Canton Before Treaty Days, 1825–1844* (London: Kegan, Paul, Trench, 1882), 117–20. [[Source: digitized book. See https://archive.org/details/fankwaeatcanton00huntgoog.]]

6. Warren Delano, quoted in Karl E. Meyer, "Editorial Notebook: The Opium War's Secret History," *New York Times* online, June 28, 1997. Warren Delano's daughter Sara was the mother of Franklin Delano Roosevelt.

7. Downs, *Golden Ghetto* (Kindle edition, 1997), locations 7738 and 8005 of 13153.

8. Massachusetts Historical Society Forbes Reel 5, Number 26, Letters from Robert Bennet Forbes, quoted in Wong, "Global Positioning," 119.

9. Hunter, *"Fan Kwae" at Canton*, 117–20.

10. Robert Bennet Forbes, *Personal Reminiscences*, 144.

11. Ian Scott, "Heroin: A Hundred-Year Habit," *History Today* 48, no. 6 (1998): www.historytoday.com/ian-scott/heroin-hundred-year-habit.

12. Ward, *Before the Trumpet* (1985), 73.

13. Hunter, *Bits of Old China*, 3, quoted in Ward, *Before the Trumpet* (1985), 74.

14. Robert Bennet Forbes to Rose Forbes, April 19, 1839, Phyllis Forbes Kerr, *Letters from China*, 120.

15. *Friend of China*, March 29, 1839, quoted in Lubbock, *Opium Clippers*, 167.

16. Robert Bennet Forbes, *Personal Reminiscences*, 153.

17. Warren Delano II to Russell Sturgis, November 24, 1840, Papers of Warren Delano II, 5, General Correspondence, 1843–1891, Forbes, John Murray-Wood, Mrs. E. Wood, FDR Library.

18. Warren Delano II to A. A. Low, December 23, 1840, Warren Delano II to Robert Bennet Forbes, November 25, 1840, Delano Family Papers, Papers of Warren Delano II, 5, General Correspondence, Russell & Company—Wood, container 34A, FDR Library.

19. Grant Jr., "Fair, Honorable, and Legitimate Trade."

20. Ibid.

21. William Jardine, quoted in Tristram Hunt, *Cities of Empire: The British Colonies and the Creation of the Urban World* (New York: Metropolitan Books, Henry Holt, 2014), 236.

22. Extract of G. Nye Jr. to R. B. Forbes, July 3, 1840, Delano Family Papers, II, Papers of Warren Delano II, 5, Generation Correspondence, box 34, FDR Library.

23. Grant Jr., "Fair, Honorable, and Legitimate Trade."

24. Warren Delano to Edward King, February 24, 1841, Delano Family Papers, Papers of Warren Delano II, 5, General Correspondence, Russell & Company—Wood, container 34A, FDR Library.

25. Warren Delano II to A. A. Low, September 30, 1840, Papers of Warren Delano II, 5, General Correspondence, 1843–1891, Forbes, John Murray-Wood, Mrs. E. Wood, FDR Library.

26. Grant Jr., "Fair, Honorable, and Legitimate Trade."

27. Warren Delano II to Russell Sturgis, May 12, 1841, Delano Family Papers, Papers of Warren Delano II, 5, General Correspondence, Russell & Company—Wood, container 34A, FDR Library.

28. Warren Delano II to Robert Bennet Forbes, November 25, 1840, Delano Family Papers, Papers of Warren Delano II, 5, General Correspondence, Russell & Company—Wood, container 34A, FDR Library.

29. Sarah Forbes Hughes, ed., *Letters and Recollections of John Murray Forbes*.

30. Grant Jr., "Fair, Honorable, and Legitimate Trade."

31. Ibid.

32. Warren Delano II to Robert Bennet Forbes, November 25, 1840, Delano Family Papers, Papers of Warren Delano II, 5, General Correspondence, Russell & Company—Wood, container 34A, FDR Library.

33. William Henry Low to Josiah Low, quoted in Augur, *Tall Ships to Cathay*, 114.

34. Shannon Butler, "The Journals of Edward Delano," Delano Papers Project, June 25, 2014, http://delanopaperproject.tumblr.com/post/89895605925/the-journals-of-edward-delano.

35. Augur, *Tall Ships to Cathay*, 117.

36. William Henry Low II to Harriet Low Hilliard, August 1, 1841, Loines, *China Trade Post-Bag*, 92.

37. Jacques Downs, *Golden Ghetto: The American Commercial Community at Canton and the Shaping of American China Policy, 1784–1844* (Hong Kong: Hong Kong University Press, 2015), 81.

38. Warren Delano II to William Hunter and Edward King, February 24, 1841, Delano Family Papers II, Papers of Warren Delano II, 5, General Correspondence, Russell and Company—Wood, container 34A, FDR Library.

39. Grant Jr., "Fair, Honorable, and Legitimate Trade."

40. "Treaty of Nanking," UCLA Asia Institute, accessed July 26, 2016, www.international.ucla.edu/asia/article/18421.

41. John Quincy Adams, *Memoirs*, 9: 30-31, quoted in Downs, *Golden Ghetto* (Kindle edition, 2015), location 5489.

42. Grant Jr., "Fair, Honorable, and Legitimate Trade."

43. Ibid.

Chapter 4: Yankees in Gotham

1. Cynthia Owen Philip, "New Englanders-on-Hudson," *About Town*, Fall 2014, 5.

2. Washington Irving, *A Knickerbocker's History of New York* (Gretna, LA: Pelican Press, 2009), 193.

3. *New York Evening Post*, October 27, 1817. *Square Riggers on a Schedule: The New York Sailing Packets to England, France, and the Cotton Ports* (Princeton, NJ: Princeton University Press, 1938), 23.

4. Walt Whitman, "Crossing Brooklyn Ferry," accessed February 13, 2017, www.poetryfoundation.org/poems-and-poets/poems/detail/45470.

5. M. C. Hallberg, "Railroads in North America: Some Historical Facts and An Introduction to an Electronic Database of North American Railroads and Their Evolution" (Harrisburg, PA: Pennsylvania Historical and Museum Commission, 2009), 19.

6. Frank Gray Griswold, *Clipper Ships and Yachts* (New York: Dutton's, 1927), 25.

7. Quoted in Ward, *Before the Trumpet* (1985), 18.

8. Colonel Duncan S. Somerville, *The Aspinwall Empire* (Mystic, CT: Mystic Seaport Museum), 8.

9. Ibid., 10.

10. Walter Barrett, *Old Merchants of New York* (New York: Knox and Sons, 1885), 158. http://files.usgwarchives.net/ny/newyork/bios/oldmerchants /griswold-nathaniel.txt.

11. Downs, *Golden Ghetto* (Kindle edition, 2015), 432.

12. Joe McMillan, "A. A. Low & Brother," House Flags of U.S. Shipping Companies, accessed March 29, 2015, http://fotw.fivestarflags.com/us~hfl .html#low.

13. Diary of Philip Hone, June 2, 1836, quoted in Martin Simmons, *Union Club of the City of New York* (New York: Union Club, 1986), 3.

14. William C. Hunter, quoted in Ward, *Before the Trumpet* (1986), 70.

15. Warren Delano II to Franklin Hughes Delano, Canton, November 11, 1838. Papers of Franklin Hughes Delano, box 3, Delano Family Papers, FDR Library.

16. Mrs. C. M. Kirland, "The Mystery of Visiting," *Sartain's* 6 (May 1850): 317.

17. Diary of Philip Hone, June 17, 1836, quoted in Simmons, *Union Club*, 9.

18. Simmons, *Union Club*, 9.

19. Charles Lockwood, "Gangs, Crime, Smut, and Violence," *New York Times* online, September 20, 1990, www.nytimes.com/1990/09/20/opinion /gangs-crime-smut-violence.html.

20. Mike Walsh, quoted in Edward K. Spann, *New York: The New Metropolis, 1840–1857* (New York: Columbia University Press, 1984), 233.

21. John Steele Gordon, "Five Myths About Millionaires," *Washington Post* online, September 21, 2011, www.washingtonpost.com/opinions/five-myths -about-millionaires/2011/09/21/gIQAvyGqqK_story.html.

22. Kevin Phillips, *Wealth and Democracy: A Political History of the American Rich* (New York: Broadway Books, 2002), 26.

23. Matthew Hale Smith, as quoted in John Steele Gordon, *An Empire of Wealth: The Epic Rise of American Economic Power* (New York: Harper Collins Publishers, 2009), 211.

24. Mary L. Knapp, *An Old Merchant's House: Life at Home in New York City, 1835–65* (New York: Girandole Books, 2012), 51–54.

25. Ibid., 15.

26. Kleeman, *Gracious Lady*, 15.

27. Knapp, *An Old Merchant's House*, 88.

28. Ward, *Before the Trumpet* (1986), 87.

29. Delano Family Papers, quoted in Ward, *Before the Trumpet* (1986), 79.

30. Anna Lyman to Edward N. R. Lyman, October 1843, quoted in Frederic A. Delano, *Warren Delano (II) and Catherine Robbins (Lyman) Delano*, 6.

31. Ward, *Before the Trumpet* (1986), 79.

32. Mary Lesley Ames, *The Life and Letters of Peter and Susan Lesley* (New York: G.P. Putnam's Sons, 1909), 137.

33. Warren Delano, April 6, 1843, quoted in Downs, *Golden Ghetto* (Kindle edition, 2015), location 3879 of 13153.

34. Diary of Edward Delano, June 16, 1841, in Downs, *Golden Ghetto* (Kindle edition, 2015), location 3921 of 13153.

35. Robert Bennet Forbes, *Personal Reminiscences*, 167.

36. Catherine Lyman Delano, quoted in Kleeman, *Gracious Lady*, 14.

37. Grant Jr., "Fair, Honorable, and Legitimate Trade."

Chapter 5: Mazeppa *and the Problem Child*

1. Alexis de Tocqueville, *Democracy in America* (1835), quoted in Benjamin W. Labaree et al., *America and the Sea: A Maritime History* (Mystic, CT: Mystic Seaport Museum, 1998), 239.

2. *Some Ships of the Clipper Ship Era* (Boston: State Street Trust Company, 1913), 12.

3. John Murray Forbes, *Letters and Recollections,* vol. 1, 67.

4. Ibid., 13.

5. Clark, *Clipper Ship Era*, 59.

6. Irving Howard Chapelle, *The Baltimore Clipper: Its Origins and Development* (New York: Dover, 1988), 3.

7. Clark, *Clipper Ship Era*, 61–62.

8. Ibid., 59.

9. Loines, *China Trade Post-Bag*, 15.

10. Low, *Some Recollections*, 9.

11. Ibid., 13.

12. Ibid., 10.

13. Michaël Barbaix to author, email, February 13, 2017. Barbaix is the former first mate of the modern-day clipper ship *Stad Amsterdam*.

14. Low, *Some Recollections*, 12.

15. Ibid., 13.

16. William Armstrong Fairburn, *Merchant Sail* (Center Lovell, ME: Fairburn Marine Education Foundation, 1945–1955), 3652.

17. Dana Jr., *Two Years Before the Mast*, 9.

18. Ibid., 5.

19. Low, *Some Recollections*, 15.

20. Dana Jr., *Two Years Before the Mast*, 10–11.

21. Richard Cadwalader to author, email, February 27, 2017.

22. Dana Jr., *Two Years Before the Mast*, 5.

23. Low, *Some Recollections*, 48.

24. A. B. C. Whipple, *The Challenge* (New York: William Morrow, 1987), 33.

25. Low, *Some Recollections*, 31.

26. Dana Jr., *Two Years Before the Mast*, 128.

27. Warren Delano II to Franklin Hughes Delano, Canton, November 11, 1838. Family Correspondence, 1838–1888, container 3, Franklin Hughes Delano Papers, FDR Library.

28. Treaty of Peace, Amity, and Commerce Between the United States of America and the Chinese Empire, July 3, 1844, accessed December 6, 2016, https://en.wikisource.org/wiki/Treaty_of_Wanghia.

Chapter 6: Captain Nat

1. Clark, *Clipper Ship Era*, 87.
2. Ibid., 86.
3. John R. Spears, *Captain Nathaniel Brown Palmer: An Old-Time Sailor of the Sea* (New York: Macmillan, 1922), 2.
4. William L. Crothers, *The American-Built Clipper Ship, 1850-1856: Characteristics, Construction, Details* (Camden, ME: International Marine, 2000), 24–28.
5. Spears, *Captain Nathaniel Brown Palmer*, 2.
6. Clark, *Clipper Ship Era*, 79.
7. Spears, *Captain Nathaniel Brown Palmer*, 2.
8. Ibid., 89.
9. Ibid., 103.
10. Albion, *Square-Riggers on Schedule*, 167.
11. Spears, *Captain Nathaniel Brown Palmer*, 166.
12. D. A. Levy, *Captain Robert H. "Bully" Waterman, 1808–1884* (Sausalito, CA: Terra /Maritime History Project, 2012), loc. 136.
13. Low, *Some Recollections*, 63.
14. Spears, *Captain Nathaniel Brown Palmer*, 167.
15. Abiel Abbot Low to Edward Allen Low, April 17, 1845, Loines, *China Trade Post-Bag*, 241.
16. Melbourne Smith, "To See Which Is *Sea Witch*," *Nautical Research Journal* 26, no. 2 (June 1930): 55–62.
17. Adam Brodsky, "Grave Injustice for NY Ship Hero," *New York Post* online, October 25, 2013.
18. Crothers, *American-Built Clipper Ship*, 14.
19. Spears, *Captain Nathaniel Brown Palmer*, 187.
20. R. B. Forbes to Nathaniel Brown Palmer, March 13, 1844, Palmer-Loper Papers, series II:1, reel 1 of 9, Library of Congress, Washington, DC.
21. Edwin L. Dunbaugh and William duBarry Thomas, *William H. Webb* (Glen Cove, NY: Webb Institute, 1987), 18–19.
22. Crothers, *American-Built Clipper Ship*, 177.
23. Ibid., 68.
24. Ibid., 139.
25. Ibid., 128.
26. Ibid., 147.

27. Ibid., 156.

28. Ibid., 229.

29. *New York Herald*, c. May 1844, quoted in Carl C. Cutler, *Greyhounds of the Sea: The Story of the American Clipper Ship* (Annapolis, MD: Naval Institute Press, 1960), 114–15.

30. A. A. Low to Warren Delano II, May 27, 1844, Loines, *China Trade Post-Bag*, 238.

31. Low, *Some Recollections*, 45.

32. Charles R. Schultz, *Life Aboard American Clipper Ships* (College Station: Texas A&M University Sea Grant Program, 1983), 8.

33. Low, *Some Recollections*, 49.

34. Ibid., 52.

35. Ibid., 55.

36. Ibid., 47.

37. Henry Low to Nathaniel Brown Palmer, September 18, 1844, Palmer-Loper Papers, series II:1, reel 1 of 9, Library of Congress, Washington, DC.

38. T. W. Ward to Nathaniel Brown Palmer, May 24, 1844, Palmer-Loper Papers, series II:1, reel 1 of 9, Library of Congress, Washington, DC.

39. Low, *Some Recollections*, 14.

40. Dana Jr., *Two Years Before the Mast*, 17.

41. Low, *Some Recollections*, 50–51.

Chapter 7: Family Pressure Under Sail

1. Benjamin R. C. Low, "Houqua, In Memoriam A.A.L.," in Loines, *China Trade Post-Bag*, 60.

2. Edward Allen Low to Abiel Abbot Low, December 23, 1844, in Loines, *China Trade Post-Bag*, 240.

3. Augur, *Tall Ships to Cathay*, 155.

4. Abiel Abbot Low to Edward Allen Low, April 17, 1845, in Loines, *China Trade Post-Bag*, 242.

5. Abiel Abbot Low to Edward Low, in Augur, *Tall Ships to Cathay*, 155.

6. Abiel Abbot Low to Edward Allen Low, April 17, 1845, in Loines, *China Trade Post-Bag*, 241.

7. Ibid., 242.

8. Clark, *Clipper Ship Era*, 67.
9. Ibid., 66.
10. Ibid., 67.
11. *New York Herald*, January 1845, quoted in Cutler, *Greyhounds of the Sea*, 113.
12. Warren Delano II to Franklin Delano, January 14, 1846, Family Correspondence, 1838–1888, container 3, Franklin Hughes Delano Papers, FDR Library.
13. Robert Forbes, *Personal Reminiscences*, p. 209.
14. Ibid.
15. Warren Delano to Franklin Delano, October 28, 1845, Delano Family Papers, Family Correspondence 1838–1888, container 3, FDR Library.
16. Ward, *Before the Trumpet* (1985), 80.
17. Kleeman, *Gracious Lady*, 14–15.
18. Spears, *Captain Nathaniel Brown Palmer*, 187.
19. "John Willis Griffiths, Designer—*Sea Witch*," *Nautical Research Journal*, undated, accessed December 15, 2016, www.sitesalive.com/ocl/public/03s/bios/johnwgriffiths.html.
20. Quoted in Albion, *Square Riggers on a Schedule*, 167.
21. Obituary of Charles H. Marshall, quoted in Ward, *Before the Trumpet* (1986), 39.
22. Robert Carse, *The Moonrakers: The Story of the Clipper Ship Men* (New York: Harper & Brothers, 1961), 47.
23. Clark, *Clipper Ship Era*, 75.
24. Ibid., 76.
25. Ibid.
26. Whipple, *Challenge*, 34.
27. *New York Herald*, December 9, 1846, quoted in Cutler, *Greyhounds of the Sea*, 121.
28. Cutler, *Greyhounds of the Sea*, 123.
29. *New York Herald*, August 15, 1847, quoted in Cutler, *Greyhounds of the Sea*, 123.
30. Cutler, *Greyhounds of the Sea*, 138.
31. "John W. Griffiths, Designer—*Sea Witch*."
32. Dunbaugh and Thomas, *William H. Webb*, 36, 46.

Chapter 8: Memnon: *Delano's California Bet*

1. Richard Wagner, *Der Fliegende Holländer*, produced by Louise Hope, Juliet Sutherland, and the Online Distributed Proofreading Team at www.pgdp.net, April 12, 2010, accessed September 20, 2016, www.gutenberg.org/files/31963/31963-h/31963-h.htm.

2. *New York Herald Tribune*, quoted in Edward J. Renehan Jr., *Commodore: The Life of Cornelius Vanderbilt* (New York: Basic Books, 2007), 158–59, https://books.google.com/books?id=Oo-FsjHw4c4C&printsec=copyright#v=onepage&q&f=false.

3. Warren Delano II, undated, Delano Family Papers II, Papers of Warren Delano II, 5, General Correspondence, Russell and Company—Wood, container 34A, FDR Library.

4. Richard C. McKay, *South Street: A Maritime History of New York* (New York: G.P. Putnam's Sons, 1934), 395.

5. "Master Mariner of Note Goes to His Final Rest," *San Francisco Call* 93, no. 18 (December 18, 1902), California Digital Newspaper Collection, accessed November 16, 2016, http://cdnc.ucr.edu/cgi-bin/cdnc?a=d&d=SFC19021218.2.114.

6. Robert Bennet Forbes, *Notes on Ships of the Past* (Boston: J. F. Cotter, 1885), 19.

7. Larrie D. Ferreiro, "A Biographical Sketch of John Willis Griffiths from Primary and Archival Sources," *Nautical Research Journal* 52, no. 4 (Winter 2007): 224.

8. Low, *Some Recollections*, 65.

9. Ibid., 70.

10. Glenn A. Knoblock, *The American Clipper Ship, 1845–1930: A Comprehensive History, with a Listing of Builders and Their Ships* (Jefferson, NC: McFarland, 2014), 101.

11. Low, *Some Recollections*, 72.

12. Ibid., 77.

13. Ibid., 81.

14. Ibid., 85.

15. Ibid., 84.

16. James K. Polk, 1848 State of the Union Address, December 5, 1848, accessed May 15, 2015, www.presidentialrhetoric.com/historicspeeches/polk/stateoftheunion1848.html.

17. DeBow, *Statistical View of the United States, Seventh Census*, 16364.

18. Matthew Hale Smith, as quoted in John Steele Gordon, *An Empire of Wealth: The Epic Rise of American Economic Power* (New York: Harper Collins Publishers, 2009), 211.

19. Helen La Grange, *Clipper Ships of America and Great Britain, 1833–1869* (New York: G.P. Putnam's Sons, 1936), 72.

20. Horace Greeley, *An Overland Journey, from New York to San Francisco in the Summer of 1859* (New York: C. M. Saxton, Barker, 1860).

21. Chester G. Hearn, *Tracks in the Sea: Matthew Fontaine Maury and the Mapping of the Oceans* (New York: McGraw-Hill, 2002), 135.

22. Nathaniel Philbrick, *Sea of Glory: America's Voyage of Discovery, The U.S. Exploring Expedition* (New York: Penguin Books, 2004), *xix*.

23. Matthew Fontaine Maury, quoted in Hearn, *Tracks in the Sea*, 135.

24. Knoblock, *American Clipper Ship*, 102.

25. Dana Jr., *Two Years Before the Mast*, 19–20.

26. Greeley, *An Overland Journey, from New York to San Francisco*.

27. "A Signal Station on Telegraph Hill: Gold Rush Communications," *San Francisco Maritime*, National Park Service, accessed December 15, 2016.

28. Warren Delano I to Warren Delano II, April 10, 1850, Papers of Warren Delano II, General Correspondence, 1843–1891, Forbes, John Murray-Wood, Mrs. E. Wood, Delano Family Papers, FDR Library.

29. Kleeman, *Gracious Lady*, 16.

30. Paine, *The Old Merchant Marine*, 161.

31. George F. Campbell, *China Tea Clippers* (New York: David McKay, 1974), 47.

32. *London Times*, 1850, quoted in Whipple, *Seafarers*, 71.

33. Octavius T. Howe and Frederick D. Matthews, *American Clipper Ships, 1833–1858,* vol. 2 (New York: Dover, 1986), 641.

34. Ibid.

35. Lieutenant Matthew Fontaine Maury, *Expeditions and Sailing Directions to Accompany the Wind and Current Charts* (Washington, DC: G. Alexander, 1852), 42.

36. Lars Bruzelius, "Sea Serpent," Maritime History Virtual Archives, last modified January 8, 2000, www.bruzelius.info/Nautica/Ships/Clippers/Sea_Serpent(1850).html.

37. *Boston Atlas*, November 20, 1850, quoted in Cutler, *Greyhounds of the Sea*, 158.

Chapter 9: Enter Donald McKay

1. Edward Everett, *Orations and Speeches on Various Occasions*, vol. 3, "Launch of the Defender" (Boston: C.C. Little and J. Brown, 1859), 363.

2. W. H. Bunting, *Portrait of a Port: Boston, 1852–1914* (Cambridge, MA: Belknap Press of Harvard University Press, 1971), 52.

3. "John F. Kennedy and Ireland," John F. Kennedy Presidential Library and Museum, accessed July 13, 2015, www.jfklibrary.org/JFK/JFK-in -History/John-F-Kennedy-and-Ireland.aspx.

4. George Francis Dow, *The Sailing Ships of New England, Series III* (Salem, MA: Marine Research Society, 1928), 17.

5. Crothers, *American-Built Clipper Ship,* 20.

6. Alex Roland, W. Jeffrey Bolster, and Alexander Keyssar, *The Way of the Ship: America's Maritime History Reenvisioned, 1600–2000* (Hoboken, NJ: John Wiley & Sons, 2008), 174.

7. Richard C. McKay, *Donald McKay and His Famous Sailing Ships* (Mineola, NY: Dover), 21.

8. "The New Clipper Packetship *Staffordshire,*" *Boston Daily Atlas*, July 21, 1851, Maritime History Virtual Archives, accessed July 6, 2015, www .bruzelius.info/Nautica/News/BDA/BDA(1851-07-21).html.

9. Charles MacIver, quoted in Howard Johnson, *The Cunard Story* (London: Whittet Books, 1987), 55.

10. Roland, Bolster, and Keyssar, *Way of the Ship*, 167.

11. Low, *Some Recollections*, 41, 43.

12. Paul Hamilton, *Donald McKay's Family* (Attleboro, MA: CreateSpace, 2010), 24.

13. Ibid., 43.

14. McKay, *Donald McKay and His Famous Sailing Ships*, 18.

15. Cutler, *Greyhounds of the Sea*, 144.

16. Edward Everett, *Orations and Speeches on Various Occasions*, vol. 3, "Launch of the Defender" (Boston: C.C. Little and J. Brown, 1859), 364.

17. Interview with Paul Hamilton (great-great grandson of Donald McKay), November 22, 2013.

18. Whipple, *Challenge*, 80.

19. Ibid., 79-80.

20. Henry Wadsworth Longfellow, "The Building of a Ship," as quoted in

Edmund Clarence Stedman, ed., *An American Anthology, 1787–1900* (Boston: Houghton Mifflin, 1900), 185.

21. Knoblock, *American Clipper Ship*, 41.

22. Crothers, *American-Built Clipper Ship*, 32–39.

23. Howe and Matthews, *American Clipper Ships*, 626.

24. McKay, *Donald McKay and His Famous Sailing Ships*, 119.

25. Howe and Matthews, *American Clipper Ships*, 627.

26. Ibid., 615.

27. Knoblock, *American Clipper Ship*, 170.

28. Howe and Matthews, *American Clipper Ships*, 616.

29. Roland, Bolster, and Keyssar, *Way of the Ship*, 146.

30. John Murray Forbes, *Letters and Recollections*, vol. 1, 132.

31. Clark, *Clipper Ship Era*, 10.

32. *A Souvenir of New York City: Old and New* (New York: New York Commercial, 1918), 289.

33. Clark, *Clipper Ship Era*, 146.

34. Knoblock, *American Clipper Ship*, 168.

Chapter 10: Grinnell Grabs the Flying Cloud

1. Henry Wadsworth Longfellow, "The Building of a Ship," Poetry Foundation, accessed September 20, 2016, www.poetryfoundation.org/poems-and-poets/poems/detail/44626.

2. Albion, *Square-Riggers on a Schedule*, 123.

3. Ibid., 121.

4. Walter Barrett, *The Old Merchants of New York City,* 4th series (New York: Carleton, 1864), 113.

5. William M. Emery, *The Howland Heirs: Being the Story of a Family and a Fortune and the Inheritance of a Trust Established for Mrs. Hetty H. R. Green* (New Bedford, MA: E. Anthony & Sons, 1919), 245–46.

6. Daniel Ricketson, *The History of New Bedford* (1858), Collection of James Grinnell Jr.

7. Thurlow Weed Barnes, ed., *Memoir of Thurlow Weed*, vol. 2 (Boston: Houghton Mifflin, 1884), 625.

8. Zephaniah W. Pease, ed. *Life in New Bedford a Hundred Years Ago: A Chronicle of the Social, Religious, and Commercial History of the Period in*

a Diary Kept by Joseph R. Anthony (New Bedford, MA: Old Dartmouth Historical Society, 1922), 5.

9. Ibid., 12.

10. Diary of Joseph Anthony, quoted in W. E. Emery, *Ancestry of the Grinnell Family* (1931), 54, Collection of James Grinnell Jr.

11. Dialogue from Captain William L. Hawes, *New Bedford in China* (New Bedford, MA: Reynolds, 1940), Collection of James Grinnell Jr.

12. Robert Bowne Minturn, *Memoir of Robert Bowne Minturn* (New York: Anson D. F. Randolph, 1871), 38–39.

13. Ward, *Before the Trumpet* (1986), 18.

14. Thurlow Weed Barnes, *Autobiography of Thurlow Weed* (Boston: Houghton Mifflin, 1884), 627.

15. Abiel Abbot Low, quoted in Augur, *Tall Ships to Cathay*, 179.

16. Robert Bennet Forbes, *Personal Reminiscences*, 145.

17. Christopher Klein, "The Warship of Peace That Fed Famine-Stricken Ireland," History in the Headlines, History.com, March 16, 2015, accessed April 18, 2016, www.history.com/news/the-warship-of-peace-that-fed-famine-stricken-ireland.

18. Robert Bennet Forbes, *Personal Reminiscences*, 194.

19. Warren Delano II to Franklin Delano, January 24, 1845, Papers of Franklin Hughes Delano, 1, Family Correspondence, 1838–1888, container 3, Delano Family Papers, FDR Library.

20. Ibid.

21. Albion, *Square-Riggers on a Schedule*, 15.

22. Ibid., 122.

23. Ibid.

24. Inventory of the Hathaway Family Business Records, New Bedford Whaling Museum, accessed April 7, 2016, www.whalingmuseum.org/explore/library/finding-aids/mss8.

25. Francis S. Hathaway to Franklin Delano, July 4, 1850, Papers of Franklin Hughes, General Correspondence, 1839–1890, Grinnell, Minturn & Company—Kissam, Philip, 1848–1878, box 10, Delano Family Papers, FDR Library.

26. George Francis Train, *My Life in Many States and Lands* (Boston: D. Appleton, 1903), 73.

27. "George Francis Train Not to Be Sent to an Insane Asylum," *New York Times*, March 27, 1873.

28. Ibid.

29. Margaret Lyon and Flora Elizabeth Reynolds, *The Flying Cloud and Her First Passengers* (Oakland: Center for the Book, Mills College, 1992), 23.

30. Henry Hall, quoted in Bunting, *Portrait of a Port*, 71.

Chapter 11: At the Starting Line

1. George Gordon Bennett, *New York Herald*, February 23, 1846, quoted in Knapp, *An Old Merchant's House*, 81.

2. "The Young Lady Who Sings," *Godey's Lady's Book*, vol. 18 (June 1839), 279, quoted in Knapp, *An Old Merchant's House*, 113.

3. "Thou Hast Learned to Love Another" (1845), quoted in Knapp, *An Old Merchant's House*, 113.

4. Clark, *Clipper Ship Era*, 165.

5. Low, *Some Recollections*, 110–11.

6. Ibid.

7. La Grange, *Clipper Ships of America and Great Britain*, 124.

8. Ibid., 114.

9. Joan Druett, *Hen Frigates: Passion and Peril, Nineteenth Century Women at Sea* (New York: Simon & Schuster, 1998), 40.

10. Sarah Smith Bowman, letter, June–September 1, 1851, Marblehead Historical Society, Marblehead, Massachusetts, quoted in Lyon and Reynolds, *Flying Cloud and Her First Passengers*, 23.

11. William Armstrong Fairburn, *Merchant Sail* (Lovell, ME: Fairburn Marine Educational Foundation, 1945), 3667.

12. David Shaw, *Flying Cloud: The True Story of America's Most Famous Clipper Ship and the Woman Who Guided Her* (New York: HarperCollins Perennial, 2001), 19.

13. Cutler, *Greyhounds of the Sea* (New York: G.P. Putnam's Sons, 1930), 183–84.

14. "Eleanor Creesy Navigates the World's Fastest Clipper," New England Historical Society, accessed December 14, 2015, www.newenglandhistorical society.com/eleanor-creesy-navigates-worlds-fastest-clipper-ship.

15. "Israel Whitney Lyon's Diary," May 31 and June 3, 1851, quoted in Lyon and Reynolds, *Flying Cloud and Her First Passengers*, 127.

16. Flora Elizabeth Reynolds, Ive Reynolds, and Laura McCreery, *A Dukedom*

Large Enough: Oral History Transcript—Forty Years in Northern California's Public and Academic Libraries, 1936–1976 (Charleston, SC: Nabu Press, 2013), 147–48, www.forgottenbooks.com/readbook_text/A_Dukedom _Large_Enough_1000652735/171.

17. Clark, *Clipper Ship Era*, 111.
18. Reverend C. M. Nickels, quoted in La Grange, *Clipper Ships of America and Great Britain*, 130.
19. Ibid., 126.
20. "Robert 'Bully' Waterman," Maritime Heritage Project—San Francisco, 1846–1899, accessed January 3, 2016, www.maritimeheritage.org/captains /waterman.htm.
21. Whipple, *Seafarers*, 86.
22. La Grange, *Clipper Ships of America and Great Britain*, 132.
23. Rich Evans, "Sailing Knives," *Sailing Magazine*, January 1, 2013, http:// sailingmagazine.net/article-1279-sailing-knives.html.

Chapter 12: Around the World

1. F. S. Hathaway, May 30, 1851, Morgan Collection, Harvard Business School, quoted in Lyon and Reynolds, *Flying Cloud and Her First Passengers*, 22.
2. "Clipper Ships," January 16, 1853, *Daily Alta California*, San Francisco, quoted in "Clipper Ships and Windjammers," Maritime Heritage Project— Maritime Nations, accessed June 18, 2016, www.maritimeheritage .org/ships/Clippers-Annals-of-San-Francisco-1852.html.
3. Bowman, letter, June–September 1, 1851, quoted in Lyon and Reynolds, *Flying Cloud and Her First Passengers*, app. 6.
4. Ibid.
5. Richard Cadwalader to author, email, dated February 25, 2017.
6. Lyon and Reynolds, *Flying Cloud and Her First Passengers*, 106.
7. Bowman, letter, June–September 1, 1851, quoted in Lyon and Reynolds, *Flying Cloud and Her First Passengers*, app. 6.
8. Ibid., 23.
9. Ibid., app. 6.
10. Ibid.
11. Whipple, *Challenge*, 121–22.

12. Dana Jr., *Two Years Before the Mast*, 26.

13. Bowman, letter, June–September 1, 1851, quoted in Lyon and Reynolds, *Flying Cloud and Her First Passengers*, app. 6.

14. Whipple, *Challenge*, 146.

15. Bowman, letter, June–September 1, 1851, quoted in Lyon and Reynolds, *Flying Cloud and Her First Passengers*, app. 6.

16. Lars Bruzelius, "*John Gilpin*," Maritime History Virtual Archives, last modified September 9, 1996, www.bruzelius.info/Nautica/Ships/Clippers /John_Gilpin(1852).html.

17. Herman Melville, *White-Jacket, or The World in a Man-of-War,* vol. 1 (London: Richard Bentley, 1850), 51.

18. Low, *Some Recollections*, 111.

19. Ibid.

20. Dana Jr., *Two Years Before the Mast*, 411.

21. Low, *Some Recollections*, 95–97.

22. "Ship *Flying Cloud*, Capt. J. P. Creesy," September 1, 1851, *Daily Alta California,* San Francisco, www.maritimeheritage.org/captains/creesy .html.

23. Low, *Some Recollections*, 111–13.

24. Abiel Abbott Low, *An Entertainment Given to Mr. A. A. Low by Members of the New York Chamber of Commerce on His Return from a Voyage Around the World* (New York: Press of the Chamber of Commerce, 1867), 11.

25. "California Gold Rush (1848–1858), *Aspiration, Acculturation, and Impact: Immigration to the United States, 1789–1930*, Harvard University Open Collections Program, accessed July 28, 2016, http://ocp.hul.harvard.edu /immigration/goldrush.html.

26. Abraham Lincoln to Joshua Speed, August 24, 1855, Abraham Lincoln Online: Speeches and Writings, accessed August 1, 2016, www.abraham lincolnonline.org/lincoln/speeches/speed.htm.

27. Whipple, *Challenge*, 146.

28. Whipple, *Seafarers*, 90.

29. La Grange, *Clipper Ships of America and Great Britain*, 134.

30. Clark, *Clipper Ship Era*, 183.

31. Whipple, *Challenge*, 161–62.

32. Ibid., 162–64.

33. Melville, *White-Jacket,* vol. 1, 152.

34. "Robert 'Bully' Waterman," Maritime History Project—San Francisco 1846–1899, accessed June 20, 2016, www.maritimeheritage.org/captains /waterman.htm.

35. Sarah Bowman to Kate Bowman, July 22, 1851, quoted in Lyon and Reynolds, *Flying Cloud and Her First Passengers*, 139.

36. Captain Josiah Creesy, Log of the *Flying Cloud*, August 31, 1851, quoted in Lyon and Reynolds, *Flying Cloud and Her First Passengers*, 145.

37. Ibid.

38. Ibid.

39. Lyon and Reynolds, *Flying Cloud and Her First Passengers*, 61.

40. Freight Bills, F. Cloud, Paid, September 2–27, 1851, Morgan Collection, Harvard Business School, quoted in Lyon and Reynolds, *Flying Cloud and Her First Passengers*, 66.

41. Alta California, September 24–October 11, 1851, as quoted in Lyon and Reynolds, *Flying Cloud and Her First Passengers*, 58.

42. Donald McKay, quoted in Mary Ellen Chase, *Donald McKay and the Clipper Ships* (Boston: Houghton Mifflin, 1959), n.p.

43. *Some Ships of the Clipper Ship Era: Their Builders, Owners, and Captains* (Boston: State Street Trust, 1913).

44. Howe and Matthews, *American Clipper Ships*, 205.

45. Robert Waterman, quoted in Whipple, *Challenge*, 200.

46. Ibid., 195.

47. *California Courier*, November 1, 1851, "Robert 'Bully' Waterman," Maritime Heritage Project—San Francisco, 1846–1899, accessed June 20, 2016, www.maritimeheritage.org/captains/waterman.htm.

48. Whipple, *Challenge*, 199.

49. Clark, *Clipper Ship Era*, 187.

50. Whipple, *Challenge*, 200.

51. "Sixteen Days Later from California," *New York Times*, December 1, 1851.

Chapter 13: *Frightful to Look Aloft:* Sovereign of the Seas

1. Clark, *Clipper Ship Era*, 228.

2. Whipple, *Challenge*, 213.

3. Ibid., 210.

4. Whipple, *Challenge*, 211.
5. Richard Crawford, "Eucalyptus Trees Have Long Roots in State's History," *San Diego Union-Tribune* online, September 4, 2008, www.sandiego uniontribune.com/uniontrib/20080904/news_1sz4history.html.
6. "Maury's Sailing Directions," *Hunt's Merchants' Magazine and Commercial Review* 30, no. 5 (May 1854): 533.
7. *London Times*, 1850, quoted in Whipple, *Seafarers*, 71.
8. Clark, *Clipper Ship Era*, 91.
9. Paine, *Old Merchant Marine*, 161.
10. Lars Bruzelius, *"Chrysolite,"* Maritime History Virtual Archive, last modified August 24, 1996, www.bruzelius.info/Nautica/Ships/Clippers /Chrysolite(1851).html.
11. Henry Blaney, Journal of Voyages to China and Return, 1851–1853 (Boston: printed privately, 1913), 78.
12. Bruzelius, *"Chrysolite."*
13. Clark, *Clipper Ship Era*, 202–3.
14. James Steers, August 15, 1851, quoted in Charles Boswell, *The America: The Story of America's Most Famous Yacht* (New York: David McKay, 1967), 72.
15. Clark, *Clipper Ship Era*, 204.
16. Ibid., 205.
17. Ibid., 222–23.
18. Carse, *The Moonrakers*, 70.
19. Low, *Some Recollections*, 119.
20. Howe and Matthews, *American Clipper Ships*, 191.
21. Low, *Some Recollections*, 120.
22. "Brief History of Punishment by Flogging in the US Navy," Naval History and Heritage Command, last modified November 18, 2015, www .history.navy.mil/research/library/online-reading-room/title-list-alpha betically/b/brief-history-punishment-flogging-us-navy.html.
23. Clark, *Clipper Ship Era*, 215.
24. Low, *Some Recollections*, 119–23.
25. Ibid., 128–37.
26. Clark, *Clipper Ship Era*, 136.
27. Robert Bennet Forbes, *Personal Reminiscences*, 359.
28. "The New Ship *Antelope* of Boston," *Boston Daily Atlas*, November 29, 1851, Maritime History Virtual Archives, accessed March 14, 2016,

www.bruzelius.info/Nautica/News/BDA/BDA%281851-11-29%29
.html.

29. Duncan McLean, "The Largest Clipper in the World," *Boston Daily Atlas*, May 25, 1852, Maritime History Virtual Archives, accessed August 24, 2015, www.bruzelius.info/Nautica/News/BDA/BDA(1852-05-25).html.

30. *Boston Daily Atlas*, 1852, quoted in Howe and Matthews, *American Clipper Ships,* vol. 2, 600–1.

31. "On Board Ship *Sovereign of the Seas*," *Boston Daily Atlas*, December 17, 1852, Maritime History Virtual Archives, accessed March 7, 2016, www
.bruzelius.info/Nautica/News/BDA/BDA(1852-12-17)b.html.

32. Basil Lubbock, *Sail: The Romance of the Clipper Ships* (New York: Madison Square Press, 1972), 47.

33. Hamilton, *Donald McKay's Family*, 76.

34. *Boston Daily Atlas*, August 5, 1852, Maritime History Virtual Archives, accessed November 14, 2016, www.bruzelius.info/Nautica/News/BDA
/BDA(1852-08-05)b.html.

35. "On Board Ship *Sovereign of the Seas*," *Boston Daily Atlas*, December 17, 1852.

36. Ibid.

37. Ibid.

38. Ibid.

39. Ibid.

40. Clark, *Clipper Ship Era*, 218.

41. Ibid., 220.

42. Ibid.

43. Johnson, *Cunard Story*, 31.

44. Helen La Grange, *Clipper Ships of America and Great Britain* (New York: G.P. Putman's Sons, 1936), 178.

45. William Armstrong Fairburn, *Merchant Sail* (Center Lovell, ME: Fairburn Marine Education Foundation, 1945–1955), 1200.

46. McKay, *Donald McKay and His Famous Sailing Ships*, 188.

47. Ibid.

48. Howe and Matthews, *American Clipper Ships,* vol. 1, 599.

49. Clark, *Clipper Ship Era*, 221.

Notes

Chapter 14: Great Republic

1. Duncan McLean, *Descriptions of the Largest Ship Our World: The New Clipper Great Republic of Boston* (Boston: Eastburn's Press, 1853), 23.
2. Francis B. C. Bradlee, *The Ship "Great Republic" and Donald McKay Her Builder* (Salem, MA: Salem Institute, 1927), 20.
3. *Boston Post,* October 5, 1853, quoted in "Great Republic," Manhattan Sailing Club, accessed January 28, 2014, www.sailmsc.com/Boats/club/Great%20Republic.htm.
4. Howe and Matthews, *American Clipper Ships*, 254.
5. Crothers, *American-Built Clipper Ship,* 114.
6. Knoblock, *American Clipper Ship*, Kindle edition, location 1958 of 9860.
7. Donald McKay to Lauchlan McKay, 1856, from Hamilton, *Donald McKay's Family*, 68.
8. Hamilton, *Donald McKay's Family*, 26–27.
9. "Council Paper," *Sydney Morning Herald*, March 28, 1854, 2, National Library of Australia online, accessed September 19, 2015, http://trove.nla.gov.au/ndp/del/article/12954149.
10. Barbaix to author, email, February 25, 2017.
11. "The Clipper Barque *Mermaid*," *Boston Daily Atlas*, June 15, 1852, Maritime History Virtual Archives, accessed June 12, 2016, www.bruzelius.info/Nautica/News/BDA/BDA%281852-06-15%29a.html.
12. Robert Bennet Forbes to Donald McKay, October 8, 1853, "The Clipper Ship That Built Snug Harbor," New England Historical Society, accessed May 18, 2016, www.newenglandhistoricalsociety.com/clipper-ship-built-sailors-snug-harbor.
13. Ibid.
14. Cadwalader to author, email, February 25, 2017.
15. Clark, *Clipper Ship Era*, 227.
16. Diary of Robert Bennet Forbes, October 4, 1853, Robert Bennet Forbes Papers, Ms.N-49.70, 1817–1967 (Bulk: 1817–1889), Diaries, 1840–1869, Massachusetts Historical Society, Boston.
17. Helen Auger, *Tall Ships to Cathay* (Garden City: Doubleday, 1951), 231.
18. Howe and Matthews, *American Clipper Ships*, 255.
19. Donald McKay to Lauchlan McKay, 1856, quoted in Hamilton, *Donald McKay's Family*, 61, 66.
20. McKay, *Donald McKay and His Famous Sailing Ships*, 237.

392

21. Sam Roberts, "New York's Crystal Palace: A Fleeting Monument to Conspicuous Consumption," *New York Times* online, April 27, 2017, www .nytimes.com/2017/04/27/arts/design/new-yorks-crystal-palace-a-fleeting -monument-to-conspicuous-consumption.html.

22. *New-York Daily Tribune*, December 26, 1853, 7, Library of Congress online, http://chroniclingamerica.loc.gov/lccn/sn83030213/1853-12-26/ed-1 /seq-7.

23. Jasmin K. Williams, "The Great Fire of 1835," *New York Post* online, November 16, 2007, http://nypost.com/2007/11/16/the-great-fire-of-1835-3.

24. "The Great Conflagration," *New York Times* online, December 28, 1853, http://query.nytimes.com/mem/archive-free/pdf?res=9E01E7D6143EE 13AA1575BC2A9649D946292D7CF.

25. "Great Conflagration," *New York Times* online, December 27, 1853, http:// query.nytimes.com/mem/archivefree/pdf?res=9503EEDF103AE334 BC4F51DFB4678388649FDE.

26. Ibid.

27. Hamilton, *Donald McKay's Family*, 143.

28. McKay, *Donald McKay and His Famous Sailing Ships*, 240.

Chapter 15: Hill and River

1. Nathaniel Parker Willis, quoted in Ward, *Before the Trumpet* (Kindle edition), location 939 of 7888.

2. Frederic A. Delano, *Algonac, 1851–1931*, Collection of the Historical Society of Newburgh and the Highlands.

3. Delano, *Algonac,* 5.

4. Kleeman, *Gracious Lady*, 38.

5. Ward, *Before the Trumpet* (1985), 63.

6. Anna Lyman to Edward N. R. Lyman, October 1843, quoted in Frederic A. Delano, *Warren Delano (II) and Catherine Robbins (Lyman) Delano*, 8.

7. Jan Potker, *Sara and Eleanor: The Story of Sara Delano Roosevelt and Her Daughter-in-Law Eleanor Roosevelt* (New York: St. Martin's Press, 2014), 14.

8. Warren Delano II, quoted in Kleeman, *Gracious Lady*, 28.

9. Franklin Delano Roosevelt, quoted in Jean Edward Smith, *FDR* (New York: Random House Trade Paperbacks, 2007), 4.

10. Ralph Waldo Emerson, *Emerson's Antislavery Writings*, ed. Len Gougeton and Joel Myerson (New Haven, CT: Yale University Press, 2002), 3.

11. Jim Nugent, "John Murray Forbes," Dictionary of Unitarian and Universalist Biography, accessed June 3, 2016, http://uudb.org/articles/john forbes.html.

12. Warren Delano II, quoted in Jan Potker, *Sara Delano Roosevelt and Her Daughter-in-Law Eleanor Roosevelt* (New York: St. Martin's Press, 2014), 14.

13. William C. Hunter, quoted in Ward, *Before the Trumpet* (1986), 70.

14. John Murray Forbes to Warren Delano II, October 4, 1848, Delano Family Papers, II, Papers of Warren Delano II, 5, General Correspondence, 1843–1891, container 34, FDR Library.

15. John Murray Forbes, *Letters and Recollections*, vol. 1, 33.

16. Interview of Llewellyn Howland III, December 15, 2016.

17. "John Murray Forbes," *Spectator*, October 28, 1899, 18, http://archive.spectator.co.uk/article/28th-october-1899/18/john-murray-forbes.

18. Ward, *Before the Trumpet* (1985), 86–87.

19. Grant Jr., "Fair, Honorable, and Legitimate Trade."

20. Dunbaugh and Thomas, *William H. Webb*, 65.

21. Ferreiro, "Biographical Sketch of John Willis Griffiths," 223.

22. John Willis Griffiths, *Monthly Nautical* 4 (August 1855): Maritime History Virtual Archives, accessed July 13, 2016, www.bruzelius.info/Nautica/Ships/Clippers/Lightning(1854).html.

23. Donald McKay to Lauchlan McKay, 1856, Hamilton, *Donald McKay's Family*, 59.

24. Ibid., 64, 68.

25. McKay, *Donald McKay and His Famous Clipper Ships*, 239.

26. Howe and Matthews, *American Clipper Ships,* vol. 1, 256.

27. Dunbaugh and Thomas, *William H. Webb*, 72.

28. Knoblock, *American Clipper Ship*, Kindle edition, location 1954 of 9960.

29. James Bradley, *The China Mirage: The Hidden History of American Disaster in Asia* (New York: Little, Brown, 2015), 29.

30. Forbes, *Letters and Recollections of John Murray Forbes*, vol. 1, 28.

31. J. A. Spencer, *History of the United States from the Earliest Period to the Administration of President Johnson*, vol. 3, bk. 7 (New York: Johnson, Fry, 1866), 542.

32. Augur, *Tall Ships to Cathay*, 242.

33. Low, *Some Recollections*, 146.
34. Charles Porter Low, quoted in Augur, *Tall Ships to Cathay*, 245.
35. Low, *Some Recollections*, 148.
36. Wingrove Cooke, *London Times*, n.d., quoted in Maggie Keswick, ed., *The Thistle and the Jade: A Celebration of 150 Years of Jardine, Matheson & Co.* (London: Octopus Books, 1982), 35.
37. Robert Bennet Forbes to Rose Forbes, January 25, 1839, Phyllis Forbes Kerr, *Letters from China: The Canton-Boston Correspondence of Robert Bennet Forbes, 1838-1840* (Mystic, CT: Mystic Seaport Museum, 1996), 87–90.
38. "History of J. M. Forbes & Co."

Chapter 16: Surprise *and Danger*

1. Smith, *FDR*.
2. Lars Bruzelius, *"Flying Cloud,"* Maritime History Virtual Archives, last modified December 14, 2003, www.bruzelius.info/Nautica/Ships/Clippers/Flying_Cloud(1851).html.
3. James L. Huston, *The Panic of 1857 and the Coming of the Civil War* (Baton Rouge: Louisiana State University Press, 1999), 30.
4. Warren Delano II, quoted in Kleeman, *Gracious Lady*, 35.
5. Ibid.
6. Commodore Matthew Perry, quoted in Peter Booth Wiley, *Yankees in the Land of the Gods* (New York: Penguin Books, 1991), 490.
7. *Entertainment Given to Mr. A. A. Low by the Members of the Chamber of Commerce on his Return from a Voyage Round the World* (New York: Abiel Abbot Low, 1867), 18.
8. Clark, *Clipper Ship Era*, 292.
9. Ibid., 341–42.
10. "Loss of the Packet Ship *Staffordshire*, and One Hundred and Eighty Lives," *Boston Semi-Weekly Atlas*, January 4, 1854, Maritime History Virtual Archives, accessed October 3, 2017, www.bruzelius.info/Nautica/News/BSWA/BSWA(1854-01-04).html.
11. Kleeman, *Gracious Lady*, 43.
12. Abraham Lincoln to Elihu B. Washburne, December 13, 1860, *Collected Works of Abraham Lincoln,* vol. 4, Library of the University of Michigan,

accessed July 5, 2016, http://quod.lib.umich.edu/l/lincoln/lincoln4/1:234 ?rgn=div1;view=fulltext.

13. Abraham Lincoln to Henry L. Pierce, April 6, 1859, accessed July 5, 2016, www.abrahamlincolnonline.org/lincoln/speeches/pierce.htm.

14. Henry Cleveland, *Alexander H. Stephens, in Public and Private: With Letters and Speeches, Before, During, and Since the War* (Philadelphia: National Publishing Company, 1886), 717–29, www.ucs.louisiana.edu/~ras2777 /amgov/stephens.html.

15. Warren Delano II, as quoted by Ken Burns and Geoffrey C. Ward, *The Roosevelts: An Intimate History,* PBS, 2014.

16. US Department of the Navy to William Henry Aspinwall and John Murray Forbes, March 16, 1863, John Murray Forbes, *Letters and Recollections of John Murray Forbes,* vol. 2, ed. Sarah Forbes Hughes (Boston: Houghton, Mifflin, 1900), 41.

17. William Henry Aspinwall and John Murray Forbes to Salmon Chase, April 13, 1863, Forbes, *Letters and Recollections of John Murray Forbes,* vol. 2, 41.

18. "The *Nightingale* of Boston and the Last Gasps of the American Slave Trade," New England Historical Society, n.d., accessed July 12, 2016, www.newenglandhistoricalsociety.com/nightingale-boston-last-gasps -american-slave-trade.

19. Mark J. Sammons and Valerie Cunningham, *Black Portsmouth: Three Centuries of African-American Heritage* (Lebanon, NH: University Press of New England, 2004), 129.

20. "Rediscovering the *Robert J. Walker*," National Marine Sanctuaries, National Oceanic & Atmospheric Administration, https://sanctuaries.noaa .gov/maritime/walker/officers.html#no7, accessed October 26, 2017.

21. Donald McKay, "The British Navy: An Interesting Letter on Iron-clad Ships by Donald McKay, *New York Times* online, December 23, 1861, www.nytimes.com/1861/12/23/news/the-british-navy-interesting-letter -on-iron-clad-ships-by-donald-mckay.html?pagewanted=all.

22. Donald McKay to Lauchlan McKay, 1856, Hamilton, *Donald McKay's Family*, 33.

23. Kleeman, *Gracious Lady*, 41.

24. David Drury, "Quinine, Morphine, and Whiskey: Tools of the Civil War Battlefield Doctor, *Hartford Courant* online, December 29, 2012, http:// articles.courant.com/2012-12-29/news/hc-civil-war-medicine -1216-20121223_1_surgeon-civil-war-medicine-doctors.

25. "Statistics on the Civil War and Medicine," eHistory, The Ohio State University, https://ehistory.osu.edu/exhibitions/cwsurgeon/cwsurgeon /statistics, accessed October 26, 2017.

26. William L. White, *Slaying the Dragon: The History of Addiction Treatment and Recovery in America* (Bloomington, IL: Chestnut Health Systems, 1998), 1, www.williamwhitepapers.com/pr/2014%20Opiate%20Addiction %20and%20the%20Civil%20War.pdf.

27. Albert Marrin, *FDR and the American Crisis* (New York: Penguin Random House, 2015), 10.

28. Clark, *Clipper Ship Era*, 208.

29. R. J. C. Butow, "A Notable Passage to China: Myth and Memory in FDR's Family History," *Prologue* 31, no. 3 (Fall 1999): www.archives.gov/publi cations/prologue/1999/fall/roosevelt-family-history-1.html.

30. Knapp, *An Old Merchant's House*, 63.

31. Butow, "A Notable Passage to China."

32. Knapp, *An Old Merchant's House*, 61.

33. Butow, "A Notable Passage to China."

34. Howe and Matthews, *American Clipper Ships*, 291.

35. Dana Jr., *Two Years Before the Mast*, 7.

36. Kleeman, *Gracious Lady*, 51.

37. Ibid., 46.

38. Ibid.

39. Ibid., 49.

40. Ibid., 55.

41. Low, *Some Recollections*, 143.

42. Campbell, *China Tea Clippers*, 71.

43. Spears, *Nathaniel Brown Palmer*, 248.

44. Low, *Some Recollections*, 156.

45. Augur, *Tall Ships to Cathay*, 246.

46. Fan Shuh Ching, *The Population of Hong Kong* (Hong Kong: Committee for International Coordination of National Research in Demography, 1974), 1.

47. Ibid.

Chapter 17: Glory of the Seas

1. Clark, *Clipper Ship Era*, 259.
2. Hamilton, *Donald McKay's Family*, 40.
3. *New York Times*, January 29, 1867, quoted in Dunbaugh and Thomas, *William H. Webb*, 117.
4. Michael Jay Mjelde, *Glory of the Seas* (Palo Alto, CA: Glencannon Press, 2000), 3.
5. *Boston Evening Traveler*, October 19–21, 1869, quoted in Mjelde, *Glory of the Seas*, 14.
6. Mjelde, *Glory of the Seas*, 25.
7. Ibid., 5.
8. Limited power of attorney executed by Houqua in favor of Warren Delano II, January 8, 1867.
9. *Boston Post*, December 5, 1868.
10. Roland, Bolster, and Keyssar, *Way of the Ship*, 197.
11. Hamilton, *Donald McKay's Family*, 40.
12. McKay, *Donald McKay and His Famous Sailing Ships*, 222.
13. Seth Low, quoted in Augur, *Tall Ships to Cathay*, 241–42.
14. Mjelde, *Glory of the Seas*, 5.
15. Ibid., 17, 19.
16. Ibid., 7.
17. *San Francisco Bulletin*, quoted in Mjelde, *Glory of the Seas*, 7.
18. Mjelde, *Glory of the Seas*, 23.
19. Ibid., 27–28.
20. Hamilton, *Donald McKay's Family*, 40.
21. Howe and Matthews, *American Clipper Ships*, vol. 1, 195.
22. Hamilton, *Donald McKay's Family*, 40.
23. Ibid., 41.
24. Ibid., 43.
25. *Brooklyn Eagle*, March 10, 1895, quoted in Hamilton, *Donald McKay's Family*, 116.
26. Hamilton, *Donald McKay's Family*, 43.
27. *Brooklyn Eagle*, March 10, 1895, quoted in Hamilton, *Donald McKay's Family*, 116.
28. John M. Leighty, "The Yacht *Thursday's Child* Sailed Under the Golden Gate . . ." UPI Archives, February 12, 1989, www.upi.com/Archives

/1989/02/12/The-yacht-Thursdays-Child-sailed-under-the-Golden-Gate
/4573603262800.

29. Jonathan M. Fisher, "Overtaking a Clipper Ship After 135 Years," *New York Times* online, February 11, 1989, www.nytimes.com/1989/02/11 /sports/overtaking-a-clipper-ship-after-135-years.html.

Chapter 18: Keeping It in the Family

1. Alden Whitman, "Adm. Morison, Historian, Is Dead," *New York Times* on-line, May 16, 1976, www.nytimes.com/1976/05/16/archives/adm-morison -88-historian-is-dead-samuel-eliot-morison-historian-is.html.

2. Household receipt dated June 20, 1864, China Accounts, 1862–1866, Delano Family Papers, II, Papers of Warren Delano II, 5, General Correspondence, 1843–1891, container 32, FDR Library.

3. C. H. Odgen to Warren Delano II, June 30, 1866, Delano Family Papers, II, Papers of Warren Delano II, 5, General Correspondence, 1843–1891, container 32, FDR Library, Hyde Park.

4. Ward, *Before the Trumpet* (Kindle edition), location 1824 of 7888.

5. Letter Book of Charles A. Lovett, 1865–1870, Delano Family Papers, 43–150: 144, FDR Library.

6. Warren Delano, April 6, 1843, in Downs, *Golden Ghetto* (Kindle edition, 2015), location 3879 of 13153.

7. Statement to George Peabody, September 26, 1864, China Accounts, 1862–1866, Delano Family Papers, II, Papers of Warren Delano II, 5, General Correspondence, 1843–1891, container 32, FDR Library.

8. Limited power of attorney executed by Honqua in favor of Warren Delano II, January 8, 1867, Delano Family Papers II, General Correspondence, 1843–1891, container 34, FDR Library.

9. Baker Forbes, Subseries III: Forbes family trust and estate papers, 1834– 1988, Boxes 16, f.10 Houqua, 1873–1879, March 17 1879, as quoted in John Wong, *Global Positioning: Houqua and His China Trade Partners in the Nineteenth Century* (Cambridge: Harvard University, 2012), 119, http://nrs.harvard.edu/urn-3:HUL.InstRepos:9282867, accessed February 17, 2017.

10. Email between Frederic Delano Grant Jr. and Steven Ujifusa, November 16, 2017.

11. Warren Delano II to Edward Delano, quoted in Ward, *Before the Trumpet* (Kindle edition), location 1845 of 7888.

12. Frederic Adrian Delano, *Algonac, 1851–1931* (printed privately, Collection of the Historical Society of Newburgh and the Highlands), 6–7.

13. Kleeman, *Gracious Lady*, 74.

14. Unpublished biographical sketch of Warren Delano by Frederic Adrian Delano, quoted in Ward, *Before the Trumpet* (Kindle edition), location 2118 of 7888.

15. Robert Bennet Forbes to Warren Delano II, February 26, 1879, quoted in Downs, *Golden Ghetto* (Kindle edition, 1997), location 8263 of 13153.

16. Ward, *Before the Trumpet* (Kindle edition), location 2016 of 7888.

17. Charles Alexander Tomes, *Autobiography* (unpublished), Charles Alexander Tomes Papers, N. 49.52, Massachusetts Historical Society.

18. Grant Jr., "Fair, Honorable, and Legitimate Trade."

19. Frederic Adrian Delano, *Algonac*.

20. Robert Dallek, *Franklin D. Roosevelt and American Foreign Policy* (Oxford: Oxford University Press, 1995), 29.

21. Low, *Some Recollections*, 179.

22. Augur, *Tall Ships to Cathay*, 249.

23. Laura Carter Holloway, *Famous American Fortunes and the Men Who Have Made Them. A Series of Sketches of Many Notable Merchants, Capitalists, Railroad Presidents, Bonanza and Cattle Kings of the Country* (Philadelphia: Garrettson & Company, 1883), 419.

24. "Mr. Aspinwall's Gallery," *Harper's Weekly*, February 26, 1859, quoted in Colonel Duncan S. Somerville, *The Aspinwall Empire* (Mystic, CT: Mystic Seaport Museum), 107.

25. Shaw, *Flying Cloud*, 265.

26. Low, *Some Recollections*, 178.

INDEX

Philadelphia, Pa., 22, 66
Philadelphia Catechism, 94
Philippines, 19, 151, 172, 251
photography, 276
Pilgrims, 12, 26
pitch, 116
Plymouth Bay Colony, 2
polio, 290
Polk, James K., 147–48, 177
Polo, Marco, 19
Pook, Samuel Hartt, 161
porcelain, xi, 13, 19, 20, 30, 134
Portsmouth (Va.) Navy Yard,
    108–9
Portugal, China and, 10, 14, 20, 39,
    60
Post Office Department, U.S.,
    Aspinwall and, 135, 156
Practical Navigator, The (Moore), 97
Prime Meridian, 96, 96*n*
Promontory Point, Utah, 330
Protestants, Protestantism, 26, 132,
    187, 221
Providence, R.I., 287
Puritans, 23, 26, 39, 158, 180, 284

Quakers (Society of Friends), 24,
    29, 180–83, 184
Queen of Nations, 324

Race Horse, 178
railroads, xi, 4, 5, 33, 68–69, 128,
    150, 157, 176, 177, 192, 196,
    268, 285, 288, 294–95, 299, 302,
    303, 327, 330, 331, 332, 341, 349
Rainbow, 124–26, 129, 134, 148,
    173, 194, 200, 234

Ranlett, Charles, Jr., 318, 319–20,
    322, 323, 325
Rat (yacht), 36
Raynes, Charles, 162
R.B. Forbes, 275
real estate, 4, 285, 332
Rebecca, 180
Red Rover, 278
Republican Party, 309, 349
Reynard, William H., 301
rhubarb, 13
Richardson, Josiah, 175–76, 210,
    308
rifles, 314
Rio de Janeiro, Brazil, 134, 182,
    222, 224
Rip Van Winkle, 65–66, 68, 128
Roland, Alex, 177
Roman Catholics, 73, 132
Romance of the Seas, 258, 268
Roosevelt, Eleanor, 347
Roosevelt, Franklin Delano, xii,
    286, 345, 347
Roosevelt, Isaac, 286
Roosevelt, James, 345, 347
Roosevelt, Martha Bulloch, 317
Roosevelt, Mary Rebecca, 286
Roosevelt, Rebecca, 345
Roosevelt, Sara "Sallie" Delano,
    1, 6–7, 284, 301, 309, 313, 316,
    319, 322, 326, 340, 344, 345, 347
Roosevelt, Theodore, Jr., 317
Roosevelt, Theodore, Sr., 317
Rose (opium clipper), 45–46
Rotch, William, 181
Rothschild's, 153
Round Hill School, 32